The Complete Guide
Big League

SCOTT COUNTY LIBRARY
SAVAGE MN 55378

by the editors of

BALLPARK*digest*

@ August Publications

Minneapolis, Minnesota

The Complete Guide to Big League Ballparks
By the Editors of Ballpark Digest

August Publications
212 N. 3rd Av., Suite 354
Minneapolis, MN 55401
612.343.5207
augustpublications.com

Copyright 2007 August Publications

Notice of Rights

All rights reserved. No part of this book may be reproduced or transmitted in any form by any means, electronic, mechanical, photocopying, recording, or otherwise, without the written prior permission of the publisher. For information on obtaining permission for reprints and excerpts, contact *info@augustpublications.com*.

Notice of Liability

The information in this book is presented on an "As Is" basis, without warranty. While every precaution has been taken in the preparation of this book, neither the authors nor August Publications shall have any liability to any person or entity with respect to any loss or damage caused or alleged to be caused directly or indirectly by the data contained in this book.

All prices, opening times, and policies quoted in this book are based on information provided to us at press time. Hours and prices may change, however, and the prudent traveler will call ahead to avoid inconvenience.

All trademarks are the property of their respective owners.

Photos of Comerica Park by Bill Zarros. Photos of Chase Field by Jack Kurtz. Thanks to both.

ISBN 0-9752706-2-1

9 8 7 6 5 4 3 2 1

Printed and bound by Sentinel Printing, St. Cloud, Minnesota, USA.

Contents

Acknowledgements

We could not have produced this book without the encouragement of our wives, significant others, and children. Writing about baseball and ballparks is one of the greatest gigs in the world, but it sometimes means significant time away from home. Thanks to all our loved ones for their love and support. Especially Courtney Ward-Reichard, who put up with the baseball travels *and* copy-edited the book. Thanks, sweetie.

Special thanks goes to Brigitte Reuther for her timely and sensitive copy-editing of the original manuscript. Cleaning up our prose is a Herculean effort and Brigitte handled it flawlessly. Any mistakes are ours, of course.

Paul Jorstad designed the cover, taking our humble photos and turning them into a striking design.

Jack and Cathy Kurtz provided comfort, support, and plenty of advice for the chapter on Chase Field. Jack, a photographer's photographer if there ever was one, took the shots of Chase Field as well.

David Pearlman was a delightful guide to Fenway Park, pointing out the nuances of the grand old dame on so many levels. We should all be so lucky to have someone as interesting and knowledgeable providing commentary to all ballpark visits.

We used the Retrosheet Website to verify names and other baseball facts. It's an invaluable resource. If you love baseball and want to spend hours perusing the records of our National Pastime, *retrosheet.org* is the place to look. As members of the Society for American Baseball Research (SABR), we had access to a wide variety of research materials and ballpark publications to augment our first-person research at all the ballparks and cities profiled in this book.

Also, thanks to these baseball employees for issuing us press credentials, offering tours of their ballparks, and providing us information about ballpark histories. Sharon Pannozzo of the Chicago Cubs was especially helpful, giving us full access to every part of Wrigley Field for a full homestand; similarly, Susan Webner of the Arizona Diamondbacks went above and beyond the call of duty. Greg Rhodes, executive director of the Cincinnati Reds Hall of Fame and Museum and team historian, was helpful in supplying photos of Crosley Field and his fine facility. Thanks also to Meghan McClure of the Boston Red Sox, Mike Swanson of the Arizona Diamondbacks, Lora Grosshans of the Kansas City Royals, Debbie Gallas of the Oakland Athletics, Matt Hodson of the San Francisco Giants, Kelly Munro of the Seattle Mariners, Todd Fedewa of the Houston Astros, and Jay Stenhouse of the Toronto Blue Jays for all their help.

Introduction

There is no better place than a ballpark on a warm summer evening, with a cool breeze coming in from left field and the smell of grilled hot dogs wafting through the grandstand. That experience has been played out every summer for over 100 years, and baseball is an integral part of the American lifestyle with tens of millions of fans attending games every year. On a daily basis, nothing captures the attention of the sporting public like baseball.

And the gathering places for those baseball fans inspire their own adulation. Indeed, it's hard to imagine the New York Yankees without Yankee Stadium, the Chicago Cubs without Wrigley Field, or the Boston Red Sox without Fenway Park. These shrines to baseball inspire and awe us. Memories for generations of people—some hardcore baseball fans, many not—are created at ballparks. When we think back to that first ballpark visit 30 years ago, we don't remember who was playing third base or who struck out; we remember being at the ballgame with our parents or grandparents, happily munching on a hot dog and overjoyed at being part of the crowd. Every day of the season ballparks across the nation serve as our new national town squares, our gathering spots, and our third places. In 1954 Jacques Barzun famously wrote, "Whoever wants to know the heart and mind of America had better learn baseball," and that's never been truer than today.

This book covers ballparks in all their glory. Every ballpark is different; while a bad night at the ballpark is always better than almost any alternative, the fact remains some ballparks are better than others. Our goal here is to provide you not only with a description of the ballpark and how to get there, but also a sense of what makes each ballpark unique and why you should visit. We also tell you about other baseball-related attractions in each major-league area (including notable minor-league and college facilities), along with tips on where to stay for the best ballpark access.

Our background: in 2002 Kevin Reichard launched a website called Ballpark Digest. The original goal was modest: provide baseball fans with information on ballparks—where to sit, what is unique about the ballpark, and what to look for outside the ballpark. Over time the site's popularity grew to where it's now recognized at the authoritative Internet resource on ballparks and the business of baseball, with tens of thousands of daily readers.

As you can tell from Ballpark Digest and this book, we're heavily into the ritual of attending a baseball game. Alas, the World Wide Web is not a portable resource and you can stare at the pixels on your screen for only so long. So a book covering ballparks seemed to us to be the natural expansion of Ballpark Digest's reach. The two resources are complementary: *ballparkdigest.com* contains many more photographs than are contained in this book. We advise you to check out the ballpark listings there in conjunction with ballpark descriptions.

Buying Seats

We advise most fans to acquire their tickets before heading to a sporting event. In most cases the cheapest way to buy a ticket is directly through a team, either from the ticket office or via the *mlb.com* web site.

In general, the best way to get the seat you want is by calling the ticket office. Web sites may be convenient, but they are limited: you are presented with a single option within your price range—take it or leave it. By calling the

Fans have been lining up for baseball since the game's earliest days. Here are fans—sandwiches in hand—waiting to see the Brooklyn team at Ebbets Field. (Courtesy Library of Congress, LC-B2-5298-14[P&P].)

ticket office and talking to a human being who knows something about the ballpark, you can be much more specific about the seats you want. Many people, for example, prefer to sit at the end of a row, and there's no way to specify that sort of placement on a team Web site. A sales rep, however, can look over all the available options and let you know where seats are available at the end of a row.

There are times when you can't buy a ticket through a team. The Boston Red Sox, famously, sell out almost every home game at Fenway Park, and most important games in major cities are sold out. At times, you will find some games you wouldn't assume are important. The Milwaukee Brewers, for instance, sell out Miller Park when the Chicago Cubs or Minnesota Twins are in town.

If you need a seat to a sold-out event, you'll need to work with a ticket reseller or head to the ballpark and negotiate with a scalper. With scalpers, you're at the mercy of the market in terms of price and availability. In theory, some states put limits on what scalpers can charge and where they can set up shop, but we've found those legal limits are routinely ignored at a popular event.

A ticket reseller can be just as ruthless as a scalper, but you generally have many more choices in terms of seat locations and price points. Plus, a host of legitimate ticket resellers are out there, so competitive market forces are at play. Our affiliated ticket reseller is: *www.ballparkdigesttickets.com*.

Some Ballpark Questions and Answers

You've decided to go to a game. You've purchased your tickets and you're getting ready for the big event. We're guessing you'll have a lot of questions about what you can bring into the ballpark and what you can do. (Don't worry: we hear those questions all the time.) Here are some of the more popular questions regarding the process of attending a big-league ballgame.

What can I bring into the ballpark?

Major League Baseball has a uniform policy about what you can bring into any ballpark.

Water bottles are allowed, but they must be sealed in their original packaging. (In other words, don't bring that Naglene sports bottle to the ballpark.) You can bring in your own food, but it must be stored in a clear plastic container or a clear plastic bag. It must also fit inside a container no larger than 16"x16"x8", such as a plastic bag or a soft-sided cooler. Be prepared to allow security to check the bag when you enter the ballpark.

What about strollers?

You can bring in a stroller, but MLB recommends you use a folding umbrella stroller that fits underneath your seat.

My child is two years old. Do I need to buy her a seat?
No, as long as she sits in your lap.

What about pets?
Only service animals are allowed in a ballgame. For some specific events pets are allowed into a game—the Chicago White Sox, for example, run a popular event where fans can bring their dogs.

What's the earliest I can get into the ballpark?
That depends on the team. In general, most teams open at least one set of gates an hour and a half before gametime, although some open a single gate two hours beforehand. The time gates open may also depend on the day of the week, with gates usually opening earlier on Fridays and Saturdays. Each team its their own gate-opening times.

When do teams take batting practice?
Home teams take batting practice at least two hours before the game, followed by the visiting team. Some home teams will skip batting practice before a Sunday afternoon game.

What's the best way to get an autograph?
That's a tricky issue. We've found most players really enjoy signing autographs for kids, but the entire autograph experience has been soured by fat, middle-aged "collectors" seeking signatures for future resale: think of Comic Book Guy from The Simpsons with a thick binder containing baseball cards elbowing his way through a crowd of kids and you'll have an idea of what players must tolerate.

Our advice is to get to the ballpark as early as you can, head next to the dugouts, and try to get the attention of players as they walk by. Some teams have designated areas where fans can gather for autographs; other teams have special events before a game where a coach and a player sign autographs. Most ushers are happy to tell kids the best place to score an autograph. Bring your own pen: players don't carry around Sharpies.

Can I smoke at the ballpark?
That depends on the ballpark. None of the MLB ballparks allow smoking in the seating areas. At Metrodome fans can smoke only in designated areas near the entry gates. At Oriole Park, fans can't smoke in the concourses but can smoke elsewhere, including the ramps. At RFK Stadium, fans can smoke on designated concourses.

What if the game is rained out? Can I get my money back?
In general, no. A game is official after the middle of the fifth inning if the home team is ahead, and after the end of the fifth if the home team is behind. If the game is postponed before that, you're entitled to use your ticket at the make-up

game. If there's no chance the game will be made up—which happens occasionally near the end of the season—the team will offer a refund or a voucher to a future game.

Why don't you cover spring-training ballparks?
We do! *The Complete Guide to Spring Training* can be found at the August Publications web site (*augustpublications.com*). Spring training is its own world, and we give that world the attention it deserves in that separate edition.

Why don't teams play more doubleheaders? When we were kids doubleheaders were scheduled all the time.
One simple reason: money. Big-league teams have 81 home games and they want to maximize the revenue from each and every one of those games. When you have a doubleheader, you allow fans to attend two games for the price of one. While it's true many fans will spend more on food if they're camped out at the ballpark for five or six hours, it's not enough to make up for the loss of the gate receipts. Today doubleheaders are a rarity on big-league schedules; most happen when a game is rained out and rescheduled.

And no one *truly* likes doubleheaders. Sure, baseball purists love the idea of sitting through 18 innings of baseball, but they're about the only ones: players hate them, most fans hate them, and most baseball team employees hate them. The romantic notion of doubleheaders doesn't square with the reality of the experience.

I like a beer or two at the game. What are the rules surrounding alcohol at baseball games?
The most important rule: you can't bring in your own alcohol. Some organizations technically outlaw alcohol consumption in surrounding parking lots as well, though many—like the Brewers, the Mets, and the Rangers—encourage tailgating.

After that, ballparks must follow the laws of the local municipality. Some municipalities offer full liquor service—beer, wine, mixed drinks—while others offer only beer. These laws also cover how many drinks you can purchase at a time: most limit patrons to purchasing only two.

MLB has some rules and guidelines. For starters, it strongly discourages teams from selling 32-ounce beers; that's why most teams cut off the largest size at 24 ounces. Generally speaking, teams cut off alcohol sales between the end of the seventh inning and the end of the eighth inning, though some do so three hours after the first pitch.

Why don't more people keep score?
The nature of the baseball fan has changed over the years. When we grew up we can recall a good chunk of any crowd—especially among season-ticket holders—keeping track of a game on a scorecard. (Heck, Twins broadcaster Herb Carneal on the radio told us how a play was scored "for those keeping

score at home," which he still does to this day.)

Today's fans typically don't spend nine innings glued to their seats, and we're as guilty as they come. For us, part of the fun of attending a game is getting up and stretching our legs to get a beer or just walk around the ballpark. Indeed, as you read our descriptions, you'll find we put a favorable premium on ballparks that allow you to move freely about. On the other hand, you have serious restrictions in places like Metrodome, where it's apparent the team would rather have you staying in your seat, scording the game.

Some Notes on the Book

We visited all the ballparks in this book in the 2005 and 2006 seasons. Some of the prices refer to the 2005 season, while others refer to 2006. We would not recommend basing your financial decisions on our price listings. In other words, don't be surprised if the hot dog we say is $3.50 is now $3.75.

One thing to remember: things change often at the ballpark, whether it be concession offerings or prices. What doesn't change much is the structure of pricing plans: even if some specific prices change, the pricing relationships between different sections don't change. We've tried to be as accurate as possible when relating ticket prices and other facts. We often update the listings at the Ballpark Digest web site; check there for the most current information.

And ballparks change, usually for the better. The information presented here is really a snapshot in time. Take Rogers Centre and Tropicana Field as prime examples of chapters updated shortly prior to publication as teams made changes in how they do business. When we first visited Rogers Centre in Toronto, we found many problems with it, including a lack of adequate kids' play areas. Between the 2005 and 2006 season the Blue Jays made a slew of ballpark changes, including the addition of a great kids' play area. Similarly, we were lucky enough to visit Tropicana Field after the Tampa Bay Devil Rays made some needed ballpark improvements, including a new sound system and a thorough cleaning of what had become a somewhat grimy facility. In those cases the changes were definitely for the better, and we're fairly confident whatever deviations you find from our descriptions will be similarly so.

Feedback

If you have any comments on or corrections to this book, please let us know at *editors@augustpublications.com*. We have worked to check every fact presented in this book; verified corrections will be posted at the August Publications web site and later editions of this book.

—Kevin Reichard, Jim Robins, and Dewayne Hankins

Ballpark Bests

Ballparks Ranked, from Best to Worst

Some ballparks may be more historic than AT&T Park, but when it comes to an intimate view of the field, a great selection of concessions, and a fantastic fan experience, there's no beating the home of the Giants.

AT&T Park
Fenway Park
Wrigley Field
PNC Park
Citizens Bank Park
Safeco Field
Petco Park
Kauffman Stadium
Coors Field
Minute Maid Park
Oriole Park at Camden
    Yards
Ameriquest Field in
    Arlington
Comerica Park
Jacobs Field
Dodger Stadium
Miller Park
U.S. Cellular Field
Great American Ball Park
Turner Field
Yankee Stadium
Chase Field
Rogers Centre
Busch Stadium
Angel Stadium of Anaheim
McAfee Coliseum
RFK Stadium
Tropicana Field
Dolphin Stadium
Shea Stadium
Metrodome

Best Ballparks for Kids

Comerica Park
Angel Stadium of Anaheim
Ameriquest Field in Arlington
AT&T Park
Citizens Bank Park
Jacobs Field
Safeco Field
U.S. Cellular Field

Best Tailgating

Miller Park
Angel Stadium of Anaheim
McAfee Coliseum

Best Ballpark Museums

*Reds Hall of Fame and Museum, Great American
    Ball Park*
Braves Museum and Hall of Fame, Turner Field
Monument Park, Yankee Stadium
Ashburn Alley, Citizens Bank Park
Legends of the Game Baseball Museum,
    Ameriquest Field in Arlington
Sports Legends at Camden Yard

Best/Most Interesting Food Items

Big Red Smokies, Great American Ball Park
Anything at the Black Muslim Bakery, McAfee Coliseum
Boiled peanuts, Tropicana Field
Cha Cha Bowl, AT&T Park
40-Clove Chicken Sandwich, AT&T Park
Legal Seafoods clam chowder, Fenway Park
Crab fries, Citizens Bank Park
Cuban fare from the Columbia Restaurant, Tropicana Field
Dodger Dog, Dodger Stadium
Fenway Frank, Fenway Park
Fish taco from Rubio's Fresh Mexican, Petco Park
Gates BBQ, Kauffman Stadium
Gilroy Garlic Fries, AT&T Park
Ichi-roll, Safeco Field
Ivar Dog, Safeco Field

Kidd Valley hamburger, Safeco Field
Montgomery Inn BBQ, Great American Ball Park
Philly cheesesteaks, Citizens Bank Park
Pierogis, Jacobs Field
Pulled pork at Boog's, Oriole Park at Camden Yards
Anything at Randy Jones' BBQ, Petco Park
Rocky Mountain oysters, Coors Field
A Primanti Brothers sandwich at PNC Park
The Schmitter, Citizens Bank Park
Skyline chili, Great American Ball Park

Best Ballpark Condiments
Bertman's Ball Park Mustard, Jacobs Field
Stadium Sauce, Miller Park
Boulevard Pale Ale Mustard, Kauffman Stadium

Best Beer Selections
Miller Park
Citizens Bank Park
Comerica Park
Coors Field
Safeco Field
McAfee Coliseum
Kauffman Stadium

Best Ballpark Experiences

Watching a Red Sox game from the Green Monster seats at Fenway Park

Taking in an afternoon game in the bleachers at Wrigley Field

Singing along to "Take Me Out to the Ballgame" during the seventh-inning stretch at Wrigley Field

Singing "Sweet Caroline" at Fenway Park

Watching the roof opening at Chase Field

Sitting a mile high at Coors Field

The roof closing at Miller Park

Viewing the Braves from the Coca-Cola Sky Field, Turner Field

Watching the exploding scoreboard at U.S. Cellular Field

Sitting in the bleachers at Petco Park

Hitting the Rain Room at U.S. Cellular Field

Sitting in the Park at the Park at Petco Park

Texas Rangers
Ameriquest Field in Arlington

Address: 1000 Ballpark Way, Arlington, TX 76011.

Cost: $191 million ($135 public funding, $56 million Rangers).

Architect: David M. Schwarz Architectural Services, design architect; HKS, architect of record.

Owner: Arlington Sports Facilities Development Authority.

Capacity: 49,115.

Dimensions: 332L, 390LC, 400C, 381RC, 325R.

Home Dugout Location: First-base line.

Ticket Line: 817/273-5100.

Playing Surface: Grass.

Other Tenants: None.

Previous Name: The Ballpark in Arlington (1994-2005).

First Game: On April 11, 1994, the Milwaukee Brewers defeated the Rangers, 4-3, in the first regular-season game at The Ballpark in Arlington, with Jaime Navarro outdueling Kenny Rogers. Baseball fan Hollye Minter was posing for pictures on the right-field home-run porch when she fell 35 feet and broke her right arm, several ribs, and several bones in her neck.

Landmark Event: The 1995 All-Star Game was played at The Ballpark in Arlington, with the National League defeating the American League, 3-2. Craig Biggio, Mike Piazza and Jeff Conine all homered for the elder circuit, with reliever Heathcliff Slocumb picking up the win.

Your Ameriquest Field Seating Crib Sheet

Best Sections to View a Game: We're fans of the outfield seats. The $14 bleacher seats in center field provide a great view of the game, and you have plenty of access to concessions and the kids' play area as well. (Another bonus: they're only $6 for kids.) The $23 Lower Reserved seats also provide great views of the game from left and right field.

Best Cheap Seats: There are no bargains at Ameriquest Field. Do what the locals do: buy a $6 Grandstand Reserved seat ($3 for kids) and then wander the ballpark. There are plenty of places to stand and watch the game on the main level. As the game wears on you can move down to the more expensive seats. If you can get an Upper Box seat at $19, go for it.

Seats to Avoid: Corner Box seats provide a generally poor view of the action and are way overpriced at $29. You may think the cheaper upper-deck seats in the Home Run Porch (at $19) are a deal, but they're not: you are a very long way from the field.

Most Underrated Sections: The Lexus Club Box seats may be $45—which seems high for an underrated seat—but on a hot day you'll want access to the air-conditioned concession stands and bars. The Club Level isn't of the same opulent quality as found in other ballparks (for some reason the Rangers passed on fully enclosing the area and putting in lounge areas), but it will do on a steamy summer day. You'll also have access to the Club amenities with a $23 Lexus Club Terrace seat. Because of the way the ballpark is constructed, Club seats are quite a ways from the action. (Really, the Crown Royal Club seats—priced at $80 a ticket—are analogous to the Club Level seats at Minute Maid Park.)

Ameriquest Field: Hot Fun in the Summertime

Our first pieces of advice when visiting Ameriquest Field in Arlington: Bring your suntan lotion and be sure to stay hydrated.

Outdoor baseball has always been problematic in Texas. The solution in Houston was to shut out the elements, first with a dome (the Astrodome) and then with a retractable-roof ballpark (Minute Maid Park).

The Texas Rangers have never attempted to block out the sun at home games. The team's first home, Arlington Stadium, featured an open design providing little relief from the scorching Texas sun. Ameriquest Field in Arlington, designed and built in an era of retractable-roof ballparks, similarly provides little relief for those in the stands, though there's an extensive concourse system where shade and air-conditioned areas can be found. Still, if you plan on watching a game on a typical Texas day, be prepared to slather on the sunscreen and keep that bottle of water handy. Even early in the season— like Opening Day—the sun is hot enough to give you a serious burn after two or three innings.

Past that, Ameriquest Field in Arlington is an interesting place to attend a baseball game: interesting because the mishmash of architectural styles will leave you puzzled over the intent of the designers, and interesting because the ballpark is so Texan. It's big, sprawling, and more than a little gaudy.

When you walk up to the ballpark, you're presented with an odd exterior architectural style for what is essentially a suburban office-park location: a federalist ballpark. The 114-foot-tall brick walls and the granite base make you feel like you're walking past a federal building in Washington, D.C., not a suburban Dallas ballpark. Festooned with Texas longhorns and tall arched windows, Ameriquest Field in Arlington doesn't exactly scream baseball, either. It's totally out of scale and sync with the surroundings, but that's what makes it so Texan.

The concourses are wide and sprawling—again, like Texas—and feature over 100 concession stands as well as multiple gift shops and restaurants. (How sprawling? The ballpark occupies 1.4 million square feet, considered a huge amount for a ballpark.) You will not be bored wandering the shaded concourses. It can definitely take a while to get from the gate to your seat, particularly if you're sitting in the Club level or the upper deck. Three sets of escalators in the ballpark—first base, third base and behind home plate—serve to move traffic smoothly, but you may prefer to walk up and down on the nearby ramps.

Once you get to your seat, you'll be surprised by how intimate the ballpark feels, especially when compared to the imposing exterior façade and sprawling concourses. Ameriquest Field in Arlington was designed as an urban ballpark despite the suburban setting, and the effect can be a little jarring. It is textbook retro, with lots of brickwork and exposed steel girders. Even the scoreboards are a little retro, with a small Jumbotron. Every seat points to the playing field, and there's very little foul space: if you're in the first few rows of the grandstand, you're definitely close to the action. The ball also carries well, making the ballpark a great place for batters but a lousy locale for pitchers. No wonder the Rangers have a hard time attracting top-notch free-agent pitchers.

Still, there's something charming and a little unsettling about a ballpark where the outfield features an office building—as if one was just sitting in suburban Arlington, waiting to have a ballpark built around it a la Oriole Park at Camden Yards—and a retro-styled home-run porch, complete with obstructed views. We imagine the effect is to persuade us a new ballpark was built around this office building and an abandoned section of ballpark seating. Sure, it's an illusion, and a rather pleasant one at that, much like Disneyland. However, the illusion is quickly shattered when you leave the ballpark and are confronted by a sea of parking lots and ponds, with the freeway in the distance.

If you're visiting the ballpark for just a game or two, sitting on the Club Level is worth the extra money. The comfort level jumps there: the seats and aisles are wider and wait service is available. In addition, the concourse behind the seating features a series of air-conditioned concession stands and bars. You can expect shorter lines for food and comfortable places to sit should you need a break from the heat. Some of the concession areas are on the absurd side—for instance, there's no Western-style saloon yet there's an Irish bar with Guinness on tap—but that fits within the generally chaotic ethos of the place.

In the end, Ameriquest Field in Arlington is an entertaining place to watch a baseball game. You'll be amused by the design and, with the cozy fences, you'll undoubtedly see a game with a lot of runs. The Rangers throw a lot of things at you in the name of entertainment baseball, and the least you can do is sit back and be entertained—with water and sunscreen in hand.

Ballpark Quirks

We've already discussed the right-field home-run porch, designed as a quirk in a ballpark filled with oddities. It's designed to look like a standalone set of seats a la Tiger Stadium, complete with supports and poles, and it does add some eye candy to the outfield.

At other ballparks, purposely designed quirks like this would be a downer. At Ameriquest Field, they're endearing.

Food and Drink

This is cattle country, as the longhorns on the exterior of the ballpark make abundantly clear. Texans love their beef and their barbecue, and the Rangers feed that appetite with over 100 concession stands in the ballpark. Though there are many general concession stands selling staples like hot dogs, fries, nachos, soda, and water, several stands have a narrower focus. The barbecue stands, for example, feature beef sandwiches, smoked turkey legs, and fries. Other stands feature catfish, Tex-Mex specialties, and hot dogs (which includes brats, Chicago dogs, and foot longs). The Starbucks stand pushes Frappacinos, not hot coffee.

Texans also love their beer, but the selection at most stands is surprisingly limited: Lite, Coors Light, Shiner Bock, and Bud. We're huge fans of the Texas-brewed Shiner Bock: it's a light, refreshing brew, and when in Texas you should

The old-fashioned seating in right field lends to the unique design of Ameriquest Field in Arlington.

drink a beer Willie Nelson would drink. The beer selection improves at the beer-only stands where Heineken, Labatt Blue, Sam Adams, and Amstel Light are sold. The best beer selection is on the Club Level, where you can find Guinness on tap.

If you're looking for a little more, there are two sit-down restaurants at Ameriquest Field. The Rawlings All-American Grille is basically a large sports bar with about a third of the seats providing a view of the action, and heavy on the paraphernalia. (Be warned: if you head to Ameriquest Field during the offseason to visit the Legends Museum or take a ballpark tour, the Grille is now closed between October and March.) The Bullpen Grill (located in The Diamond Club, above Section 5) features an all-you-care-to-eat buffet.

For the Kids
The Rangers placed all the kids' attractions in center field, in back of the bleachers and the batters' eye. The Coca-Cola Sports Park features a Wiffle-ball diamond where kids can play their own ballgames (there's a small fee to play, but children get to keep the souvenir bat), as well as a speed-pitch booth, a temporary-tattoo stand, a photo booth, and a batting cage. This is also a place for families to gather: adults can watch the game while sitting at picnic tables and kids can cool down occasionally by standing under a mister. The nearby Captain's Corral features kid-sized concessions.

Ballpark Tours
The Rangers offer guided tours of Ameriquest Field along with admission to the Legends of the Game Baseball Museum (discussed in the next section) hourly between 9 a.m. and 4 p.m. on non-game days and 9 a.m. and 1 p.m. on game days. The charge for both is $10 for adults, $8 for seniors and students, and $6 for youth (ages 4-18), with free parking on non-game days.

Local Baseball Attractions
The best local baseball attraction is also located in the ballpark: Legends of the Game Baseball Museum, located behind the right-field home-run porch. While it's a little spendy—$10 for adults, $8 for seniors and students, $6 for youth— it's an extensive collection of baseball memorabilia (the Rangers claim it's the largest collection outside of the National Baseball Hall of Fame, and many of the items are on loan from Cooperstown) and a repository of Rangers baseball history, dating back to the team's days as the second Washington Nationals. Also covered in exhibits: the Negro Leagues, women in baseball, and the Texas League. Kids will enjoy the upstairs Learning Center, which isn't nearly as boring as it sounds.

During the season the museum is open between 9 a.m. and 5:30 p.m., Monday–Saturday, and between 11 a.m. and 4 p.m. on Sunday (until 7:30 p.m. on game days). During the offseason the museum is open Tuesday–Saturday between 10 a.m. and 4 p.m.

There is plenty of minor-league baseball in the area. The Frisco

RoughRiders of the Class AA Texas League play at Dr Pepper/Seven Up Ballpark, one of the more scenic ballparks in America. *Dr Pepper/Seven Up Ballpark, 7300 RoughRiders Trail, Frisco; ridersbaseball.com.*

For many years the real center of baseball in the Metroplex was Fort Worth's LaGrave Field, home to the original Fort Worth Cats from 1926 through 1964. For many years the Cats was a Dodgers farm team, and future stars Bobby Bragan, Duke Snider, Maury Wills, Sparky Anderson, Carl Erskine, and Rogers Hornsby spent time in a Cats uniform.

The Fort Worth Cats of the independent American Association play at the new LaGrave Field, built in the same location as the original LaGrave Field—in fact, home plate is exactly where it was in 1926 when the old facility opened. It's the only ballpark in minor-league ball with four dugouts: two dugouts from the original LaGrave Field were unearthed and renovated, and today they're used as dugout suites. Also, Cats officials make a point of featuring "fair" poles, not foul poles—after all, a ball hitting the pole is considered a home run, not a foul ball. *LaGrave Field, 301 NE 6th St., Fort Worth; fwcats.com.*

Getting There

Ameriquest Field is located in suburban Arlington, halfway between Dallas and Fort Worth, making freeway access a snap. The location also makes it easy to find a paid parking spot close to the ballpark.

Most fans will arrive at the ballpark from I-30, which runs between Dallas and Fort Worth. Take the Six Flags Drive exit (if coming from Dallas) or the Nolan Ryan Expressway (if coming from Fort Worth) and head south to the ballpark—the signs will make the path to the ballpark abundantly clear. If you're flying in for a game or two, you'll want to rent a car: it's only 12 miles from the airport to the ballpark, all on the freeway. In theory, you could take a bus to the ballpark, but you won't: schedules are inconvenient.

Speaking of flying in: the Metroplex sports two popular airports. The first, Dallas-Fort Worth International (*dfwairport.com*; 972/574-6000), mentioned above, is close to the ballpark. It's a huge airport—one of the busiest in the United States—and serves virtually every airline, and all major car-rental companies have operations there.

Southwest Airlines operates out of Love Field (*dallas-lovefield.com*; 214/670-6073). We're not going to get into the history of Southwest Airlines, except to note that weird federal policy growing out of the Texas political culture—developed mainly to protect American Airlines—forcing a small startup named Southwest Airlines to fly in and out of Love Field, a small airport near downtown Dallas used mainly for cargo shipments. Southwest thrived at Love Field and the rest is history; American and Continental are adding flights there as well. You won't need to compromise anything by flying into Love Field, as all the major car-rental companies have operations there.

INSIDER'S TIP
Many car-rental companies charge one-way fees if you pick up at one location and drop off at the other. They usually don't do this in Dallas, so don't worry about flying into one airport and leaving from the other.

Despite the suburban location, parking at Ameriquest Field is surprisingly limited. The Rangers control nine lots surrounding the ballpark, but many of them are small and some are remote—so remote the Rangers run a shuttle bus. The Rangers charge $10 in the closest lots and $20 for valet parking, while local businesses charge $5 for lot parking. If there's a huge crowd on hand and

you arrive close to gametime, be prepared to park on a street far from the ballpark and walk in. (In these cases, the Rangers usually run a shuttle bus to transport fans.)

Where to Stay

The ballpark is located in an entertainment district of sorts in Arlington, with Six Flags Over Texas and a convention center nearby. A number of hotels are located within walking distance (which we define as a mile or so) of all three attractions, and we'd recommend the Wyndham Arlington DFW Airport South (1500 Convention Center Dr.; *wyndham.com*; $125-$200), Courtyard by Marriott Arlington Ballpark (1500 Nolan Ryan Expressway; *marriott.com*; $85-$125), the Holiday Inn Express Hotel and Suites Arlington (2451 E. Randol Mill Rd.; *holiday-inn.com*; $75-$100), the Springhill Suites by Marriott Arlington Near Six Flags (1875 E. Lamar Blvd.; *marriott.com*; $100-$200), or the Homewood Suites (2401 E. Road to Six Flags; *hilton.com*; $100-$150). You're on your own with the overpriced Howard Johnson Express-Arlington Ballpark (2001 E. Copeland Rd.; *hojo.com*; $120-$200), the two-star Best Western Great Southwest Inn (3501 E. Division St./Hwy. 80; *bestwestern.com*; $60-$100), or the Sleep Inn Maingate Six Flags (750 Six Flags Dr.; *choicehotels.com*; $80-$125). There are also dozens of hotels within five miles of the ballpark and even more 12 miles away, near the major airport.

Since it's highly likely you will drive to and from the ballpark, it really doesn't matter if you stay near the ballpark. Fans of classic hotels will flock to downtown Dallas's Adolphus Hotel, built in 1912 by Adolphus Busch, the Anheuser-Busch beer magnate. It is pure Texas, a little larger than life, and a mix of the majestic and the profane: every aspect of the decorating is excessive, as if a hotel featuring dark, imported wood paneling and French tapestries really belongs in downtown Dallas. *The Adolphus Hotel, 1321 Commerce St., Dallas; hoteladolphus.com; $175-$300.*

The Magnolia Hotel may be one of the most unusual hotels in Dallas. For starters, it's located in the former headquarters of Magnolia Petroleum Company, which became Mobil Oil, and the famous winged Pegasus can be seen at the top of the building, forever enshrined in neon. The Magnolia Hotel is geared mainly toward business travelers, but you can take advantage of some whimsical touches, such as late-night milk and cookies, while the second-floor Magnolia Room features a bar, library and billiard table. *Magnolia Hotel Dallas, 1401 Commerce St., Dallas; magnoliahoteldallas.com; $150-$250.*

For those looking for a more modern experience, the Hotel Zaza is more Manhattan than Texas. The rooms are themed, but in a postmodern ironic way. It's not the place to take the kids, but cool for those parents who want to feel young for a weekend. *Hotel Zaza, 2332 Leonard St., Dallas; hotelzaza.com; $200-$300.*

Your hotel options are more limited in smaller Fort Worth. For those seeking a memorable experience, the Ashton Hotel is expensive but unique. Created by combining two historic buildings (including the posh Fort Worth

Club), the Ashton is a luxury hotel in old surroundings. The downtown location is prime as well. *Ashton Hotel, 610 Main St., Fort Worth; theashtonhotel.com; $250-$350.*

Also historic: the Stockyards Hotel, originally built in 1907 and renovated in recent years. This is where cowboys would come at the end of the drive to take a bath, play poker and drink whiskey (and, presumably, take up with the likes of Miss Kitty). This is also where Bonnie and Clyde laid up after their crime spree, and the room where they stayed can be yours. The experience today is a little more refined—in other words, don't be afraid to put your back to the door. *Stockyards Hotel, 109 W. Exchange Av., Fort Worth; stockyardhotel.com; $125-$250.*

While You're There

You're smack dab in the middle of what the locals call the Dallas-Fort Worth Metroplex, the sprawling area containing both Dallas and Fort Worth. They're not quite twin cities—they're 30 miles apart and Dallas is by far the larger of the two, sprawling over 400 square miles—but they make a nice study in contrasts. Dallas is the upscale, rather Eastern city boasting Neiman Marcus and big business; Fort Worth is the cowtown where pickup-driving locals proudly live in the gateway to the Wild West. Of course, this makes a better analogy than a real-life experience: there's actually more culture in Fort Worth than Dallas, and there certainly are enough pickup-riding rednecks in Dallas. Still, the physical Continental Divide may be farther to the West, but the Metroplex embodies the psychic American continental divide.

If you're in town for a couple of days you can easily see the best of both worlds and experience the contrast on your own. You can begin with the attractions closest to Ameriquest Field and then make your way east and west.

Six Flags Over Texas is within walking distance of the ballpark and many of the hotels listed in the previous section. It's part of the popular Six Flags chain (which means it has the same rides as most other Six Flags parks), but it's heavy on the thrill rides and roller coasters, albeit with a Texas twang: the 14-story wooden Texas Giant roller coaster, the classic wooden Judge Roy Scream roller coaster, a local installation of the popular Batman: The Ride, and the intense Mr. Freeze. You'll also find the usual attractions, like a water flume and bumper cars. The price is a little high, even by amusement-park standards ($41.99 for adults and children over four feet tall, $26.99 for children under four feet tall and seniors, and $9 for parking), but you'll save $12 off general admission if you buy a ticket via the park's Web site and print it out at home. *2201 Road to Six Flags, Arlington; sixflags.com.*

Nearby is Six Flags Hurricane Harbor, open summers. It's a standard water park, with 50 acres of rides and attractions. *1800 E Lamar Blvd.; sixflags.com. Adults, $30; children under four feet tall, $20; parking, $7.*

Though Dallas is a fairly cosmopolitan city—more sophisticated than outsiders assume, but less sophisticated than locals maintain—you'll want to "do" old Texas while in town. In terms of restaurants, that means beef (steak

and barbecue), Southwestern, and Mexican.

Dallas is a masculine city, and that side is well-served by the many steakhouses in town. One of the best is Bob's Steak and Chop House, winning a national following with its wet-aged steaks and smashed potatoes. Nothing is small at Bob's: you won't get out with anything smaller than 12 ounces unless you wuss out and order fish. The 20-ounce bone-in ribeye steak is a signature item. *Bob's Steak and Chop House, 4300 Lemmon, bobs-steakandchop.com.*

Texas barbecue is heavy on the beef, and Sonny Bryan's Smokehouse is regarded as the most authentic barbecue joint in Dallas. The menu is limited, but there's really only one dish worth ordering: beef on a bun with a side of onion rings, washed down with a Shiner Bock. The original location near Love Field and downtown Dallas is a delight; be prepared to eat standing up because seating (consisting mostly of one-armed school chairs) is extremely limited. If you must, try some brisket at one of their other locations, including the upscale Galleria shopping center. *Sonny Bryan's Smokehouse, 2202 Inwood Road (at Harry Hines Blvd.); sonnybryansbbq.com.*

Even the Mexican food in Dallas is heavy on the beef: there are 10 kinds of fajitas served at Matt's Rancho Martinez, and chicken-fried steak is on the menu as well. Sip a margarita and head to the back patio. *Matt's Rancho Martinez, 6312 La Vista Drive.*

Mexican food in Dallas has gone upscale in recent years. Take La Duni Latin Cafe as an example: appetizers include arepas criollas (corn masa patties filled with avocado and chicken, ham and cheese, and pork tenderloin), while the entrees feature an assortment of marinated and grilled meats. *La Duni Latin Cafe, 4620 McKinney Avenue; laduni.com.*

If your palate is too sophisticated for barbecue or Mexican, there are a number of famous fine-dining establishments in Dallas. The best-known is The Mansion on Turtle Creek, where sophisticated Southwestern cuisine reigns in the form of tortilla soup and lobster tacos. The effect is a little less stunning now that virtually every metropolitan area features a restaurant with similar Southwestern cuisine. Be warned a jacket is required for men; no sneakers or shorts. *The Mansion on Turtle Creek; 2821 Turtle Creek Blvd,,; mansiononturtlecreek.com.*

In terms of must-see Dallas attractions, quite honestly, there aren't many. You'll want to walk through the flagship Neiman Marcus department store to see Texas excess at its best, though the effect is a little diluted now that Neiman Marcus stores can be found across the country. *Neiman Marcus, 1618 Main; neimanmarcus.com.*

History buffs will want to drop by the Sixth Floor Museum at Dealey Plaza, commemorating a pivotal event in Dallas history: the assassination of President John F. Kennedy. You'll see the spot where Lee Harvey Oswald pulled the trigger and killed the immensely popular JFK, but the museum is more than just a morbid history market: it puts the entire Kennedy presidency in context (the rise of Camelot, the looming Vietnam War crisis). The exact place on Elm Street where Kennedy's car was when he was shot is marked with a red X; the plaza (including the infamous grassy knoll) is pretty much the same as it was in 1963. *The Sixth Floor Museum at Dealey Plaza, 411 Elm Street; jkf.org.*

Having said all that, we would recommend spending most of your time in Fort Worth. Who needs a stinkin' Neiman Marcus when you can visit the Texas Cowboy Hall of Fame or the National Cowgirl Museum and Hall of Fame?

The Texas Cowboy Hall of Fame is exactly what you'd expect: a tribute to the best rodeo and bull riders of all time. Bull riding is quickly rising in popularity and this museum, located at the Fort Worth Stockyards, pays tribute to contemporary riders like Ty Murray and veterans like Larry Mahan. (Despite the name, women are honored as well.) *Texas Cowboy Hall of Fame, 128 E. Exchange Av., Barn A; texascowboyhalloffame.com; $4 for adults, $3 for seniors, $3 for children 3–12.*

The Cowgirl Hall of Fame is a tribute to the great cowgirls of past and present. Of course, Annie Oakley is enshrined in the Hall of Fame, but so is Ann Lowdon Call, a talented rider, and Elaine Kramer, a Wisconsin trick rider whose signature move involved six horses. For those who assume the West was won solely by the likes of Wild Bill Hickok and Buffalo Bill Cody, this museum is an enlightenment. *The National Cowgirl Museum and Hall of Fame, 1720 Gendy St.; cowgirl.net; $6 for adults, $5 for seniors, $4 for children ages 6–18, free for children under 6.*

The Cowboy Museum is part of the 125-acre Stockyards National Historic District, honoring Fort Worth's history as cattle capital of the world. Twice a day a herd of longhorns is driven down Exchange Avenue, and most of the older buildings have been converted to shops and restaurants. If you go, a mandatory stop is the historic Stockyards Hotel, where the bar stools are decked out with saddles. Nighttime is also the time to drop by the Stockyards, where you'll find musicians playing Western swing and honky-tonk tunes; the downtown Sundance Square is also a popular spot for nightlife.

You'll want to check out the restaurants in the Stockyards District as well. Talk about fresh off the hoof: the Cattlemen's Steakhouse has been serving char-broiled steak for more than 50 years. It's a low-key kind of place. Unlike many high-end steakhouses in the Metroplex, taking your family to the Cattlemen's Steakhouse won't break the bank. *Cattlemen's Steakhouse, 2458 N. Main St., Fort Worth; cattlemenssteakhouse.com.*

Kids will love the Wild West décor at Lonesome Dove Western Bistro, and parents will love the sophisticated menu selections—in addition to the obligatory steak selections, you'll also find lobster cakes, wild boar ribs and deer chops. (Be forewarned it's a foodie hangout, and dinner reservations are a must.) *Lonesome Dove Western Bistro, 2406 N. Main St., Fort Worth; lonesomedovebistro.com.*

For a quick bite, head to Joe T. Garcia's Mexican Dishes. There are no menus and only two dishes are served: fajitas or enchiladas. Simplicity means quick service, but you won't feel rushed. Bring your cash; no credit cards or checks accepted. *Joe T. Garcia's Mexican Dishes, 2201 N. Commerce St., Fort Worth.*

Western wear is fairly mandatory no matter if you're in Dallas or Fort Worth. We prefer the Western shopping in Fort Worth, however; you can find all you need either in the Stockyards District's Stockyards Station or the Cultural District.

Team Ballpark History

The expansion Washington Senators began play in 1961 at Griffith Stadium. The new Senators came into being when Calvin Griffith moved the original Washington Senators to Minnesota. The second-gen Sens played at Griffith Stadium until RFK Stadium opened in 1962. (We discuss Griffith Stadium and RFK Stadium in our chapter on the Washington Nationals.)

After the Senators moved to Texas in 1972, the team played at Arlington Stadium through 1993. Built in 1965 as 10,500-seat Turnpike Stadium, the smaller ballpark housed the Class AA Texas League Dallas-Fort Worth Spurs until the Rangers arrived in town. Arlington officials expanded the ballpark to 35,698 seats by the 1973 season, and later expansions put capacity at 43,508 by 1985.

Arlington Stadium was known for its extensive bleacher seating, stretching from foul pole to foul pole. There, the Rangers fought the same problem they fight today: how to keep fans cool in one of the hottest ballparks in the majors. The ballpark was also known for one more signature item: a huge Texas-shaped scoreboard behind the bleachers.

However, Arlington Stadium lacked most of the amenities fans expect from a modern ballpark, and after it became clear it would be easier to build a new ballpark than renovate Arlington Stadium, the decision to build anew was easy for Arlington and Rangers officials. It took just 23 months to build the new ballpark on a site southeast of the old Arlington Stadium site.

The Complete Guide to Big League Ballparks

Los Angeles Angels of Anaheim
Angel Stadium of Anaheim

Address: 2000 E. Gene Autry Way, Anaheim, CA 92803.
Cost: $24 million (1966); $118 million (1996-1997 renovations).
Architect: 1996-1997 renovation overseen by HOK Sport and Robert A.M. Stern
Architects.
Owner: City of Anaheim.
Capacity: 45,050.
Dimensions: 330L, 387LC, 400C, 370RC, 330R.
Ticket Line: 888/796-HALO (4256).
Home Dugout Location: Third-base side.
Playing Surface: Grass.
Other Tenants: The NFL's Los Angeles Rams played here from 1980 to 1994.
During this period the outfield was totally enclosed with seats.
Previous Names: Anaheim Stadium (aka "The Big A"), 1966-1997; Edison
Field, 1997-2003.
First Game: On April 19, 1966, the California Angels lost to the Chicago White
Sox 3-1 before 31,660 fans—less than a sellout. Rick Reichardt homered
for the only Angels run of the game. Tommy John earned the win with seven
solid innings of work, while Marcelino Lopez was tagged with the loss.
Veteran Lew Burdette pitched 1.1 innings of scoreless relief; other Angels in
the game included Joe Adcock, Jimmy Piersall, and Buck Rodgers.
Landmark Event: The Anaheim Angels won the 2002 World Series, defeating
the San Francisco Giants four games to three in an all-California finish to
the season. The Angels won the final two games, played at Edison Field, to
pull out the Series and make a national celebrity out of the Rally Monkey.
The ballpark also hosted the 1967 and 1989 All-Star Games.

Your Angel Stadium Seating Crib Sheet

Best Sections to View a Game: The Dugout Suites are located between the dugouts on the field level. They're great, but really, really expensive, so they're not an option for the rest of us. Anything between the bases anywhere in the grandstand is a pretty good seat (even in the upper deck) as well. We're also fans of the cheap seats in left field.

Best Cheap Seats: At $9 for adults and $5 for kids, the left-field Family Pavilion seats are a tremendous deal. They sell out almost every night despite having one major problem; no beer allowed. The seats are set off a ways from the action (both bullpens are situated between the outfield wall and the beginning of the section), but it is amazing to see a major-league team place a family section in such a prime area and to charge so little for the seats.

Worst Seats: You'll be fighting the sun in the Right Field Pavilion on a typical evening, making the low price of $12 seem like less of a bargain. (Those are great seats during a day game, however.) The 200-level seats on the main concourse are marred by the overhang from the Club Level; your view of the field will be seriously diminished. We're also not fans of the Club Level past the bases: for the money ($45, $34, $30) you expect more than ordinary concessions and average views. The ballpark curves around the foul poles; these seats are nicely oriented but overpriced at $25. To be honest, the way the Angels draw, there are some nights when you'll be happy just to be in the ballpark.

Most Underrated Sections: The Family Pavilion scares folks off, but those are great seats. If you really need a beer at a game, just head to the center-field picnic area and down a quick one; the resulting views of the game from the Family Pavilion will be worth the small sacrifice.

Angel Stadium: Endless Summer

You can't say the folks in California don't embrace change: just look at Angel Stadium, home of the Los Angeles Angels of Anaheim. Since opening in 1966, the ballpark has been altered several times, most notably coinciding with the arrival and departure of the NFL's Los Angeles Rams as a tenant, though the infamous California earthquakes also played a role. The ballpark is now on its third name and its most famous tenant is on its fourth name.

Still, Angel Stadium gets no respect, due in part to the Angels perennially being the number-two team in the Los Angeles region behind the Dodgers. Add to that the general consensus that Angel Stadium isn't as nice or as historic as Dodger Stadium—despite being only four years younger, Angel Stadium isn't regarded as a classic ballpark in the same manner Dodger Stadium is.

And, quite honestly, it isn't as nice as Dodger Stadium. For many years Anaheim Stadium was a perfectly adequate, if somewhat bland, suburban facility, popular with players but failing to draw large crowds. There was a lot made about the Disneyfication of Angel Stadium in 1996-1997 when then-Angels owner Disney Corp. hired HOK Sport and cutting-edge architect Robert A.M. Stern to remodel the aging facility. Though hailed as a success—the former mixed-use facility was finally reconfigured to a baseball-only venue—one thing is crystal-clear now that the facility has been in use several years: the Disneyfication didn't go far enough.

Under Disney ownership, the outfield seating was reconfigured, new seating was added in the grandstand, concourses were enclosed and connected, and a new center-field concession area was added. All of these come right out of a playbook for anyone building a new MLB ballpark.

Angel Stadium

What's lacking at Angel Stadium is any sense of history or whimsy, aside from the Rally Monkey appearing in the late stages of games. Yes, you have the huge caps outside the ballpark, but these are there as much for marketing purposes (one houses a concession booth) as for decoration. Walk inside the ballpark and there's nothing about the Angels' past (or the rich history of Los Angeles Angels PCL baseball, for that matter), nor is there any whimsical element to anything—concession stands, decorative elements, nothing. (A major exception: the Angels run a very entertaining video on sportsmanship before the game.) One really must wonder exactly what Robert A.M. Stern, who once famously lectured the world on what the glitz of Las Vegas could teach architects, contributed to the design.

While we were growing up in the last 40 years, California got old. California once represented the new and cutting edge, but today Los Angeles is a town that seems frozen in time, a showcase of historical styles from the 1920s through the 1970s. Angel Stadium fits within this spectrum. Ballparks moved back to the city, but the Angels never made that move, with Disney preferring (for business reasons) to keep the team close to Disneyland and its Anaheim base.

Despite the ballpark remodeling, it is a classic example of a suburban ballpark, with all the good and bad that entails. (We hesitate to call it a cookie-cutter stadium as the original design was a pure baseball configuration.) The Big "A" once installed past center field still advertises the ballpark to freeway drivers and a sea of parking surrounds the facility. Virtually everyone attending a game will get there via car on the freeway, though there is a train station near the ballpark.

Wisely, Disney made no attempt to turn Angel Stadium into a faux urban facility a la what the Texas Rangers did with Ameriquest Field—an urban ballpark plunked into a suburban office park. Angel Stadium is a suburban ballpark through and through, featuring a fairly open layout and many very good sightlines. The joint is usually

INSIDER'S TIP

There are two tributes at Angel Stadium worth noting. A statue of Gene Autry can be found near Gate 2, while a statue of Michelle Carew is installed outside Gate 3.

Gene Autry was the original owner of the Los Angeles Angels. Best known as a singing cowboy (he wrote and recorded "Back in the Saddle Again" and "The Yellow Rose of Texas," though his biggest hit was "Rudolph the Red-Nosed Reindeer") who sang and rode his way through 93 movies and 91 television shows, Autry was also an astute businessman who saw the potential of radio and television before most. Sadly, he died in 1998 without ever seeing his beloved Angels win the World Series.

Michelle Carew, daughter of former Angels Hall of Famer Rod Carew, died in 1996 at the age of 18 after a battle with leukemia. She made national headlines after a public plea for a matching bone marrow transplant: over 70,000 offered, but no match was found.

rocking because the team comes close to selling out every night.

However, there are some things a remodeling simply couldn't address. For starters, rows in the grandstand are still too close together, though the seats installed were wider and cupholders were added. The upper concourses are still too narrow, as are the staircases leading into the stands. The fake rocks and fountains in the outfield don't go far enough: we're sitting next to a freeway in

INSIDER'S TIP
There's a fairly active tailgating scene in the Angel Stadium parking lot
before games. The Angels encourage this, albeit with some limitations: in
theory, no alcohol is allowed and charcoal grills are prohibited. The alcohol
ban appears to be a rule that's not strictly enforced (judging by our jaunt
through the parking lot before a game), unless Heineken sells soft drinks in a
green keg-shaped can.

Southern California, not cavorting in the middle of Yosemite and nothing about
it approximates the California experience. One of the lessons Stern supposedly
took from Vegas was the effectiveness of excess; a little more excess is needed,
however.

But you know what? Fans could care less. Attendance has been up sharply
the last few years and the Angels attract some pretty passionate fans; weekend
games routinely sell out. During our visit we hung around the ticket lines to see
where folks wanted to sit. A surprising number wanted to be in the best seats
available, and they were uniformly disappointed when told only the cheap seats
in the upper deck were available. There are 29 other MLB teams who would
love to be in the position of turning away dollars at the gate because they don't
have enough premium seats available. (A word to the wise: buy tickets before
you head to the ballpark.)

Once inside the ballpark you'll find Angels fans are intelligent. The Angels
under Mike Scioscia are entertaining and competitive, and fans appreciate the
likes of Vladimir Guerrero, even if they're seeing a diminished version these
days. You won't run into many crowds in the concourses during a game: fans
really do stay in their seats and watch the games closely.

Angel Stadium is divided into three levels: Terrace, Club (which includes
the suites), and View. All three follow the same pattern, with a concourse in
back of the seating area. We spent most of our time on the Club Level, which
wasn't as exclusive or lush (or expensive, for that matter) as Club Levels in
other ballparks (such as Coors Field). The concourse in back of the seating was
enclosed and the seats were padded, but in all other ways the club level was not
very special. On the field level, the concourse rings the entire ballpark, leading
to concession and seating areas in center field dubbed the Outfield
Extravaganza.

Because much of the ballpark is structurally the same as it was when first
built in 1966, there are some unpleasant remnants of that era. If you're sitting in
back of the field level, overhang interferes with your view of the field. Even
though the concourse wraps around the entire field of play, there are very few
places to just stand around and watch the game except for some limited areas in
the outfield (and none between the foul poles). Only two escalators bring fans
to the upper levels.

Angel Stadium suffers from being caught between two eras. Remodeling
could not address the problems with bad seats in the field level, while the 1996-

The center-field picnic area is a popular gathering spot for families.

1997 remodeling didn't go far enough in adding any whimsy or magic to the ballpark. The Big A sign has been relegated to serving as a big freeway sign. It should have been installed in its rightful spot in center field and made the centerpiece of the ballpark. Angel Stadium is definitely worth a visit, but don't expect to find much magic off the field.

Ballpark Quirks

Rally Monkeys sell well at the ballpark. A little history: when the Angels won the 2002 World Series, team management played a silly video in the later innings of games to rally the team and the crowd—and so the Rally Monkey was born. They still show Rally Monkey videos at the game and sell Rally Monkey dolls at the concession stands. We're guessing the Angels front office had no idea a quirky little video would take off to the extent it has; fans can do some pretty cool things if you let them, a fact frequently lost on MLB management.

This is a designed quirk: both bullpens are located between the left-field concourse and the playing field, with the home bullpen closest to the field. Otherwise, there's really nothing quirky about the ballpark itself. Everything is where it should be.

Food and Drink

The food offerings at Angel Stadium are on the ordinary side. You have three sizes of hot dogs made by Farmer John—the same outfit that makes Dodger Dogs—and you've got a pretty decent selection of beers on tap and in the bottle, including Corona, Sierra Nevada, Sam Adams, Michelob Ultra, Sapporo, Firestone, Beck's, and Foster's. Angels owner Arte Moreno made a big deal about slashing beer prices when he bought the Angels. A small beer is still only $4, although you'll reach over $6 when drinking a premium version. There are over 50 stands selling beer so you're never too far from a cold one. If beer is too weak for you, mixed drinks and Jose Cuervo margaritas are available at multiple stands on each level.

Other offerings include deli sandwiches, a Mexican cantina (Angelitos) in center field, and a slew of branded concessions—Carl's Jr., Dominos, Panda Express, et al.

The Angels also offer two food courts at the first- and third-base entrances; at both you'll find a BBQ Courtyard, a Carl's Jr., and an Udder Yogurt frozen-yogurt stand. There are no specialty concession stands on the Club Level, interestingly enough.

If you want a full meal with sitdown service, there are three restaurants at the ballpark: The KnotHole Club (a sports bar on the Club Level, limited to those with Club Level seats), the Diamond Club (featuring outdoor seating on the field level; seating is limited to those with tickets to the area or those with suite access), and the Home Plate Club (another Club Level restaurant, limited to those with Club Level seats).

For the Kids

Angel Stadium is one of the most kid-friendly ballparks in the majors. This isn't much of a surprise when you consider the present layout was concocted by Disney officials; wisely, owner Arte Moreno kept the emphasis on pleasing youth.

Most families will want to check out the outfield Family Zone, which includes the Family Pavilion in left field and the right-field Perfect Game Pavilion, a slew of attractions for kids and adults: batting cages, tee-ball field, a run-the-bases game, and a speed-pitch area. (You'll need to buy tokens for the attractions.) In between there's an open picnic area where kids of all ages roam around.

The Family Zone also features a kid-sized concession stand offering PB&J sandwiches and corn dogs.

There's also a special team store for kids located near Section 247 on the Terrace Level. We spent quite a bit of time decrying the lack of kid-sized apparel in the main store before being told about it.

Ballpark Tours

The Angels offer ballpark tours on Tuesday and Wednesday when the Angels are out of town. (Alas, this won't help most readers of this book, as we expect you'll want to combine a tour with a game.) The tour includes the Angels dugout, the press box, the visiting clubhouse, and more. Tours are offered at 9:30 a.m., 11 a.m. and 1 p.m.; the cost is $3 for adults and $2 for kids. Call 714/940-2070 for more information.

Local Baseball Attractions

The biggest local baseball attraction is Dodger Stadium, home of the Los Angeles Dodgers. Dodger Stadium is covered in its own chapter.

Pacific Coast League baseball once ruled Los Angeles and the region, with the original Los Angeles Angels leading the way. We'll discuss Wrigley Field and the original Angels a little later in this chapter, but they weren't the only team in town: The Hollywood Stars was the glamour team of the Pacific Coast League, regularly drawing stars to Gilmore Field, located in the heart of Hollywood at 7800 Beverly Boulevard. Celebrities like Walt Disney, Bing Crosby, and Gary Cooper invested in the team and were regulars at the cozy ballpark. How cozy? The grandstand was only 34 feet from the plate, and the grandstand was only 24 feet away from first and third bases. Most fans didn't go to Gilmore Field for the baseball; they came out to watch the stars. Gilmore Field was torn down in 1958, with the site becoming the home of CBS's Television City. You can see some historic photos of Gilmore Field outside Studio 46, where the former ballpark entrance stood, but be warned you must get a pass to enter the premises.

There are a few other historical markers in the area honoring the former sites of ballparks. In Burbank's George Izay Park (West Olive Avenue and Mariposa Street) sits a plaque honoring Olive Memorial Stadium, the former spring-training home of the St. Louis Browns from 1949 through 1952.

Several minor-league teams play in the Los Angeles area. There are three California League teams within a close drive: the Rancho Cucamonga Quakes play at the Epicenter (8408 Rochester Av., Rancho Cucamongo; *rcquakes.com*), the Lake Elsinore Storm play at The Diamond (500 Diamond Dr., Lake Elsinore; *stormbaseball.com*), and the Inland Empire 66ers play at Arrowhead Credit Union Park (280 South "E" Street, San Bernardino; *ie66ers.com*). When entering the Epicenter, you'll walk by a statue of the late Jack Benny. Besides being a baseball fan, Benny is forever remembered by locals for a famous line on his television show when a railroad conductor calls out the next stops: "Anaheim, Azuna, and Cucamonga!"

Blair Field at Long Beach State hosts baseball from February through August. From February through June the ballpark hosts the Long Beach State Dirtbags, one of the more successful college programs of the last 20 years. After the Dirtbags season ends, the independent Golden Baseball League's Long Beach Armada take over and play through August. The ballpark is located at 4700 Deukmejian Drive in Long Beach.

When you think of Jackie Robinson, you might not instantly associate the Hall of Famer with his native Pasadena. In fact, Pasadena was noticeably slow in recognizing him. Robinson was a four-sport letter winner at UCLA, but he really was a star only in track (long jump), basketball, and football. His .097 one-year collegiate batting average provided no hint of the .311 career talent he exhibited despite the pressure he endured by breaking the MLB color barrier in 1947. Now, of course, his #42 is retired throughout the Major Leagues. UCLA has honored him with the naming of Jackie Robinson Stadium (located on Constitution Avenue on the campus)—catch a college game if your trip is early enough in the MLB season. As for Pasadena, two bronze sculptures honor not only Jackie, but his older brother Mack, who would have set a world record but still took the 200-meter dash silver medal close behind Jesse Owens at the 1936 Olympics in Hitler's Berlin. You can see the two sculptures across from Pasadena City Hall on Garfield Avenue, just north of Union Street.

Getting There

The ballpark is located on South State College Boulevard between Katella Avenue and Orangewood Avenue. (Gene Autry Way runs off State College Boulevard.) There are entrances on all four sides of the ballpark grounds.

Most fans will arrive at the ballpark via car: after all, Angel Stadium is directly north of where a major freeway and two major state highways meet, and mass transit in Anaheim is extremely limited. Plus, parking is only $8—a bargain by major-league standards.

Where to Stay

Despite the suburban location next to the freeway, there is a decent selection of hotels within walking distance of the ballpark. One dirty little secret you won't find promoted by the local Chamber of Commerce: most local hotels are older

INSIDER'S TIP
If you're coming in solely for an Angels game, you won't want to fly into Los Angeles International Airport and deal with the resulting hassles to rent a car and find lodging. Instead, fly into the smaller Orange County Airport, located 13 miles from Angel Stadium.

and don't provide an upscale experience. These are pure tourist hotels and you're expected to spend little time in them past sleeping and preparing for a full day at a local theme park. As such, the standards are fairly low—but so are the prices.

The Best Western Anaheim Sportstown may not be the spiffiest hotel in the area, but it does hold the honor of being the one closest to Angel Stadium, located northwest of the ballpark area. *1700 E. Katella Av.; bestwestern.com; $50-$125.*

Families will want to check out TownePlace Suites by Marriott, located north of the ballpark. The TownePlace chain is geared mainly toward business travelers, but families will want to consider the one- and two-bedroom suites, complete with full kitchens. *1730 W. State College Blvd.; marriott.com; $90-$120.*

A similarly appropriate spot for families is the Hilton Suites Anaheim, located south of the ballpark. It's more like an Embassy Suites than a true Hilton, with one-bedroom suites the order of the day. *400 N. State College Blvd.; hilton.com; $125-$200.*

The Ayres Hotel-Anaheim is located close to the northeast entrance to the ballpark and is the most luxurious hotel close to Angel Stadium: the rooms are decorated in a northern French style, a notch above the average suburban hotel. *2550 Katella Av.; ayreshotels.com; $100-$200.*

Angel Stadium

INSIDER'S TIP
We may not sound thrilled about the condition of the hotels surrounding Disneyland, but they uniformly have one huge advantage: they are a lot less expensive than staying at one of the Disneyland resorts, where room prices regularly run more than $200 a night.

For those who like to mix baseball and the beach, a good option is the Hotel Carmel (201 Broadway; *hotelcarmel.com*; $130-$210) in the heart of Santa Monica just two blocks from the ocean. Although thoroughly renovated, the hotel provides you a good idea of early 20th century southern California architecture and provides you the basic amenities in a fun location at a reasonable price. Santa Monica has a relaxing small-town feel inside a big city. Shopping, good dining, the beach, cinema, and people-watching on the Third Street Prominade are among the activities available close to the hotel without getting in the car.

If you're combining a game or two with visits to Disneyland, consider staying near the theme park. There's a wide range of accommodations near the resort area, with most rooms priced below $100 a night for doubles and $150 a night for suites. It's ridiculously easy to get to the ballpark from Disneyland: just head east on Katella Avenue.

While You're There

Anaheim is suburbia, and as such there's no downtown to hang around before or after the game. Still, there are two things worth checking out.

The first, obviously, is Disneyland, the cornerstone of the Disney empire. We're not going to spend any time describing it here—you would have to live under a rock not to know about it—but Disneyland is a relatively short drive to and from the ballpark. (Just head east on Katella Avenue from Disneyland and

Many of us remember the Big A, formerly located in the ballpark's center-field area. Today it sits next to the ballpark on the freeway.

you'll find the it.) Disneyland itself really isn't that big, but the development surrounding it seems to sprawl forever to the south and east. It was disgust with this sprawl (which can be on the tacky side) that caused Walt Disney to forego any future development in California and instead seek a new development in Florida, which became Disney World.

There are now two theme parks at Disneyland: the original Disneyland Park and the new California Adventure Park. The original Disneyland is now 50 years old and amazingly unchanged—remember, we said Los Angeles had not been modernized much in recent years, and here's a prime example of something transitioning from cutting edge to retro before our eyes. Boomers who grew up watching The Wonderful World of Disney and wishing they could visit Tomorrowland or Frontierland can show up today and still ride Mr. Toad's Wild Ride or the Jungle Cruise.

INSIDER'S TIP
The assumption is you'll need a car if you stay in the area; the ballpark is located next to a freeway and Anaheim really is the epitome of California suburbia.

But that assumption would be incorrect. Yes, your stay would be more convenient if you had a car at your disposal, but it's entirely possible to head to Anaheim for a weekend Angels series and not rent a car. It will require a little planning on your part, but it's doable so long as you fly into Orange County Airport and stay at a hotel within walking distance of the ballpark. (We list a few in the next section.) Most hotels in the ballpark area run shuttles to the airport, and once you're at the hotel you can walk to Angel Stadium and area restaurants.

The new California Adventure Park has a Golden State theme and is a mix of new attractions and those appearing first in another Disney theme park, such as Muppet Vision 3D. California Adventure Park is also heavier on the thrill rides, which include Tower of Terror and California Screamin'. *Disneyland, 1313 S. Harbor Blvd., Anaheim; disneyland.com; ages 10 and above, $56; ages 3-9, $46. From the ballpark, head west on Katella Avenue and follow the signs.*

The second local attraction is the Crystal Cathedral, located south of the ballpark. The Rev. Robert Schuller's television studio/church is an amazing piece of work on so many levels: Schuller's optimistic brand of religion—nondenominational in nature—has been embraced over the years by a wide variety of politicians (Hubert Humphrey and Ronald Reagan both endorsed Schuller's teachings) and is an echo of the sunny optimism that permeated the state in the 1950s. The Crystal Cathedral, designed by flaky architect/critic Philip Johnson, serves better as a television studio than a place of worship. The entire complex, comprising the cathedral itself, a visitor's center, cafe, and bookstore, is open to the public daily. *Crystal Cathedral, 12141 Lewis St., Garden Grove; crystalcathedral.org.*

If you stay in the area, J.T. Schmid's Restaurant and Brewery is a popular gathering spot before and after games. Located between the ballpark and the Honda Center (formerly Arrowhead Pond)—in fact, it's known as a hangout for Anaheim Ducks players—the brewpub features a popular patio. *J.T. Schmid's Restaurant and Brewery, 2610 E. Katella Av.; jtschmids.com.*

Team Ballpark History
The expansion Los Angeles Angels played their 1961 season in Wrigley Field (42nd Street and Avalon), former home of the Pacific Coast League Los Angeles Angels. This was the original Wrigley Field, built in 1925 and owned by William Wrigley, the chewing-gum magnate who also owned the Chicago Cubs and renamed Chicago's Wrigley Field in 1926. The Los Angeles Wrigley Field was partially modeled after Chicago's Wrigley Field, and hosted the Angels from 1927 through 1957 and the Hollywood Stars from 1926 through 1935 and 1938. Because of its location in the film and television capital of the world, Wrigley Field was prominently featured in many baseball movies over the years, serving as a stand-in for Yankee Stadium in *Pride of the Yankees* and Griffith Stadium in *Damn Yankees*. It was also the home of television's *Home Run Derby*, originally filmed in the 1960s and occasionally repeated today on ESPN Classic.

The Los Angeles/California Angels played at Dodger Stadium from April 17, 1962 to September 22, 1965. Team officials and announcers always referred to the ballpark as Chavez Ravine (not Dodger Stadium) in radio and TV broadcasts, a practice persisting to this day—the Angels Web site specifically lists Chavez Ravine as the team's previous home.

San Francisco Giants
AT&T Park

Address: 24 Willie Mays Plaza, San Francisco, CA 94107.
Cost: $357 million.
Architect: HOK Sport.
Owner: San Francisco Giants.
Capacity: 41,584 (plus standing room for 1,500).
Dimensions: 339L, 382LC, 399C, 421RC, 309R.
Ticket Line: 888/326-7297.
Playing Surface: Kentucky bluegrass with rubberized Tartan warning track.
Dugout Location: Third-base side.
Other Tenants: None. The XFL's San Francisco Demons played there in 2001.
First Game: The Giants hosted archrival Los Angeles on April 11, 2000 and suffered a 6-5 loss before a crowd of 40,930. The Dodgers took a 4-2 lead off Giants starter Kirk Reuter thanks in part to two Kevin Elster home runs, and then hung on for the win. The Giants ended up being swept by the Dodgers in that opening series. In fact, it took the Giants seven tries to notch their first home win against the Montreal Expos on April 29.
Landmark Event: Barry Bonds has provided most of the landmark events, hitting his 500th, 600th, and 700th home runs at AT&T Park, as well as his record-breaking 71st home run in 2001 and his 715th career homer in 2006. The Giants hosted three games in the 2002 World Series (winning two), eventually losing Game Seven to the Anaheim Angels. AT&T Park has also hosted several concerts, including Bruce Springsteen and the E-Street Band, the Rolling Stones, and the Dave Matthews Band. The 2007 All-Star Game will be played here.

Your AT&T Park Seating Crib Sheet

The Giants offer one of the most complex pricing schemes in the majors: Monday-Thursday prices, Friday-Sunday prices, and premium prices for Opening Day and select Oakland Athletics and Los Angeles Dodgers series. For the sake of clarity we're using Friday-Sunday prices here; note the premium prices are slightly higher and Monday-Thursday prices are slightly lower.

Best Sections to View a Game: We're partial to the Club Infield seats ($67): you're high enough to have a good view of the whole field, are ensured comfort with wider seats, and have the amenities of the Club Level behind you—a must if it's a cold and misty night. Also worth seeking out: the Left Field Bleachers ($25). It can be a little hectic getting in and out of these seats—the heavy traffic next to the kids' play area ensures that—but they also provide great access to the center-field concessions.

Best Cheap Seats: The best things in life are free, and that extends to the free area outside the right-field fence. It's a standing-room-only area, but there are tables and chairs in the vicinity as well as a concession stand. This is by far the best bargain in baseball: you can see most of the action from the fenced vantage point. If you want to actually be in the ballpark, the Center Field Bleachers are only $16 ($7 for children). Like the Left Field Bleachers, you have good accessibility to the center-field concessions on both the field and promenade levels.

Most Underrated Sections: The bleachers are great. We highly recommend them. Though they are spendy, access to the Club Level is a worthwhile splurge if you don't often visit AT&T Park: the concessions are great, the shelter is welcome on a typical Bay Area evening, and the service is tremendous.

Seats to Avoid: The Arcade seats in right field aren't as good as you'd think: you're right in front of the standing-room-only area and you'll have plenty of folks standing right beside you, no matter how many security guards are out there. Those seats work better in theory than in reality. Speaking of the SRO tickets, the rowdies tend to gather and we've come upon more than one incident involving an intoxicated fan and security guards. Unless you really, really want to be at a sold-out game or are part of a large crowd, we do not recommend them.

AT&T Park: Welcome to the Neighborhood

The concourses are surprisingly narrow for a new ballpark, the traffic outside the ballpark can be stifling, and you'll likely spend part of a game peering at the action through a light mist.

Having said this, one thing is clear: watching a San Francisco Giants game at AT&T Park is one of the greatest experiences in Major League Baseball. The ballpark is a beautifully designed gem perfectly integrated into the City skyline. It manages to evoke nostalgia without being cloying, providing modern amenities while retaining a majestic sense of permanence. It is already a much-loved symbol of The City, taking advantage of a gorgeous bayside location to provide the best views in the majors. Sure, there's always the chance of an evening mist, and ticket and concession prices are among the highest in the majors—but that's the price of doing business in the big city.

Some of those high prices have to do with the unique way the ballpark came to be: it was the first privately financed ballpark in the major leagues since 1962's Dodger Stadium. Giants owner Peter Magowan may have irritated some of his fellow major-league owners when he went forward with a privately financed ballpark, but he really had no choice. Attempts at public financing in San Francisco had failed in previous years and, while there could have been public money if the Giants had moved south to San Jose, Magowan and his group decided to forge ahead with private financing in San Francisco proper. They did receive a small measure of public money in the form of tax-increment financing, but in the end they raised the bar on private financing and forced other owners to take more responsibility.

So you can excuse the team if the prices are a little high. The Giants seem

to walk the line when it comes to spending money on the team: Barry Bonds has been one of the highest-paid players in the majors and the team payroll is above the league average. But the surroundings are definitely worth the money. Put together a great ballpark and an above-average front office and you've got an outstanding combination—a win-win for the baseball fans of San Francisco.

Despite occupying a relatively small footprint on the waterfront, AT&T Park has plenty of public spaces. We'd recommend arriving early at the ballpark to give yourself plenty of time to wander the grounds before the game starts. There's plenty to see even before you step in the ballpark.

At the corner of Third and King streets, near the main entrance to the ballpark, is a nine-foot-high statue of Hall of Famer Willie Mays, caught admiring one of his 646 home runs hit during his 22-year stint as a Giant. You'll find reference to the "Say Hey" kid throughout the ballpark, though the branding of hot-dog stands with his familiar catchphrase does seem a little inappropriate.

Head down Third Street and stop at the much more interesting statue of former Giants pitcher Juan Marichal (shown below), caught in the midst of his distinctive windup. Marichal won 238 games for the Giants between 1960 and 1973; the Dominican Republic native won 20 games in a season six times and threw a no-hitter against the Houston Colt .45s in 1963. He was, arguably, the greatest pitcher in San Francisco Giants history. (Perhaps not in franchise history: Christy Mathewson still holds most of the team's career records.)

Juan Marichal's distinctive leg kick is captured forever in time in this statue outside AT&T Park.

The harborside entrance to AT&T Park.

Cross the Lefty O'Doul Bridge and head to an overlooked area: McCovey Point and China Basin Cove, directly across McCovey Cove from the ballpark. Walk up the shoreline from Third Street and take a look at the sea wall: every so often there's a commemorative marker honoring the San Francisco Giants teams playing at Seals Stadium and Candlestick Park, complete with team roster and statistical highlights. At the end of the point is a statue of Willie "Stretch" McCovey, the most prolific left-handed home-run hitter in National League hisory, with 521. The public open space features a T-ball diamond and picnic area.

Walk back across the Lefty O'Doul Bridge and along McCovey Cove and the right-field wall. This is where fans can watch games through a field-level fence for free: the covered area features a concession stand and tables for snackers. On a nice night you'll find a crowd down here, mostly fans arriving on bikes.

Keep walking to the center-field ballpark entrance where the ferries arrive and depart. Here you'll find a great view of the Bay, as well as a statue of a seal balancing a ball on its nose. This is an homage to the old San Francisco Seals, Joe DiMaggio's first team and one of the flagship franchises of the old Pacific Coast League.

Go ahead and enter the ballpark. Interestingly, this is a nook and cranny most fans miss: a small concession area featuring a Safeway (!) stand. Head up to the concourse level and take in the spacious center-field area: here you'll find a BBQ area named after former Giants slugger Orlando Cepeda and other concession stands.

Walk down the right-field concourse and tour the ballpark on a clockwise

path. This is a great place to look at McCovey Cove, the small stretch of water outside the ballpark. When you're watching a game on television this cove looks large, but in real life it's smaller than you'd think. On a night when Barry Bonds is in the lineup, the cove is crowded with small watercraft. When he's not, you'll still find the occasional kayaker or fisherman. Only seven Giants have hit the ball directly into the cove as of the 2006 season. As you might suspect Bonds has hit the vast majority of the McCovey Cove homers.

The concourse is also where most of the standing-room-only ticketbuyers congregate and it is usually quite jammed by the second inning. It is, alas, also the place in the park where there's likely to be trouble of some sort. We've never been to a game at AT&T Park where policemen didn't need to deal with at least one drunken rowdy out there.

As you enter the grandstand, you'll encounter most of the concession stands. We'll cover the food offerings later in this chapter, but keep in mind this is the area where you can find almost everything good served at the ballpark. You can walk through the entire grandstand on this concourse. If you've been to any of the newer MLB megaparks—such as Minute Maid Park or Ameriquest Field—you may be surprised at the small AT&T Park concourses. No surprise: the ballpark occupies a relatively small footprint when compared to these new megaparks.

As you leave the grandstand, in the left-field corner you'll find bleachers to the left and the Coca-Cola Fan Lot to the right. We cover the Fan Lot later in this chapter, but spend some time there: it will be pretty obvious kids of all ages are enjoying themselves on the slide and playing on the miniature field.

Now you're ready to take your seats, and you have the advantage of

already scouting all the concession stands in search of a pregame nosh. There are not many bad seats in the ballpark, so you'll have good or great views of the field no matter where you sit. If you're like us, you may not be impressed with the ballpark's dimensions at first glance, with the right-field fence only 309 feet down the line. Then you'll come to your senses and realize the right-field wall is 25 feet high, meaning there are no cheap home runs hit in AT&T Park. Say what you will about potential steroid abuse and bad attitude: Barry Bonds was not helped much by the design of AT&T Park in his pursuit of Henry Aaron's career home-run mark.

During the game the Giants are all business: baseball is the main entertainment here. There's a minimum of between-inning shenanigans, and the likes of Crazy Crab—surely one of the most hated mascots ever in Major League Baseball—has been replaced by the more cuddly and kid-friendly Lou Seal. (Want your own Lou Seal? There's a Build-A-Bear Workshop at the ballpark where you can buy or make your own.)

AT&T Park is one of the great ballparks of the majors: some say it's the best modern ballpark in baseball and we can't argue too much with that assessment. Customer service has never been less than exemplary during any of our many visits here. It's clear people who love baseball designed and run AT&T Park, and you can share that love with a visit to the ballpark at China Basin.

Ballpark Quirks

Take a close look at the baseball mitt in the Coca-Cola Fan Lot: it has only four fingers. No, it's not meant for a cartoon character: it was patterned after a 1927 glove owned by the father of Giants senior vice president and general counsel

Jack Bair, and that old glove had only four finger slots. The glove weighs 20,000 pounds and is made of fiberglass-coated foam.

Food and Drink

Interestingly, the Giants don't club you with an overabundance of concession stands, especially on the main concourse. Indeed, there are only 25 permanent concession stands (though they are almost all fairly large), and there are temporary concession stands on the main concourse and throughout the Club Level, though the Giants took some of them out before the start of the 2006 season to allow for better traffic flow in the concourses. Despite the decreased number of concession stands, AT&T Park is a foodie's dream come true, a place where the simple hot dog is exalted and more sophisticated fare awaits at every turn.

The main concession offering that will make you drool: the Gilroy Garlic Fries. It's impossible to be anywhere at AT&T Park without getting a whiff of them. Other ballparks offer garlic fries, but AT&T Park was the first in the majors, and in these parts it's a local delicacy. If the garlic on the garlic fries isn't enough, the Stinking Rose Restaurant stand on the main floor sells a 40-clove garlic chicken sandwich. If you eat one, better buy one for your date if you want some lovin' after the game. (The Stinking Rose is a famous restaurant in San Francisco's North Beach area—325 Columbus Avenue, to be exact.)

Center field—both on the Field and Promenade levels—is where you can find almost any food items. Yes, there's the obligatory celebrity BBQ at AT&T Park: here it's Orlando's, named for former Giant great Orlando Cepeda. The marketing here is a little over the top: Cepeda was known as the "Baby Bull" during his playing days and one of the specialties at Orlando's is the Baby Bull Tri-Tip Sandwich. Don't buy it—it's not very good. A better bet is the Cha Cha Bowl, made up of blackened chicken, pineapple salsa, rice, and beans. Here you'll also find the Fresh Catch stand, where the menu is centered on fish sandwiches made with famous San Francisco sourdough bread. Downstairs on the field level you'll find the Big Guy Barbecue; we recommend the pulled-pork sandwich.

> **TRIVIA**
>
> It might be fair to assume that Orlando Cepeda gained his "Baby Bull" nickname as the contemporary of Willie McCovey, but that isn't the case. Orlando's papa Perucho was a Puerto Rican baseball slugger in his own right, nicknamed "The Bull." In his earliest playing years, Orlando was also known as "Cha Cha," and the explanation for that nickname is far more predictable: he was known as a good dancer in the nightclubs. Nightlife gave way to a more serious side by the 1980s when Cepeda converted to Buddhism, and he became the first Buddhist inducted into Cooperstown.

If you've guessed the Giants are aiming for a foodie demographic, you'd be correct. Whenever the team adds a menu item, it seems to always come on

the high end of the foodie spectrum. To wit: in 2006 the Giants added a Cailifornia Cookout concession stand down the first-base line, specializing in local cuisine. On the menu: an Ahi tuna filet sandwich.

Despite being located in such a health-conscious city and state, the Giants sell a lot of meat at the ballpark; there are three popular Say Hey! Willie Mays Sausages stands and 10 Doggie Diners. (Yes, the marketing is most definitely over the top.) Regular Giants dogs compete for your attention with quarter-pound Superdogs, a third-pound dog, and various sausages: Italian, bratwurst, Polish, and Louisiana hot links. A Budweiser Brew Pub serves mainstream and microbrewed beers as well as fresh-roasted peanuts, while a deli serves sandwiches and sushi. If you like Mexican food, a number of stands specialize in soft tacos, burritos, taco salads, and quesadillas. Other standard ballpark food items, like pizza, burgers, Ben & Jerry's ice cream, and popcorn, are also available. On a cool night, you might want to buy coffee or hot chocolate at the Doggie Diner or indulge at the Ghirardelli Hot Fudge Sundae stand. For vegetarians veggie dogs and portabello-mushroom burgers are available at the John J. McGraw Derby Grills.

The Club Level features some unique concessions: we loved the brisket sandwich at a carvery, and we were tempted by the fresh lemonade at the Farmers Market stand. The four Farmers Market stands, operated by Bon Appetit, features fresh produce brought in twice weekly from the Ferry Building Farmer's Market in San Francisco. With the emphasis on fresh produce, offerings at these four stands varies. Other favorites at the Farmers Market stands: strawberry shortcake, organic yogurt parfait, and baguette sandwiches.

Acme Chophouse is the signature restaurant on the Third Street side of the ballpark, and it's quite unlike any other ballpark restaurant. For starters, it's not a sports bar (which would have been the safest moneymaker for the team); it's a fine-dining establishment with trendy chef Traci Des Jardins' menu putting an emphasis on sustainable agriculture and grass-fed beef. There probably is no other market where a restaurant like this would succeed in a ballpark, but you'll find crowds here on game nights.

Handicapped Access
Wheelchair-accessible seating is available on every level and at every price range. Elevators run to all levels at the Willie Mays Plaza entrance at Third and King and the left-field corner by the Second Street entrance.

Ballpark Tours
The Giants offer daily tours at 10:30 a.m. and 12:30 p.m., except when day games are scheduled. The tours begin in the Dugout Store and last approximately one hour and 15 minutes. The cost: $10 for adults (anyone 13 or older), $8 for seniors (55 and over), $5 for children between 2 and 12 years old, and free for children under 2. Tour stops include the warning track, dugouts, indoor batting cages, the visitors' clubhouse, the press box, and a luxury box. Group tours are also offered.

For the Kids

The Coca-Cola Fan Lot is one of the best activity centers in the majors. Normally, activity centers for children (when they exist) are consigned to fringe areas, but the Fan Lot is firmly ensconced in a prime location in left field. Part of that is marketing—the iconic Coke bottle is visible from all parts of the ballpark—but we'd like to think Giants ownership wanted to make a great ballpark even better by stressing the family experience.

The location works. You'll usually find the activity area crammed with kids before the game, going down the Superslide located within the 80-foot-long Coke bottle or running the bases in a mini-ballpark. A raised mezzanine allows parents to watch their kids and the game at the same time; the mezzanine also provides great views of the Bay and the San Francisco skyline. Three telescopes let fans zoom in on their favorite players during the game.

(The Coke bottle adds to the festive experience at the ballpark: when a Giant hits a home run, the bottle is the focal point of a light display.)

The Little Giants ballpark is a 50-by-50-foot replica of AT&T Park where aspiring major leaguers can hone their craft during the game. Also helpful to potential Giants: a speed gun.

Where to Stay

There are an abundance of hotels in downtown San Francisco, with almost all of them of them over a mile from the ballpark. A few hotels technically are within a mile of the ballpark, but that's as the crow flies. By the time you navigate the city streets and avoid the freeways and the Embarcadero you'll find the real distance is considerably more.

So do what we did: stay elsewhere in the city and take a cab to the ballpark. San Francisco, especially the core city, is like New York City in that cabs are in abundance, even after the game when a large crowd leaves the ballpark. We've never left AT&T Park without a long line of cabs waiting at the Second Street exit.

The area near Moscone Center, San Francisco's convention center, features

INSIDER'S TIP

If you're into historic properties, San Francisco is the city for you. We're partial to the stately Westin St. Francis (335 Powell St.; *westinstfrancis.com*; $225-$500): it opened in 1904 and has served as the center of San Francisco social life ever since. (Even if you don't stay there, the Oak Room is a wonderful place for an evening meal or cocktail.) The Omni San Francisco (500 California St.; *omnihotels.com*; $225-$325), with a lobby built in 1926 as a bank with all the appropriate flourishes, is in the city's Financial District—bustling on weekdays, deserted on weekends. And there's always the grand Fairmont Hotel on Nob Hill (950 Mason St.; *fairmont.com*; $250-$500); the rooms may be a little worn, but the lobby and the public spaces are among the most majestic in the city.

The walkway between the ballpark and McCovey Cove allows the ultimate in knothole access.

a slew of surrounding hotels a little more than a mile from the ballpark. The Four Seasons Hotel (757 Market St.; *fourseasons.com*; $415-$500) is typical of the chain, with an emphasis on service and luxury. The St. Regis Hotel (125 3rd St.; *stregis.com*; $399-$650) is even more expensive and luxurious. W Hotel San Francisco (181 3rd St.; *whotels.com*; $254-$400) is typical of that chain: small, preciously decorated rooms with models moonlighting as doormen.

Union Square is a popular area near downtown San Francisco, featuring lots of shopping (Saks, Tiffany's, Macy's, and Neiman Marcus all have large stores there), a great location next to Chinatown, and lots of hotels. Some of the city's largest tourist hotels are located near Union Square, including the Grand Hyatt San Francisco (345 Stockton St.; *grandsanfrancisco.hyatt.com*; $200-$300), the Four Seasons (757 Market St.; *fourseasons.com*; $400-$600), the Hotel Monaco (501 Geary St.; *monaco-sf.com*; $200-$250), the massive Hilton San Francisco (333 O' Farrell; *hilton.com*; $150-$250), and the Pan Pacific Hotel (500 Post St.; *panpacific.com*; $235-$300). There are also a host of smaller boutique hotels near Union Square, including the Inn on Union Square (440 Post St.; *unionsquare.com*; $200-$300), the affordable Kensington Park (450 Post St., *kensingtonparkhotel.com*; $175-$300), the White Swan Inn (845 Bush St.; *jdvhospitality.com*; $171-$236), the Warwick Regis (490 Geary St.; *warwicksf.com*; $145-$400), the Villa Florence (225 Powell St.; *villaflorence.com*; $150-$250), and the highly affordable Hotel Rex (562 Sutter St.; $125-$225).

For families on a budget, consider staying closer to Fisherman's Wharf or Pacific Heights. The Nob Hill Motor Inn (1630 Pacific Av.; *staysf.com/nobhill*;

$75-$165) has a convenient location to both Union Square and Fisherman's Wharf, a reputation for service, and free parking and Internet access. The Argonaut Hotel (485 Jefferson; *argonauthotel.com*; $200-$500), located at Fisherman's Wharf, bills itself as a luxury boutique hotel, but like every hotel in the Kimpton chain it manages to deliver luxury at a reasonable price.

Local Attractions

You would assume that with one of the most affluent crowds in the majors and the Giants playing in a rejuvenated area, more bars and restaurants would have popped up close to the ballpark. But so far AT&T Park has had a negligible effect on the local neighborhood. Some gentrification was happening with or without the ballpark, but nothing extensive ever took root. You'd expect some sort of sports-related bar to have opened up across the street from the ballpark; instead, you have a Borders bookstore at the corner of King and Third streets.

Still, there are some notable restaurants in the area. Jack Falstaff (598 2nd St.; *plumpjack.com/falstaff1.html*; 415/836-9239) may be one of the best, though a 2006 change of the executive-chef saw an overhaul of the menu to feature more Latin- and Indian-flavored dishes at lower prices. Paragon Restaurant and Bar (701 2nd St.; *paragonrestaurant.com*; 415/537-9020) is a block away on Townsend, and it's a solid place for cocktails (especially martinis), though less so for food. Primo Patio Café (214 Townsend St.; *primopatiocafe.com*; 415/957-1129) features Cuban and Jamaican specialities. Go before the game: it closes at 9 p.m.

Maybe it's because the concession offerings at the ballpark are so good and that anyone wanting a good meal can eat at the Acme Chophouse before the game. Maybe it's because fans spend so much at the ballpark they don't have much left over afterwards. Whatever the case, the area around the ballpark isn't one where you'll be able to go bar-hopping or spend a wad on a great meal.

Let's face it, San Francisco already has more than enough things to do before and after the game. For starters, it's one of the great restaurant towns in the country: California cuisine was basically invented here and it seems like every corner features a great neighborhood bistro.

It's also one of the great walking cities. The North Beach neighborhood along Columbus Avenue is perfect for walking: the many sidewalk cafes and restaurants have been there for decades, giving it a true sense of community. If you go, a mandatory stop is Mario's Bohemian Cigar Store (566 Columbus Av.; *mariosbohemiancigarstore.com*; 415/362-0536), which (despite the name) is a cappuccino café located opposite Washington Square Park. After an espresso at the original Caffé Trieste (601 Vallejo St.; *caffetrieste.com*; 415/392-6739), which opened in 1956, or Caffé Greco (423 Columbus Av.; 415/397-6261), drop by City Lights Books (261 Columbus Av.; *citylights.com*; 415/362-8193) to see what's left of San Francisco Bohemian literary society.

Or visit the Gap clothing store at the corner of Haight and Ashbury and lament the loss of innocence and passion displayed during the Summer of Love.

Getting There

Despite being in the midst of one of the most congested cities in America, the ballpark is fairly accessible. Driving is probably the most frustrating way to get to the ballpark, especially on a weeknight: the normal congestion associated with San Francisco is multiplied by baseball fans.

Having said that, the three major highway/freeway entries into the city provide fairly good access to the ballpark. Coming from the south is easiest: take I-280 north to the Mariposa Street exit and follow the signs on Mariposa (hanging a left on Third Street) to the parking lots, or stay on I-280 until it ends at King Street and take your chances in one of the privately operated lots or parking ramps near the ballpark. From the East Bay, take I-80 to the Fifth Street exit and follow the signs to the ballpark. (It's not a very direct route, but it's not complicated, either.) From the North Bay, take Hwy. 101 across the Golden Gate Bridge to the Marina Boulevard exit. Stay on Marina Boulevard until you hit Bay Street; hang a left and then turn right on the Embarcadero. The Embarcadero turns into King Street; stay on it and then hang a right on Third Street.

Once you're there, 4,800 parking spots await you in three lots south of the ballpark. The cost is not cheap—$25 for the closest lots, $20 for a more distant lot—but nothing about going to a Giants game is cheap.

Because of the cost and hassle, we recommend you look at alternative ways of getting to the ballpark. If you're coming in from out of town, consider staying downtown and taking a cab to the game: a cab can drop you off in a special loading area next to the ballpark, and there will be plenty of cabs waiting to take you back after the game. You can stay at one of the hotels near Moscone Center and walk down Third Street to the game, though we wouldn't necessarily recommend it.

Caltrain, BART, and the San Francisco Muni system also serve the ballpark. The Muni N line goes directly to the ballpark while the 10, 15, 30, 45, and 47 lines stop within one block. The Muni buses load and unload near the intersection of King and Second streets north of the ballpark. If you're out in the Valley in Santa Clara or San Mateo, you can take a train directly to the Fourth and King streets station a block from the ballpark. Going via BART is a little more complicated: the train can get you into downtown San Francisco, but you'll then need to take a Muni N bus at Civic Center, Powell, Montgomery, or Embarcadero to the ballpark.

One of the more unique ways to get to AT&T Park is via ferry. Three ferry lines pick up and drop off at the center-field Bay entrance: the Alameda/Oakland Ferry Service runs from Oakland's Clay Street Pier, Golden Gate Transit's ferry leaves the Larkspur Ferry Terminal in Marin County, and the Vallejo Baylink Ferry runs from the Vallejo Ferry Terminal to the San Francisco Ferry Terminal on the Embarcadero. It's not necessarily cheaper to take a ferry—the Golden Gate Ferry charges $7 each way per adult with kids under five free, and the Vallejo Baylink Ferry charges $10 per adult each way, so a family of four would pay more to take the ferry than driving to the ballpark and parking in a Giants lot. The ferries are convenient if you're a resident of the community served via ferry service, not so much so if you're a tourist looking to take in a baseball game.

Team Ballpark History

The Giants began life as the New York Giants and played in several different East Coast ballparks before moving to the West Coast: Oakland Park in Jersey City (1889, for two games), St. George Grounds in Staten Island (1889, for 25 games), Hilltop Park (1911), and four different versions of the Polo Grounds (1883-1888, 1889-1890, 1891-1911, 1911-1957).

The first Polo Grounds was actually used for polo, as owner James Gordon Bennett—the owner of the *New York Herald* newspaper—opened the huge expanse of land for the sport of kings. By 1883 baseball was popular enough that two diamonds were laid out: one served as the home of the Giants (then known as the Gothams) and the other as the home of the American Association's Mets. The two fields were divided by a 10-foot-high canvas fence and, as both teams played on the same days, occasionally balls would end up on the other field. At the time the American Association was a major league, and the first National League/American Association championship was played in 1884 with the Mets hosting the Providence Grays. The Giants' stay at the first Polo Grounds ended when the city took their field to make room for 111th Street, and the team played games in Jersey City and Staten Island while a new ballpark was built.

That ballpark, Polo Grounds III, was open for less than a season. It was adjacent to Brotherhood Park, the home of the New York Giants of the Players League, a short-lived attempt by players to control their own destiny. Polo Grounds III was known for a steep embankment in the outfield; it ended up being used as a cricket field well into the 1930s.

When the Players League collapsed, the National League Giants moved into Brotherhood Park and renamed it the Polo Grounds, even though it was never used for polo. The 16,000-seat ballpark featured a large covered grandstand and a hodgepodge of additions. The Giants drew a colorful clientele: the center-field bleachers were known as the cigar boxes and Burkeville because of the large number of Irish immigrants buying tickets to sit there. Originally, center field stretched out 500 feet, and the oddities of the left-field corner must have given umpires nightmares. Part of the left-field stands jutted out into in fair territory and any ball hit there was ruled a homer, and the bullpens behind the stands were in play—each area having its own foul pole. Polo Grounds IV went down in flames on April 14-15, 1911, forcing the Giants to finish out the season at Hilltop Park, the home of the New York Highlanders (later the Yankees).

Polo Grounds V is the version of the Polo Grounds most people associate with the Giants: it opened on June 28, 1911 and served as the team's home until Horace Stoneham moved the franchise to San Francisco. Due to the ballpark's distinctive horseshoe shape and spacious dimensions—with center-field fences extending beyond 500 feet during several periods in Giants history—many assume polo was played here, but that's not the case. It was perhaps one of the most poorly designed ballparks in the majors: the outfield was slanted so badly the outfield wall was eight feet lower than the infield, and the overhangs down each line meant a pop fly traveling 250 feet could end up as a cheap homer. The bullpens were cut out of the stands in both power alleys and were in play, and a five-foot-high memorial to former Giant Eddie Grant (killed in World War I) was in play in center field.

A lot of baseball history was made at the Polo Grounds: Bobby Thomson's "shot heard 'round the world" happened there on Oct. 3, 1951, and Willie Mays' famous over-the-shoulder catch in the 1954 World Series occurred there as well. Only four players homered to center field: Negro League legend Luke Easter, Boston's Joe Adcock, Milwaukee's Henry Aaron, and—surprisingly—the Chicago Cubs' Lou Brock, better known as a base-stealing king with the St. Louis Cardinals. Ironically, none of the great Giants sluggers—Mays, Johnny Mize, Bill Terry, George Kelly, Mel Ott—ever homered to straightaway center.

At the Polo Grounds, the earliest box seats were literally box seats. (Courtesy Library of Congress, LC-B2- 2720-6[P&P].)

Above: The Polo Grounds in 1912. Note the ornate facade work. (Courtesy Library of Congress, LC-B2- 2438-8[P&P].)
Below: A crowd in the final game of the 1908 season at Polo Grounds III. (Courtesy Library of Congress, LC-B2- 480-11[P&P].)

Above: In the early days of the Polo Grounds the quickest way to get information out of the ballpark was via the telegraph. This photo shows the hordes of telegraph operators at the 1912 World Series, won by the Boston Red Sox. (Courtesy Library of Congress, LC-B2-2539-14[P&P].)
Below: The Polo Grounds in 1923. Note the spacious surroundings. (Courtesy Library of Congress, LC-B2-5982-2[P&P].)

Candlestick Park.

When the Giants moved to San Francisco, it was clear the Polo Grounds was a dilapidated shell of its former self. The New York Mets played two seasons there as Shea Stadium was being built, and then the Polo Grounds met the inevitable wrecking ball. Ironically, the same wrecking ball—painted with the seams of a baseball—was used to take down both Ebbets Field and the Polo Grounds.

The Polo Grounds Towers now stand on the site, and all that's left is a small marker in front of Tower D showing the former location of home plate and a staircase that once transported fans down from Edgecombe Avenue to the Polo Grounds. (If you poke around you can see a marker commemorating the John T. Brush stairway, presented by the New York Giants. The Polo Grounds was originally called Brush Stadium after team owner John T. Brush.)

After moving to San Francisco, the Giants played two seasons at Seals Stadium (1958-1959), the former home of the Pacific Coast League's San Francisco Seals, before moving into Candlestick Park in 1960. Candlestick was known by that name until 1996 when 3Com bought naming rights. Today it's known as Monster Stadium after Monster Cable bought naming rights in September 2004.

The "Stick" was one of the most unloved stadiums in baseball by both players and fans, mainly because of the swirling winds that would cool everyone down—even on a sunny day—and occasionally knock a pitcher off the mound. This happened to the Giants' Stu Miller in the ninth inning of the 1961 All-Star Game. (Well, *knock* is a strong word. Technically, Miller never fell off the mound, but there was enough wind to cause him to move. The umps called a balk because of the movement. Still, the story has achieved apocryphal status because most versions have Miller violently thrown off the mound by wind gusts.) Every pop fly was an adventure, to say the least. To reward fans who actually made it through an entire game and extra innings, the Giants would give out little commemorative stickpins, the Croix de Candlestick. The Giants never drew exceptionally well at Candlestick and, at one point, were headed out of town to St. Petersburg, Fla., until local investors stepped in to buy the team and prevent the move.

Located on the San Francisco Bay at Candlestick Point, Candlestick Stadium was built as a multiuse stadium with the NFL's San Francisco 49ers also a tenant. It wasn't really a cookie-cutter stadium the same way Veterans Stadium and Shea Stadium were; the original design was clearly for a ballpark, with a curved grandstand suited for use with a diamond. Ironically, the 49ers still play there. Since the Giants moved, some changes were made to make it more football-friendly, but the stadium won't likely have a long life as the 49ers are actively seeking a new facility.

How will history judge Candlestick Park? Some great players exhibited their skills there: Juan Marichal, Orlando Cepeda, Willie McCovey, Willie Mays, John Brodie, and Joe Montana all spent their best years there. But one special distinction will live on when history has forgotten the names of these great athletes: the Beatles played their final live concert there on Aug. 29, 1966.

Local Baseball Attractions

The Oakland Athletics play across the Bay at McAfee Coliseum. We cover the team and its ballpark in a separate chapter.

San Francisco had a rich baseball history before the Giants ever moved westward. The San Francisco Seals were a mainstay in the original Pacific Coast League (PCL) since before the turn of the century, playing at Recreation Park (15th and Valencia) from 1906 through 1913 and 1915 through 1930, Ewing Field (Turk and Masonic) in 1914, and Seals Stadium (16th and Bryant) from 1931 through 1957. (The Giants played for two seasons at an expanded Seals Stadium before Candlestick Park opened in 1960.) Another PCL team, the Mission Reds, also played at Recreation Park from 1926 through 1930. Seals Stadium was one of the great ballparks of the Pacific Coast League, located next to the Hamm's Brewery in downtown San Francisco (in fact, the Hamm's tower was a landmark clearly visible to most game attendees). The Seals drew well, and owner Paul I. Fagan was one of the owners agitating to declare the PCL a major league, going after talent from the East. If Fagan and his fellow owners had succeeded, baseball history would have changed. Thanks to great weather, the PCL played longer seasons, and with the increased number of games would have come increased revenues. With teams in Los Angeles and Hollywood, the PCL would probably have had access to a lucrative television contract at some point. With the Angels and Seals firmly ensconced in Los Angeles and San Francisco, the Dodgers and Giants would probably never have headed West.

The Seals are best known as the team with whom a teenage Joe DiMaggio made his first mark in the baseball world. A slew of famous players spent much of their careers with the Seals, who regularly filled 18,600-seat Seals Stadium. Sadly, no markers or plaques commemorate these ballparks in the Old Navy or Petco stores currently occupying the site. (For the record, home plate would be in the Old Navy and Petco is where center field was located.) Before the ballpark was demolished its seats and light towers were shipped to Cheney Stadium in Tacoma; the stanchions and some of the seats are still in use. (We discuss Cheney Stadium in our chapter on Safeco Field and the Seattle Mariners.)

Still, there are some reminders of Seals Stadium and the San Francisco Seals. For starters, there's an ancient bar across the street from the former Seals Stadium site, Double Play Bar & Grill (2401 16th St., at Bryant Street), featuring a host of Seals memorabilia: a 1939 jersey, old baseball gloves, and the top of the Seals Stadium flagpole. In the back room a mural shows how Seals Stadium looked in its heyday with the Seals hosting the cross-bay rivals Oakland Oaks. The food isn't half-bad either.

Many San Francisco tourists will walk by Lefty O'Doul's (333 Geary Street) in San Francisco's trendy Union Square area and not realize the bar was founded in 1958 by the Bay Area baseball legend. O'Doul was born and died in San Francisco, but in between he made the bigs as a pitcher, blew out his arm, and then made his mark as a outfielder, compiling a .349 batting average in 11 seasons spent with the Yankees, Red Sox, Giants (in two different stints), Phillies, and Dodgers—a record that should put him in the National Baseball Hall of Fame, according to some. He returned to the Bay Area as a player-manager with the Seals and later became Joe DiMaggio's first manager. Walking into Lefty O'Doul's after leaving one of the hip Union Square shops can be a jarring experience; the place hasn't changed much since O'Doul passed away in 1969, but that's part of the charm. If you're staying in the Union Square area, the bar is your best bet for a quick, inexpensive breakfast.

Several minor-league teams play in the region. Worth a drive is Raley Field (400 Ballpark Drive, West Sacramento; *rivercats.com*; 916/376-4700), the home of the Sacramento River Cats, the Triple-A affiliate of the Athletics. Raley Field is not the flashiest of ballparks, lacking the sort of signature items found in top-tier ballparks. But it is certainly one of the most beloved ballparks in the minors: during the night of our most recent visit the temperature was over 100 degrees, and yet the ballpark was packed with an actual crowd over 10,000. (It was the eighth consecutive crowd of over 10,000, including the Triple-A All-Star Game and All-Star Monday.) Any ballpark and team drawing these sorts of numbers are doing something right; Raley Field has been the most popular new minor-league ballpark built in the last 10 years.

Also worth a drive, albeit a longer one: Banner Island Ballpark (404 W. Fremont St., Stockton; *stocktonports.com*; 209/644-1900), the home of the Class A Stockton Ports of the California League. The model is basic: there's a single level of seating with a concourse wrapping the entire ballpark. Though the effect is a little sparse—the 4,200 fixed seats are between the foul poles, while there's additional berm and patio seating in the outfield—the end result is

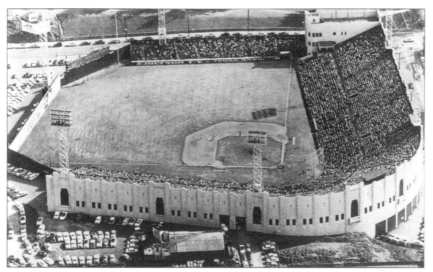

Seals Stadium when it was the home of the Pacfic Coast League's San Francisco Seals.

that most fans will have a good view of the game without feeling too confined.

The San Jose Giants of the Class A California League play at Municipal Stadium (588 E. Alma Av., San Jose; *sjgiants.com*; 408/297-1435), which opened in 1942. The WPA-era ballpark may seem small and quaint by today's standards, but that's part of the appeal. If you go, definitely have some Turkey Mike's Barbeque—it's among the best in the minors.

The Complete Guide to Big League Ballparks

St. Louis Cardinals
Busch Stadium

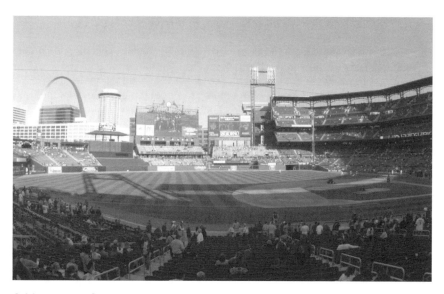

Address: 250 Stadium Plaza (8th and Poplar), St. Louis, MO 63102.
Cost: $365 million.
Architect: HOK Sport.
Owner: St. Louis Cardinals.
Capacity: 46,861.
Dimensions: 336LL, 390LC, 400C, 390RC, 335RL.
Ticket Line: 314/345-9000.
Home Dugout Location: Third-base side.
Playing Surface: Bluegrass.
Other Tenants: None.
First Game: On April 10, 2006, the St. Louis Cardinals christened the new
Busch Stadium with a 6-4 win over the Milwaukee Brewers before a sellout
crowd. Mike Mulder was a double threat for the Cards that day: he threw
eight innings to snare the win and helped out his own cause with a two-run
homer. Albert Pujols hit the first home run in the new Busch Stadium and
Scott Rolen contributed a key two-out, two-run double.
Landmark Event: Not a bad debut for the newest Busch Stadium: the Cardinals
won the 2006 World Series there. Not since 1970 has a team moved to a
new ballpark and made it to the World Series, when the Cincinnati Reds
moved from Crosley Field to Riverfront Stadium and won the National
League title. (The Reds dropped the World Series to Baltimore.)

Your Busch Stadium Seating Crib Sheet

The St. Louis Cardinals use a premium pricing plan with prices increasing for weekend and special games. In general, the ticket prices at Busch Stadium are the third-most expensive in Major League Baseball, trailing the Red Sox and the Yankees. In this section we'll use premium prices.

Best Sections to View a Game: Let's make one thing clear: Redbird Nation will buy most of the seats to the ballpark for the near future, so you'll need to be happy with whatever seats you can score. Having said that, there are obviously some seats better than others. You'll get the best views of the downtown skyway and the St. Louis Gateway Arch when sitting behind home plate or down the third-base line. Not many regular open seats are available behind home plate: much of the seating there is given over to suites and club-level seating. (Speaking of club seats: those go for $90.)

Best Cheap Seats: The cheapest seats for an adult at the new Busch Stadium are $18, and those Outfield Terrace Reserved seats are at the back of the upper deck. You won't be battling the sun there, which you will when sitting in the outfield bleachers. (Those are real bleachers in the outfield, by the way, and not the most comfortable seating in the ballpark.)

Most Underrated Sections: Try as we might, we couldn't think of any in terms of view and amenities. There are three sections where ticket prices are seriously discounted for children: Outfield Terrace Reserved, Pavilion Reserved, and Infield Terrace Reserved—the three sections in the far back of the upper deck. We question the wisdom of marketing these seats to children when the Family Pavilion is a country mile away

Seats to Avoid: The 1st and 3rd Field Box seats go for $78, but they're really borderline. They're somewhat angled toward home plate, but they're set back from the field—there's another section of 12 rows in front of you.

Busch Stadium: Third Time's the Charm

In designing the new Busch Stadium, the St. Louis Cardinals really didn't have a big target to hit: just make it better than the previous Busch Stadium. Redbird Nation is so passionate about their Cardinals that any little improvement would send them into a collective swoon.

Which the new Busch Stadium does. We—that is, book authors, ballpark enthusiasts, and general baseball fans—are not necessarily the target audience for the new Busch Stadium. The passionate Cardinals fans of St. Louis are the target, and we're guessing the new ballpark does not disappoint them. But when compared to other big-league ballparks profiled in this book, Busch Stadium is a utilitarian facility that comes up short of dazzling ballparks like Citizens Bank Park or AT&T Park.

To be totally blunt, we're not sure the Cardinals really care about keeping up with the Joneses when it comes to ballpark amenities found elsewhere. Yes, there are some requisite homages to the past, but there's nothing like Ashburn Alley, the amazing historical displays found in Citizens Bank Park, and they certainly are not central to the Busch Stadium experience. There's the requisite number of concession stands, but you'll find surprisingly little variety given the newness of the facility. The elements are all there, but that last little attention to detail—the kind that makes Citizens Bank Park or AT&T Park such delights—is missing.

Does that absence matter? Not in the least. The Cardinals ownership probably figured out long ago their fan base is one of the most sophisticated and loyal in the majors. The Cardinals rule St. Louis. There's precious little need to woo the casual fan: Cardinals tickets are among the hottest in the majors. There's no need for frou-frou concession stands or flashy memorials to

Busch Stadium

the past at Busch Stadium: build a comfortable ballpark where baseball rules and the sophisticated Cardinals fans will return.

As they did to the second Busch Stadium, designed by Edward Durrell Stone and Sverdrup & Parcel & Associates. The second Busch Stadium, which opened in 1966, was a circular cookie-cutter stadium also hosting the NFL's St. Louis Cardinals. It was hailed as state of the art when it opened but very few players remember it fondly. Because it featured artificial turf, the second Busch was regarded as a tough place to play: tough on the joints and tough on the rest of the body because the artificial turf sucked up heat from the sun. After the NFL's Cards left for Phoenix, the second Busch Stadium was reconfigured for baseball, complete with real grass and retro scoreboards.

A temporary solution, to be sure. Over the years, Cards management realized the second Busch just didn't have the infrastructure—plush suites, club level, premium seating—to financially compete with the big hitters in baseball. And while Cards fans are indeed fanatical in their devotion to their team, they are also demanding. They want a winner.

So the Cards front office did the logical thing: pursue a new ballpark. When state and city funding failed to materialize, the Cards pursued private financing, finally ending on designs for a $365-million ballpark adjacent to the second Busch Stadium.

We're guessing the Cardinals exercised some value engineering as designs evolved because the end result was a ballpark with very few bells and whistles. The St. Louis Cardinals Hall of Fame and Museum is located across Eighth Street from the ballpark; plans are to move it to the Ballpark Village slated for the former Busch Stadium space across the street. A famous statue of Stan

Musial was moved from old Busch Stadium; Stan the Man now stands guard at the Gate 3 entrance. Nifty medallions from Wishstone Chisel & Mallet are scattered through the park and at the entrances; the medallions highlight uniforms and logos used by the Cards throughout the years. (You can buy replicas at the Cardinals gift shop.)

There is really only one direct homage to the second Busch Stadium (and none at all to the first): the installation of the manual scoreboards from Busch (shown on the opposite page), left in the same configuration as they were the day the ballpark closed down in the fall of 2005. Ironically, their presence highlights one of the deficiencies of the new Busch: the new scoreboards convey far less information than these old hand-operated scoreboards. Thank goodness organist Ernie Hays made the move to the new ballpark as well.

The real stars at Busch Stadium are the fans. Yes, the concourses are a little cramped, but that's okay: that means less space between a Cardinals fan and his or her seat. Outside you'll find thousands of bricks engraved with the names of Cardinals fans; we noticed hundreds of fans looking through the engraved bricks to see their family inscriptions. Other new ballparks feature engraved bricks; here it seems to mean more.

Busch Stadium is really two different ballparks: premium seating and ordinary seating. Unless you have a club or suite ticket you're limited to two concourses: a main concourse and an upper concourse. The main concourse rings the ballpark, but not in a way that allowed you to watch the action while heading out for a snack. The outfield bleachers are real bleachers (and there are a lot of them; this is what we mean by value engineering), and a lack of scoreboards in the grandstand gives fans sitting there little data about the game's progress. The bullpens are cut into the outfield bleachers, giving fans plenty of access to middle relievers.

In the end, Busch Stadium was designed to fill the needs of Redbirds Nation. There are no signature items in the ballpark: no rockpile, no spouting geysers, no roof. It's a utilitarian ballpark that's a vast improvement over the old Busch Stadium: the views of downtown and the Arch are superior, the concourses and concessions are better, and the seats are more comfortable. In the end, improvement was all the Cardinals brass had to deliver—and they did.

Ballpark Quirks

Busch Stadium opened in 2006 in an unfinished condition, so it's hard to say what was a quirk and what was simply unfinished. In general, the Cardinals eschewed quirks or whimsical touches: the fences are symmetrical, for example.

One quirk did make it to the first exhibition game, however. Outside the ballpark is a statue (shown above) of former Cardinals great Stan Musial, arguably the best hitter to put on a St. Louis uniform (though that designation may end up going to Albert Pujols in time). A plaque near the statue lists Musial's accomplishments, including five home runs hit in a May 2, 1954 doubleheader. Trouble is, the opponent is listed as the San Francisco Giants. All good baseball historians know at the time the team was the New York Giants. We're guessing the plaque will be fixed pronto and will probably be correct by the time you visit the ballpark.

Food and Drink

The concessions are surprisingly limited. The vast majority of concession stands are variations on a grill and a run-of-the-mill stand featuring hot dogs, nachos and the like. Three Hardee's stands—two in the main concourse, the other on the top level—serve cheap hamburgers (at least cheap by ballpark standards, not by Hardee's standards). There's a single BBQ stand, with a few Italian and kosher-hot-dog stands thrown in for variety.

Better like Bud if you're going to Busch: the only concession stand not selling Bud, Bud Light, Busch, or Bud Select is the Backstop Bar behind home plate, where more exotic beers like Sam Adams and Anchor Steam can be found—provided you can find them among the many bottles of Bud. Now, we're not going to begrudge Anheuser-Busch some monster pouring rights—they did step forward to buy naming rights to the ballpark, after all, keeping the Busch Stadium name intact—but A-B does brew and/or distribute other good beers, like Widmer, Red Hook, and the Michelob line, and those beers should be showcased a bit at the ballpark. It just seems wrong to pay $8.25 for a Busch.

The center-field Plaza Grill serves up toasted ravioli, chicken fingers, and burgers. Toasted ravioli is hailed as a great St. Louis culinary treat, but we were not impressed: when toasted, the ravioli dries out, unredeemable by the accompanying marinara sauce.

For the Kids

We're guessing the U.S. Cellular Family Pavilion in right center is going to be one of the most popular areas in the ballpark, especially with families. There are batting cages (both free and paid) and pitching machines, as well as a separate concession area, miniature Fredbird playground, and table seating.

Speaking of Fredbird: you can build your own lovable stuffed mascot at a stand in the main concourse behind third base. The Build-a-Bear Workshop folks sell pre-stuffed Fredbirds, or you can build your own. Given the long lines in the build-it-yourself line, we're guessing the stand will remain a huge success.

Ballpark Tours

The St. Louis Cardinals offer ballpark tours seven days a week except for New Year's Eve, New Year's Day, Thanksgiving Day, Christmas Eve, Christmas Day, and when day games or other daytime special events are scheduled. They are offered at 9:30 a.m., 11 a.m., 12:30 p.m., and 2 p.m. Tours depart from Gate 5, located on Clark Street on the north side of Busch Stadium. Stops on the tour include the U.S. Cellular Family Pavilion, the Redbird Club, the press box, the Cardinals Club, the warning track, and the Cardinals dugout.

Tickets are available only on the day of the tour (no advance sales) and sell for $10 (adults), $8 (seniors and military), and $6 for children 15-years-old and younger (children 3-years-old and younger are free). For more information call the Busch Stadium Tour Line at 314/345-9565.

Getting There

Busch Stadium sits near the intersection of I-64 and I-55 on the southeastern edge of downtown St. Louis. An exit off I-64 serves the ballpark directly.

While there's no parking right at the ballpark, plenty of ramps and surface lots are available on all four sides. On Eighth Street, for instance, there's a large ramp between Walnut and Clark, as well as large ramps on Broadway between Walnut and Poplar. Large surface lots are also located directly underneath the freeway.

As we note in the section on hotels, a slick way to visit Busch Stadium is to fly in and take the Metro Link to the ballpark area. There is a Busch Stadium stop on the Metro Link light-rail line running directly from the airport; the fare is $3.25 each way.

Where to Stay

An abundance of hotels are located a close walk from both the ballpark and the Metro Link stop. Your best plan of action is to fly in, take the train to the ballpark, and stay at a local hotel. As a bonus, the hotels near the ballpark are also close to the Gateway Arch area.

The three nicest hotels near the ballpark are a block or less from Busch Stadium and Ballpark Village, and we'd recommend any of the three. The closest is the Westin (811 Spruce St.; *starwoodhotels.com*; $90-$250), located right across Eighth Street from the third-base entrance and built into a former Folgers Coffee warehouse-style brick building. (The odd-numbered rooms are on the ballpark side if you want to gaze upon Busch Stadium from your room.) The Hilton St. Louis at the Ballpark (1 S. Broadway; *hilton.com*; $185-$200)—formerly the Pavilion, a Marriott property—has been completely remodeled and sits a block away. It's a larger hotel, with all the amenities you'd expect. The Hilton

> **INSIDER'S TIP**
> Downtown St. Louis isn't the greatest place to stay unless you're incredibly close to the ballpark. There are cheaper accommodations farther away from the ballpark, but to be honest many are borderline establishments—like the Roberts Mayfair, a Wyndham hotel. If you can't score a hotel close to the ballpark and have a family in tow, you may want to consider staying out by the airport and driving in.

> **INSIDER'S TIP**
> St. Louis Union Station (1820 Market St.; *stlouisunionstation.com*; 314/421-6655) is a marvelous facility housed in a restored train station on the southwest edge of downtown St. Louis. It includes a very affordable Hyatt Regency on site, as well as lots of restaurants, shops, and bars. Best of all, there's a Metro Link station on site so you can take the train to and from the game (it's only two exits away).

Outside the ballpark are commemorative bricks purchased by Cardinals fans; they surround plaques honoring important events in Cardinals history.

offers Cardinals packages at $275 that include two outfield seats, a room with a view of the ballpark, and a free Fredbird from the ballpark Build-a-Bear store. The hotel also offers Sunday breakfasts where Fredbird makes an appearance. The St. Louis Drury Plaza (2 S. 4th St.; *druryhotels.com*; $140-$170) combines three old office buildings into one hotel, and while it's the least expensive of three recommended hotels, it contains a lot of extras (free Internet access, happy hour, and breakfast) not found in the other two higher-class establishments.

Other hotels can be found within a few blocks of the ballpark. The Millennium St. Louis (200 S. 4th St.; *millenniumhotels.com*; $130-$200) also features views of the ballpark—it's located straight out center field. Adam's Mark St. Louis (315 Chestnut St.; *adamsmark.com*; $125-$200) is billed as a moderately priced hotel, but beware of the lack of parking there, save expensive valet parking.

While You're There

Two nearly mandatory stops for Redbirds fans should be on your list before and after the game: the St. Louis Cardinals Hall of Fame and Museum, and Mike Shannon's.

The Hall of Fame (111 Stadium Plaza; 314/231-6340; $7.50 adults, $7 seniors, $6 children under 16) currently shares space with the International Bowling Museum in what is surely one of the weirdest museum pairings on the planet. (Your admission entitles you to four free frames of bowling in the basement lanes, no matter your level of interest in bowling.) The museum is fairly complete, highlighting the history of professional baseball in St. Louis; besides a raft of Cardinals memorabilia, the St. Louis Browns and the Negro Leagues' St. Louis Stars are the subjects of prominent displays as well. As you might expect, the stellar career of Stan Musial is discussed in some depth, and there's lots of memorabilia associated with Mark McGuire's home-run exploits. This includes the 1962 Corvette presented to McGuire when he broke Roger Maris's single-season home-run record, as well as a bench made of bases and bats used by McGuire that season. (Yes, you can sit on it.)

Eventually the Hall of Fame will be moved to a new space in Ballpark Village; we're a little irritated the Cardinals aren't incorporating parts of it into the new ballpark a la Ashburn Alley in Philadelphia, but expect to see the Plaza of Champions statues from the old Busch Stadium in Ballpark Village. The museum is open 9-5 during the baseball season, and 9-6:30 on game nights.

Mike Shannon's Steaks and Seafood (620 Market St.; *mikeshannonssteaksandseafood.com*; 314/421-1540) is now next to the Hilton St. Louis at the Ballpark, directly across Walnut from Ballpark Village. While the décor is sleek and modern—punctuated with lots of sports photos from Shannon's personal collection—the cuisine is old-fashioned steakhouse: sirloins, tenderloins, prime rib, porterhouses, lobster, creamed spinach, and a traditional wedge salad. We were amused when we dined there at lunchtime and the waitress recommended the fish sandwich; we had the French dip and were pleased. Mike Shannon is a Missouri sports legend: a local prep star, he signed with the Cardinals out of high school and made the major-league roster by 1964, becoming a key member of the great 1960s Cardinals teams as a clutch-hitting third baseman. He later became a Cards' broadcaster, a position he's held for 35 years; today he broadcasts a talk show live from the restaurant after home games. We'd recommend reservations for dinner before or after the game; there's also a large outdoor deck at the new Mike Shannon's for those wanting a cocktail before the game.

Mike Shannon's isn't the only celebrity steakhouse close to the ballpark. Dierdorf & Hart's (701 Market St.; *dierdorfharts.com*; 314/421-1772) is owned by former Cardinals greats Dan Dierdorf (who later made his mark as a Monday Night Football broadcaster) and Jim Hart. The menu is a little more limited at Dierdorf & Hart's—though you can always have that wedge salad, tenderloin, and creamed-spinach dinner. Al Hrabosky's Ballpark Saloon (800 Cerre St.; *hraboskys.com*; 314/241-6969) is in the shadow of the ballpark. Named for former Cardinals reliever (whose fierce nature on the mound led to the moniker of the "Mad Hungarian") and current Cards broadcaster, the saloon's patio is a popular gathering spot. Cards fans also head to Bernie Federko's Steak & Sports Grill in the Sheraton City Center (400 S. 14th St.; 314/613-6490), where the former NHL great holds court.

A neighborhood bar with few pretensions and a heavy dose of Redbird Nation is Jack Patrick's (1000 Olive St.; 314/436-8879), located several blocks from Busch Stadium.

If you want a little red sauce with that meat, Tony's (410 Market St.; *tonysstlouis.com*; 314/231-7007) is the only four-star restaurant in the state. It's probably not the place to wander in wearing your Cardinals jersey and blue-jean shorts, so be forewarned.

Kemoll's Italian Restaurant (#1 Metropolitan Sq.; 314/421-0555; *kemolls.com*) has an almost irresistible offer: have dinner there before the game and park your car for free. Plus, Kemoll's will accept fans in casual attire—i.e., a Cardinals jersey and blue-jean shorts.

One of the nicest things about the new Busch Stadium is the view of the Gateway Arch in center field for those sitting behind home plate or down the third-base line. A visit to the Arch is recommended for families and individuals interested in American history and the American West. The Gateway Arch exists as a symbol of St. Louis's status as the gateway to the west, as designed by legendary architect Eero Saarinen: as the centerpiece of Jefferson National Expansion Memorial, the Arch is now a universal shorthand for St. Louis, and its graceful curves were echoed in the arches atop the second Busch Stadium. You can take a tram to the top of the 630-foot-high Arch and treat yourself to some spectacular vistas. Also in the Jefferson National Expansion Memorial: the Museum of Westward Expansion (focusing on the Lewis and Clark Expedition, where President Thomas Jefferson sent the pair to catalogue the Louisiana Purchase and find a water route to the Pacific Ocean) and St. Louis's Old Courthouse, where Dred Scott originally won his case for freedom

Sportsman's Park, from the air.

(ultimately the U.S. Supreme Count ruled otherwise, holding that slaves had no rights). (*Jefferson National Expansion Memorial, 11 N. 4th St.; 314/655-1700; nps.gov/jeff/about.html.*)

Team Ballpark History

The St. Louis Cardinals can trace the team's lineage to Chris Von der Ahe's St. Louis Browns, who were a hit playing at the original Sportsman's Park. Von der Ahe was a St. Louis saloon owner ignorant about the game of baseball, but he knew about beer and baseball's immense appeal to the German immigrants of St. Louis. He bought a controlling interest in the St. Louis Brown Stockings and their home, Grand Avenue Park, eventually installing a beer garden right on the playing field.

When the National League banned Sunday games and beer from ballparks in 1879 (surprisingly surviving the ban), Von der Ahe picked up his marbles and defected to the American Association. That league, dubbed by many as the "beer and whiskey" league, became the first serious competitor to the National League. And while many of the teams in the American Association were borderline economic propositions, the Browns led the majors in attendance from 1885-88. When the American Association folded at the end of 1891, Von der Ahe's Browns returned to the National League.

By 1893 the Browns had outgrown the original Sportsman's Park (at Grand

and Dodier) and Von der Ahe moved to a new ballpark—New Sportsman's Park (at Vandeventer and Natural Bridge avenues). But the move and poor showings on the field led a bankrupt Von der Ahe to sell the team to brothers Frank and Stanley Robinson in 1898. They made a series of changes, dumping the Browns moniker in favor of the Perfectos and renaming Sportsman's Park to League Park. Public reaction to the Perfectos name was mixed, although fans seemed to like the red uniforms. After a St. Louis sportswriter overheard a lady fan say, "What a lovely shade of cardinal" upon first seeing the uniforms, a new name was born, and the team officially became the St. Louis Cardinals in 1900.

In the meantime, an upstart American League team—playing in 1901 as the Milwaukee Brewers—eagerly appropriated St. Louis's baseball history in 1902, taking the name of the St. Louis Browns and moving into the old ballpark at Grand and Dodier, calling it Sportsman's Park.

League Park was renamed Robinson Park in 1911 after the team's owners. The name didn't stick: by 1917 it was renamed Cardinal Field and a young Branch Rickey was installed as the league's GM and president.

Rickey was a sharp operator and, when Sam Breadon took control of the team in 1920, he took the radical step of selling Cardinal Field and becoming a tenant of the Browns at Sportsman's Park. Using the proceeds of the ballpark sale Breadon and Rickey set up the first farm system in baseball. For the first time minor-league baseball teams were directly affiliated with a major-league club, thus ensuring the Cardinals a steady stream of prospects. It was a more expensive approach to the game (the practice had been for major-league teams to buy the contracts of minor leaguers—a system that encouraged bidding for prospects), but it ensured stability both for the Cardinals and the minor-league teams. (For the record: the first Cardinals farm team was the Houston Buffs.)

Sportsman's Park after it was renamed Busch Stadium.

During the same time the St. Louis Browns thrived and was actually the better box-office draw, leading the team to expand the capacity of Sportsman's Park from 18,000 to 30,000 in 1926. George Sisler was the big star for the Browns and a decent box-office attraction, hitting .420 in 1922. It was an era of great players in St. Louis: the Cardinals' Rogers Hornsby hit .424 in 1924, snared a Triple Crown in 1925, and as a player-manager won a World Series in 1926.

Over time, the agreement to share Sportsman's Park worked out well financially for both the Browns and the Cardinals, though the Cardinals became the better box-office draw. That changed somewhat when legendary promoter Bill Veeck bought the Brownies in 1951 and infused some life into the franchise. Veeck, however, saw the writing on the wall when Gussie Busch and Anheuser-Busch bought the Cardinals in 1952, soon after announcing he would seek to move the Browns to either Milwaukee or Baltimore. Lou Perini beat Veeck to Milwaukee with the move of the Boston Braves, and in 1953 Major League Baseball owners voted to deny Veeck's request to move the Browns to Baltimore. That denial essentially put Veeck out of business and he knew it: he sold Sportsman's Park to Anheuser-Busch and the Browns to a Baltimore group. The Browns became the Baltimore Orioles for the 1954 season and St. Louis became a one-team town for the first time since 1901. Busch also made a little history by dropping the Sportsman's Park name in favor of Busch Stadium beginning with the 1953 season.

The 1960s weren't kind to old ballparks like Sportsman's Park, and by the early part of the decade Anheuser-Busch and city officials were working on a new ballpark, which opened in 1966. Busch Stadium was one of the dreaded multipurpose cookie-cutter ballparks, hosting both the Cardinals and the NFL's St. Louis Cardinals, relocated from Chicago. With a hard Astroturf that soaked up the hot Missouri sun and some awkward seating arrangements, Busch Stadium was beloved not because of the physical configuration—heavy on the concrete, light on the amenities—but because of the great Cardinals players and managers who thrived in St. Louis: Lou Brock, Joe Torre, Mark McGuire, Ozzie Smith, Bob Gibson, Mike Shannon, Orlando Cepeda, Ted Simmons, Jack Clark, Whitey Herzog, Tony LaRussa, and Albert Pujols. Those are the players who created the memories that made Busch Stadium great.

Local Baseball Attractions

Two of the biggest local baseball attractions were already discussed in this chapter: the St. Louis Cardinals Hall of Fame and Museum, and Mike Shannon's.

We also mentioned Sportsman's Park in the previous section. Located at Grand and Dodier (2901 N. Grand Av., to be exact), Sportsman's Park was the center of St. Louis baseball when both the Browns and the Cardinals played there. It was host to every game in the 1944 World Series when the Cards defeated the Browns four games to two.

When the Cardinals moved to Busch Stadium, the team turned the site over

Busch Stadium

to a community group, and eventually the Herbert Hoover Boys and Girls Club was built on the site. Part of the old Sportsman's Park outfield is still a park, but a tennis court occupies the space where home plate was located. A plaque and other displays mark the history of the old ballpark. (Be forewarned the club is not in the best part of town.)

While neither is worth a special trip, two roads in St. Louis are named for former greats. James "Cool Papa" Bell was a star of the Negro Leagues, a fast center fielder who spent time with the St. Louis Stars and once stole 175 bases in a season. The former Dickson Street, now Cool Papa Bell Street, is between Martin Luther King Jr. Drive and Jefferson Avenue, northwest of downtown St. Louis.

When Mark McGuire broke the single-season home-run record, Missouri legislators renamed a six-mile stretch of I-70 after him.

Speaking of Bell: a 10-foot high memorial marks his gravesite at St. Peter's Cemetery (2101 Lucas & Hunt Rd.), constructed when Bell was elected to the National Baseball Hall of Fame in 1974.

Two teams in the independent Frontier League play in nearby cities southeast and east of St. Louis. The Gateway Grizzlies play at GMC Stadium (2301 Grizzlie Bear Blvd., Sauget, Ill.; *gatewaygrizzlies.com*; 618/337-3000), while the River City Rascals play in O'Fallon, Mo., about 35 miles west of St. Louis. T.R. Hughes Ballpark (900 Ozzie Smith Dr., O'Fallon; *rivercityrascals.com*; 636/240-2287;) is considered one of the nicer ballparks in minor-league baseball, but both ballparks are worth the drive. To reach GMC Stadium, take I-255 to Mousette Lane (Exit 15). Go west to the stop sign onto Sauget Industrial Park Drive, then left at the stop sign to Goose Lake Road. The ballpark will be on the right. To reach T.R. Hughes Ballpark, take I-70 west to the T.R. Hughes Blvd. exit. Take a right (north) from the off-ramp and continue on for approximately one mile. T.R. Hughes Ballpark is on the right-hand side at the corner of T.R. Hughes Blvd. and Tom Ginnever Avenue.

Arizona Diamondbacks
Chase Field

Address: 401 East Jefferson Street, Phoenix, AZ 85004.
Cost: $354 million.
Architect: Ellerbe Becket.
Owner: Maricopa County Stadium District.
Capacity: 49,033.
Dimensions: 328L, 402C, 335R.
Ticket Lines: 602/514-8400, 888/777-4664.
Home Dugout Location: Third-base side.
Playing Surface: Grass.
Other Names: Bank One Ballpark (The BOB), 1998-2005.
Other Tenants: None currenly. The Insight Bowl was played at the BOB
    between 2000 and 2005.
First Game: On March 31, 1998, the Colorado Rockies defeated the expansion
    Arizona Diamondbacks 9-2 before an above-capacity crowd of 50,179.
    Rookie Travis Lee (who also collected the first Diamondbacks hit, a single in
    the first) and Karim Garcia homered for the D-Backs; Andy Benes started
    the game for Arizona and suffered the loss. Two days previously a capacity
    crowd was on hand to see the first exhibition game played at Bank One
    Ballpark as the Chicago White Sox defeated the D-Backs, 3-0.
Landmark Events: The National League champion Arizona Diamondbacks held
    the home-field advantage for the 2001 World Series, won by the
    Diamondbacks in dramatic fashion in Game 7 when Luis Gonzalez's flare to
    center field plated the winning run with the bases loaded in the bottom of
    the ninth.

Your Chase Field Seating Crib Sheet

Best Sections to View a Game: Most of the seating at the game provides a great view of the action. On the lower level you'll want to stick between sections 110 and 134; any further out and you'll feel like you're in another part of the ballpark. In the upper level, virtually every seat between sections 305 and 327 is decent.

Best Cheap Seats: The seats are bad, but $1 will get you into the ballpark. The seats are way up in the corners and beyond the TGI Friday's in left field, but at least you're in the ballpark. The Diamondbacks are pretty good about letting you wander around Chase Field, so you can watch a few innings at the remote seats and then view the game from one of many vantage points scattered throughout.

Most Underrated Sections: Believe it or not, the Clubhouse seats—the most expensive in the park at $110 ($114 on weekends)—may be a little underrated. They're great seats, right against the backstop with an unbelievable view of the action. With them, you also gain access to the private lounges under the grandstand. If you're feeling the need to splurge a little, these are the seats for you.

Seats to Avoid: The $8 seats in the upper level and lower-level seats down the lines (109 and below, 135 and above) are not very good compared to the rest of the ballpark. In theory, every seat is angled toward the infield, but those angles can be a little pronounced in some sections.

Chase Field: Fun Shaded from the Sun

You simply cannot escape an air-conditioned existence when spending any time in Phoenix in the summer: the desert atmosphere so welcome for spring training in March becomes rather tiresome by the beginning of June when it's just too darn hot to be outside.

At the end of the day, air conditioning is perhaps America's greatest contribution to the world, and air conditioning makes Chase Field an oasis. We know Phoenix natives aren't afraid of being outside in the hot summertime, but that doesn't mean they're willing to spend three hours outside on an August evening. Major-league baseball couldn't exist in Phoenix without an air-conditioned ballpark like Chase Field—which is good news for the rest of us.

Chase Field is built for comfort, not flashiness, engineered by the kind of folks who sought to solve a slew of problems and then didn't have the energy left to address issues like ornamentation. In other words, Chase Field feels like it was designed by engineers, not architects. Not that this is a bad thing: it took a lot of engineering to solve the many challenges of bringing major-league baseball to the Valley of the Sun.

Chase Field features a retractable roof, air conditioning, and a grass playing field, the first such combo in major-league history. (The original Astrodome design sported natural grass under a glass roof, but the experiment was a huge failure when not enough sunlight pierced the roof. Hence Astroturf.) The 8,000-ton air-conditioning system takes only about four hours to cool down the stands and concourses from 110 degrees to 72 degrees. (The playing area is not cooled.)

That's not the only engineering feat at the ballpark. Growing decent grass in Arizona in the summertime is hard enough, especially when it's partially shaded much of the time. Even when opening the roof during the day to allow in sunshine, it took a few months for the grounds crew to come up with the right grass—in this case, a blend of Bull's Eye Bermuda, Kentucky blue grass, and rye grass—to withstand the scorching sun and extremes between hot days and cool nights. (Sections of turf lacking enough sunlight get their own special treatment with the help of incandescent grow lights.) More recently, Seattle and Houston have successfully combined a retractable roof with natural grass.

Speaking of the roof: despite the scale, the 9-million-pound roof is a fairly simple mechanism. Two halves—made up of three trusses—are opened or closed using four miles of cable pulled by two 200-horsepower motors. It takes only four minutes to open or close the roof (because the roof is so light, it costs the team only $2 in electricity to open or close it). The Diamondbacks do it in style: they hold a countdown to the opening of the roof, performed to special theme music. (Alas, the roof remains closed for most of the season; if you want to see it open be sure to head to Phoenix in April or May.) Technically, the roof doesn't seal: one side fits on top of the other, and there's enough of a gap to allow air to flow through. (It's enough space to allow rain to fall through, too, which happens from time to time.) During the day, you'll often see only half of the roof open to allow sunlight on the field but not in the stands. The

Diamondbacks have sole authority over the roof opening decisions, and the team usually maps out several days in advance whether or not the roof will be open. (You can check the team's Web site at *mlb.com* for the roof-opening status or call 602/379-7663). At other ballparks, such as Rogers Centre in Toronto, the umpires and opposing managers are notified when a roof is to be opened or closed, with the umpires able to overrule the decision if a protest is lodged by the opposing manager. On hot nights, the roof is not opened; in the past Diamondbacks pitchers (especially Randy Johnson) were vociferous in their belief the roof should be closed for almost every game. When the roof opens, six large window screens in left field open as well. Although you never feel like you're at an outdoor event at Chase Field, you can get a decent approximation of it when the roof and windows are open.

In many ways, Chase Field plays against type. Phoenix is square in the desert, but nothing really approaches a Western or Southwestern motif in the ballpark (unless you count the new uniforms the D-Backs are slated to wear in the 2007 season). Most of Chase Field is understated, to say the least, but in center field there's a pool designed for groups of 35 or more. When the ballpark was built, the Diamondbacks were mocked for the pool, but now it's become a signature item.

In fact, the whole ballpark is a little bland, though not fatally so. As we've pointed out, it's built for comfort, not for flash. The exterior is your standard retro brick and steel, which is out of place in the Valley of the Sun no matter how much the team and the ballpark designers say it fits into the old warehouse area of Phoenix. (One old warehouse was incorporated into the façade of the south side of the ballpark.) When you think of Phoenix architecture, you think of these wonderful, low-slung buildings designed to fit within the desert environment, shaded and cool. You think of the Biltmore, you think of Taliesin West, you think modern (as in the spiffed-up exterior of next-door US Airways Arena), you think of the Heard Museum, you think of the Wild West—you don't think ballpark retro.

Once inside, there's little flash to the décor. It's cool when the roof opens, and it's always fun to wander the concourses and gawk at the bikini-clad women in the center-field pool. The layout is a standard three-level design: a main level, a club/suite level, and an upper deck. Almost 90 percent of the seating is between the foul lines; small sections of bleachers are located in left field and right field—though the left-field area is more suited to groups and just standing around.

One thing about Chase Field: despite the massive footprint, it doesn't feel like a huge park. It's never a pain to move from level to level (enough elevators and escalators are in place) and wandering through the ballpark doesn't take the day-and-a-half it does in some other new facilities. Score one for intimacy.

Perhaps the reason you don't feel like it takes a lot of time traversing the concourse is the display of baseball history. Baseball-history nuts will also appreciate the displays of historical memorabilia throughout the main concourse. Take note of the small gloves the old-timers used, as well as programs and memorabilia from the old Phoenix Firebirds minor-league franchise. The team logo was simply outstanding.

It seems doubtful Chase Field will ever be considered a classic ballpark: it's a little plain, with an emphasis on function over form. But it's a comfortable ballpark and well worth a visit if you'll be in the Phoenix area.

Ballpark Quirks

There really are none: the quirks were all engineered out, and major-league baseball hasn't been played long enough in Phoenix for the fans to develop any endearing traditions.

The closest thing to a quirk is to listen to the cheers when the roof is opened. The Diamondbacks instituted a theme of sorts for opening the roof in 1999, but the one-year theme was extended indefinitely after fans called for the return of the music. That's about as quirky as it gets at Chase Field.

Food and Drink

As with any newer ballpark, an abundance of food and drink options are available. With 39 fixed and 35 portable concession stands (a relatively small number by modern ballpark standards), the concourses are usually crammed with folks waiting for a beer or food.

We've found the local vendors offer the best food. If you stroll the concourses, you can also find items like vegetarian Gardenburgers, turkey burgers, chicken sandwiches, chicken tenders, Mexican specialties and the standard ballpark fare: hot dogs (quite good, by the way), brats, pizza, candy, etc. One interesting concession twist: the Diamondbacks offer signature food items from other ballparks, including Dodger Dogs from Los Angeles.

The view from the Lexus Club—white-linen dining at the ballpark.

The beer selection runs the gamut from microbrews to offerings from the giants. The prices are right—$4 for a small, $7 for a large—and you can find Foster's, MGD, Lite, and Bud Select at various stands. For those who want to stand around and quaff a brew while watching the game, two beer gardens are located in the upper deck. If beer isn't your thing, you can get Jose Cuervo margaritas at your seat via roaming vendors.

Two restaurants offer differing experiences within the ballpark. The Lexus Club is a white-table-linen buffet with seats overlooking the action in right field. The rules for entry have relaxed since it opened as the Arizona Baseball Club: it's now open to anyone attending a game, not just club-seat patrons. During our visit, the spread was pretty luxurious (you could spend quite a few innings sampling the fare) and the price is reasonable: $27.95 plus beverage, tax, and tip. There are two sittings per game; the second shift is definitely the better of the two, as there's no deadline to vacate your table and the view. The Friday's Front Row Sports Grill is located in the left-field corner; no table linens there, and the food is not quite as upscale.

If you prefer bland chain food, check out the Panda Express, Blimpie's, and McDonald's stands; Panda Express is the only place in the ballpark serving sushi.

For the Kids

A visit to the play area beyond the center-field scoreboard is highly recommended for families. There, your children will be tired out by a miniature diamond where they can run around to their joy's content, as well as peruse the home of Baxter, the genial mascot of the Diamondbacks. Baxter's Den features family pictures of Baxter, as well as descriptions of his family and history with the team. It's a little hokey, but the kids love Baxter and he regularly drops by his den during the fourth and fifth innings. The Peter Piper Playhouse also features interactive video games, a batting cage, and skeet ball.

Ballpark Tours

The Diamondbacks offer ballpark tours. The cost—$6 for adults, $4 for children ages 7-12 and seniors, and $2 for children ages 4-6—directly benefits Arizona Diamondbacks Charities, the fundraising arm of the team.

The extensive tour covers the following areas: the Rotunda entrance, the grass field, the pool party pavilion, the Lexus Club, a luxury suite, the visitor's clubhouse, an underground batting tunnel, the press box (except on game days), dugouts, and the team shop.

Tours are offered year-round, but the exact times vary. Call 602/514-8400 or 888/777-4664 for more information and for a specific date and times when tours will be given.

Local Baseball Attractions

Few baseball attractions are located close to the ballpark. Your only real choice is Cooper's Town, located two blocks west of Chase Field. Cooper's Town was created by baseball fanatic and longtime rocker Alice Cooper, who had settled in Phoenix after his shock-rock days and was looking for a new challenge.

Cooper's Town is an entertainment complex featuring a restaurant and outdoor stage sometimes hosting live music. The themes are sports and rock and roll: think of a Hard Rock Cafe run by sports geeks and you have a pretty good vision of the sports and rock memorabilia dominating the interior.

The fare is fairly eclectic for a theme restaurant: there's the "Ty Cobb Salad," the "Ryne Sandburger," and the "Megadeth Meatloaf." Cooper's Town does its own smoking on the premises, so the ribs are recommended. Fans of home cooking will appreciate the tuna-noodle casserole made from Mama Alice's recipe. And yes, Alice Cooper does spend quite a bit of time hanging around when he's not at the ballpark. *Alice Cooper's Town, 101 E. Jackson St., Phoenix; 602/253-7337; alicecooperstown.com.*

Also close to Chase Field: Majerle's Sports Grill. Dan Majerle was a star basketball forward for the Phoenix Suns, and when US Airways Arena (originally known as America West Arena) was completed in 1992, Majerle went into the sports-bar business and opened up Majerle's in the oldest commercial building in downtown Phoenix. *Majerle's Sports Grill, 24 N. 2nd St.; 602/253-0118; majerles.com.*

Another sports bar in the general vicinity worth visiting is Jackson's on

3rd, south of US Airways Arena and to the west of Chase Field. It's really three clubs in one: a sports bar, a live-music club, and a dance club. *Jackson's on 3rd, 245 E. Jackson; 602/254-5303; www.jacksonsonthird.com.*

There is also a bar directly between Chase Field and US Airways Arena. When it first opened, the Leinie Lodge—serving Leinenkugel Beer—was an odd, but welcome addition to the area: Odd because there probably wasn't much call for a Wisconsin-themed microbrewery in the Valley of the Sun, but welcome because Leinie beers are so good. But the Lodge closed, and the space has devolved into this anonymous Hooter's-wannabe-kinda place. If you have a shred of dignity, skip it. If you have kids, definitely skip it.

Getting There

Phoenix's mass-transit system is rudimentary, to say the least: it consists of buses: no light rail (yet), no subways. If you're visiting Phoenix, you'll probably need to rent a car unless you're staying with friends or plan on staying downtown and walking to the ballpark. It's very expensive to rent a car in Phoenix, thanks to the almost 50 percent rental-car tax rate that funds a whole slew of services in the Valley of the Sun.

If you drive, our tip is to follow the highway signs to the ballpark. No single way is really the best way to the ballpark: Phoenix was built around the freeway and all roads— like I-10 and I-17—lead to

INSIDER'S TIP
Many folks park in the ramp at Arizona Center, north of the ballpark on 5th Street between Van Buren and Taylor, and then walk to the game or ride back via rickshaw. We'll cover Arizona Center in a following section.

INSIDER'S TIP
Though mass transit in Phoenix isn't the greatest, two noteworthy services could come in handy during your stay.

The first is a free shuttle bus circulating in the downtown area. During the evening the shuttle runs between 5:30 and 11 p.m., stopping at Chase Field, the Civic Plaza, Collier Center, various restaurants on Washington and Jackson streets, and the Orpheum Theater.

The second is the presence of rickshaws that gather on Jefferson Street on the north side of the ballpark. Rickshaws involve no set fees so you're free to make an offer when you approach a driver. They can take you anywhere in the downtown area.

downtown. Your exact route will depend on your approach to the ballpark.

Despite its sprawling nature, the Valley of the Sun is surprisingly easy to navigate. Once you master your location relative to the freeways or to one of the major streets in the region, you stand a much better chance of not getting lost in a new area. Why? Because the entire Phoenix-area region is built in a grid system that extends to the far suburbs. Freeways and bypasses intersect the grid at convenient points, making Phoenix easy to navigate.

Two major freeways service the area: I-10 and I-17. I-10 enters the region from the west (where it's known as the Papago Freeway), runs through the center of Phoenix, and then heads south to Tempe and Tucson. This is the one freeway you'll spend some time driving. I-17 (Black Canyon Freeway) comes in from the north and loops south of downtown before merging with I-10 (the merged stretch is called the Maricopa Freeway) near Sky Harbor International Airport.

Once in the city, some major streets will get you places: Washington Street, Buckeye Road, Van Buren Street, McDowell Road, Thomas Road, Indian School Road, and Camelback Road are all major east-west streets that will usually get you close to where you want to go.

Parking is not a problem near Chase Field. Within blocks some 30,000 spaces are available. You can easily find something for $10 or less, including the 1,500-car ramp attached to the ballpark on Fourth Street (a skyway connects the ramp with the suite level of Chase Field). A lot is located directly south of the ramp; parking at either is $8. The Civic Plaza East Garage (across the street, on Washington and 5th Street) is one of the spendier downtown lots at $8, but it allows you to park your car in the shade, as does the attached garage located on the south side of the ballpark. Otherwise, pick from a slew of surface lots to the west along Jackson Street.

Sky Harbor International Airport is the major airport in the region. It is also one of the most confusing airports in the United States, thanks to a poor design that splits the airport into three unconnected terminals. If you plan to meet buddies in the Phoenix airport, don't merely arrange your meeting by the luggage pickup or car-rental areas. With three autonomous terminals, you also have three separate car-rental booth areas (though the lots are all located offsite). *Sky Harbor International Airport, 3400 E. Sky Harbor Blvd., Phoenix; (602) 273-3300; phxskyharbor.com.*

If you're coming in just for baseball, we'd recommend you stay downtown. (See the following section for more information on downtown hotels.) Despite little to do in downtown Phoenix, some definite signs of life are emerging. A section of south downtown, Copper Square features hotels, restaurants, and other services, benefiting from a recent marketing push.

Where to Stay

Downtown Phoenix features several hotels within an easy walk of the ballpark. There's also a wide price range between the hotels so you can choose what best fits your pocketbook.

Our recommendation is the Hotel San Carlos (202 N. Central Av.; *hotelsancarlos.com*), the first modern, air-conditioned hotel in Phoenix. Opening in 1928, the elegant Hotel San Carlos—then considered a high-rise at seven stories, complete with an elevator—attracted more than its share of dignitaries and celebrities, including the likes of Mae West, Clark Gable, and Jean Harlow. Cocktail lounges and card rooms attracted the locals as well. The room rates vary widely depending on demand: we've seen rates as high as $220 a night during the high season and as low as $59 in the offseason. In a city with little of historical importance, the Hotel San Carlos is the real deal.

If historic is not your bag, pick from a host of newer hotels downtown within a half-mile (and easy walking distance) of the ballpark, including the Hyatt Regency (122 N. 2nd St.; *hyatt.com*; $175-$225), Wyndham Phoenix Downtown (50 E. Adams St.; *wyndham.com*; $150-$200), Springhill Suites Phoenix Downtown (802 E. Van Buren; *marriott.com*; $100-$150), and the

Ramada Inn Downtown (401 N. 1st St.; *ramada.com*; $75-$100).

An alternative is staying out by the airport, which is fairly close to downtown. You can use cabs to get to and from games or bite the bullet and rent a car. Virtually every chain—Super 8, Days Inn, Econo Lodge, Travelodge, Holiday Inn, Ramada, Crowne Plaza, Extended Stay, Radisson, Doubletree, Hampton Inn, Hilton, Marriott, Sleep Inn, and La Quinta—has at least one hotel in the general airport vicinity.

If you're committed to driving anyway, you can look at staying at one of Phoenix's several resorts. After the Hotel San Carlos was built and attracted fame, other entrepreneurs stepped in and built large-scale resorts in the area. The most famous such resorts are the Arizona Biltmore Resort (2400 E. Missouri Av.; *arizonabiltmore.com*), The Phoenician (6000 E. Camelback Rd., Scottsdale; *thephoenician.com*), the Fairmont Scottsdale Princess (7575 E. Princess Dr., Scottsdale; *fairmont.com*), and the Royal Palms Resort (5200 E. Camelback Rd., Scottsdale; *royalpalmshotel.com*). Partially financed by chewing-gum magnate William Wrigley, Jr., the Biltmore's design was influenced by Frank Lloyd Wright, dating to 1929. (Despite urban legend, the resort was not designed by him; however, Taliesin Associates did oversee a 1973 renovation and later work was designed explicitly patterned after Wright's furniture and building designs.) The low-slung design is made up mostly of "Biltmore Blocks," precast concrete blocks from sculptor Emry Kopta.

The Phoenician isn't quite as old or historic, but it's more opulent: the rooms are large, the private balconies feature great views, and the staff is accustomed to providing a high level of service. The rates at the area resorts

usually begin at $200 a night and can run into four figures for a villa at the Biltmore, but if you schedule a stay for the slow seasons in July or August you can save a little.

Even if you don't stay there, head to the Biltmore and take in the atmosphere with a cocktail in the lobby lounge.

The resorts all run on roughly the same model: your days are expected to be filled with leisure as Mom and Grandma hit the shops, the kids hit the large pool areas, and Dad and Grandpa hit the golf course. Simple, no?

Local Attractions

The Arizona Biltmore has its own nearby shopping mall: the Biltmore Fashion Mall (2502 E. Camelback Road; *shopbiltmore.com*), featuring a slew of upscale shops (Saks Fifth Avenue, Oilily, Cartier, Betsey Johnson) and restaurants (Capital Grille, Bamboo Club).

Other resorts are closer to the shopping mecca of Scottsdale. Four major districts divide downtown Scottsdale: Fifth Avenue, Main Street, Old Town, and Marshall Way. Fifth Avenue features upscale shopping and dining; the Marshall Way Arts District features art galleries specializing in contemporary art from local artists, as well as a wide variety of regionally produced jewelry; Main Street is one of the largest concentrations of art galleries in the world; and Old Town features the Wild West kitsch.

Shopping is one of the major attractions of Phoenix; golf is another. We're not going to list the many golf courses in the region—many resorts have their own courses and, if they don't, they have affiliations with nearby courses—and with such a wide range of course skill levels and price ranges, we'll leave it up to you to make your own tee times.

That isn't to say there's not a lot to do in downtown. We've already mentioned Cooper's Town and some other eateries within a close walk of the ballpark, but those are not the only downtown spots worth visiting.

Coach & Willie's, strictly speaking, is not a sports bar, though it caters to sports fans heading to Chase Field and US Airways Arena. It sports a definite Southwestern spirit—the stone-and-wrought-iron deck is the big attraction— and the portions are huge. It's within a block of the ballpark, which makes it popular both before and after the game. *Coach & Willie's, 412 S. 3rd St.; coachandwillies.com; 602/254-5272.*

If it's a Sunday morning and you've imbibed a few too many at the game, the best place for a hangover cure is the Matador Restaurant, family-owned and fairly unchanged over the last 30 years. Go for the huevos rancheros; the chorizo is truly spicy. *Matador Restaurant, 125 E. Adams St.; 602/254-7663.*

If your tastes run a little more upscale, Kincaid's is a stylish steakhouse. The one-page menu is simple with an emphasis on elegantly prepared steaks, chops, poultry, and seafood. Alas, there's no late-night dining, so it's not a place to head after the game. *Kincaid's, 2 S. 3rd St.; kincaids.com; 602/340-0000.*

If you prefer your meat more downscale, La Mesa Pit BBQ is probably more your style. Owned by local entrepreneurs, La Mesa Pit BBQ offers hearty smoked ribs, pulled pork, beef brisket, and beer-butt chicken. If you're coming from the South, be prepared for Western-styled BBQ with more nuanced flavors, to say the least. *La Mesa Pit BBQ, 20 W. Adams St.; lamesapitbbq.com; 480/214-0048.*

For those who just can't resist a chain, there's the Hard Rock Café. It's just like all the other Hard Rock Cafés around the world: good burgers and lots of memorabilia. *Hard Rock Café, 3 S. 2nd St., Suite 117; hardrockcafe.com; 602/261-7625.*

The best pure sports bar close to the ballpark is Lucky Break Game and Grill, a huge pool hall/restaurant/dueling-piano bar/restaurant. With 30 TVs scattered throughout, you're bound to find a game of some sort to watch. *Lucky Break Game and Grill, 3 S. 2nd St., Suite 113; luckybreakphoenix.com; 602/307-5825.*

We mentioned Arizona Center as a place where many D-Backs fans gather before and after games. It's only four long blocks from the ballpark (easily within walking distance) and the food offerings are definitely on the casual side. Mi Amigo's Mexican Grill is the place for authentic Mexican fare, while Lombardi's features upscale, wood-fired Italian fare. For those looking for a different kind of entertainment with their meal: Hooter's. *Arizona Center, 400 N. 5th St.; arizonacenter.com; 602/229-1228.*

If you want to cast your net a little wider, the Barrio Café is relatively close to downtown Phoenix and worth the short drive. Silvana Salcido Esparza offers the most imaginative fare in the Valley of the Sun: the conchinita pibil (slow-roasted Mayan pork) is to die for, while the guacamole is prepared tableside to ensure the maximum freshness. They don't take reservations; our recommendation is heading there before the doors open at 5:30 p.m. to snare a table at the first seating before going to a game. *Barrio Café, 2814 N. 16th St.; barriocafe.com; 602/636-0240.*

Also worth the drive: Lo Lo's Chicken & Waffles. It's only a mile from the ballpark so, in theory, you could walk there. And after gobbling down a full plate of chicken and waffles you may want to burn off some of those calories. For those not from the South or Los Angeles (two areas where the pairing of fried chicken and waffles is not ridiculed), there's something sublime about golden-colored soul food prepared right. Also on the menu: fish, some great sides (like mac and cheese), and red velvet cake. The place can get crowded so be prepared for a wait after a Friday night game, and don't go there if you're in a hurry: it takes time to properly fry chicken, and everything at Lo Lo's is made from scratch. *Lo Lo's Chicken & Waffles, 10 W. Yuma St.; 602/340-1304.*

Team Ballpark History
The Arizona Diamondbacks have played every home game in team history at Bank One Ballpark/Chase Field since entering the National League as an expansion team in the 1998 season.

Other Area Baseball Attractions

Nearby Scottsdale features plenty of upscale shopping and Western art. It also features one of the best restaurants in the Valley of the Sun for baseball fans: Don and Charlie's (7501 E. Camelback Road; *donandcharlies.com*; 480/990-0900). Owner Don Carson opened shop in 1981 and immediately established a sports theme before the rise of the strip-mall sports bar: it's a classy place, to say the least. During spring training it's a favorite haunt for Giants and Cubs players; it's also a favorite spot for retired players in the area. You could spend hours looking at the sports memorabilia throughout the place. Despite its corporate ownership—it's part of the Lettuce Entertain You chain—you can find Don patrolling the premises much of the time.

The Tucson Sidewinders of the Pacific Coast League play at Tucson Electric Park, located 110 miles southeast of Phoenix. The Sidewinders are the Triple-A affiliate of the Diamondbacks. *Tucson Electric Park, 2500 E. Ajo Way, Tucson; tucsonsidewinders.com.*

If you do head down to Tucson, stop at Casa Grande and check out the Francisco Grande Hotel (2600 Gila Bend Hwy.; the route is marked from the freeway), the former spring-training home of the San Francisco Giants. It was built by Giants owner Horace Stoneham with a baseball theme: the swimming pool is shaped like a baseball bat and the parking lot is shaped like a glove. Out beyond the hotel is an observation deck where the Giants coaching staff would watch the action on four surrounding diamonds. The current hotel management plays up the Giants angle with plenty of historic photos throughout. If you head to the roof you can see remnants of the complex in all its glory.

One of the oldest ballparks still standing is Warren Ballpark in Bisbee (on Ruppe Avenue between Arizona Street and Bisbee Road). The ballpark location dates to 1909, when the venue hosted railroad teams and barnstormers. It was rebuilt in 1930 and played host to minor-league baseball through 1955.

The Complete Guide to Big League Ballparks

Philadelphia Phillies
Citizens Bank Park

Address: One Citizens Bank Way, Philadelphia, PA 19148.
Cost: $346 million.
Architect: EwingCole, Philadelphia; HOK Sport.
Owner: City of Philadelphia.
Capacity: 43,500.
Dimensions: 329L, 374LC, 409 "The Angle," 401C, 369RC, 330R.
Ticket Line: 215/463-5000.
Home Dugout Location: First-base line.
Playing Surface: Grass.
Other Tenants: None.
First Game: On April 12, 2004, the Philadelphia Phillies opened Citizens Bank
    Park with a 4-1 loss to the Cincinnati Reds before a crowd of 41,626. Bobby
    Abreu homered for the only Phillies run of the game. Reds ace Paul Wilson
    gave up that single run in 7.1 innings of work to earn the victory. The
    Phillies earned their first win at Citizens Bank Park the following day with a
    6-4 victory over the Reds, rallying for six runs in the seventh and eighth
    innings. David Bell and Mike Lieberthal homered for the Phillies.
Landmark Event: None. The ballpark opened in 2004 and in their first three
    seasons at Citizens Bank Park the team has not made the playoffs or
    hosted an All-Star Game.

Your Citizens Bank Park Seating Crib Sheet

Best Sections to View a Game: The Diamond Club seats are wonderful, but they're also usually sold out. Our recommendation is to sit down the first-base line in the Field sections (115-132) as you'll see the action and always have the scoreboard in plain view.

Best Cheap Seats: The cheapest seat at Citizens Bank Park is $15, so there's no such thing as a true cheap seat. Seats in the corners that should be closer to $10 are $15, and seats down the line that are $35 really should be $25. Then again, you can sit between the dugouts for $40—and compared to most MLB ballparks, that would qualify as a cheap seat. Attending a game at Citizens Bank Park is an expensive proposition if you're not careful about seat selection.

Most Underrated Sections: At the prices you're paying, no section really is underrated. At $22, the Field seats in the outfield are a bargain—you're close to the action. But sit in right field to get the best view of the left-field scoreboard. We're also partial to sections 419-422: you have a great view of all the action, and because of the vertical orientation of the ballpark you don't feel too far from the action.

Seats to Avoid: There are no really bad seats at Citizens Bank Park: every section and seat is angled toward second base, and sections that are typically wastes of time in ballparks, such as the corner sections, are severely angled to face second base. Because the Citizens Bank Park is built up vertically rather than horizontally like most new ballparks, it sometimes feels more like a tennis stadium than a ballpark. Be forewarned, though, the last two or three rows in the grandstand should really be sold as obstructed-view seats because of the severe overhang of the deck above. If you do sit in the Terrace (upper) Level, sit behind home plate or down the first-base line.

Citizens Bank Park: A Shining Star

There is no reason why Citizens Bank Park shouldn't be sold out every night: the ballpark is lovely and the Phillies field a competitive team.

So why was it so easy for us to score tickets in 2005 while the team was in the midst of a wild-card race? True, crowds did return to some extent during the 2006 pennant race, but it seems odd to us that an intimate, state-of-the-art ballpark in a city filled with passionate fans doesn't attract more paying customers.

This issue weighs on the minds of local sports pundits, who point out Philadelphia is really a football town at heart. They also point out the Phillies need to actually win something before fans hand over their hearts.

But the lack of sellouts has nothing to do with Citizens Bank Park, a beautiful addition to the family of big-league ballparks. Though it has retro features like brickwork and cozy dimensions, Citizens Bank Park isn't a true retro ballpark. Its location in the same South Philadelphia sports complex housing Lincoln Financial Field, the Spectrum, and Wachovia Center gives it a definite suburban feel: it's basically adrift in a sea of parking, a ballpark without context. (The downtown Philly skyline can be seen from the ballpark, but it is not an exceptionally distinguished skyline.) Given the site limitations, Citizens Bank Park is designed to be insular: it's a fairly vertical ballpark designed to interact as little as possible with the rest of the city.

But it works. The reddish brickwork gives the ballpark a warm feel, while the large scoreboard in left provides a great focal point off the field. The abundance of small touches—Ashburn Alley, above-average concessions, public art—and some unique design decisions make Citizens Bank Park one of the most interesting ballparks in the majors.

When you go—and if you love ballparks, you absolutely must—take some time to walk around the ballpark before the game. From a distance, Citizens Bank Park isn't very impressive: it is a ballpark without much context, surrounded by a sea of parking and other sports facilities. Walk all the way around the ballpark before you enter and you'll see the four main gates are designed differently. Outside the ballpark you'll see 10-foot-tall bronze statues of Richie Ashburn, Robin Roberts, Steve Carlton, and Mike Schmidt—all members of the National Baseball Hall of Fame in Cooperstown—done by local sculptor Zenos Frudakis. Also on the west side of the ballpark is the statue of Connie Mack that once graced the Veterans Stadium and Connie Mack Stadium grounds.

Once inside, head right to the outfield area and spend time in Ashburn Alley. It opens early—2.5 hours before evening games and three hours before weekend games. The atmosphere celebrates Philadelphia baseball, from the earliest days of the Philadelphia Quakers, to Richie Ashburn's era, to the great teams of the 1970s and 1980s. Memory Lane provides timelines of Philadelphia baseball highlights, including the Phillies, Athletics, and the Negro League teams in the city. Every Phillie All-Star is honored with a commemorative marker, while members of the Phillies Hall of Fame are honored with a bronze

WATCHING SHIBE PARK 1910

Taking in a game for free from a rooftop next to Shibe Park was a grand old tradtion, echoed in the design of Citizens Bank Park. This shot from 1910 shows a crowd gathered for an important game. (Courtesy of the Library of Congress, LC-B2-2286-13[P&P]).

plaque. There are food choices galore (we cover them later in this chapter) and you'll also be able to watch both starting pitchers warm up in the bilevel bullpens before the game.

In this section you'll also find bleacher seats on top of the buildings, designed to invoked the rooftop seats surrounding Shibe Park after the ballpark opened. Rooftop seating is actually a grand baseball tradition, dating to the first days when promoters started charging admission to games and enterprising fans sought to circumvent those admission charges. It's nice to see that knothole spirit celebrated at the ballpark, albeit limited to groups. (Before we get too weepy with nostalgia, let's also point out it's a really clever way to monetize space a great distance away from the playing field.)

The ballpark is aggressively asymmetrical. The outfield fence goes beyond being merely that: it contains an "Angle" that juts into play. (We discuss it more in the next section.) The upper deck and the lower deck don't match up, there's a break in the grandstand near section 210 (with the right-field pavilion sitting lower than the grandstand), and there's more seating in the right-field corner than the left-field one. The break is more than a design quirk: its platform provides views of the game and the Philadelphia skyline.

You'll notice plenty of eye candy once the game starts. When the Phillies homer, a neon Liberty Bell high above right-center field "rings." The clapper

and the bell appear to move, and a ringing sound is played over the sound system. The Liberty Bell is large—35 feet by 50 feet—and it occupies a perch 100 feet above street level.

And, of course, there's the massive scoreboard, featuring the largest videoboard in baseball when installed in 2004 (since eclipsed more than once). The scoreboard dominates the view from any seat (save those in Ashburn Alley and the left-field bleachers, of course). Out-of-town scores are tracked on a videoboard in front of the right-field bleachers: in addition to scores, the game status in terms of runners on base and the number of outs is displayed. The immense scoreboard stands out because signage is sparse at the ballpark, with no race-track displays. The small display boards above the club level are discreet, to say the least.

One good thing about Citizens Bank Park: It seems to attract a better class of fan than the Vet did. Philadelphia fans are passionate about their sports, and while that passion sometimes can manifest itself in alarming ways—remember, Philadelphia is where the fans once booed Santa Claus at an Eagles game. We didn't see too much evidence of boorish behavior at Phillies games played at the new venue, even with larger crowds fueled by playoff fever.

In the end, we had a great time attending Phillies games and much of that had to do with Citizen Bank Park. It's a ballpark where all the little touches shine through, from the historic displays in Ashburn Alley to the emphasis on local offerings in the concession stands. There's nothing generic about Citizens Bank Park—which should make it a destination for anyone wanting a great ballpark experience.

Ballpark Quirks

The quirk that impacts play most is the outfield "Angle," a portion of the outfield fence that juts into play between the left-field power alley and center field. To be honest, it's a little overboard. In old ballparks odd fences were in response to external factors, not created for sheer entertainment value. When the fence jogged at Griffith Stadium, it was because the owners of the original Washington Nationals couldn't acquire all the properties on the block and needed to build around existing properties. At Citizens Bank Park the fence is contrived and unnecessary. In a ballpark where almost every detail is perfect, the fence layout is jarring, and although the Phillies adjusted the fences before the 2006 season, it's still a distraction.

Food and Drink

Apparently it is mandatory for a new ballpark to have a BBQ stand, a precedent set by Boog Powell's stand at Oriole Park. In Philadelphia the barbecue is served up under former Phillie Greg "The Bull" Luzinski's name in Ashburn Alley. Now, Bull Luzinski is the kind of guy who looks like he's never walked away from a rack or two of ribs in his life, and apparently he was quite the rib connoisseur before he signed on as the celebrity name at the Citizens Bank Park barbecue pit. It was a smart signing for concessionaire Aramark: we couldn't get near the place because of the long lines.

However, that left us with probably a dozen other solid food choices, including several in Ashburn Alley. Sandwiches are big in Philadelphia, and in Ashburn Alley you have your choice between Philly cheesesteaks from Geno's Steaks and Philly-style sandwiches (including cheesesteaks and pork sandwiches) from Tony Luke's. Both have their adherents, judging by the long lines in front of both stands.

Neither are as excessive as The Schmitter, sold at the stand behind Section 139. Basically, a Schmitter is a cheesesteak on steroids, comprised of fried salami, steak, three slices of cheese, tomatoes, and a special sauce. It originated at McNally's Tavern in Chestnut Hill.

Also represented in Ashburn Alley and other Citizens Bank Park concession stands: crab fries from local watering hole Chickie's & Pete's, hoagies from local chain Planet Hoagie, pizza from Ardmore's Peace A Pizza, and Turkey Hill ice cream, also found at multiple stands on the main concourse. Microbrews and sandwiches are sold at the Brewerytown stands.

There are, of course, additional concessions past those in Ashburn Alley. Most of the specialty concession stands on the main level have the same

---

INSIDER'S TIP

In an effort to bring fans to the ballpark earlier, the Phillies now offer concession specials for the first hour Ashburn Alley is open. (It opens 2.5 hours before gametime.) The specials change game by game, and they're posted at the Ashburn Alley entrance and the Left Field Gate.

The historical displays in Ashburn Alley provoke many discussions; it's the perfect place for young and old to gather before the game.

offerings: Hatfield Grills feature Hatfield hot dogs (also sold throughout the park) and Italian sausages, while Philadelphia Water Ice stands offer the local variation on a sno-kone. You can also find generic Philly cheesesteaks at several other stands. Fresh-roasted peanuts are offered at stands behind sections 104 and 137. The standard-issue Hatfield hot dogs sold at most concession stands are tasty. For those who prefer meatless items, several concession stands offer veggie burgers and veggie dogs.

The beer selection is varied with an emphasis on the local: you can find Flying Fish Extra Pale Ale, Victory Hop Devil IPA, Dock Street Amber, Yards Philly Pale Ale, Troegs Sunshine Pils, Sly Fox Pikeland Pils, Straub, and Yuengling on tap and in bottles throughout the park, with other national brands—Blue Moon, Red Hook, Foster's—available as well. Other stands feature mixed drinks and martinis.

If you want something a little more formal, there are three popular sitdown areas at the ballpark. Before the game there's usually a huge line at Harry the K's, the Ashburn Alley eatery named after longtime Phillies announcer Harry Kalas (perhaps better known as the "Voice of God" on countless NFL Films presentations). McFadden's Restaurant and Saloon is located outside the third-base gate and has its own entrance. It's a popular spot before the game as live music attracts a horde of fans on the outside patio. On the Terrace Level is the High & Inside Pub, a surprisingly elegant bar featuring original artwork. (You can order Bull's BBQ there as well—a bonus if you don't want to wait in line at the main stand.)

Basically, there's very little reason to go hungry at Citizens Bank Park. We didn't feel like concession prices were out of line, either, so arrive hungry at the ballpark.

Handicapped Seating

Citizens Bank Park features 700 seats designated for the handicapped. Some are larger spots designed for wheelchairs, while other wider seats are located at the end of rows and featuring movable armrests for easier access. These seats should be a model for anyone looking at accessibility issues in ballparks.

For the Kids

There is an abundance of attractions at Citizens Bank Park geared toward kids. In the right-field corner—near the Right Field Gate entrance—are several games, including a monster-sized Baseball Pinball (yes, part of our misspent youth was behind the flippers of a Williams Line Drive pinball game; the giant version is a wonderful reminder of the original), a climbing wall, a pitching cage, and other games.

The Phillies merchandise the heck out of the Phillie Phanatic, but it's all in good taste and the kids just eat it up. There's no way a kid will attend a game and not walk away with some sort of Phanatic souvenir: various concession stands sell Phanatic dolls and T-shirts, while the second level of the Majestic Clubhouse Store is devoted to Phanatic merchandise. Also, the smaller set will enjoy building their own Phillie Phanatic at the Build-A-Bear Workshop located on the Main Concourse near Section 135. (Citizens Bank Park was the only ballpark we visited where an entire concession stand is devoted to DVDs and books. To *books*. We were awestruck.)

The Phanatic Phun Zone, geared for kids aged eight and below, is a giant play area. The Phillies say it's the largest in Major League Baseball.

Finally, two concession stands are devoted to kid-sized foods: the Phanatic Phood Stand in Ashburn Alley and the Kid's Corner, located behind Section 318. Both offer Phanatic Phun Meals, kid-sized hot dogs, drinks and more.

This is only a partial listing of the kid-oriented attractions at Citizens Bank Park. Heck, most kids would be happy with a hot dog and the opportunity to watch the Phillie Phanatic race around the ballpark on his ATV. These additional attractions are icing on the cake.

Ballpark Tours

During the season the Phillies offer tours of the ballpark daily at 10 a.m. Stops include both dugouts, the outfield bullpens, and the Hall of Fame Club. Tickets are $8 for adults and $5 for children (ages 3-14); expect to spend 90 minutes touring. You must preorder your tickets either via the Phillies Web site or by calling 215/463-1000.

Local Baseball Attractions

You will get all the local baseball history you need in Ashburn Alley. Schedule plenty of time before the game to wander through the historic exhibits covering the Phillies, the Athletics, and the local Negro Leagues teams.

Outside the ballpark there are plenty of local baseball attractions. Within the Philadelphia city limits are markers honoring the former homes of the Philadelphia Phillies and Philadelphia Athletics, Shibe Park/Connie Mack Stadium and Baker Bowl, located within blocks of each other on 21st. To be totally honest, they're probably not worth a pilgrimage unless you're a big

The Camden Riversharks play in the shadow of the Ben Franklin Bridge.

ballpark geek or a huge Philly baseball fan. (We're the former, not the latter, so we visited both.) Neither site has anything relating to baseball besides the markers: the Baker Bowl site was converted to warehouse spaces decades ago, while Connie Mack Stadium was torn down in 1976, replaced by an evangelical church.

If you have a car, a drive to suburban Hatboro and the Philadelphia Athletics Historical Society is in order. People outside Philadelphia forget that for much of their history the Athletics was the more successful franchise in Philly, with the Phillies running a poor second. Connie Mack led the Athletics to nine American League pennants and five World Series championships. The Historical Society warehouses a trove of Athletics memorabilia: Shibe Park seats, plaques memorializing Athletics of the past, replicas of uniforms, and more. *Philadelphia Athletics Historical Society Museum, 6 N. York Rd., Hatboro, PA; 215-323-9901; philadelphiaathletics.org. Open Monday through Saturday, 10 a.m. to 3 p.m., Sunday 11 a.m. to 2 p.m.*

Across the Delaware River in downtown Camden is an absolutely charming minor-league ballpark: Campbell's Field, the home of the Camden Riversharks of the independent Atlantic League. Located at the base of the Ben Franklin Bridge, the ballpark provides great views of the Philadelphia skyline and the riverfront. Many have named it the most scenic minor-league ballpark in baseball; who are we to argue? *Campbell's Field, 401 N. Delaware Av., Camden, N.J.; riversharks.com; 866-SHARKS9 (1-866-742-7579).*

Getting There

Citizens Bank Park is located in the same south Philadelphia sports complex with Lincoln Financial Field (home to the NFL's Philadelphia Eagles), Wachovia Center (home to the NHL's Philadelphia Flyers and the NBA's Philadelphia 76ers) and the Wachovia Spectrum (home to the AHL's Philadelphia Phantoms). Because of this confluence of sporting facilities, you'd expect great car and mass-transit access.

You'd be correct.

It is a breeze taking mass transit to the ballpark: the SEPTA Broad Street Subway Line terminates at the sports complex at Pattison Avenue. The Broad Street Line runs north-south through Philadelphia, beginning to the north at the Fern Rock Transportation Center and terminating to the south at the Pattison Avenue stop next to the sports facilities. The sports complex is only two miles from downtown Philly, so taking the train is a cinch. If you pay cash on the train the cost is $2, but prepurchased tokens are only $1.30. You can see schedules and maps at *septa.org.*

Driving is easy: the sports complex is located between I-75 and I-95, so as long as you know how to

INSIDER'S TIP
There's one additional reason not to rent a car during your stay in Philadelphia: it costs serious bucks to park a car overnight at most center-city hotels. Charges of $20 or $30 are not atypical.

Citizens Bank Park **95**

get to either freeway you can make it to the ballpark. When on I-95 exits 17 and 19 will take you directly to the ballpark. If you're staying downtown, take Broad Street south and you'll be right there. With 21,000 parking spots surrounding the ballpark, you can usually get fairly close to an entrance without a lot of maneuvering. Parking is $10.

Where to Stay

The only hotel within walking distance of the ballpark is the Holiday Inn Philadelphia Stadium (10th Packer Av.; *holiday-inn.com*; $150-$200), located on the edge of the sports-facilities complex. It's a fairly new facility but nondescript as well. If all you want to do is live and breath Phillies baseball, this is the place for you.

Citizens Bank Park is only two miles from Philadelphia's Center City, and with the convenient mass transit to the ballpark there's no reason not to stay there. It also puts you close to all the historic sites.

All the major chains have outposts in Philadelphia's Center City and historic areas: Sheraton Society Hill (1 Dock St.; *sheraton.com*; $250-$350), Hyatt Regency at Penns Landing (201 S. Christopher Columbus Blvd.; *hyatt.com*; $200-$200), Doubletree Philadelphia (237 S. Broad Rd.; *hilton.com*; $200-$300), Rodeway Inn (1208 Walnut St.; *rodewayinn.com*; $100-$200), Holiday Inn Express (1305 Walnut St.; *holiday-inn.com*; $110-$150), Omni Hotel at Independence Park (401 Chestnut St.; *omnihotels.com*; $225-$325), the underrated Best Western Independence Park (235 Chestnut St.; *bestwestern.com*; $150-$250), Radisson Plaza Warwick (1701 Locust St.; *radisson.com*; $125-$225), Embassy Suites (1776 Benjamin Franklin Pkwy.; *hilton.com*; $100-$175), the swanky Four Seasons (1 Logan Square; *fourseasons.com*; $200-$400), the all-suite Hotel Windsor (1700 Benjamin Franklin Pkwy.; *windsorhotel.com*; $125-$200), and the plush Hotel Sofitel (17th and Samson sts.; *sofitel.com*; $200-$300). Of special historic note is Park Hyatt Philadelphia at the Bellevue (1415 Chancellor Court at Broad and Walnut; *hyatt.com*; $225-$325): Thomas Edison designed the fixtures, and the Library Lounge Bar is still a well-regarded meeting spot.

The Reading Terminal has been a Philadelphia landmark for decades, and there are several hotels either connected to the terminal and the adjoining Convention Center or just a short walk away. These include the 500-room Courtyard by Marriott (13th and Filbert; *marriott.com*; $170-$300), the 1,410-room Philadelphia Marriott (12th and Market; *marriott.com*; $175-$275), Crowne Plaza Philadelphia City Center (18th and Market sts.; *crowneplaza.com*; $125-$250), and the lovely Loews Philadelphia (1200 Market St.; *loewshotels.com*; $150-$250).

For a more intimate experience, consider the Alexander Inn (12th and Spruce; *alexanderinn.com*; $100-$200), a small, 48-room boutique hotel in a restored Art Deco-style building. Room rates include a decent breakfast buffet. Similar is The Latham (135 S. 17th St.; *lathamhotel.com*; $100-$150), set in a 1915 apartment building. On the other end of the spectrum is the luxurious

Several statues of former Phillies great grace the grounds of Citizen Bank Park.
Pictured above: Hall of Famer Steve Carlton.

Rittenhouse Hotel (210 W. Rittenhouse Square; *rittenhousehotel.com*; $300-$450), the grand dame of Philadelphia hotels. Each room is a suite, and the location can't be beat.

If you're on a tight budget and are driving in, consider staying near the airport. Hotels in the general airport area (which is just a couple of miles from the ballpark) include the Philadelphia Airport Hilton (4509 Island Av.; *hilton.com*; $125-$225), the Sheraron Suites Philadelphia (4101b Island Av.; *sheraton.com*; $125-$225), and the Philadelphia Airport Marriott (One Arrivals Rd.; *marriott.com*; $129-$179), attached directly to the airport. Be warned these hotels tend to be a little isolated: there's nothing in terms of convenience stores or restaurants within walking distance.

As you'll note, Philadelphia hotels tend to be on the spendier side, and you can probably find cheaper digs if you stay farther outside of town. Still, if you're splurging on a Philly trip anyway, find lodging in the Center City or historic areas. You don't want to spend too much of your trip commuting between attractions and then paying a lot for parking anyway.

While You're There

Philadelphia is rightly called the Cradle of Liberty, and there's enough in the Center City and historic areas to occupy your time for a long weekend (at least). Most of the historic attractions are kid-friendly as well, so you can combine education with entertainment.

Many of Philadelphia's historic attractions are contained in Independence National Historical Park. Your first stop there should be Independence Visitor Center (6th and Market; *independencevisitorcenter.com*) where you'll get a great overview of the attractions in the area and obtain tickets to local attractions. Don't spend too much time there as there are so many things to see within a short walk. Independence Hall (*nps.gov/inde*) is a must-see: it served as the first capitol of the newly independent United States, the Second Continental Congress met there, and most of the signatories to the Declaration of Independence and the Constitution did the honors there (in fact, most of them used Philip Syng's inkstand, still displayed there). Other iconic items displayed include the famous Rising Sun Chair used by George Washington when presiding over the Continental Congress.

Nearby is the pavilion containing the Liberty Bell, the most famous icon associated with Philadelphia. Originally part of Independence Hall, the Liberty Bell was commissioned in 1751 to commemorate the chartering of Pennsylvania as a colony. It cracked while undergoing testing and was subsequently recast twice; in 1846 it cracked while being rung to commemorate George Washington's birthday and has never been rung since.

The National Constitution Center puts much of what happened in Independence Hall in perspective, explaining how the Constitution was developed and how it's still very relevant in the everyday life of America.

Be forewarned that although the tours of Independence Hall, the National Constitution Center, and the Liberty Bell pavilion are free, you must have a

reservation for a specific tour time: you can make reservations up to 12 months in advance by calling 800/967-2283 or visiting *reservations.nps.gov*. In theory tickets are available on a daily basis, but the Liberty Bell is Philadelphia's most popular attraction (over 1.6 million visitors make the pilgrimage yearly), so having a ticket is essential.

Franklin Court is another essential visit. Benjamin Franklin is one of the most fascinating figures in American history, a reluctant convert to the notion of American independence (he preferred keeping ties with the British) but once converted he became an essential player, helping to draft many of the stirring documents declaring independence and helping to arrange vital funding for the war effort. He was also a storyteller and inventor, making an early name for himself with *Poor Richard's Almanack* and later serving as Postmaster General. Franklin Court gives an idea of how Franklin lived (the foundation of his former home was excavated) and provides a fascinating overview of his life and writings. No tickets are necessary for the self-guided tour.

Religious institutions played a vital role in the American independence movement; one of the most important groups was the Society of Friends, better known as Quakers. The Arch Street Meeting House (4th and Arch sts.) is an historic meeting house, first operating in 1683. Exhibits there honor the role of Quakers over the centuries. Christ Church is worth seeing for two reasons: George Washington and other revolutionaries worshiped here, making it historically significant; and Benjamin Franklin and his wife are buried there. For good luck, toss a penny on old Ben's gravesite.

Of course, one cannot live by historical sites alone. At some point you'll need to stop for refreshments. We've already discussed Philly cheesesteaks in the context of what's available at the ballpark. It's fascinating how this relatively simple foodstuff (thinly sliced ribeye or top round, Amoroso Italian rolls, fried onions, Cheese Whiz) is so intertwined in the culture of a city and how passionately the locals argue about who serves the best cheesesteak in town. There's also a proper ordering etiquette: order a "cheesesteak wit" to indicate you want the essential Cheese Whiz (although provolone or American are often offered as worthwhile alternatives).

We've always been fans of Jim's Steaks (400 South St.; *jimssteaks.com*), where the Art Deco surroundings are as pleasant as the cheesesteaks, though some locals decry Jim's as being overly touristy. Whatever. Also highly regarded by locals are Geno's (1219 South St.; *genosteaks.com*) and Pat's King of the Steaks (1237 Passyunk Av.), located across the street from one another.

We mentioned Reading Terminal (12th and Arch; *readingterminalmarket.org*) in our previous section on hotels, and if you're staying near the historic venue you should drop by for a meal or two. Basically, the food court at Reading Terminal is where you can find the best of Philadelphia at any number of counters. Rick's Philly Steaks is run by a descendent of the founders of Pat's Steaks, while fresh seafood is available at Pearl's Oyster Bar. There's also surprisingly good Southern food available at Delilah's at the Terminal (try the fried chicken, and mac and cheese), while the Dutch Eating Place features pancakes, scrapple, and apple dumplings.

Also worth a visit if you're staying downtown: Morimoto's (723 Chestnut St.; *morimorestaurant.com*). Normally we're not big on celebrity restaurants, but how many Iron Chefs have their own American outposts? The last time we were there Masaharu Morimoto personally made our sushi, so we're fans for life. The place is also gorgeous and worth a visit even if the Iron Chef isn't personally making sushi.

This overview should help you begin your planning for a Philadelphia trip. We're barely scratching the surface, with a lot more interesting attractions (such as Betsy Ross's house) contained in historic Philadelphia. Do some research before you head out and you'll have a very rewarding experience.

Team Ballpark History

Considering how long Philadelphia has supported professional baseball, it's surprising there have been basically four venues for two baseball teams since 1909: Shibe Park (which opened in 1909), the Baker Bowl (which opened in 1887), Veterans Stadium (which opened in 1971), and Citizens Bank Park.

There are parts of Citizens Bank Park designed to evoke memories of Shibe Park, the home of the Philadelphia Athletics from 1909 through 1954 and the Phillies from 1938 through 1970, and Baker Bowl, the home of the Phillies between 1887 and 1937. Both ballparks were close to 21st Street in north Philadelphia.

We cover Shibe Park in more detail in our chapter on the Oakland Athletics and McAfee Coliseum.

The Philadelphia Phillies began life as the National League's Worcester Brown Stockings before Al Reach and Col. John Rogers bought the franchise in

1883 and moved the team to Philadelphia, adopting the Phillies moniker.

The team played at 6,500-seat Recreation Park, located at the corner of 24th and Columbia avenues, before moving to Baker Bowl in 1887. The Phillies were a good draw and owner Reach saw the building of 12,500-seat Philadelphia Base Ball Park as a good investment.

And it was an investment: $101,000. Reach spared no expense, using expensive brick for exterior walls and choosing a location in a rapidly expanding residential neighborhood north of downtown Philadelphia. The corner of Broad Street and Lehigh Avenue also provided one additional enticement: it was well-served by mass transit in the form of rail lines and trolley cars. On Opening Day, Reach managed to cram a crowd of 20,000 into the ballpark.

Sadly, Philadelphia Base Ball Park suffered the same fate as many other ballparks of its era: on Aug. 6, 1894, the wooden structure burned to the ground, leaving behind only the brick wall. Reach's response was predictable: he pushed the envelope further and commissioned a cutting-edge ballpark that would be impervious to fire.

National League Park, which opened for the 1895 season, was the first of a wave of modern ballparks opening between 1895 and the 1920s. Wood was eschewed in favor of the more durable and lasting brick and steel, and the new ballpark could seat 18,000.

Adding more seats, however, meant some compromises were made elsewhere. At a time when center-field distances of 500 feet were not uncommon, National League Park was an uncommonly intimate ballpark, with the left-field foul pole 341 feet from home plate and the right-field wall only 280 feet out. As you might expect, the unusual dimensions gave the Phillies a tremendous home-field advantage. So did Reach's installation of a underground

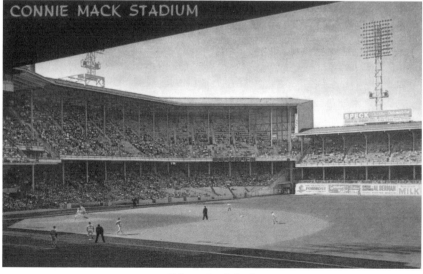

Citizens Bank Park **101**

TRIVIA

The Phillies nickname is the longest-running team name in pro sports, although in 1944 and 1945 the Philadelphia front office tried marketing the team as the Blue Jays, placing both nicknames on team jerseys.

wire between the outfield clubhouse and the third-base coaching box, allowing the Phillies to tip off batters.

One thing about Reach: he was not afraid to spend a buck to make a buck, and he invested enough in the on-field product for the team to be constantly competitive. The 1915 Phillies, for instance, drew 449,898 fans en route to the National League pennant and a World Series loss to the Boston Red Sox. (That World Series was known for two firsts: Woodrow Wilson was the first president to attend a championship game, coming up to Baker Bowl for the second game and throwing out the first pitch, while a young Babe Ruth pinch-hit in the first game.) Reach's successor, former New York City Police Commissioner William Baker, was the opposite: after taking control of the team in 1913, Baker sold off his stars, slashed costs (using two ewes and a ram to keep the grass low), and renamed National League Park as Baker Bowl.

Baker literally drove Baker Bowl into the ground with his parsimonious ways, putting off needed maintenance and continuing to operate the ballpark when safety issues were clearly present. By 1927 the ballpark was literally falling down: the pavilion collapsed when a crowd gathered there during a rainstorm, injuring 50 and killing one. The Phillies managed to play several more seasons at Baker Bowl without killing anybody, but the Great Depression and a long string of losing seasons forced the Phillies to Shibe Park in 1938, where the Phillies and the Athletics could share costs. Despite all the safety issues associated with Baker Bowl—one press pundit called it the "Toilet Bowl"—it remained opened until 1950 when it was finally torn down.

It was a sad end to a once-great ballpark. Hall of Famers Grover Cleveland Alexander and Ed Delahanty had the best years of their storied careers while playing there. The Hilldale Daisies of the Eastern Colored League, a Negro Leagues powerhouse, won the 1925 Negro World Series there, defeating the mighty Kansas City Monarchs.

TRIVIA

Baker Bowl's most historic moment may have come in 1923 when an 11-year-old fan caught a foul ball. At the time many teams insisted foul balls be returned, but the kid demurred. Baker's front office had the child arrested for larceny and insisted he be taken to jail. A local judge dismissed the charges the following day, and soon after the commissioner's office decreed all balls hit into the stands be released as souvenirs.

Most recently the Phillies played at Veterans Stadium, a mixed-used cookie-cutter ballpark built in 1971 for the Phillies and the NFL's Philadelphia Eagles. Like most cookie-cutter facilities of the era, Veterans Stadium excelled in neither

Shibe Park in 1973, after the Phillies vacated the ballpark. (Courtesy of the Library of Congress, HABS PA,51-PHILA,683-1.)

configuration, but even by cookie-cutter standards the place was a wreck. The Vet was unloved by all; the Phillies sell a DVD commemorating the Vet, but it's really a celebration of the best-loved players from the Vet era, including Mike Schmidt, Larry Bowa, and Steve Carlton. There's also a plaque near Citizens Bank Park honoring the Vet.

The Complete Guide to Big League Ballparks

Detroit Tigers
Comerica Park

Address: 2100 Woodward Av., Detroit, MI 48201.
Cost: $300 million.
Architect: Architect of record, SmithGroup (Detroit); design architect, HOK Sport; entertainment architect, Rockwell Group.
Owner: Detroit-Wayne County Stadium Authority.
Capacity: 40,120.
Dimensions: 346L, 402LC, 422C, 379RC, 330R.
Ticket Line: 248/25-TIGER.
Playing Surface: Grass.
Home Dugout Location: Third-base side.
Other Tenants: None.
First Game: On April 11, 2000, the Tigers opened Comerica Park on a high note with a 5-2 win over the Seattle Mariners before a less-than-capacity crowd of 39,168. Tigers starter Brian Moehler earned the win despite giving up 10 hits in six innings of work; Todd Jones earned the save. Gregg Jeffries and Bobby Higginson each drove in two runs off Mariners starter Freddy Garcia.
Landmark Event: In the 2005 All-Star Game, the American League jumped out to a 7-0 lead behind homers from game MVP Miguel Tejada of the Baltimore Orioles and Mark Teixeira of the Texas Rangers, and then held on for a 7-5 win. And, of course, there was the amazing showing by the Detroit Tigers in the 2006 season, culminating with the first-ever Series games at Comerica.

Your Comerica Park Seating Crib Sheet

Best Sections to View a Game: There are few bad seats in the ballpark. Given the location of the scoreboard in center field and the Detroit skyline beyond, the best seats from a purely aesthetic viewpoint are located in the grandstand closest to home plate.

Best Cheap Seats: You can get into the ballpark for $5, but those seats are limited to a single section down the left-field line. Instead, spring for the $8 right-field bleacher seats or the $15 Rightfield Grandstand seats. Also, sitting in the closer left-field pavilion seats will run you $15.

Most Underrated Sections: The $20 Upper Box and $35 Infield Box seats are quite good—a decent compromise between your desires and your credit card.

Seats to Avoid: Despite the name, the Club seats at Comerica Park aren't like club-level seats in other ballparks, giving you access to a climate-controlled area with private concessions and bathrooms. At Comerica Park, the Club Seats are merely the first five rows of the upper deck, and they go for $25. The Tiger Den, complete with freestanding teak chairs in a traditional baseball box, fulfills the role of club seating at Comerica Park.

Comerica Park: Tiger, Tiger, Burning Bright

Despite opening the same year as Fenway Park and a few years before Wrigley Field, Tiger Stadium never achieved the same mythic stature among baseball fans as those two shrines. We're not quite sure why: Tiger Stadium was a great old ballpark, but the Tigers never had the likes of WGN broadcasters touting the Friendly Confines or generations of newspaper columnists claiming Fenway Park as their personal turf. Detroit never attracted the glamourous crowd.

So when the Detroit Tigers ownership decided to push for a new ballpark instead of renovating Tiger Stadium, there was an outcry from some Tigers fans, but by and large most went along with the move. Downtown Detroit needed something to reinvigorate the depressed local economy and a new ballpark was seen as an essential tool for that growth.

Now, several years after Comerica Park opened, the downtown economy is a little better off, but not overly so, although there is some semblance of an urban village surrounding Comerica Park that includes some office buildings and the restored Fox Theatre (all part of Ilitch Holdings). Tigers fans finally started turning out in droves after Jim Leyland injected some life into the roster, but the ballpark never achieved the status of standalone attraction the way Oriole Park at Camden Yards did. Meanwhile, public officials debated whether to tear down venerable old Tiger Stadium (and, as of this writing, it looks like they will). All in all, the new ballpark didn't really accomplish what locals expected, though (admittedly) urban renewal is often a glacier-slow process.

This is a shame because there is a lot to like about Comerica Park. Yes, it has a lot of sideshows, but you certainly can't say there's not something for

Comerica Park

everyone. The kids will enjoy the amusement-park rides. The teenagers will like
the center-field water fountains and the large scoreboard. The adults will like
the food and beverage selections, as well as the lovely view of the Detroit
skyline from the grandstand. And, if all is well in Motown, everyone will enjoy
the game on the field.

So why didn't fans turn out in droves to Tigers games after the ballpark
opened? Tigers fans are pretty savvy, and despite some headline-generating
free-agent signings that supposedly improved the team, the Tigers were

consistently awful right after the ballpark opened. Detroit fans were just not going to support a losing team no matter how palatial the surroundings. These days the team is much more competitive and, as a result, attendance is improved—in fact, it's not uncommon to find scalpers around the ballpark during a big series.

Plus, Tigers fans were smart enough not to be manipulated by team ownership. Owner Mike Ilitch didn't even make a pretense of studying a remodeling of Tiger Stadium before announcing pursuit of a new ballpark. (Then again, the Tigers and Ilitch paid over 60 percent of the total price tag for the ballpark, so he certainly deserved wide latitude.) Fans wondered whether ownership was truly committed to winning: first Comerica Park was designed as a pitchers' paradise, and then the fences were moved in when batters complained. Truth is, the park's dimensions were probably a little too spacious when Comerica Park opened in 2000; when the fences were moved in before the 2005 season the ballpark played more fairly.

Either way, Comerica Park is a distinctive ballpark. There's no doubt you're in the home of the Tigers, as there are enough Tiger logos and statues in the ballpark to outfit a small jungle. Giant Tiger statues stand at the entrance, tiger claws mark the walls, there are tigers on the huge scoreboard (their eyes light up when a Tiger homers), and tiger heads hold lighted baseballs on the ballpark's exterior. And, of course, you have a tiger roaring every time the Tigers score a run.

Though the Tigers gave up a lot on the historic front with the decision to abandon Tiger Stadium, they did redeem themselves with an emphasis on the great Tigers of the past at Comerica Park. On the main concourse the great history of the Tigers is highlighted by the Walk of Fame, where important moments in Detroit baseball history from the 1800s to the present are presented: photos, artifacts, and other historical relics are displayed. In center field are statues of six former Tiger greats: Ty Cobb, Charlie Gehringer, Hank Greenberg, Willie Horton, Al Kaline, and Hal Newhouser. Sadly, two of the most important historic relics for the Tigers—the 1968 and 1984 World Series trophies—are stashed away in the private Champions Club.

In fact, walking around the ballpark and taking in all the historical displays is one of the great joys of Comerica Park. Like most newer ballparks, Comerica Park features a concourse wrapping around the ballpark, and the concourse is open all the way around, giving you a view of the action no matter where you are. (Heck, you can even glimpse a view of the ballgame from outside the ballpark.)

We knew Tiger Stadium, and Comerica Park is no Tiger Stadium. But with an emphasis on Tigers history and a design geared for those who love to move around a ballpark, Comerica Park is a better-than-average major-league ballpark.

Ballpark Quirks

When the ballpark opened, the flagpole in center field was in play. When the fences were moved in 2003, the flagpole remained in the same spot, this time outside the center-field fence.

Food and Drink

If you can't find some kind of food to your liking at Comerica Park, you aren't looking hard enough. The Big Cat Food Court, located near the main Comerica Park entrance, features standard ballpark foods (hot dogs, Coney Islands, ice cream), carnival foods (elephant ears, pretzels), and more substantial fare (gyros from local vendors, deli sandwiches). You can also find ballpark fare at the Brushfire Grill picnic area.

The Comerica Park Beer Hall is one of the best places in the majors for beer lovers, with a slew of beers on tap and bar-style food on the menu.

Fifth Avenue Downtown is located inside Comerica Park, but isn't really part of the ballpark. The upscale pool hall and bar also features live music. Despite the location, it's not billed as a sports bar.

If the weather is a little extreme during your visit, head upstairs to the Upper Deck Lounge. This climate-controlled facility (cooled in the summer, heated in the spring and fall) has its own bar and concessions.

Handicapped Access

Only 360 wheelchair-accessible seats are available at Comerica Park—a rather small number for such a newer ballpark.

For the Kids

This is the best ballpark in the majors for kids, containing both a carousel and a Ferris wheel. The carousel was built specifically for Comerica Park, with 30 hand-painted tigers; it's located down the first-base line. The Ferris wheel features cars shaped like baseballs; it's located down the third-base line.

Ballpark Tours

The Tigers offer tours of Comerica Park on Tuesdays and Fridays at 10 a.m., noon, and 2 p.m. between June 7 and Sept. 2 on non-game days. The cost is $6 for adults and $3 for children between 5 and 17. You can buy tickets at the box office; tours begin and end at the Tiger Club entrance at Witherell and Elizabeth. Call 313/471-2000 for more information.

Getting There

Comerica Park is located in downtown Detroit, just south of I-75. To get there from anywhere in the Detroit metro area, make your way to I-75 north or south. Take exit 50 and follow the signs to the ballpark.

There is plenty of parking in the general Comerica Park vicinity. Olympia Entertainment manages about 5,000 spots close to the ballpark, while there are other ramps and lots nearby as well. You should expect to pay upwards of $15-

$25.

    Mass transit is a dirty concept in the Motor City, so don't expect to stay out in the suburbs and catch light rail or a bus to the game. However, a People Mover in Detroit makes it possible to stay just about anywhere downtown and make your way to the ballpark. The People Mover is an elevated light-rail line looping through downtown Detroit, running until midnight on weeknights and 2 a.m. on Fridays and Saturdays. The cost: 50 cents. Closest to Comerica Park is the Grand Circus stop; you can learn more at the People Mover website—*thepeoplemover.com*.

Where to Stay

Downtown Detroit hotels can be a little dicey, so choose carefully before making a reservation. For instance, the Milner Hotel and The Leland (formerly the Ramada Inn Downtown Detroit) are billed as the two closest hotels to Comerica Park. Don't stay at either: they're both scary places.

    Our recommendation is to stick with the premium chains. With that in mind, the closest decent hotel is the Hilton Garden Inn Detroit Downtown (351 Gratiot Av.; *hilton.com*; $160-$181). It's new and clean and contains a very good restaurant, the Hunter House. A little farther away, but similarly well kept up, is the Holiday Inn Express Downtown (1020 Washington Blvd.; *holidayinn.com*; $92-$112). The Atheneum Suite Hotel (100 Brush Av.; *summithotels.com*; $210-$250) is an all-suite hotel located next to the new Greektown Casino, minutes from the ballpark.

    The Renaissance Center, located on the other side of downtown from Comerica Park, features two hotels: a Courtyard by Marriott (333 E. Jefferson

INSIDER'S TIP
If you're in town for the weekend with the kids and are looking for activities to go along with the ballgame, consider staying at the Dearborn Inn (20301 Oakwood Blvd., Dearborn; *marriott.com*; $129-$300). Built in 1931 on the grounds of the Ford Motor Company, the Dearborn Inn is located across from the Ford Museum and is more a resort than a hotel. It actually opened as the first airport hotel and, although the airport is long gone, the hotel is a treasure.

Av.; *marriott.com*; $200-$210) and the Detroit Marriott (Renaissance Center; *marriott.com*; $240-$260).

You should also consider staying outside the city, either in Dearborn (where high-end chains like the Ritz-Carlton and the Hyatt Regency are located) or out by the airport. Quite honestly, Detroit is not a great hotel town: the urban renewal in other cities that has led to the restoration of grand old hotels hasn't yet happened in Detroit.

While You're There

Sports in the form of the Tigers, the NFL's Detroit Lions, and the NHL's Detroit Red Wings are probably the three biggest attractions in downtown Detroit. Sure, there are cultural amenities like the Detroit Opera House, but aside from a few casinos, there really isn't a lot to do downtown.

Don't feel compelled to spend a lot of time downtown, aside from your trips to see the Tigers. For families, one of Detroit's best attractions is The

Henry Ford (20900 Oakwood Blvd., Dearborn; *hfmgv.org*; 800/835-5237), which actually comprises several different attractions, including a museum and Greenfield Village. The Henry Ford Museum presents the personal collection of Henry Ford, who amassed a vast fortune as founder of the Ford Motor Company. No, Ford didn't invent the automobile, but he created the assembly line that allowed automobiles to be manufactured in a cost-effective manner (15 million Model Ts were manufactured), making them affordable to the middle class; the last one built is displayed in the museum. As you might expect, the collection at the Henry Ford is heavy on automotive and transportation history, but there's more to the collection than just cars. For instance, the bus on which Rosa Parks refused to move to the back is on display.

That assembly-line approach to auto manufacturing can be seen in the Ford Rouge Factory Tour, illustrating the history of car assembly and including a tour of Ford's F-150 manufacturing plant.

A series of historic districts comprises Greenfield Village. Some, like Henry Ford's birthplace and garage where he put together the first Model T, are local, while others, like Thomas Edison's various working spaces, came from elsewhere—Menlo Park, N.J., and Fort Myers, Fla. The emphasis here is on the inventor as an important member of society: the bicycle shop where the Wright Brothers designed and built their first flying machine is included. *Pricing and hours vary by attraction and time of the year.*

Detroit is Motown, and the automobile isn't the city's only famous export. The Motown sound, as conceived by Berry Gordy, Jr., was cool and brash, with artists like Diana Ross and the Supremes, Stevie Wonder, the Four Tops, Marvin Gaye, Smokey Robinson and the Miracles, Martha and the Vandellas, the Temptations, and the Jackson 5 combining smooth vocals and Detroit street grit. Motown Records long ago moved to Los Angeles, but the Motown Historical Museum (2648 W. Grand Blvd.; *motownmuseum.com*; 313/875-2264), located in the modest house Gordy, Jr. dubbed "Hitsville U.S.A.," keeps the sound alive. Motown Records was an amazing enterprise: it was located in several houses near Hitsville U.S.A., and often you'd find Motown Records artists preparing their own records for shipment across the world. Most of the great Motown songs were recorded in Studio A, and you can see that famous studio as part of the tour. *Adults, $8; children, $5.*

If you do stay downtown, there are a host of bars and restaurants close to the ballpark worth checking out. Our personal favorite is the Elwood Bar & Grill (300 Adams Av.; 313/962-BEER *elwoodgrill.com*), behind the left-field Comerica Park scoreboard. This Art Deco diner was built in 1936 on the Comerica Park site, was moved to make way for ballpark construction, and lovingly restored as a bar and reraurant. The menu isn't anything special— sandwiches, burgers, salads, and appetizers—but the atmosphere is.

Also worth a visit for a pregame or postgame cocktail: Detroit Beer Company (1529 Broadway; *beercos.com*; 313/962-1529), the State Bar (2115 Woodward Av.; *statebardetroit.com*; 313/961-5451), the Hockeytown Café (2301 Woodward Av.; *hockeytowncafe.com*; 313/965-9500), and Cheli's Chili

Bar (47 E. Adams Av.; *chris-chelios.com*; 313/961-1700). The Detroit Beer Company is a better-than-average brewpub with a fairly standard selection of pub grub—burgers, pasta, beer-battered fish and chips, and pizzas. Many of the beer offerings are seasonal, though you'll always find available an excellent red, a unique Dwarf Ale, and tasty oatmeal stout. The State Bar is attached to the State Theatre and becomes a sports bar before a Tigers game. The Hockeytown Café is located across the street from Comerica Park (go figure— Joe Louis Arena, the home of the NHL's Detroit Red Wings, is several blocks away), with plenty of beers on tap and, of course, Red Wings (which are basically Buffalo hot wings) on the menu. Despite the name, there's plenty of Tigers memorabilia on display. There's always a crowd at the Hockeytown Café so expect a long wait for a table; on a nice night head to the patio. Cheli's Chili is owned by Red Wings star Chris Chelios; the chili is the perfect repast on a cool spring or fall evening.

Detroit is a sports town, and there are other notable sports venues a little further afield. Nemo's (1384 Michigan Av.; *nemosdetroit.com*; 313/965-3180) is in the Tiger Stadium neighborhood and was the psychic center of Detroit sports for decades. The walls are covered with sports memorabilia. It's still worth a visit, with free parking and shuttle-bus service to Tigers games.

Centaur (2233 Park Av.; *centaurbar.com*; 313/963-4040) is a trendy hotspot a few blocks from Comerica Park, near the Fox Theatre. The Art Deco bar features a menu of martini concoctions and finger foods like miniburgers and fish tacos. Similarly hip: the Town Pump Tavern (100 W. Montcalm St.; *thetownpumptavern.com*; 313/961-1929). If want to get away from the hipsters, the Comet Bar (128 Henry St.; 313/964-1508) is your basic neighborhood pub.

Team Ballpark History

One huge shadow looms over Comerica Park: Tiger Stadium. Opened in 1912, Tiger Stadium was an important spot for baseball in America, always revered as one of the great ballparks of the game. That it still stands says much about its nostalgic importance to many Detroiters hesitant to let go of such a great facility. (It also shows the heavy inertia of Detroit city government, but that's another story.)

"The Corner"—or, rather, a lot at the corner of Michigan and Trumbull— was the home of Detroit baseball between 1895 and 1999. George Vanderbeck owned the Detroit Tigers of the old Western League (which became the American League in 1901) and built Bennett Park on the former grounds of a dogpound and the Western Market haymarket. Seating 5,000 when built and later expanded to 14,000, Bennett Park featured an L-shaped wooden grandstand and several trees in the field of play. It was named for Charlie Bennett, a popular player with the National League's Detroit Wolverines who lost both feet in a train accident.

Tigers baseball was popular, and team ownership faced the same issue as other team owners of the era: wildcat bleachers were constructed by adjacent landowners so fans could see the action but avoid paying for a game. The

Tigers put up screens to block the bleachers, but landowners built them higher and higher.

Seeing the demand, Tigers owner Frank Navin decided to tear down Bennett Park after the 1911 season. He was inspired by Pittsburgh's Forbes Field, considered then to be state-of-the-art ballpark design, and approached Osborn Engineering to design a concrete-and-steel structure.

Navin Field opened in 1912 on the same day as Fenway Park, with both events overshadowed by the sinking of the Titanic. Navin Field was a slightly larger and reconfigured facility, originally seating 23,000, but over the years the Tigers expanded it to 53,000. It was renamed Briggs Stadium in 1938 before being formally dubbed Tiger Stadium in 1961.

In terms of ballpark eras, it sits beside Fenway Park and Wrigley Field as landmarks of the first great steel-and-concrete ballparks in professional baseball still standing. Ironically, when today's ballpark designers look for a model as they prepare plans for a retro ballpark, they look to Tiger Stadium for inspiration.

Many greats plied their wares at Tiger Stadium: Ty Cobb roamed center field and was a terror on the base paths; sluggers like Mickey Cochrane, Hal Newhouser, Hank Greenberg, Willie Horton, Al Kaline, and Norm Cash wowed crowds with long and dramatic home runs; and Denny McLain (the last 30-game winner in the majors), Mickey Lolich, and Jack Morris silenced opposing bats with their powerful arms.

And, for whatever reason, Tiger Stadium brought out the best in visiting players as well. Fans still talk about Reggie Jackson's dramatic home run in the 1971 All-Star Game, a blast off Pittsburgh's Dock Ellis that hit the light stanchion on top of the right-field bleachers.

Tiger Stadium still stands at the corner of Michigan and Trumbull (2120 Trumbull Avenue, to be exact), about a mile from Comerica Park. Alas, it's not open to the public (or the press, either). While it's occasionally used for a special event or movie filming (Billy Crystal's *61* was partially filmed there), the venerable ballpark is allowed to deteriorate while city officials wait for the perfect redevelopment plan. The final game at Tiger Stadium was played on Sept. 27, 1999, with the Tigers defeating the Kansas City Royals, 8-2. Immediately after the game, home plate was dug out to be transferred to Comerica Park.

Local Baseball Attractions

If Tiger Stadium was still open, it would be the biggest local baseball attraction besides Comerica Park. But it's not, so you'll have to make do with other points of interest after you make your pilgrimage.

Recreation Park was the first center of baseball in Detroit, serving as the home of the National League's Detroit Wolverines between 1881 and 1888. It wasn't an especially distinguished facility, but some good ballplayers—such as Hall of Famers Sam Thompson and Dan Brouthers—stood out on the field for the Wolverines. Recreation Park was torn down in 1894 after the Wolverines shifted operations to Cleveland at the end of the 1888 season. There's a marker commemorating the ballpark on the Brush Street Mall behind Harper Hospital.

Michigan is also home to several minor-league teams, but you'll need to jump in a car and drive outside the city to catch a game.

Colorado Rockies
Coors Field

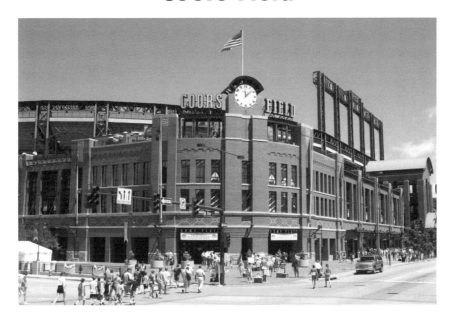

Address: 2001 Blake Street, Denver, CO 80205.
Cost: $215 million.
Architect: HOK Sport.
Owner: Denver Metropolitan Baseball Stadium District.
Capacity: 50,381.
Dimensions: 347L, 390LC, 415C, 375RC, 350R.
Ticket Line: 800/388-ROCK (7625).
Playing Surface: Grass.
Home Dugout Location: First-base side.
Other Tenants: None.
First Game: On April 26, 1995, the Colorado Rockies defeated the New York Mets 11-9 in a game that set the tone for Rockies history. Billy Swift started the game for the Rockies and gave up five runs on 10 hits in five innings of work; the two teams combined for 33 hits, 10 doubles, and three homers, including a grand slam from the Mets' Todd Hundley.
Landmark Event: The Rockies made the playoffs once in the team's existence. In 1995, the third-year expansion team moved to Coors Field and made the playoffs as a wild-card team, finishing a game behind the Los Angeles Dodgers in the National League West Division standings. The first two games of the opening round of the playoffs were played at Coors Field, with the Atlanta Braves winning both, 5-4 and 7-4. The Rockies would win Game Three before being eliminated from the playoffs when the Braves won Game Four, 10-4, in Atlanta.

Your Coors Field Seating Crib Sheet

Like many teams, the Colorado Rockies have adopted a variable-pricing plan based on the day of the week and the opponent. Here we're using the lower prices, since they're in effect for most games.

Best Sections to View a Game: The Infield and Midfield Box seats aren't the most expensive seats in the ballpark, but they provide the best views of the action. Also notable: the pavilion seating in left field.

Best Cheap Seats: You may be seduced into sitting in the center-field bleachers, marketed by the team as the Rockpile. And for $4 (the price drops down to $1 for kids) the price is right. But you are a long, long way from the action: you're a mile high, and it seems like you're a mile away from home plate and a half-mile from concession stands and restrooms. Even at a buck it would be hard to keep kids focused on a game out there. There are never many folks sitting in Rockpile seats. Denver residents have realized they are very bad, and most folks buying those tickets do so just to get into the ballpark and sit somewhere else. So our choice of best cheap sections at Coors Field are the upper-deck sections in right field: you feel closer to the action and at $7 ($9 for priority games), they are almost as cheap as the Rockpile seats while giving you access to more concessions and restrooms. You also get a great view of the Rocky Mountains sitting that far up. Be warned that these seats are not always available: in an effort to make Coors Field feel more intimate the Rockies have started blocking off entire sections when smaller crowds are anticipated.

Most Underrated Sections: That would be our choice for best cheap seats: the upper-deck sections in right field.

Seats to Avoid: Along with the aforementioned Rockpile, you'll want to avoid the Upper Reserved Outfield and Upper Reserved Corner seats.

Coors Field: Rocky Mountain High

Coors Field is at the top of MLB ballparks: literally. Sitting one mile above sea level (the purple rows in the upper deck are exactly a mile high), Coors Field is one of the most stunning ballparks in baseball as well as one of the most exciting. If your idea of a good time is watching a game with the Rocky Mountains in the background and scoring more resembling a pinball game than a baseball game, Coors Field is for you.

We exaggerate a little, of course. Actually, scoring at Coors Field has been down in recent years (Fenway Park now leads major-league ballparks in terms of runs scored), but Coors Field is incredibly scenic. Perhaps the best use of brick and exposed steel beams among all the retro ballparks is the design at Coors Field. Situated on the edge of the century-old warehouses of Denver's Lower Downtown, Coors Field was seamlessly integrated into an area already full of character and managed to lift standards in the whole area. Coors Field didn't just fit into the neighborhood: it improved it both physically and economically, creating the model for using ballparks as an economic-development tool.

If you've never been to Coors Field, schedule some open time before and after the game to look around the neighborhood. Drop by the Tattered Cover and peruse the offerings of one of the best independent bookstores in the United States. Have a martini at the Cruise Room Bar at the Oxford Hotel; the oddball Art Deco bar is a replica of a bar on the Queen Mary ocean liner. Buy a vintage Western shirt from Rockmount Ranchwear, housed in a 97-year-old warehouse; if you're lucky, 104-year-old company founder "Papa Jack" Weil will be there to take your order. Walk into Union Station, built in 1914 and once the front door to Denver, with 80 trains a day passing through. When you approach

Coors Field

Coors Field on Blake Street, it will seem like the ballpark and its classic clock tower have been there as long as everything else in the area.

All of these old buildings and warehouses existed before Coors Field; the point is they became much more economically viable as a slew of new restaurants and companies moved into Denver's LoDo area after Coors Field opened. Today Coors Field doesn't command the throngs of sellout crowds it once did (good for us, bad for the Rockies and local bar owners), but it has developed into a Denver institution.

At an elevation of 5,200 feet above sea level, Coors Field is by far the MLB ballpark at the highest elevation, beating out Bank One Ballpark (1,100 feet above sea level) and Atlanta's Turner Field (a surprising 1,050 feet above sea level). Because of the thin mountain air, balls carry better at Coors Field than other ballparks: scientists say a ball hit 400 feet at sea-level Yankee Stadium would travel 408 feet in Atlanta and 440 feet in Colorado (the old Atlanta-Fulton County Stadium was known as "The Launching Pad" for good reason). Because of this, baseball statisticians estimate the field dimensions in terms of "real" play at Coors Field are actually 315'-377'-318'—which would be one of the coziest parks in baseball.

Winds frequently plays havoc with balls; a good wind can add or subtract 10 feet from a ball headed to the stands, as well as change its trajectory. It's not easy being an outfielder at Coors Field, but you have the consolation of playing half your games there as a batter.

The high altitude also affects pitchers. Because of thin air, a curve ball loses some of its bite while fast balls don't lose velocity as quickly. The perfect

Coors Field pitcher is a broad-shoulders guy who relies on fast balls and changeups, saving curve balls and sliders for special situations.

That's why Coors Field is the MLB ballpark that most directly impacts the day-to-day play of a team, even more so than the Metrodome, where the Twins build for speed and defense on the artificial turf. While a team built for the Metrodome can play adequately on the road, a team used to playing in Coors Field can't make the adjustment that easily. It's come up quite often: the Rockies will finish a long homestand and then hit the road to face a pitcher sporting a nasty curve or slider. Because the team was so used to seeing below-average curveballs, they'd fail miserably in these situations. Former Rockie Dante Bichette brought in a pitching machine designed to throw vicious curveballs to prepare for these situations.

But most fans—at least those making a pilgrimage to Denver—don't really care about how the Rockies are doing. They want to see a gorgeous ballpark in action, and it will be the rare fan who is disappointed.

Despite all of our accolades, there's actually an understated feel to Coors Field. Features designed to be old-fashioned, such as the lighting stanchions, seem to fit naturally in the area. Take the center-field waterfall: while other ballparks feature hokey-looking outfield fountains (i.e., Angel Stadium), the fountains and rockpile here feels completely natural, like a ballpark was constructed around them.

Before the game, keep an eye on this center-field area. It houses seven fountains shooting water almost 40 feet in the air; the fountains also shoot after a Rockies homer and a Rockies win. Colorado spruce, concolor (white) fir, limber pine, gamble oak, curl-leaf mahogany, and bristle cone pine are planted out among the 350 tons of local Navajo ruby sandstone and granite river boulders.

If anything, the ballpark is a little too large these days and should serve as a lesson to ballpark designers who get too much of what they wish for. The ballpark certainly sprawls, taking up a whopping 76 acres in Denver, so bring your walking shoes if you plan on seeing it all. The original design of Coors Field called for only 43,500 seats. However, after the expansion Rockies drew well at Mile High Stadium, Rockies ownership shifted direction and asked the ballpark capacity be set at more than 50,000. In retrospect, the Rockies should have stayed with the smaller ballpark and pumped demand: the team's all-time attendance record came at Mile High Stadium in 1993 (4.483 million), but the attendance slumped to 2.334 million in 2003 and today Colorado is among the bottom five in MLB attendance.

In response, the Rockies close off whole sections of the ballpark for lightly-attended games, moving fans closer together in the lower levels and behind home plate. The closures also take away some of the better cheap seating in Coors Field.

The ballpark is on three basic levels: a main concourse, a club level, and an upper deck, certainly nothing out of the ordinary. The main concourse wraps around the entire ballpark, giving you multiple vantage points when you start wandering around; in particular, the outfield concourse is wide and attracts lots of families and groups just standing around and chatting. (The outfield concourse is the place to see the downtown Denver skyline; the ballpark is situated with its back to downtown, an unfortunate side effect of ensuring the diamond would be oriented correctly.) There are real bleachers in the outfield and Rockpile area with backs but no arms. The club level is about what you'd expect in a modern ballpark: the seats are outside and the concourse is enclosed, featuring lots of concessions you can't find in the rest of the ballpark, including espresso, fresh-tossed salads, hand-carved sandwiches, and more.

The ballpark signage is more than adequate and a little understated, highlighted by a manual scoreboard in right field posting out-of-town results. The left-field scoreboard, featuring a large video board and clock, could have ended up dominating the scene due to its sheer scale, but it was designed with the same look as the lighting stanchions and blends in perfectly.

That sort of understated elegance—so prevalent in Coors Field—makes the ballpark one of the best in the majors. The retro style of brick and ornamental iron may be done to death elsewhere, but in Denver it still strikes the perfect note.

Ballpark Quirks
There are many, and we've already mentioned most of them in plain view.

Perhaps the biggest quirk is one not seen by fans. As you've already read in this chapter, the Rockies have been facing a serious challenge in making Coors Field less of a hitters' paradise and more of a competitive ballpark. Their solution: store baseballs in a humidor to increase their humidity and (in theory) keep them in the ballpark.

So far the move has worked. Since bedginning the practice Coors Field has slipped from being the MLB ballpark where the most runs are scored to second behind Boston's Fenway Park. Of course, the Rockies did go with a youth movement at the same time.

Food and Drink
Coors Field is surprisingly light on concession stands, with only 43 scattered through the ballpark. Still, there's a wide variety of foodstuffs available, with some very unique offerings.

The most unusual are the Rocky Mountain oysters. No, they're not seafood: they're calf testicles, skinned and deep-fried. We don't imagine they taste all that good, although folks who have tried them say they're lighter and less dense than you'd imagine. You can make almost anything edible by deep-frying it, but we suspect the Rocky Mountain oysters stand at Section 153 is more a promotional venture than a money-making machine.

Denver is a pretty good beer town and the beer offerings reflect that sophistication. Beer from Fort Collins' Fat Tire Brewery can be found throughout the ballpark, while a number of stands also feature the microbrewed Sandlot Brewery Beer. Several Beers of the World stands offer a wider variety of beers as well.

One unique feature of Coors Field is the onsite Sandlot Brewery microbrewery run by Coors Brewing. It's located behind Section 112 and it's a real bar with real beer and real brewing equipment. The Sandlot Brewery fits within the general design of Coors Field—lots of brick and exposed ductwork—and there's an outside deck for those who want to soak up some sun before or during a game. If you want to watch the game, there are windows between the brewery and the field. Upwards of a dozen beers are on tap at all times (including the offseason), ranging from light pilsners to heavier ales and bocks. During game days the brewery is restricted to game attendees, but it's open to the public the rest of the time.

The signature food item at Coors Field is the Rockie Dog, a foot-long hot dog with the works (fresh and grilled onions, grilled red and green peppers,

Coors Field

sauerkraut and mustard). It can be found throughout the ballpark, and it's basically heartburn on a bun.

Other popular food offerings include various Mexican specialties (nachos, burritos, soft tacos, quesadillas), grilled-chicken sandwiches, garlic fries, soft-serve and hand-dipped ice cream (go to Madeline's in Section 150 for the best selection), foot-long bratwursts, regular and kosher hot dogs, pizza, and more. Though the emphasis is on beer when it comes to alcoholic beverages, you can find daiquiris on the main concourse (Section 137) and margaritas on the club and upper levels. The Hillyard Deli stand behind Section 137 offers deli sandwiches, and half-pound burgers.

If you want to eat healthy at the ballpark—and given the general healthiness of Denver residents, that's not an unreasonable expectation—you can find chicken sandwiches at all Grill Works stands, while the Hillyard Deli offers Chinese chicken salad, Gardenburgers, panini deli sandwiches, and veggie wraps.

Smaller portions designed for kids are offered at the Buckaroos concession stand opposite the play area at Section 149.

For the Kids
The kids play area is located down the left-field line on the main concourse, behind Section 147. Parents can see the game and watch their kids in action; as mentioned earlier you can order kid-sized concessions at the Buckaroos concession stand.

Kids of all ages will enjoy the Coors Field Interactive Area, located behind Section 120. The various games focus on baseball skills—there's a video batting cage, a pitching video game, a speed gun to test your arm speed, and a home-run derby. Younger kids can test their skills in a T-ball cage. Two other activities are appropriate for anyone: a special computer allows you to place a personal message in a photo of the scoreboard of any MLB ballpark, while a fantasy broadcast booth lets you call the game for a half inning and take home a recording of your effort.

If your child is young, the Rockies offer booster seats. You can check them out at the Guest Relations Center behind Section 127.

Ballpark Tours

The Colorado Rockies offer tours of Coors Field year-round. They last about 75 minutes and hit popular spots throughout the ballpark, including the dugout, the visitor's clubhouse, the club level, and suites. Times vary based on the time of year and whether there's a game that night; call 303/ROCKIES for more information. The cost is $6 for adults, $4 for children (12 and younger) and seniors. Proceeds go to the Colorado Rockies Baseball Club Foundation.

Getting There

One great thing about Denver: there's an emphasis on mass transit with good light-rail and train lines. Unless there's an absolute need for you to drive to the game, consider taking mass transit.

The RockiesRide Express buses run from 14 area Park-n-Ride lots (from as far north as Longmont and Boulder to as far south as Littleton). There's no set formula: some lines run more than once before a game while other do not. In general, you can assume you'll be at the ballpark at least 30 minutes before game time. Buses do not begin leaving until after the conclusion of the game, with the last bus leaving 45 minutes after the last out. For more information on the RockiesRide lines, call 303/299-6000.

Denver's light-rail system also services the ballpark. The C Line terminates at Union Station, a short two-block walk from the ballpark. The D Line terminates at 16th Steet, where you can catch a free downtown train closer to the ballpark and then walk the final few blocks.

If you must drive, there are 3,800 parking spots adjacent to Coors Field in two separate lots. Parking at Lot A is $10 and $8 at Lot B. There are many other parking spots in the general vicinity of Coors Field, however, many within a short walk of the ballpark. You can also seek out one of the 18,000 parking spots within a 15-minute walk of the ballpark, but be warned the meter restrictions near the Coors Field are strictly enforced.

By car, Coors Field is relatively easy to find, with routes well-marked on the freeway. No matter your starting point, you'll want to take I-25 to Exit #213 (Park Av. West) and follow the signs.

If you want to bike to the game, the Rockies offer bike parking adjacent to the Wynkoop ticket windows at Gate E, across from Gate B at 22nd and Blake Streets, and outside Gate A.

Where to Stay

There are not many hotels within LoDo proper, but there are plenty on the edge and within a short ride away on the 16th Street Trolley.

In fact, there are several smaller-scale, hip hotels within a relatively short walk of the ballpark. The Oxford Hotel (1600 17th St.; *theoxfordhotel.com*; $150-$250) once catered to train travelers looking to crash for the night; it is defenitely not fancy, but it is homey. A trendier bet is the Luna Hotel (1612 Wazee St.; *thelunahotel.com*; $170-$220), an all-new hotel featuring flat-screen TVs, a modernist decor and upscale beddings. (In other words, don't bring the kids.) The Hotel Monaco (171 Champa St.; *monaco-denver.com*; $200-$300) is typical of the excellent pet-friendly Kimpton chain: it feels like an upscale bed and breakfast, complete with evening wine reception, yoga supplies, and pet goldfish on demand. And the Magnolia (818 17th St.; *magnoliahotels.com*; $150-$225) is part of the same chain restoring old office buildings in Houston and Denver, converting them to hotels. The Magnolia's angle is providing luxury accommodations for businesspeople at a lower room rate; that business plan also allows for plenty of open (and cheaper) rooms on weekends.

The Brown Palace Hotel (321 17th St.; *brownpalace.com*; $200-$400) is the most historic hotel in downtown Denver: former President Theodore Roosevelt stayed there in 1905 and subsequent Presidents have taken up in the Presidential Suite. Built in 1892 by hotelier Henry C. Brown, the Palace stood apart in a time when Denver was still a rough-and-ready Western city. Even if you're not staying there, the Brown Palace's eight-story atrium is worth a gawk.

Also close to the ballpark—and the best bets for families—are the Embassy Suites (1881 Curtis St.; *hilton.com*; $175-$250) and the new Residence Inn (1725 Champa St.; *marriott.com*; $100-$200).

There are other corporate hotel chains represented within a mile of the ballpark: the Westin Tabor Center (1672 Lawrence St.; *westin.com*; $150-$250), Courtyard by Marriott (934 16th St.; *marriott.com*; $100-$150), the Grand Hyatt Denver (1750 Welton St.; *hyatt.com*; $125-$200), the Hampton Inn & Suites Downtown (1845 Sherman; *hilton.com*; $150-$200), and the Holiday Inn Denver Downtown (1450 Glenarm Place; *holiday-inn.com*; $90-$125).

Local Attractions

Denver's LoDo district is fairly large and features many restaurants and shops presenting plenty of diversions for adults and kids. All the establishments we list here are an easy walk of Coors Field. Navigating LoDo is relatively simple: the 16th Street Mall runs a mile through the heart of downtown Denver, with Union Station on the north end and the Capitol district on the south. Coors Field and the most popular attractions are on the north end.

Though the food selection at Coors Field is pretty decent, we'd recommend eating out before or after the game—the wealth of great restaurants in the area makes that an easy decision.

We dined before our Rockies game at the Vesta Dipping Grill, where the food presentation is simple: you choose from an extensive list of sauces, aiolis

and chutneys, as well as entrees to dip. It's fusion at its most extreme—our dips included chocolate mole, smoked tomato sage, rosemary ginger sauce, Asian peanut sauce and harissa sauce. The always-crowded dining room and bar make Vesta the place to see and be seen in LoDo. Reservations are recommended. *Vesta Dipping Grill, 1822 Blake St.; vestagrill.com.*

We also dined and drank at the Wynkoop Brewing Company, one of the first businesses that helped revitalize the area. The bar is renowned for its microbrewed beer but the food is good as well. It's an extremely popular place to meet before and after a game, so expect a crowd. *Wynkoop Brewing Company, 1634 18th St.; wynkoop.com.*

The Wazee Lounge and Supper Club isn't quite as old as it looks—it dates back only to the 1970s—but almost all the architectural elements of the place have a long provenance in Denver: the back bar was removed from Denver's American Hotel shortly before its demolition, while the benches came from the downtown Denver Elks Club before it relocated. The food is basic pub grub—burgers, sandwiches, and pizza—but you go to the Wazee for the atmosphere, not the food. *Wazee Supper Club, 1600 15th St.; wazeesupperclub.com.*

Shoppers will also delight in LoDo. Two establishments stand out: the Tattered Cover bookstore and Rockmount Ranch Wear.

The Tattered Cover is one of the great independent bookstores still fighting against the onslaught of Borders and Barnes & Noble. Located in an old downtown warehouse, The Tattered Cover is also a pleasant place to just hang out and leaf through the extensive periodical collection. *Tattered Cover, 1628 16th St.; tatteredcover.com.*

In many respects Denver is a cowtown, with Western influences throughout. That's what makes Rockmount Ranch Wear, located in LoDo since

1946, so special. Jack Weil, the company's founder, is still around (he's now 105 years old). He helped create a distinct Western look: shirts with piping and snaps, bolo ties, and more. If you want the Western look, this is the place. *Rockmount Ranch Wear, 1626 Wazee St.; rockmount.com.*

Team Ballpark History
The Colorado Rockies played their first two seasons (1993-1994) at Mile High Stadium, best known as the home of the NFL's Denver Broncos. But Mile High Stadium wasn't built to house an NFL team; ironically, it opened in 1948 as 17,000-seat Bears Stadium, home of the baseball Denver Bears of the Class A Western League. The Bears already were a huge hit when the ballpark was built, and by 1949 Denver was attracting 463,039 a season, outdrawing the National League's St. Louis Browns and every higher-classification minor-league team east of the Rockies save the Montreal Royals. In 1955 the Bears moved to the American Association and drew 426,248 fans under manager Ralph Houk (outdrawing the Washington Senators in the process).

By 1959 the ballpark was expanded to 34,000 with the American Football League's Denver Broncos beginning play for the 1960 season. The ballpark was expanded once again in 1968 and renamed Mile High Stadium, while another 1977 expansion put capacity at 75,000.

Pro baseball never left Denver, and, in fact, thrived during the late 1980s and early 1990s before the arrival of the Rockies (the Denver Zephyrs drew over 550,000 fans in 1991). The grandstand remained in the same place since the facility opened as Bears Stadium, but the surrounding stands did not: the east stands would move in for football and out for baseball using a track of water.

Mile High Stadium was torn down after the 2001 football season; the site is now a parking lot for Invesco Field at Mile High, the new home of the Broncos. A memorial plaque honoring Mile High's history as a baseball venue was installed in 2006.

Other Baseball Attractions
The Colorado Springs Sky Sox of the Class AAA Pacific Coast League play in nearby Colorado Springs. Sky Sox Stadium (4385 Tutt Boulevard; *skysox.com*) was built in 1988 and gives prospects a chance to get used to playing in the high altitudes of Colorado.

The Fort Collins Foxes of the Mountain Collegiate Baseball League play a short season between June and the beginning of July. The MCBL (*mcbl.net*) is like the Cape Cod League or the Northwoods League: it gives college players a chance to hone their wares using wood bats instead of the wretched aluminum version.

Los Angeles Dodgers
Dodger Stadium

Address: 1000 Elysian Park Avenue, Los Angeles, CA 90012.
Cost: $23 million.
Architect: Captain Emil Praeger.
Owner: Los Angeles Dodgers.
Capacity: 56,000.
Dimensions: 330L, 383LC, 395C, 385RC, 330R.
Ticket Line: 866/DODGERS.
Playing Surface: Grass.
Home Dugout Location: Third-base side.
Other Tenants: None currently. The Los Angeles/California Angels played at
Dodger Stadium from April 17, 1962 to September 22, 1965.
First Game: On April 10, 1962, Kay O'Malley tossed the ceremonial first pitch to
catcher John Roseboro to open the new ballpark. The Dodgers lost to the
Reds, 6-3, with Cincy's Wally Post hitting the first homer. Though there were
some early problems (only two drinking fountains were working on Opening
Day), overall Dodger Stadium was well-received by the local sporting
community.
Landmark Event: Dodger Stadium has hosted eight World Series with the
Dodgers winning four (1963, 1965, 1981, and 1988). In 1963, the Dodgers
swept the Yankees 4-0 behind Sandy Koufax, who threw complete games in
Games One and Four (striking out 15 in Game One). In 1965, the Dodgers
needed seven games to dispatch the Minnesota Twins, winning all three
Series games played at Dodger Stadium. In 1981, the Dodgers once again
faced the Yankees, coming out on top four games to two: this Series may
be better remembered for Yankees reliever George Frazier losing three of

the four games. The 1988 World Series featured one of the more memorable moments in championship history when gimpy pinch-hitter Kirk Gibson homered off Oakland reliever Dennis Eckersley to give the Dodgers the opening-game victory. The real hero for the Dodgers, however, was pitcher Orel Hershiser, who won Games Two and Five in complete-game performances. The 1980 All-Star Game was played there as well, with the National League winning 4-2. Steve Stone threw three shutout innings, but the Senior Circuit squad took the lead for good when Phil Garner scored on a Willie Randolph error. Ken Griffey Sr., who homered off Tommy John, was named MVP. Also, Pope John Paul II celebrated Mass in 1987 and the Three Tenors reunited there in 1994.

Your Dodger Stadium Seating Crib Sheet

Best Sections to View a Game: There are not many bad seats in Dodger Stadium; in fact, most are great. Obviously you'll have the best views between the bases (and you'll pay for the privilege of being close to the field; the loge boxes are not cheap), but Dodger Stadium was designed solely for baseball and the seat orientations reflect that.

Best Cheap Seats: In general, the Dodgers offer a wide array of affordable seats. We're partial to the $6 Top Deck seats located behind home plate: from there you can see the on-field action from a great vantage point as well as take in the lovely California sunsets. At $10, Pavilion seating is a great bargain as well: there's not a bad seat in the intimate outfield seating areas.

Most Underrated Sections: The outfield Pavilion seating area is only $10, and you feel like you're in your own separate little ballpark. Actually, you are: you can't enter the Dodger Stadium grandstand with a Pavilion ticket (similarly, those with tickets to grandstand seating can't enter the Pavilion), and that section features its own concessions and restrooms; the only drawback is the limited view of DodgerVision scoreboards. Similarly, we think the Top Deck seats are underrated: since they rarely sell out, you can stretch out and have a great view of the ballpark and the game.

Seats to Avoid: Really, we can't think of any. Dodger Stadium features a slight horseshoe shape so any seats down the lines will be oriented to the infield as the grandstand curves in. One can argue the Club Level is a little overpriced at $55 (the views are great behind the plate, but the amenities are lacking when compared to club levels in other MLB ballparks), as are the infield loge boxes at $45, but in general there are very few seats to avoid in Dodger Stadium.

Dodger Stadium: The Blue Standard

Many in baseball revere Dodger Stadium as representing all that's right with baseball. At a time when ballpark designers are straining to impart a sense of history with retro designs, historic credibility is automatically part of the Dodger Stadium experience.

Dodger Stadium is a gorgeous, classic, well-maintained ballpark set on 300 acres; an oasis in the midst of Los Angeles. It's interesting that the ballpark was designed by Captain Emil Praeger (not known primarily as a ballpark designer), who toured several ballparks while designing Dodger Stadium and decided not to copy any of them, preferring instead what critics today would call an organic architecture. The ballpark is built into the side of Chavez Ravine, more like a classic auditorium built into the side of a hill than a ballpark rising from the ground.

In theory, this allows you to walk off the parking lot and head directly to your section without needing an elevator or escalator—even in the upper deck. The formula gets screwy these days because you're not allowed to park where you want or in a section that corresponds with your seat location: the parking-lot attendants force you to the parking area of their choice, and if you must walk up the side of a hill to enter in your assigned section, so be it. (In the past you matched the color of the baseball on the parking-lot light pole with the color of your ticket, but that format has been dumped.) Given 16,000 parking spots occupy the 21 Dodger Stadium lots, not allowing you to park close to your section is simply ludicrous.

At a time when ballparks are run as relatively open venues and new ballparks feature lots of places to mill around and watch a ballgame from different angles, Dodger Stadium is run the same way it was in the 1960s and 1970s—with an iron fist. Fans are expected to enter the gate closest to their seating area; tough luck if the parking lot attendants place you on the opposite side of the ballpark from your gate. Fans are expected to stay in their seats for the entire game: sure, you can go to the bathroom or a concession stand, but you really shouldn't wander too far. Want to watch some of the game from the outfield Pavilion? Forget it if you don't hold a ticket to that section; an usher will turn you away at the gate, even if the game is in the bottom of the eighth and the Dodgers are getting blown away by the Diamondbacks. (Apparently losing makes the ushers surly.) The way the

TRIVIA

In 2005 Dodger Stadium actually got younger—relatively speaking. When the Montreal Expos moved to Washington's RFK Stadium, Dodger Stadium was superseded as the second-oldest ballpark in the National League. Dodger Stadium opened on April 10, 1962; District of Columbia Stadium opened on April 9, 1962, making it the second-oldest park in the National League behind Wrigley Field. When the Washington Nationals move to a new ballpark for the 2008 season, Dodger Stadium will once again be the second-oldest ballpark in the Senior Circuit.

Dodgers front office runs the ballpark is opposite how most major-league teams now run their ballparks, and it's not clear whether the front office knows it or really cares. Being treated well by the Dodgers is not why you head to Dodger Stadium.

If you've gotten the idea we're not fans of the way the Dodgers run Dodger Stadium, you're correct. Dodger Stadium is a treasure and should be treated as such, but given what the Dodgers get for tickets and parking fees, the fans paying the freight should be treasured as well.

Like many transplants in southern California, the Dodgers carry some baggage from their former home. The name *Los Angeles Dodgers* is somewhat nonsensical: the original name of the franchise came from the practice of Brooklyn residents dodging trolley cars. To many, Brooklyn slid into irrelevancy when the Dodgers moved to Los Angeles; it became just another borough.

But Brooklyn's loss was Los Angeles's gain. The site of Dodger Stadium was offered to owner Walter O'Malley before he committed to move the team to Los Angeles: city leaders took O'Malley on a helicopter ride and showed him potential ballpark sites. Given the way Los Angeles was sprawling even in the 1950s, his choice of Chavez Ravine (at that time a working-class Latino neighborhood) was a curious one until you realize how many freeways intersected near the ballpark. At a time when baseball was fleeing to the suburbs, O'Malley chose to stay near downtown Los Angeles—and a tangled web of highways and freeways.

It took four years for the Dodgers to build Dodger Stadium as lawsuits and

landslides postponed construction several times. We don't know whether Praeger intended to build a ballpark totally suited for pitchers, but he did. The ball doesn't carry well in Dodger Stadium when compared to most major-league ballparks, and with the spacious outfield dimensions, Dodger Stadium rewards moderately talented pitchers and penalizes power hitters. Despite the fact that many great sluggers have played in Dodger Stadium (like Duke Snider and Frank Howard), only one batter has ever hit the ball out of the ballpark: Willie Stargell of the Pittsburgh Pirates. He did it twice. In 1969 he pulled the ball 506 feet over the Pavilion roof, and he did it again in 1973 when the ball traveled 470 feet, bounced on top of the Pavilion roof and went out of the ballpark.

INSIDER'S TIP

Nancy Bea is part of a shrinking number of ballpark employees: She's the organist at Dodger Stadium. Fewer than half of the major-league teams employ an organist, and Bea's has largely been supplanted by loud music and other sound effects. After a loss, the Dodgers play "Tomorrow" (from *Annie*), but by that time Bea has left the ballpark—it's a recorded version.

The layout of Dodger Stadium is a familiar one: a field level is topped with a mezzanine level and an upper deck. The bleachers in the outfield have their own entrances and concessions—you instantly know you're seeing Dodger Stadium when you see the pavilion roof over the bleachers in the outfield, the familiar palm trees beyond the line and the San Gabriel Mountains in the distance. (In person, the view is even more spectacular: you can see the downtown Los Angeles skyline as well.) There are two scoreboards in the outfield: the classic Dodgervision in right field and a newer, flashier video display in left. In 2005, the Dodgers added a race-track display strip on the fascia between the upper and lower sections: it tends to distract when you first arrive, but then you tune it out. Despite Dodger Stadium's urban location, it is the model of a bucolic California ballpark.

And it is clean, though not as well maintained as in the past. The O'Malleys were known for repainting the entire ballpark in every offseason; the current owner has apparently missed a few years. The capacity of Dodger Stadium has remained steady since day one at 56,000. We suspect it's not truly that number as the Dodgers have removed seats on the mezzanine level and installed suites over the years. (Before the 2005 season the Dodgers added 1,600 seats behind home plate and didn't appear to remove any. The addition of these seats meant the removal of the old lower-level windows in the grandstand. Two generations of baseball fans can remember the white-suited Mike Brito in the background of every televised pitch, speed gun in hand. Before the 2006 season the team eliminated multiple rows, but the capacity of Dodger Stadium is still the same—56,000.) Praeger designed the ballpark to be expandable to 85,000 by extending the grandstand around the foul poles and into the outfield, but luckily the Dodgers never felt the need to add so many seats despite some golden years when sellouts were common. (They are not now, though the team draws very well.)

If there's one additional drawback to Dodger Stadium, it's the ballpark's relative isolation despite being in the center of Los Angeles. There's a fairly large buffer zone of trees and streets between Dodger Stadium and any of its neighbors, and while the relative isolation can make the ballpark experience a timeless one, it can be a jarring thrust back to reality when you leave the premises and see how poor the surrounding neighborhood is. The Dodgers have

Dodger Stadium

made some noise in recent years under owner Frank McCourt about developing land they control around the ballpark; they should consider doing so with an eye toward revitalizing the entire area. Through extensive writings and the music of Ry Cooder, the long-term impact of Dodger Stadium on its ethnic community surroundings has probably drawn more attention and debate than the location of any other sports facility.

We will give McCourt and his crew some credit for putting big bucks into Dodger Stadium between the 2005 and 2006 seasons: during that time all the ballpark's seating was replaced, as the familiar blue and orange seats were removed and seating matching the original pastel colors was installed. It was time: those plastic seats dated back to the mid-1970s (they replaced the original wooden seats) and were pretty worn. Replacing the seats also allowed the Dodgers to reconfigure the ballpark seating. In some sections two rows were replaced with a single row of unique seating and in front of a single row of seats is a table. Replacing seating and reconfiguring the bowl was a good idea; aisles needed to be widened and the rather odd way the Dodgers numbered seats had to go.

We don't want to be too negative about Dodger Stadium: anyone who cares about ballparks and baseball needs to make a pilgrimage as it's one of the loveliest and most historic ballparks in baseball. The Dodgers deserve a lot of credit for leaving Dodger Stadium much as it was when it first opened—they were smart not to mess with a good thing.

Ballpark Quirks

Builders placed the foul poles in the wrong location when Dodger Stadium opened in 1962: they were completely in foul territory. The Dodgers received special permission from the National League office to play the season with the foul poles in foul territory. In the off season the Dodgers didn't move the foul poles, but instead slightly moved home plate and the infield backward slightly to reposition the poles in fair territory.

Food and Drink

Concession areas are located behind the seating on a concourse level, both on the field level and in the upper deck. Alas, Dodger Stadium was built so compactly it's hard to get a view of field while you're walking on the concourse level, and the views of the field are completely cut off from the upper-deck concourse. You can expect to miss some of the action when heading for concessions.

Which are fairly limited at Dodger Stadium in terms of variety. Dodger Dogs are available everywhere and you'll want to try one: the franks are made by Farmer John specifically for the Dodgers and having a Dodger Dog is a great Los Angeles tradition. Cary Grant ate them; so should you.

The Dodgers are heavy on branded concession stands—Subway, Panda Express, Wetzel's Pretzels, Carl's Jr.—with only one truly regional vendor: the ever-tasty Saag's Sausage. Otherwise, you'll find your basic ballpark staples: pizza, frozen yogurt, ice cream, nachos, pop, et al. Worth seeking out: the Gordon Biersch stands on the field and upper levels, where you can find the famous garlic fries.

For the Kids

The kids should be happy enough to simply be at the ballpark. What more could they possibly want? Seriously, the Dodgers don't offer much for kids at the ballpark: the team caters to an adult clientele and does little to attract children. While this can be refreshing (you don't need to worry about a silly mascot roaring around the ballpark on an ATV every half inning), it also tends to lend a somber tone to the proceedings.

Ballpark Tours

The Dodgers do not offer ballpark tours.

Getting There

Drive. Drive. Drive.

Let's be real: this is Los Angeles and everyone drives. Everyone drives to the corner store for milk, and everyone drives to run the smallest of errands. The only time people walk is when they're walking to their cars.

So it's no surprise Dodger Stadium is totally geared to those arriving by car. Be prepared to pay the $10 parking fee. You cannot easily park outside the ballpark and walk in, and no one takes the bus unless they're too poor to own a car. In fact, the Los Angeles bus system doesn't serve Dodger Stadium proper very well: you can take the 2, 3 or 4 lines to Sunset Boulevard and Elysian Park Avenue and walk the half mile to the ballpark.

Chavez Ravine is northeast of downtown Los Angeles. As multiple freeways converge near Dodger Stadium, multiple routes go to the ballpark and most of them are well marked with signage. From I-101: exit Alvarado, go north, then turn right on Sunset. Go approximately one mile and turn left on Elysian Park Avenue, taking you to Dodger Stadium. From I-110: take the Dodger Stadium exit and go straight off the off-ramp, taking you directly to Dodger Stadium. From I-5 South: exit on Stadium Way, then turn left and follow the baseball signs to Dodger Stadium. From I-5 North: exit Stadium Way and turn left on Riverside Drive. Turn left onto Stadium Way and follow the baseball signs until you enter Dodger Stadium off Academy Road.

The closest airport to the ballpark and the largest airport in the region is Los Angeles International Airport (LAX; *lawa.org/lax*). It can be a zoo: the horseshoe layout of the eight terminals ensures traffic bottlenecks and some long lines at security (particularly for those flying on Southwest Airlines, where lines can snake far outside the terminal).

It may be more convenient for you to fly into one of the smaller airports in the region. If you're planning on hitting Angel Stadium as well, look at flying into Anaheim's John Wayne Airport (*ocair.com*). It tends to be more sedate but is still served by all the major airlines. If all you're doing is attending a ballgame and staying downtown, the Bob Hope Airport (also known as the Burbank-Glendale-Pasadena Airport; *burbankairport.com*) is served by Alaska, US Airways, American, Delta, JetBlue, Southwest, and United.

Where to Stay

There's really only one hotel within walking distance of the ballpark: the Super 8 (1341 W. Sunset Blvd.; *super8.com*; $70-$90). It is everything you would expect out of a Super 8 on Sunset Boulevard. And we're not talking about a hotel that's exactly close to the ballpark: it's still quite a hike from there to a Dodger Stadium gate.

Since you'll be driving anyway, don't feel compelled to stay near the ballpark.

Downtown Los Angeles features a number of good hotels within a few miles of the ballpark, including the Marriott Los Angeles (333 S. Figueroa; *marriott.com*; $125-$200), the Sheraton Los Angeles (711 S. Hope St.; *sheraton.com*; $175-$250), the underrated Hotel Figueroa (939 S. Figueroa; *figueroahotel.com*; $89-$125l), the massive Westin Bonaventure (404 S. Figueroa; *westin.com*; $195-$300), and the stately Millennium Biltmore (506 S. Grand Av.; *millennium-hotels.com*; $150-$350). A favorite is the four-star Hilton Checkers (535 S. Grand Av.; *hiltoncheckers.com*; $100-$250), originally built in 1927 and preferred by many visiting movie stars who want a more sedate and plush stay. Be prepared to pay for parking when staying at an upscale downtown hotel.

The beautiful crowd stays in Beverly Hills at places like the plush Avalon (9400 W. Olympic Blvd.; *avalonbeverlyhills.com*; $199-$300), the Beverly Hilton (9876 Wilshire Blvd.; *hilton.com*; $125-$350), the inexpensive Carlyle Inn (1119 S. Robertson Blvd; *carlyle-inn.com*; $109-$159), and the iconic Beverly Hills Hotel (9641 Sunset Blvd.; *beverlyhillshotel.com*; $300-$500). (In fact, drop by the Fountain Coffee Shop at the Beverly Hills Hotel and have breakfast at the famous curved counter to get a real sense of Hollywood glamour.) If you want to go funky in Beverly Hills, check out the historic and quirky Chateau Marmont (8221 Sunset Blvd.; *chateaumarmont.com*; $250-$400), where John Belushi overdosed and where Jim Morrison was a regular visitor. Also on the quirky side: the Farmer's Daughter (115 S. Fairfax Blvd.; *farmersdaughterhotel.com*; $125-$200), done up in a post-retro, wholesome country theme (think calico) near CBS Television City (a place that's significant for several reasons, as you'll find out later in the chapter).

If you're flying in and find the rich and famous in Beverly Hills to be a little intimidating, consider staying at one of the many, many hotels near LAX, such as the Westin (5400 W. Century Blvd.; *westin.com*; $159-$300) or the Sheraton Gateway (6101 W. Century Blvd.; *sheraton.com*; $109-$200).

While You're There

Downtown Los Angeles doesn't have a whole lot of charm. On the whole, it's rather depressing, with rows of former movie houses now converted to cheesy stores, which is why the hotels tend to be self-contained fortresses—so we'd recommend you spend some time in nearby Hollywood and Beverly Hills.

Remember, this is the entertainment capital of the world. And while there's a very seamy and depressing side to Hollywood (remember, most of those fresh-scrubbed youths seeking fame and fortune will fail), there is a lot of history and beauty in Los Angeles everywhere you turn. Los Angeles—more specifically, Hollywood—has been the center of the entertainment world for decades and we'd recommend taking in some of that glamour and glitz during your trip.

The most visible symbol of that glamour and glitz is the famous Hollywood sign. There are many vantage points in Los Angeles from which to view the sign, but the best view is at the corner of Sunset Boulevard and Bronson Avenue. (Don't bother trying to get close to the sign—it's at the end of a 5-mile trail and protected by a fence and motion detectors.) It was erected in 1923 as an ad for the HOLLYWOODLAND housing development, but landslides wiped out the latter portion of the sign. Take a picture or two with the sign in the background for the folks back home.

After that, check out the general Hollywood and Vine area, the historic center of Tinseltown. Grauman's Chinese Theatre (6925 Hollywood Blvd.) is one of the most famous movie houses in the world and the backdrop to many a movie opening. The place is all glitz, and the entryway features the handprints and footprints of many Hollywood stars. Hollywood Boulevard is also home to the Hollywood Walk of Fame, where thousands of celebrities are honored with a star. It's not that exclusive a club—basically, if you have $15,000 and a modicum of name recognition, you too can have a star—and most of the names are already forgotten. The most famous names are on Hollywood or Vine, and Gene Autry has five stars of his own. For an equally tacky experience, check out the Frederick's of Hollywood Lingerie Museum (6608 Hollywood Blvd.; *fredericks.com*), where you can see bras worn by Milton Berle on television and Tony Curtis in the movies. This is the original Frederick's of Hollywood; Los Angeles history at its best.

You could also be on television if you play your cards right. Several shows tape in Los Angeles. One of the most popular is CBS's The Price is Right, which tapes at CBS Television City (7800 Beverly Blvd.) in Hollywood. You can order tickets weeks in advance via the Internet at *cbs.com/daytime/price/tickets*, or you can call 323/575-2458 during business hours to inquire about upcoming tapings at CBS Television City. (There's a very pragmatic reason to try to get into CBS Television City: it's built on the former site of Gilmore Field, home of the Hollywood Stars. We discuss this later.) Most networks use a service called Audiences Unlimited (*tvtickets.com*) to distribute tickets to sitcom tapings; check the Internet site to score some tickets.

While in Hollywood, check out the nearby Musso and Frank Grill (6667 Hollywood Blvd.). It's the oldest restaurant in Hollywood, dating to 1919, and many of the menu items (as well as some of the waitstaff) seemingly date back to opening day. It's got a definite club feel: Orson Welles was a regular, while Ernest Hemingway was known to throw back a few in the bar. Come hungry: the specialties are grilled meats of all sorts, as well as hearty dishes like spring lamb.

Many of these attractions are on or near Hollywood Boulevard, giving you the best (and the worst) Los Angeles and Hollywood have to offer. Here's an interesting itinerary for you: make a loop from Dodger Stadium to the ocean via Hollywood Boulevard and Sunset Boulevard. Sunset Boulevard runs northwest of the ballpark and splits into Hollywood Boulevard (to the north) and Sunset Boulevard, running parallel three blocks apart. The journey will show you the seamier side of Los Angeles in the east before ending up at a public beach on the Pacific Ocean. (Consult a map before you set out on this journey; Hollywood Boulevard ends well to the east of the ocean, so you'll need to heard south to Sunset Boulevard to continue to the west.)

If you want the Hollywood experience in a pure form, check out a studio tour. Universal Studios Hollywood combines an hour-long tour of the lot with a theme park. You'll see lots where movies famous and forgotten were shot, and you may see some stars wandering around as well. After the legendary tour you can spend the rest of the day hitting rides like Waterworld (reportedly better than the movie) and Revenge of the Mummy. *Universal Studios Hollywood, Universal City (take the Universal Center Drive or Lankershim Boulevard exit off the Hollywood Freeway); universalstudioshollywood.com. Adults, $53; children, $43.*

If you don't need a theme park and want just the essential movie-lot tour, consider a tour from Sony or Warner Brothers. Sony Pictures offers a studio tour at its Culver City studio (10202 W. Washington Blvd.; *sonypicturesstudios.com*). It's the former Columbia Studios lot where films like *The Wizard of Oz* and *Men in Black* were filmed. It's also the busiest movie lot in Hollywood with both movies and television shows (tapings include *Jeopardy* and *Wheel of Fortune* are both taped there) increasing your chances of seeing a star. A tour is a real movie-lot tour lasting two hours. Call 323/520-TOUR for times and availability; the cost is $25 and kids under 12 years old are not allowed. Warner Brothers offers two levels of tours at its Burbank studios (4301 W. Olive Av.; *wbstudiotour.com*), with one at two hours long and the other at five hours in length, including lunch in the commissary. A highlight of any tour: the Warner Brothers Museum, which features memorabilia from TV shows and movies shot on the lot. The VIP Tour operates Monday through Friday with tours starting every half hour between 8:30 a.m. and 3:30 p.m. The price is $39 per person, and children under eight years old are not allowed. For a more in-depth studio tour experience, Deluxe VIP Tours are offered daily at 10:30 a.m. for $125.

Kids will enjoy a visit to the La Brea Tar Pits and the Page Museum (5801 Wilshire Blvd.; *tarpits.org*; adults, $7, seniors 62 and older and students with I.D., $4.50, youths 13-17, $4.50, children 5-12, $2, children under 5, free); tar bubbling to the surface has ensnared many animals, including extinct species such as saber-tooth cats and mammoths. Today the tar pits still bubble as they did 30,000 years ago and scientists have identified 400 species of mammals, amphibians and birds excavated from the various pits. That these tar pits exist in what's become a large urban area is a little surreal.

Team Ballpark History

The Los Angeles Dodgers began life in Brooklyn, N.Y., operating under a variety of names (the Brooklyn Robins and the Brooklyn Superbas were used before the Brooklyn Dodgers moniker was adopted), The team played first at Washington Park (1890-1912) and then at Ebbets Field (1913-1957).

Ebbets Field was an opulent palace of baseball when it opened on April 9, 1913 as the home of the Brooklyn Dodgers. When the working-class Brooklynites showed up to cheer on the Dodgers, they entered the ballpark through a legendary 80-foot-wide rotunda, walking across a floor of Italian marble decorated like the stitching on a baseball, their path illuminated by a mammoth chandelier featuring 12 arms shaped like baseball bats.

Why the show? The Dodgers weren't the top attraction in New York baseball in the 1910s: in 1913 the New York Giants ruled the roost. The team had moved into its own baseball showcase, the fireproofed Polo Grounds, and the Giants' attendance picked up while the Dodgers' attendance slipped away at Washington Park, at Third Street and Fourth Avenue in the Red Hook area of South Brooklyn (which isn't actually the southernmost part of Brooklyn, but that's another other story). Washington Park was small, so Dodgers owner

Above: The first game at Ebbets Field on April 8, 1913. The regular season began the following day, so this was an exhibition game; we're guessing the "Caldwell" identified on the photo was Ray Caldwell, who pitched that season for the New York Yankees, a likely exhibition opponent for the Brooklyn Superbas. (Courtesy of Library of Congress, LC-B2-2669-11[P&P].)

Below: Fans were placed along the fence during games attracting large crowds. Note the manual scoreboards in the right of the picture. (Courtesy of Library of Congress, LC-B2-5311-7[P&P].)

Charlie Ebbets decided to build something grand and magnificent to draw attention to what had become a pretty decent team. After obtaining some land in the borderline—but inexpensive—area of Flatbush called Pigtown, Ebbets mapped out a new ballpark. It was a grand dream and beyond Ebbets' financial wherewithal: he ended up selling half the team to the McKeever brothers, who built Ebbets Field.

Ebbets and the McKeevers didn't do a great job of designing a ballpark or opening it, though. When Ebbets Field opened for an exhibition game against the New York Yankees in early April 1913, team officials and incoming reporters realized that for some reason a press box was never planned or constructed. In those days press boxes were true box seats near the action, not the lofty perches designed for the press today. (It is possible that Charlie Ebbets wasn't that fond of the press: it wasn't until 1929 that a press box was constructed.) As of Opening Day 1913, no one could get into the left-field bleachers because they were locked up and no one had a key. More curious was the omission of a flag pole in center field, a tradition in ballparks of the era.

Despite the borderline Pigtown site, Ebbets Field had a great location. Flatbush Avenue was the main drag through Brooklyn and two subway/rail stations were located within three blocks of the ballpark. The area was served by nine trolley lines that connected to 32 others. This is how the Dodgers got their name: Brooklyn residents were forever dodging the trolley cars.

The original design of Ebbets Field was a two-story grandstand that curved in back of home plate, extending all the way down to the foul pole on the first-

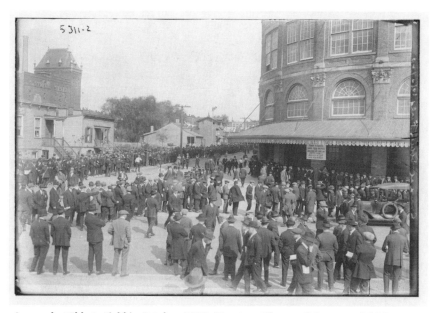

A crowd at Ebbets Field in October 1920. (Courtesy Library of Congress, LC-B2-5311-2[P&P].)

base side and to just past the infield on the third-base side; a deck of bleachers went from there to the foul pole. Initially there were no outfield bleachers, but there sure was a lot of playing surface: left field extended 419 feet down the line and 477 feet to dead center. Only right field was friendly to batters with the fences only 301 feet down the line.

During the heyday of the Dodgers, Brooklyn was the melting pot of New York City. The swells lived in Manhattan and the working class lived in Brooklyn. This particular working class had a collective chip on its shoulder as big as the Ritz: Brooklynites were permanently underdogs and dared the rest of the city—and the world—to knock it off. Yes, they may be bums, but they're the Brooklyn Bums. The Dodgers took this notion to heart and reveled in it: "Dem Bums" became the team's rallying cry and the team commissioned New York World-Telegram artist Willard Mullin to put his archetypal Brooklyn Bum on the cover of team publications. Though the average Brooklynite may have felt marginal in the grand scheme of things, he was king at Ebbets Field, entering through the grand rotunda and then occupying a seat close to the action. (Of course, in a ballpark so small, all the seats were close to the action. "The fans, you joked with them on a first-name basis," said Pee Wee Reese. "You were friends.") And the typical crowd could only have come from the neighborhoods of Brooklyn. Hilda Chester is still renowned in baseball circles as the ultimate Dodgers fan: she sat out in the left-center-field bleachers with her cowbell after her doctor forbade her to yell after she suffered a heart attack. (The cowbell was actually a scaled-back instrument for her: she began by banging a frying pan with an iron ladle.) The Brooklyn Sym-phony Band, whose enthusiasm outpaced their musical skills, still exists to this day: consisting of a trumpet, trombone, cymbals, bass drum, and snare drum, the band roamed through Ebbets Field.

By the 1950s, however, Walter O'Malley grew dissatisfied with Ebbets Field, first proposing a new ballpark for the Dodgers elsewhere in Brooklyn and then elsewhere in New York City. City officials, led by the legendary Robert Moses, weren't too thrilled about building a new stadium for the Dodgers or even donating some desirable real estate for a privately funded stadium. Instead, Moses offered a tract of land in Queen's Flushing Meadows. (No, O'Malley replied: "We'll not be the Brooklyn Dodgers if we're in Queens.") But in the end, O'Malley threw in the towel when Los Angeles made an offer he couldn't refuse: free land and a ton of civic support. Brooklyn didn't give up on the Dodgers (attendance in 1957 was well over a million—pretty good for its day); the Dodgers gave up on Brooklyn.

Upon moving to the West Coast, the Dodgers played four seasons at the Los Angeles Coliseum while Dodger Stadium was under construction. Dodgers officials decided on the problematic Coliseum over the decrepit Wrigley Field, long-time home of the Pacific Coast League's Los Angeles Angels: the Coliseum held over 90,000 fans, much more than 20,000-seat Wrigley Field (which, sadly, sat unused). Some basic work was done to make the Coliseum appropriate for baseball: dugouts, three banks of lights, and a press box were added. Because of the orientation of the diamond, there was a ton of space in foul ground down the left-field line, but very little space between the right-field line and the bleachers. The baseball diamond was crammed into one end of the stadium, resulting in a left-field line measuring only 250 feet. A 40-foot screen was constructed to counter the intimate dimensions, but it didn't do that much good: the balls flew out of the park because of its small size. In fact, the disparity between home runs hit to left and those hit to right field was staggering. In 1958, 193 home runs were hit in the Coliseum—182 to left, three to center, and eight to right.

On April 18, 1958, the Dodgers played their first game at the Coliseum, defeating the Giants 6-5 before 78,672 fans. On that day the Coliseum became the largest stadium ever in major-league baseball—a record that still stands. The size of the stadium allowed the Dodgers to set the all-time single-game attendance record on May 7, 1959: a crowd of 93,105 showed up to see former Dodger great Roy Campanella honored during an exhibition game between the New York Yankees and Dodgers. In 1958, the Dodgers drew over 1.8 million fans (good enough for second in National League attendance—the Milwaukee Braves drew over 1.9 million fans to County Stadium), and in 1959 and 1960 the team drew over 2 million fans—records at the time.

For more on Walter O'Malley and that era of Dodgers baseball, check out the excellent Walter O'Malley Web site at *walteromalley.com*.

Local Baseball Attractions

Baseball fans will be in ecstasy in Los Angeles with a host of baseball attractions and minor-league baseball teams. There's also a rich baseball history in the area and you'll want to know a little about it before making a trip.

Long before the Dodgers and the Angels moved to Los Angeles, the city hosted several Pacific Coast League (PCL) teams. At one point the PCL was considered a competitor to the major leagues (star players could make more money on the West Coast, thanks to longer seasons made possible by favorable West Coast weather), and at one point PCL owners were poised to make a run as a third major league before they were appeased by a special open classification in the minors.

The Los Angeles Angels were a flagship team in the Pacific Coast League, playing their home games at Wrigley Field (42nd Street and Avalon). This was the original Wrigley Field, built in 1925 and owned by William Wrigley, the chewing-gum manufacturer who also owned the Chicago Cubs and renamed Chicago's Wrigley Field in 1926. The Los Angeles Wrigley Field was partially modeled after Chicago's Wrigley Field and hosted the Angels from 1927 through 1957 and the Hollywood Stars from 1926 through 1935, and 1938. Because of its location in the film and television capital of the world, Wrigley Field was prominently featured in many baseball movies over the years, serving as a stand-in for Yankee Stadium in *Pride of the Yankees* and *Griffith Stadium* in Damn Yankees. It was also the home of television's *Home Run Derby*, originally filmed in the 1960s and occasionally repeated today on ESPN

Classic.

When the Dodgers moved to Los Angeles, they eschewed Wrigley Field in favor of the larger Los Angeles Coliseum, discussed in the previous section. The expansion Los Angeles Angels gave Wrigley Field one last hurrah in 1961 when the American League squad played a single season there before moving to Dodger Stadium (referred to as Chavez Ravine by Angels announcers). Wrigley Field was demolished in 1966; sadly, there is no marker commemorating the site.

Speaking of the Coliseum: it is still standing and still the home of the University of Southern California Trojans football team.

The PCL Angels wasn't the only baseball team in the area. The Hollywood Stars was the glamour team of the Pacific Coast League, regularly drawing celebrities to Gilmore Field in the heart of Hollywood (7800 Beverly Blvd). Notables like Walt Disney, Bing Crosby, and Gary Cooper invested in the team and were regulars at the cozy ballpark. How cozy? The backstop was only 34 feet from the plate, and the grandstand was only 24 feet away from first and third bases. Many fans didn't go to Gilmore Field for the baseball; they came out to watch the stars. Gilmore Field was torn down in 1958 and the site became the home of CBS's Television City. You can see some historic photos of Gilmore Field outside Studio 46, where the former ballpark entrance stood, but be warned you must get a pass to enter the premises.

A few other historical markers in the area honor the former ballpark sites. In Burbank's George Izay Park (West Olive Avenue and Mariposa Street) sits a plaque honoring Olive Memorial Stadium, the former spring-training home of the St. Louis Browns from 1949 through 1952.

And, of course, there are the Los Angeles Angels of Anaheim, who play at Angel Stadium, located about 30 minutes south of downtown Los Angeles. We cover the Angels in a separate chapter; we also discuss other area baseball attractions in that chapter as well.

Florida Marlins
Dolphin Stadium

Address: 2269 Dan Marino Blvd., Miami, FL 33056.
Cost: $115 million; $10 million in renovations for baseball use.
Architect: HOK Sport.
Owner: Miami Dolphins.
Capacity: 36,331.
Dimensions: 330L, 385LC, 410C, 434C, 385RC, 345R.
Ticket Line: 877/MARLINS.
Playing Surface: Grass.
Home Dugout Location: First-base side.
Other Tenants: The stadium was originally built by owner Joe Robbie for his NFL Miami Dolphins, opening in the 1987 season.
Previous Names: Joe Robbie Stadium (August 1987-August 1996), Pro Player Park (August 1996-September 1996), Pro Player Stadium (September 1996-2005), Dolphins Stadium (2005-2006).
First Game: The Baltimore Orioles and Los Angeles Dodgers played an exhibition game here on March 11, 1988. The expansion Florida Marlins opened their history at home on April 5, 1993, with a 6-3 win over the Los Angeles Dodgers before a crowd of 42,334. Veteran knuckleballer Charlie Hough went six innings for the Marlins to earn the victory, defeating Orel Hershiser. Jeff Conine went 4-for-4 and scored two runs for the Fish.
Landmark Event: The Florida Marlins won the 1997 World Series at Pro Player Stadium, defeating the Cleveland Indians 3-2 in the seventh game. Edgar

Renteria singled in Craig Counsell with two out in the bottom of the 11th to secure the win. In 2003 the Marlins won another World Series, snaring two victories at home before clinching the series four games to two with a 2-0 win over New York at Yankee Stadium. Josh Beckett threw a complete-game shutout and Luis Castillo drove in the eventual winning run. Curiously, the Marlins have never won a division title; in both seasons the Fish were a wild-card entry in the playoffs. Many other notable events in the stadium's history include three Super Bowls (1989, 1995, and 1999), and the yearly Orange Bowl (since 1996).

Your Dolphin Stadium Seating Crib Sheet

Best Sections to View a Game: In one sense any section is the best: because the Marlins don't draw well you can have your pick of sections and move down to a more expensive seat by the seventh inning or so. Obviously, the best seats are between the bases in the grandstand; past that every section has its pros and cons.

Best Cheap Seats: The Marlins adopted the obnoxious practice of premium pricing: ticket prices for Opening Day, Friday, and Saturday games are more expensive, up to $10 extra per seat. Fish Tank seats—those in sections 125, 126, and 127—go for $10 on premium dates, $8 during the week. The Fish Tank prices are halved for kids aged between 2 and 12, so a family of four in the Fish Tank can get in the gates for $24.

Most Underrated Sections: There are three club sections—A (243-256), B (240-242, 201-210), and C (211-215). They have a huge advantage: they're sheltered from the hot sun and inevitable late-afternoon rainstorm. They're not overly expensive ($28-$45), and if you're going to Dolphin Stadium for a single game or two, they're worth the investment.

Seats to Avoid: We're not fans of sections 101 or 142 (seats there go for $33/$38, by the way) or sections 102, 103, 140, and 141. They're too far down each line and are angled toward center field, which means you'll be spending much of the craning your neck to see the action. The same goes for sections 401-404 and 440-442. For an afternoon game, almost any seat in the sun is one of the worst in the ballpark. Also, beware the outfield terrace box seats ($21/$25): because of the football configuration of the stadium they sit very high off the action, so you feel like you're in a different time zone. The same is not true of the right-field bleachers, by the way, which are cheaper.

Dolphin Stadium: Baseball on a Gridiron

Four professional facilities house both major-league football and baseball teams: McAfee Coliseum, Rogers Centre, Metrodome, and Dolphin Stadium.

Of those four, none is so dedicated to football as Dolphin Stadium, the home of the Florida Marlins and the NFL's Miami Dolphins. No surprise: the stadium was built by and is owned by the Dolphins, and the Marlins are a poor cousin to the Dolphins in every respect. When both the Dolphins and the Marlins were owned by H. Wayne Huizenga, the specifics of the leases didn't matter—all the money ended up in the same pocket. But when Huizenga sold the Marlins to John Henry and his investment group, the details did matter.

Financially, the Marlins always seem on the brink of disaster, despite usually excelling on the field, winning World Series in 1997 and 2003. What's holding back the Marlins, of course, is Joe Robbie/Pro Player/Dolphin Stadium, a great place to catch a football game but so far unsuccessful in sustaining any kind of fan base for baseball. In fact, three separate ownership groups have tried and failed miserably to build their own baseball-only facility.

The problem with Dolphin Stadium is that you are constantly reminded you're are at the Dolphins' stadium. From the retired numbers of former Dolphins players inscribed on the upper-deck bowl to the endless sea of orange seats, you are know this football stadium has been turned into a "temporary" place for baseball.

Ballparks are places you fall in love with for all of their different and unique reasons, but if you never believe you are, in fact, in a baseball park, how can you ever sell yourself on the whole experience?

"Miguel Cabrera hits a drive! Way back! And it's off the Dan Marino plaque in left field. Home run!"

See what we mean?

As a natural football complex, Dolphin Stadium comes with all the quirks involved in trying to fit the luxuries of a modern ballpark into a football-first facility. The outfield dimensions have power allies where home runs go to die. Then there's the stadium's trademark Bermuda triangle in left-center field, which juts out to 434 feet. Not surprisingly, quite a few inside-the-park-homers have been hit in Dolphin Stadium (Clint Barmes of the Colorado Rockies hit one during one of our visits).

As a football facility, Dolphin Stadium is great. It's geared for large crowds spending seven or eight hours at the stadium: in other words, its scale is meant for events. A Florida Marlins game is not an event. The things that make Dolphin Stadium great for an NFL game—the relatively remote location, a sea of parking located next to the freeway, the rectangular configuration—make it a bad venue for baseball.

The football seats fold back in left field to create what used to be called the "Teal Monster" (the name has mysteriously disappeared ever since the Marlins took teal out of their color scheme). The left-field scoreboard, expanded for the 2006 season, is the only other trademark of the stadium.

Intimacy is not what you'll get when you see a baseball game at Dolphin

Stadium. The facility seats roughly 65,000 for baseball, so when the Marlins announce a sellout (which is 36,331 officially), the sea of orange seats in the upper deck is still very apparent. Most of the seats aren't very close to the action, and the only intimate baseball-designed seating is the high-priced seats behind home plate referred to as Founder's Field. Those will cost you up to $95 a game.

The seating configuration is also set up for football, so you usually have to sit at a funny angle to get a good view of the game—especially when you have seats near the foul pole. The Marlins try to make up for their expansive seating selection and interesting arrangements with some of the cheapest tickets in Major League Baseball. The Fish Tank, located in the outfield, has plenty of seats for $8 apiece. You get a great view of the game for the price.

Go to a 1:05 p.m. game and there's no doubt about it: it's hot. The endurance required for staying a full nine innings is something one must fully prepare for. When the Marlins discuss the necessity for a retractable roof at a potential new stadium, it's those day games that make you realize it's just as much for the sun as it is for the daily rain showers.

Maybe weather is the mitigating factor for the Fish and a retractable roof would solve all of their attendance woes, but maybe, just maybe, baseball wasn't meant to be played in Florida past those mild days of spring.

Ballpark Quirks

Putting a baseball field in the midst of a football stadium may be the biggest quirk: it leads to all sorts of issues. We've already mentioned the left-field wall, made larger than normal because of the way the diamond is crammed into the football field. Generally speaking, this arrangement has never really worked: the Blue Jays suffered through some weird games and small crowds when playing at Exhibition Stadium, the Dodgers enjoyed large crowds and cheap

home runs when playing at the Los Angeles Coliseum, and the Minnesota Twins can't attract a loyal following because of the absurdity of playing in a football stadium.

Food and Drink

Dolphin Stadium has your standard ballpark fare plus a few regional touches, such as Cuban food. Finding a Cuban sandwich is not hard to do in Miami—it seems there's a sandwich stand every four or five blocks—but we will admit the version at the ballpark is pretty good, if only because it's fresh off a grill. (For those from northern climes with little exposure to Cuban food, a Cuban sandwich contains ham, pork, Swiss, mustard, and pickles on Cuban bread.) There's not much else special on the menu, so eat before you head to the ballgame or—better yet—throw some brats in the cooler and grill them in the sea of parking outside the ballpark.

The same goes for the beer selection. You can walk around and find some specialty beers, such as Samuel Adams, but the majority of concessions stands sell Bud. Mixed drinks and wine also can be found.

Water, a definite necessity at a Marlins game, is rather high-priced (as is everything on the menu). Our advice: drink plenty of fluids before you get to the stadium, especially if you plan on trying to sit through a matinee game. One plus: every seat has a cupholder, so you can make that expensive bottled water last.

Handicapped Access
There are 300 seats designated for disabled access.

For the Kids
The Fanzone area features some basic ballpark novelty games geared for older kids: a batting cage, a pitching game, and a home-run derby game. The Fun Zone, meanwhile, is designed for kids younger than 12 and is located in sections 130 and 131. Unfortunately, the Fun Zone is open only on Sundays.

Billy the Marlin is one of the better mascots in the majors, if only because he's everywhere during all the game, spending a lot of time wandering the concourses and being very accessible. He does a meet and greet at Section 138 as well.

Older kids will enjoy the Florida Marlins Mermaids, a cheerleading squad (or, as the Marlins say, a "female rally team").

Ballpark Tours
The Florida Marlins and Miami Dolphins do not offer tours of Dolphin Stadium.

Getting There
You are expected to drive to the ballpark. With a location near three major freeways and parking for more than 20,000 vehicles, Dolphin Stadium does afford easy access for those arriving by car.

Dolphin Stadium is near the northern border of Dade County, just south of Broward County. The Florida Turnpike runs directly east of the stadium, so getting there is easy: just map your route to the Florida Turnpike north of the I-95/turnpike interchange and take exit 2X.

In past years the Marlins offered a park-and-ride programs in conjunction with Miami-Dade Transit. The service was offered only on weekends, with buses running between four Metrorail stations and the stadium. To see if the service is running in the current season, call 305/770-3131 for information.

Gates to the parking lot open 2 1/2 hours before gametime, while gates to the ballpark open 1 1/2 hours before gametime. Parking is $10.

Where to Stay
Quite honestly, Dolphin Stadium isn't in the greatest part of town and we don't recommend staying close to the facility. Since there's nothing within walking distance, you'll need to drive to the game anyway.

INSIDER'S TIP
Be warned, most online map services and travel sites don't recognize the 2269 Dan Marino Boulevard address used by the Marlins. If you're mapping a route via a service like Mapquest, use an address of 2269 NW. 199th St., Opa Locka, Florida.

INSIDER'S TIP
If you insist on staying closer and want to get in some golf, the Fairmont Turnberry Isle Resort & Club is about six miles from the stadium, near the Aventura Mall. It is not cheap: you'll be spending over $400 a night just for the room. Golfing at one of the Robert Trent Jones Sr. courses is extra.

Miami is the trendy city of the moment and there's no trendier part of the city than South Beach, where the Art Deco hotels have been renovated and given new life as boutique establishments. Take, for example, the trendy Aqua Hotel and Lounge, located on Collins Avenue in the heart of South Beach. It's small—only 45 rooms—but the décor is sleek and the guests sleeker. The price is right, too: between $150 and $400 a night on the weekends. There are a host of establishments in South Beach along these lines, and while they're not necessarily ideal for families—the scene isn't exactly geared toward the toddler set—they're great for singles and couples. *Aqua Hotel and Lounge, 1530 Collins Av., Miami Beach; aquamiami.com.*

While You're There
Your best bet before the game is to bring a grill and cooler to tailgate in the expansive parking lot. There is nothing of interest within walking distance of the stadium to do before or after the game—another example of why it's a great facility for football and one that doesn't work so well for baseball.

Afterwards: get the heck out of Dodge and head into town. Miami is a great city: there are family attractions like museums and zoos and grown-up attractions like the late-night party scene at South Beach. For a complete list of attractions, check out the Greater Miami Convention & Visitors Bureau Website at *gmcvb.com.*

Team Ballpark History
The Florida Marlins have played at Dolphin Stadium for the team's entire history since joining the National League in 1993.

Stadium History
Dolphin Stadium is an anomaly as a baseball ballpark, and in some ways it is an anomaly as a football stadium.

Over the last 30 years NFL team owners have been adept at obtaining subsidies from local governments to build new stadiums. Not Joe Robbie, the owner of the Miami Dolphins: he built Dolphin Stadium on his own, using revenues from suite and seat licensing to finance construction. And the revenues were substantial: $30,000-$90,000 per year for suites and $800-$1,800 per year for seat licenses—with a 10-year commitment. (The San Francisco Giants and St. Louis Cardinals used similar financing methods to build their new ballparks in recent years.) Those sorts of revenues from the rabid Dolphins fan base made construction possible, and the stadium opened in time for the 1987 NFL season.

Sadly, the Minneapolis lawyer—who owned the Dolphins since its entry into the American Football League in 1965—wasn't around long to enjoy his new stadium: he died of respiratory failure on Jan. 7, 1990. His death put the remaining family members in a bind, and within two months H. Wayne Huizenga, the CEO of Blockbuster Video, had purchased half of Robbie Stadium Corp. (the corporation owning Robbie Stadium) and 15 percent of the Dolphins. By January 1994 Huizenga had agreed to purchase the rest of the stadium and the Dolphins from the Robbie family. With ownership in hand, Huizenga pursued a Major League Baseball team and was awarded an expansion franchise for the 1993 season.

As part of the award Huizenga agreed to several renovations to Joe Robbie Stadium to make it more baseball friendly. Several concession stands were added to the main concourse, while retractable seating was added to the north side of the stadium and a baseball press box to the southwest corner. On the field, dugouts were built, a retractable pitcher's mound was installed, additional lighting was hung, and a synthetic warning track was put down.

On Aug. 26, 1996, the apparel company Pro Player purchased naming rights to Joe Robbie Stadium, ending the public celebration of the man who brought pro football, Don Shula, a new stadium, and the Super Bowl to south Florida. The deal was worth $2 million a year, but the Dolphins and Huizenga never collected on the whole amount. Pro Player's parent company, Fruit of the Loom, declared bankruptcy in 1999 and the Pro Player division was sold to Perry Ellis International in 2001.

Under Huizenga the Marlins were successful on the field, winning the 1997 World Series in a stunner over the Indians. Huizenga invested heavily in payroll and the front office, bringing in stars like Moises Alou, Bobby Bonilla, Cliff Floyd, and Kevin Brown and a coaching staff led by Jim Leyland. But Huizenga claimed huge losses on the team—$29.7 million in 1997—and put the team up for sale before the 1998 season after slashing payroll.

Boca Raton investor John Henry bought the Marlins in November 1998 for an announced $150 million. He immediately sought a new ballpark, saying the team's deal in Pro Player Stadium was inadequate. Henry first vowed to build a new ballpark with his own funds, but backed off that promise and asked for government assistance. By February 2002 Henry had his eye on a bigger prize—the Boston Red Sox and its media empire—and worked out a deal with Major League Baseball where he and Tom Werner (and an ownership group that included the New York Times) would buy the Red Sox, MLB would buy the Montreal Expos, and Expos owner Jeffrey Loria would buy the Marlins for $158.5 million.

Loria didn't endear himself to the Florida fan base: on the same day he closed on the purchase of the Marlins he laid off 60 Marlins employees. The entire player development staff was fired, including scouts, administrators and minor league managers and coaches. Loria then brought in many Expos employees, leaving the shelves at the MLB-owned franchise bare.

The future of the franchise remains in doubt: Loria has made clear a new ballpark is needed for the Marlins to succeed in south Florida. The Marlins have identified locations for a new ballpark, but as this book went to press those efforts have come up short.

Local Baseball Attractions

The local baseball attractions in Miami are limited, to say the least. The Baltimore Orioles train at Fort Lauderdale Stadium, but the facility is unused during the regular season.

Sadly, there's nothing to mark the site of Miami Stadium/Bobby Maduro Stadium at 2301 NW 10th Av., the former home of the Miami Marlins of the International League and the Florida State League. With a distinctive canopy designed to protect fans from the sun and murals celebrating local baseball heroes of the past, the ballpark was the center of baseball in Miami for decades.

TRIVIA
When it comes to minor league baseball in Miami, the Orange Bowl doesn't come to mind—unless, of course, you're a premier baseball showman like Bill Veeck. In the Miami Marlins' first year as an International League franchise, executive VP Veeck promoted a charity event at the Orange Bowl that set the all-time minor league attendance record at the time by drawing 57,713 and featured four bands led by the likes of Cab Calloway and Merv Griffin. Another big draw for the Aug. 7, 1956 game was 50-year-old starting pitcher Satchel Paige. He lasted into the eighth inning and knocked in three runs with a double at the plate as the Marlins defeated the Columbus Jets, 6-2.

Miami Stadium (later renamed Bobby Maduro Stadium), the former home of minor-league and spring-training baseball in Miami.

Built in 1949, the ballpark was also the spring home of the Brooklyn Dodgers and the Baltimore Orioles; it was torn down in 2001.

The closest minor-league baseball to Miami is about 60 miles to the north in Palm Beach. Roger Dean Stadium is the spring home of the Florida Marlins and the St. Louis Cardinals, and it's the regular-season home to two Class A Florida State League teams: the Jupiter Hammerheads (a Marlins farm team) and the Palm Beach Cardinals (a Cardinals farm team). It's located in the midst of the Abacoa development, which contains retail and restaurant space nearby. You can easily make a day of it with a pleasant meal and a game at one of the nicer minor-league ballparks in the state.

The Complete Guide to Big League Ballparks

Boston Red Sox
Fenway Park

Address: 4 Yawkey Way, Boston, MA 02215.
Cost: The original cost was $650,000, though it's been upgraded and renovated repeatedly over the years.
Architect: Osborn Engineering.
Owner: Boston Red Sox.
Capacity: 33,871.
Dimensions: 310L, 379LC, 390C, 420RC, 380RC, 302R.

Ticket Line: 877/REDSOX9.

Home Dugout Location: First-base side.

Playing Surface: Grass.

Other Tenants: There have been many tenants over the years, mostly on the football side. In what will come as a shocking horror to Red Sox fans, even a "Yankee" tenant occupied the ballpark: the NFL's Boston Yanks played at Fenway from 1944 to 1948. (That team moved to several cities before settling as the Baltimore Colts and later the Indianapolis Colts.) The NFL's Boston Braves/Redskins played at Fenway from 1932 through 1936 before moving to Washington, D.C. Both Boston College and Boston University played home games in Fenway Park. And the 1914 "Miracle Boston Braves" played their World Series games in Fenway.

First Game: On April 20, 1912, the Boston Red Sox defeated the New York Highlanders (the predecessor to the New York Yankees) 7-6 in 11 innings before a crowd of 27,000, with Hall of Famer Tris Speaker driving in the winning run. It was the third attempt at an opening day as games were rained out the previous two days. Also opening the same day: Navin Field, home of the Detroit Tigers, which later became known as Tiger Stadium. Neither opening got much attention from the press the following day as the big headline was the sinking of the "indestructible" Titanic.

Landmark Event: The 2004 World Series, won by the Boston Red Sox to break the Curse of the Bambino, is surely the event held most dear by Red Sox fans. But a host of landmark events have held in Fenway Park over the last 90-plus years, far too many to recount in this limited format, ranging from Ted Williams' .400 season to David Ortiz setting a franchise season record for home runs in the 2006 season.

Your Fenway Park Seating Crib Sheet

Best Sections to View a Game: Nearly every seat is the ballpark is a great place to view a game. Vantage points for some seats are limited because of overhang (including the $40 Infield Grandstand seats) and some seats where the angles are awkward (such as the Outfield Grandstand seats), but let's be real: we're talking Fenway Park here. You should be happy to be in the gates.

Best Cheap Seats: The cheapest seats are the $12 Upper Bleacher seats, comprising the last few rows in the outfield bleachers. They'll get you in the ballpark, and as there aren't many bad seats in Fenway (though there are some, as we discuss in the following section), we highlight them as the best cheap seats.

Seats to Avoid: Believe it or not, some seats are in Fenway not worth pursuing. Sections 32 and 33 are alcohol free; good for the kids, not so good for the rest of us. A multitude of seats are obstructed by pillars or girders, but this condition is noted on the tickets (which can be a handy tool when bargaining with a scalper—always ask to see a ticket before buying it!). In addition, the Right Field Rooftop seats (priced at $65/$90) may seem appealing (you have your own private concessions and access), but there's one huge condition: you're over 500 feet from home plate, which completely wipes out one big reason to attend a Red Sox game at Fenway: intimacy. However, since the Red Sox sell almost every ticket they print, just getting in the ballpark most nights will be a triumph.

Most Underrated Sections: We're fans of the $23 Lower Bleachers in the outfield: the price is right (by MLB standards, these seats are reasonably priced) and you're close to the best concessions and restrooms at the ballpark.

Fenway Park: A True Classic

You're not a true ballpark fan until you've made the pilgrimage to Fenway Park, the oldest ballpark in the majors. It's small, featuring narrow aisles and narrower seats. Tickets can be infuriatingly difficult to acquire. Unless you know what you're doing, you could drop hundreds and hundreds of dollars on tickets, concessions, and parking, and walk out with nothing but your memories.

And it would be worth every penny.

There's nothing so beautiful as Fenway Park on a clear Massachusetts night, with the sun retreating behind the grandstand at gametime and the sun reflecting off the Prudential Building in the Back Bay. Little by little, the sun recedes and the Citgo sign past left field achieves more prominence as night falls. It is timeless, a ballpark where the ghosts of baseball compete for your attention. Close your eyes and you can practically see Ted Williams patrolling right field, Luis Tiant launching into his trademark windup on the mound, and Carlton Fisk waving a World Series homer fair in left field. At the end of the game, virtually the entire crowd is still in their seats, unwilling to end the experience.

Yes, the entire experience is more ritualized than Kabuki theater, but so what? Fenway Park presents pro baseball in its most essential form. If you do make only one baseball-related trip in your life, make sure it's to a Red Sox game at Fenway Park.

But be ready to jump through a few hoops.

The Red Sox are the only team to count more fans at the game than capacity allows. The whole operation is a textbook example of supply meeting demand: the supply of tickets isn't close to meeting the demand. This hikes up the price of tickets, both for the Red Sox (BoSox ducats are among the highest priced in baseball) and for scalpers, who buy season tickets and then resell them during the course of the year.

We are not fans of scalpers (although some full disclosure is in order: our parent company runs a Website, *ballparkdigesttickets.com*, where tickets are sold beyond face value where legal), but if you can't get good tickets to a game before heading to Fenway, dealing with scalpers is a must. You can find them wandering any street surrounding the ballpark, though many congregate between the ballpark and the Kenmore Square T transit stop to

INSIDER'S TIP
The Red Sox release a small number of tickets two hours before game time. Head to Gate C and try your luck there if you're in the area.

catch folks walking to the game. Scalpers make their best money an hour or so before the game and then drop prices as the game approaches; if you're patient, you'll score the best tickets for the lowest price if you wait until after the game starts. Technically, scalping (selling a ticket for more than face value) is illegal in Boston, but that law is never enforced, especially when the Yankees are in town and you're wearing a New York cap.

Diversions are plentiful before you get to Fenway Park, with a number of bars and restaurants in the general vicinity. We're not going to cover them all, but two local watering holes are worth noting. Stop at the newly renovated Cask and Flagon (62 Brookline Av.; *casknflagon.com*), a Red Sox landmark. A sports bar before sports bars become a cliché, the Cask and Flagon's walls are covered with Red Sox memorabilia and clippings, and (surprisingly) the food isn't half-bad either. Our other fave is Boston Beer Works (61 Brookline Av.; *beerworks.net*), where the beer is fresh and the pickles are deep-fried.

If this is your first visit to Fenway Park, head there at least two hours before game time when the Red Sox set up entertainment and food concessions on Yawkey Way. The Red Sox have taken several measures to relieve the crowding in Fenway Park, and one of the biggest was to move security gates and several vendors outside onto Yawkey Way, limiting access to ticketholders. It's a great place to meet your friends or just take in the action.

After spending some time on Yawkey Way, head to your seat and get your bearings. Take a good look at the Green Monster and the famous hand-operated scoreboard. The Green Monster didn't come about because of any grand architectural plan; rather, it was designed to prevent outsiders from viewing the action on the field (which apparently was a problem endemic to Boston sporting events; the owners of the Braves also put up large screens to prevent outsiders from viewing the action at South End Grounds). When built, there was a 10-foot embankment in front of the Green Monster where fans could sit. Red Sox outfielder Duffy Lewis became so skilled at playing the ball off the embankment it became known as Duffy's Cliff.

When it was unveiled in 1934, the scoreboard wasn't the first in Boston to use lights to denote balls, strikes, and outs—the Boston Braves used similar lights to broadcast game information at South End Grounds. Over the years the

BoSox never quite got around to dumping the scoreboard, although it's been altered somewhat with expansion.

Head to the outfield to gawk at Seat 21 in Row 37 of Section 42, 502 feet from home plate. It's painted red for a reason: it marks the longest home run hit in Fenway Park history. Though the Red Sox have featured many prodigious home-run hitters over the years—Manny Ramirez, Jim Rice, David Ortiz—Ted Williams still holds the record for the longest blast, set on June 9, 1946, in the first inning of the second game of a doubleheader against the Detroit Tigers, with Fred Hutchinson on the mound. Williams hit a changeup into the right-field bleachers (at the time there were bleachers in the outfield), with the ball hitting Fenway Park regular Joseph A. Boucher on the head. It shattered his straw hat, and the ball bounced a dozen or so rows back. After the game, Boucher told a Boston Globe reporter he never saw the ball coming,

"How far away must one sit to be safe in this park? I didn't even get the ball," he said. "They say it bounced a dozen rows higher, but after it hit my head, I was no longer interested. I couldn't see the ball. Nobody could. The sun was right in our eyes. All we could do was duck. I'm glad I didn't stand up."

The commemorative red seat is fairly new, installed in 1984.

While out there, take a look at the outfield bullpens. In 1940 new bullpens were constructed in right field, bringing the fences 23 feet closer to home plate. One prime reason prompted the change: in 1939 a young left-handed slugger

Fenway Park in 1914. (Courtesy of Library of Congress, LC-USZ62-103058.)

named Ted Williams made his Red Sox debut with a bang, hitting .327 with 31 home runs and 145 RBI. The new bullpens became known as Williamsburg.

On your way back, stop by the right-field foul pole, referred to by locals as Pesky's Pole. It's named for former Red Sox shortstop Johnny Pesky, ostensibly in honor of a home run he hit that curved around the foul pole to win a game for the BoSox. No one seems to remember exactly which home run actually inspired the moniker; it doesn't really matter. The name comes out of the deep affection felt by Red Sox fans for Pesky, who's still on the Red Sox payroll and serving for years as the perfect ambassador for the team. (The left-field pole was officially named the Fisk Pole by the Red Sox in honor of Carlton Fisk's famous 1975 World Series home run and the indelible TV images of him waving the hit fair. For some reason the name hasn't quite taken: the Pesky Pole name evolved organically, and arguably more legitimately.)

Finally, take your seat and enjoy the action. You'll sing the National Anthem before the game and "Take Me Out to the Ballgame" during the seventh-inning stretch, but the weirdest tradition takes place in the middle of the eighth when the crowd starts singing along to Neil Diamond's "Sweet Caroline." No one knows exactly why this song is a hit with the Red Sox audience: Diamond has no particular link to Beantown and this song was never a huge hit locally. Chalk it up to Ann Tobey, who programmed music at Red Sox games in 1998. She played "Sweet Caroline" one night and it resonated with fans; it also seemed to her the Red Sox played better after the song. (Former Red Sox pitcher Pedro Martinez seemed to like the song as well, imploring the crowd to stand when it was played.) It wasn't a regular occurrence until the John Henry group bought the Red Sox and requested the song be played every night in the middle of the eighth. And, of course, if the

Red Sox win, the Standells' "Dirty Water" is played, with its famous line, "Well I love that dirty water / Boston you're my home." That's another recent tradition, dating only to 1997.

For the most part the ushers at Fenway Park are pretty cool about letting you move around during the game and sit in seats that may not be yours. There are some exceptions. First, don't bother trying to head up to the Green Monster seats to sneak a view: even journalists need a special pass to get up there. (We were turned away.) Second, sections 58 and 59 are considered VIP sections: this is where the long-time season-ticket holders sit, as well as celebrities and political heavyweights (Gov. Mitt Romney sits there). Under no circumstances will the ushers allow you to cruise in for a good view of the action: during one visit we were lucky enough to sit in one of these sections and the ushers were escorting squatters from the section with two out in the top of the ninth, literally a minute before the Red Sox won the game. Just imagine what would have happened if the Red Sox had been losing.

Otherwise, if you want to head to the outfield sections or the back of the grandstand to stand and watch the game, feel free. Apparently fire codes are suggestions, not hard rules when it comes to keeping the aisles clear in back of the grandstand (the Red Sox sell a fair number of standing-room tickets to each game).

This leads us to one important rule when moving around the ballpark: be polite. The aisles are narrow, barely wide enough for two people. If you're heading to another section, go first to the concourse and use that route. Anyone walking in the aisle is going to block the views from at least two rows, so you'll want to minimize your time there.

As we mentioned before, be prepared to stay the entire game. Red Sox fans simply do not leave the game early, no matter how lopsided the score in the ninth inning. Yes, you can easily beat the rush by leaving an inning early, but that would be counter to the real Fenway Park experience. If it's a nice night, skip the train and walk back to the Back Bay: you won't be alone, as a good chunk of the crowd will be by your side.

Ballpark Quirks
Besides the big quirks mentioned so far, there are a load of smaller quirks for the discerning fan. For one, look out toward left field and the scoreboard at the base of the Green Monster. You'll see a series of dashes and lines separating the sections of the scoreboard. Those dashes are Morse code for Thomas A. Yawkey (TAY) and Jean R. Yawkey (JRY), the former owners of the Red Sox.

Food and Drink
Despite the lack of space in the grandstand, there's an abundance of foodstuffs available at the ballpark. You simply must have a Fenway Frank: those from outside New England will be amused by what passes for a hot-dog bun in Boston, and the dogs are pretty flavorful despite being boiled. If it's a cool evening, buy some clam chowder at the Legal Seafoods stand behind home

plate; across the way you can buy a Guinness or a Harp at the most unauthentic Irish bar in Boston. Concession stands on Yawkey Way sell Cuban sandwiches, BBQ, pizza, and fresh-roasted peanuts.

A newer addition to Fenway Park is a concession area under the right-field bleachers. This area used to house TV trucks and other team equipment, but the Red Sox cleared out the area and installed a sea of concession stands and large new bathrooms. It's worth the walk, even if you're not seated out there: the lines are usually short for both food and bathrooms. Beer is not sold by vendors in the stands, so you'll need to head to the concession areas for a Sam Adams— and then only two to a customer.

For the Kids
Space is at a premium in Fenway Park, which is why there's no designated kids' play area. The average Boston family doesn't need no stinkin' play area: kids are taught early in life to respect the BoSox and the Fenway Park experience, and hate the New York Yankees—but not in that order.

Ballpark Tours
The Boston Red Sox offer tours of Fenway Park daily throughout the year. Popular stops include the Green Monster seats, the press box, and the playing field. Check the Fenway Park Tours Hotline at 617/226-6666 for information on specific dates and times.

Getting There
Most of you will not be driving to Boston, which means you'll either be flying into town or taking the train in. Both have their advantages.

Any discussion of getting around in Boston begins with a discussion of the Massachusetts Bay Transit Authority, or MBTA (*mbta.com*), which locals call the "T." There are four main lines, but because of the compactness of the Boston area you're never more than a transfer away from Fenway Park. It is a safe, clean way to get around Boston, and the price ($1.25 per ride) is irresistible. Plus, the T connects with other popular ways of getting into Boston, providing that final last mile of transportation.

Those on the East Coast should consider driving (which has its own disadvantages, as we'll discuss later) or catching the train. Amtrak (*amtrak.com*) serves three stations in Boston: the South Station, the Back Bay Station, and the North Station. As you'll see in the following sections, staying in the Back Bay—a great neighborhood close to Fenway Park—is highly recommended. The Back Bay Station is in the center of things, connected via walkway to the Boston Marriott Copley Place and the Westin Copley Square. You can

INSIDER'S TIP
You can avoid some of the crowds by taking the Orange Line and getting off at the Ruggles station. There's a free shuttle bus between this station and Fenway Park.

get from New York City's Penn Station, Washington's Union Station, or Philadelphia's 30th Street Station (among others) to the Back Bay Station via the high-speed Acela Express train. It's not cheap (often costing just a little less than an airline flight), but it is certainly a less hectic way to travel.

Flying into Logan International Airport is easy: an airport expansion in recent years has made flying in and out a less stressful process. Every major airline flies into Logan, save Southwest, and the airport's convenient location means you can catch a hotel shuttle into town or take a short bus ride to the T. (Technically, the subway doesn't run all the way out to the airport, but shuttle buses run from all airport terminals to the Blue Line's Airport station; from there you can hit the Government Center stop and catch a transfer to your ultimate destination.)

Boston is a very pedestrian-friendly city. The easiest way to do Fenway is to stay in the Back Bay (as we discuss in later sections) and then walk to and from the ballpark. It's both safe and easy.

The T is the easiest and cheapest way to get to Fenway Park. The Green Line's Kenmore Square stop serves Fenway Park; you'll know you're there when everyone else on the train heads out the doors. All Green Line trains, save the E line, stop at Kenmore Square. When you buy a token, buy one for the way home to avoid the long lines at the Kenmore Square token line after the game.

If you insist on driving, getting to Fenway Park is easy in terms of

INSIDER'S TIP
Normally we're huge fans of Southwest Airlines, but Boston is one city where flying Southwest is not an advantage. Southwest doesn't fly into Logan, but rather into two regional airports in Warwick, R.I. and Manchester, N.H., each located about 60 miles from Boston. You'll either need to rent a car and drive into Boston or catch a bus to South Station. Either is a huge hassle.

directions, but a pain when it comes to fighting traffic. You can either take 93 North or South to Storrow Drive and take the Fenway South exit; you could also take the Massachusetts Pike (90) to the Cambridge tolls, then follow the signs to the ballpark. (If you need a monument to measure progress, watch for the Citgo sign, which sits a block from the ballpark.) If you're close to the ballpark near game time, *do not* attempt to drive on the streets within a block of the ballpark: they'll be crammed with game attendees and navigating your way through will take you forever.

Parking is at a premium near the ballpark: you can expect to pay $30 or more for a middling spot several blocks from Fenway. And, yes, the kind officers of the Boston Police Department will write you up—and maybe even tow your car—if you park illegally, though in many cases the charge for the parking ticket is less than the fees charged by parking-lot owners.

INSIDER'S TIP
There are some definite minuses to having a car in Boston: parking is never inexpensive. At most of these Back Bay hotels you'll pay at least $15—and probably closer to $30—for the nightly privilege of parking your car. Unless you have an absolute need for a car (if you drove in from out of town or will be driving to your next destination), don't bother renting one: the public transit system is safe, clean, and reliable.

Where to Stay

One imagines Boston as this huge urban oasis, the Hub writ large. Truth is, the area around Fenway Park isn't all that hospitable when it comes to hotels, though you can expect that to change in the coming decade. Light industrial is the prevailing land use in the general Fenway Park area, which means there are relatively few choices within a block or two of the ballpark. This will change in the next five to 10 years, as the Red Sox and other development partners invest hundreds of millions to transform the area.

The closest hotel is the Hotel Commonwealth (500 Commonwealth Av.; *hotelcommonwealth.com*; $200-$300). Ignore the price tag (which is fairly moderate for Boston): this is an upscale hotel perfect for the Red Sox fan looking to do nothing but attend a weekend series and spend the rest of the time in the lap of luxury. Highly recommended; ask for a room facing Fenway Park.

You can stay in the Back Bay and have a pleasant, safe walk to and from the ballpark, as there are a host of hotels at different price points near Copley Square and the Hynes Convention Center. We'd recommend any of these establishments: the Eliot Suite Hotel (370 Commonwealth Av.; *eliothotel.com*; $250-$450), a European-style hotel featuring comfy suites and plenty of antiques; the huge Sheraton Boston (39 Dalton St.; *sheraton.com*; $150-$400); the Hilton Boston Back Bay (40 Dalton St.; *hilton.com*; $200-$400); the intimate Newbury Guest House (261 Newbury St.; *newburyguesthouse.com*; $150-$300), providing great access to the shopping paradise known as Newbury Street); the European-style Colonnade Hotel (120 Huntington Av.; $175-$300), which features a rooftop pool and resort; the huge Boston Marriott Copley Place (110 Huntington Av.; *marriott.com*; $160-$275), connected via skyway to several shopping centers; the historic but smaller (both in terms of number of rooms and size of the rooms) Copley Square Hotel (47 Huntington Av.; *copleysquarehotel.com*; $189-$300); the upscale Westin Copley Square (10 Huntington Av.; *westin.com*; $250-$600); and the even more upscale Fairmont Copley Plaza Hotel (138 St. James Av.; *fairmont.com*; $250-$500), located directly on historic Copley Square and across from scenic Trinity Church.

Other popular hotel clusters are farther away, but easily accessible via the Boston T. Cambridge lies across the Charles River from Fenway Park and the Back Bay, and there are many hotels within a short walk of the Harvard Square MTBA stop at 1400 Massachusetts Av.: the inexpensive Harvard Square Hotel (110 Mount Ashburn St.; *harvardsquarehotel.com*; $99-$200), the upscale Charles Hotel (1 Bennett St.; *charleshotel.com*; $200-$400), the Inn at Harvard (1201 Massachusetts Av.; *theinnatharvard.com*; $125-$250) and the colonial-style Sheraton Commander (16 Garden St.; *sheratoncommander.com*; $125-$300).

You'll also find easily accessible hotels in downtown and in Brookline, the suburb to the west of Boston. Really, you should feel comfortable staying in any hotel close to a train station: all lines seemingly lead to Fenway when the Red Sox are in town.

Fenway Park in September 1914. (Courtesy of Library of Congress, LC-B2-2447-11.)

While You're There

Boston residents call their city the Hub, reflecting their belief in the city's rightful place as the center of everything. While that's not necessarily true any longer (the publishing industry by and large has abandoned Boston, for instance), it's still a fascinating city to visit. You won't be bored between games at Fenway, even if you limit your sightseeing to historically significant sites.

Many of the more historically significant buildings in Boston are strung together on the Freedom Trail (*thefreedomtrail.org*), a 2.5-mile path (marked with either red brick or a red line) connecting sites on Beacon Hill, downtown Boston, the North End and Charlestown. The Trail starts at the Boston Common Visitor Center in the northeastern corner of Boston Common, itself worth a visit: the area has been preserved as open space since 1640 and been used as a cow pasture and a public-hanging area. Those with kids will want to head to the sculpture commemorating the brave ducks in *Make Way for Ducklings*, while kids will also enjoy riding one of the swan boats.

We'll not cover all the stops on the Freedom Trail, though we would highly recommend setting aside an entire day to meander along the red line. Here are our recommendations for stops along on the Freedom Trail:

Park Street Church and **Old Granary Burial Ground** (Park and Tremont streets) were home to many firsts—the first Sunday School was held there, as was the first singing of "My County 'Tis of Thee"—but the more interesting thing is the adjoining graveyard, first used when the site housed a granary and was part of Boston Common. Buried here are Samuel Adams, John Hancock, Paul Revere, Benjamin Franklin's parents, and Elizabeth Vergoose, the woman believed to be "Mother Goose," the author of nursery rhymes.

King's Chapel and **King's Burial Grounds** (Tremont and School streets) came about when King James II ordered an Anglican church be built in America; when the locals refused, the king's troops seized land and constructed the church. The burial ground is the oldest in Boston.

The Old Corner Bookstore (School and Washington streets) was once home to the publisher of classics such as *The Scarlet Letter* and *Walden* and then became a legendary bookstore (it still exists after moving to Cambridge).

INSIDER'S TIP

Almost all the churches in this section house active congregations and are open to visitors wanting to look at historic sites. Many of these congregations freely open their doors to visitors, but remember it does cost them money to open the churches and offer information. It's good form to donate money if you visit; most churches will have a contribution box discreetly placed somewhere near the church entrance. Also, if you're doing your sightseeing during a church service, please respect the proceedings; you're always welcome to worship, but don't walk in and out.

Today, the building is home to a *Boston Globe* retail store.

The Old South Meeting House (310 Washington St.) began life as a Puritan house of worship, but is best known historically as where Americans began the process of independence with the Boston Tea Party, planned at a Dec. 16, 1773 meeting attended by over 5,000 colonists. After a spirited debate, the colonists marched to the waterfront and dumped three shiploads of tea into Boston Harbor. The history of this revolutionary act is detailed in multiple displays. (Side note: look across the street at 17 Milk Street. This is where Benjamin Franklin was born.)

The Old State House (206 Washington St.; *bostonhistory.org*) is where the Declaration of Independence was read aloud to a gathered crowd for the first time on July 18, 1776. It's now home to a museum devoted to Boston history. The Boston Massacre took place outside the state house on March 5, 1770 when angry colonists clashed with British redcoats who fired into the crowd, killing five.

Faneuil Hall (Congress and North streets) is the central marketplace and meeting place for Boston since 1742: speeches exhorting support for the Revolutionary War were delivered here by the likes of Samuel Adams. The second floor is still used for important public debates, while the first floor is still a market. The nearby **Faneuil Hall Marketplace** (*faneuilfallmarketplace.com*) features a food court filled with local delicacies, but if you desire a full meal there are two restaurants to consider. **Durgin-Park** (340 Faneuil Hall Market Place; *durgin-park.com*) dates back to 1827 and serves classic meals like Yankee pot roast, potted beef, roast turkey, and scrod. Definitely order baked beans as a side. Top off your meal with Indian pudding: cornmeal and molasses are baked and then served with ice cream. The **Union Oyster House** (41 Union Street) is even older (opening in 1826) and features a wealth of great fresh seafood: the broiled scrod and oyster stew are New England traditions. If you don't have time for a full meal, grab a piece of pizza from **Bertucci's**.

The Paul Revere House (19 North Square; *paulreverehouse.org*) is one of the most underrated attractions on the Freedom Trail, but it's well worth a visit. This house, which dates back to 1680, was the home of Paul Revere and his family from 1770 to 1800. Paul Revere is best known for his famous midnight ride warning the colonists the British were coming, but he was a central figure in the entire Revolutionary War movement and also a very skilled silversmith whose work is featured in the best American art museums. You can walk through the house and learn about life during the Revolutionary War era, but ask a guide for more information: they're full of fascinating information about Revere and his times.

Old North Church (193 Salem St.; *oldnorth.com*), Boston's oldest church, is where most tourists end their Freedom Trail tour. It was at Old North Church where Revere received his signal as to the route of the British—"One if by land, two if by sea"—and in recent years renovations have uncovered the window where historians believe Robert Newman hung his lantern. Most of the church, such as the pew used by the Paul Revere family (pew 54), is original, but alas the steeple is not (the original fell in 1954). Today, the North End is known for its many Italian restaurants, though most are of the checkered-cloth spaghetti-and-meatball ilk. A step above is **Mamma Maria** (3 North Square; *mammamaria.com*), specializing in regional cuisine. If a quick bite will suffice, stop for a cannoli and an espresso at **Mike's Pastry** (300 Hanover St.; *mikespastry.com*), though purists recommend the pastries at **Caffe dello Sport** (308 Hanover St.) or **Caffe Vittoria** (296 Hanover St.). As you can tell from the addresses, these businesses are all in a row.

If this isn't enough, there's a whole host of other historic attractions in Boston. Those staying in the Back Bay have their own set of must-visit sites. Trinity Church (*trinityboston.org*), located on Copley Square, was designed by H.H. Richardson and served as an iconic representation of what became known as the Richardsonian style: a massive style of architecture featuring stone exteriors, little ornamentation and broad arches. The Mary Baker Eddy Library (200 Massachusetts Av.; *marybakereddylibrary.org*; $6 adults, $4 children and seniors) honors the founder of Christian Science. Kids will love the Mapparium, a three-story stained-glass globe offering a view of the world from inside. The Mapparium was built in 1935 and the borders of the world's countries reflect the political boundaries of the day, while the adjacent Hall of Ideas honors influential writings and ideas through the ages.

Being in the Back Bay also puts you close to two additional attractions: the Boston Duck Tour and Boston's best shopping. Boston Duck Tours (*bostonducktours.com*; $25 adults, $22 students 12-18, and $16 children ages 3-11) run on renovated World War II amphibious landing vehicles and drive by all the popular local attractions, including most of the ones listed in this chapter, before splashing into the Charles River and touring Boston and Cambridge via water. The tours leave next to Shaw's Supermarket,

INSIDER'S TIP

Red Sox Nation may seem like a heavily commercialized phrase, but there really is a Red Sox Nation. Polls indicate the New York Yankees are the most popular major-league team—and there are a lot of passionate Yankees partisans out there—but members of Red Sox Nation are a little different in their approach to the team. There are places where you can approximate the Red Sox Nation/Fenway Park experience without actually shelling out the big bucks for a seat. Almost any neighborhood bar in Boston will do the trick—the older the better, of course. In Cambridge, head to Cardullo's in Harvard Square (6 Brattle St.). Owner Francis Cardullo installed a television set in the front window of her gourmet shop and when the Red Sox are playing a crowd gathers to cheer on their team. Cardullo supplies the folding chairs; fans provide Swedish fish and cigars.

across the street from the Prudential Center on Huntington Avenue.

Shopping is also a big attraction in the Back Bay: the aforementioned Prudential Center features lots of local and chain stores. There's also an outpost of Legal Sea Foods in Prudential Center; it's worth the wait for great fresh seafood.

Boston is also a great museum town in keeping with the large number of education institutions nearby. The most popular art museum is perhaps the quirkiest: the Isabella Stewart Gardner Museum (280 The Fenway; *gardnermuseum.org*) features art collected by Isabella Stewart Gardner and displayed in her Italian-style palace. After her death the palace was opened as a museum and works by the likes of Raphael, Rembrandt, Matisse, Sargent, and Whistler are now on display. The Museum of Fine Arts (465 Huntington Av.; *mfa.org*; $15 adults, $13 students and seniors) is more formal, attempting to bring a more comprehensive view to art history. The collection is especially strong in Impressionist art; other highlights include a Gilbert Stuart portrait of George Washington and Childe Hassam's popular *Boston Common at Twilight*.

Boston Ballpark History

Despite Fenway Park's advanced age, it was not the original home of the BoSox. The team began play at Huntington Avenue Grounds (1901-1911) on the campus of Northeastern University. When the nascent American League announced it was expanding into a major league to compete with the established National League, Connie Mack (best known as the longtime owner and manager of the Philadelphia Athletics) came to his hometown to scout out ballpark sites. At that time, there were two crucial factors driving ballpark sites: the land had to be affordable and located on a train line. Mack came up with a location at the intersection of Huntington Avenue and Rogers (known today as Forsyth) Street next to the New York, New Haven and Hartford Railroad line. (It was not a location that required a genius to find: the South End Grounds, the home of the Boston Braves, was across the street.)

Charles Somers, vice president of the American League, ended up financing the construction of Huntington Avenue Grounds to house the Boston Americans. It was a small ballpark, seating only 9,000 with standing room behind ropes in the outfield. (There was plenty of room: center field was originally 530 feet, later expanded to 635 feet.) The ballpark was a success as the Americans charged only 25 cents for admission versus the 50 cents charged by the more established Braves. By 1903 the Boston Pilgrims—then owned by Milwaukee attorney Henry Killilea—hosted the Pittsburgh Pirates in the very first World Series, won by the Boston team five games to three.

However, by the end of the 1911 season the Red Sox (as they were known by then) had outgrown Huntington Avenue Grounds, despite many miscues by new owner Gen. Charles Taylor. Taylor built the larger Fenway Park and sold the team to James McAleer. Huntington Avenue Grounds was torn down and the site hosted a YMCA before Northeastern University built a physical-education center on the site. A plaque commemorates the grounds and the 1903

World Series won by Boston.

We mentioned the South End Grounds earlier. This ballpark housed the Boston Braves from 1876 through 1914 and featured a castle-like grandstand and early instances of fencing erected to prevent neighboring houses from renting roof space to fans not wishing to pay admission fees to the house. There were three versions of South End Grounds (fire was a common problem for ballparks) before the Braves abandoned the site for Braves Field in 1915. (The Braves played at Fenway Park for parts of two seasons when South End Grounds burned down in August 1914 and before Braves Park was completed in August 1915.) A commemorative marker can be found in the Ruggles T Station, built on the site of the three ballparks.

The Braves moved to Braves Field (285 Babcock St.) in 1915 and stayed there until the end of the 1952 season when the team moved to Milwaukee. When built, Braves Field was quite the spiffy facility, seating 40,000 fans in relative luxury, although the largest recorded crowd there was 52,000. The Red Sox were a regular inhabitant of Braves Field, playing the 1915 and 1916 World Series there as well as Sunday games from 1929 to 1932. While the Braves initially drew well there, the fortunes of the team—and resulting attendance— declined over the years to the point where the Braves drew only 280,000 fans in their final year, 1952. The grandstand at Boston University's Nickerson Field was originally the right-field bleachers at Braves Field, while the original ticket office and exterior wall still stands and a marker commemorates the historical significance of the site. The AFL's Boston Patriots played there in 1960-1962, and today BU's soccer and lacrosse squads use the field. We discuss Braves Field in more detail in our chapter on Turner Field: the Atlanta Braves are the descendent of the original Boston Braves.

Local Baseball Attractions

An abundance of minor-league baseball can be found in the Boston area. The Pawtucket Red Sox, the Triple-A affiliate of the BoSox, play at historic McCoy Stadium (Ben Mondor Way, Pawtucket; *pawsox.com*). Built in 1942, McCoy Stadium maintains the ambiance of its early days and adds the modern amenities fans of today expect. The Lowell Spinners are the short-season affiliate of the Red Sox: the team is immensely popular and continually sells out games at LaLacheur Park (450 Aiken Street, Lowell; *lowellspinners.com*). The newest team in the region is the New Hampshire Fisher Cats, playing at MerchantsAuto.com Stadium (One Line Drive, Manchester; *nhfishercats.com*).

Independent baseball is also well-represented in the Boston area. The Can-Am Association has three entries in the area: the North Shore Spirit play in nearby Lynn's historic Fraser Field (365 Western Av.; *northshorespirit.com*), the Brockton Rox play at newer Campanelli Stadium (One Lexington Av.; *brocktonrox.com*), and the Worcester Tornadoes play at a renovated Hanover Insurance Park at Fitton Field (One College St.; *worcestertornadoes.com*) on the Holy Cross campus.

If you visit in June through the beginning of August you'll want to check out one of the many summer college wood-bat teams in the region. All 10 teams in the Cape Cod League (*capecodleague.org*) play in Massachusetts, mostly in modest facilities, but it consistently features the best gathering of college baseball players every summer. The New England Collegiate Baseball League may not approach the same talent level, but the teams play in more interesting facilities: the Newport (R.I.) Gulls play at Cardines Field (20 Americas Cup Av.; *newportgulls.com*), one of the oldest North American baseball facilities still in use (the diamond dates back to 1908, although the grandstand came much later). The exact age of the ballpark is under some debate—the Gulls front office puts the opening at 1908, while some historians (based on some sketchy information, we feel) argue the ballpark's opening should be put back farther, to 1889. It doesn't matter: Cardines Field is a great atmosphere for summer baseball.

The Complete Guide to Big League Ballparks

Cincinnati Reds
Great American Ball Park

Address: 100 Main Street, Cincinnati, OH 45202.
Cost: $280 million.
Architect: HOK Sport.
Owner: Hamilton County.
Capacity: 42,059.
Dimensions: 328L, 379LC, 404C, 370RC, 325R.
Ticket Line: 513/381-REDS or 877/647-REDS.
Home Dugout Location: First-base line.
Playing Surface: Grass grown on plastic micromesh.
Other Tenants: None.
Other Names: None. The local newspaper tried to come up with a nickname or two for GABP, but nothing seems to have stuck.
First Game: On March 31, 2003, the Pittsburgh Pirates scored six runs in the second inning off Reds starter Jimmy Haynes and cruised to a 10-1 victory before 42,343 fans. In that inning both Reggie Sanders and Jason Kendall homered for the Bucs. The Pirates swept the three-game season-opening series, so it wasn't until April 4 until the Reds earned their first win at Great American Ball Park, a 10-9 victory over the Chicago Cubs. Barry Larkin knocked in Jason LaRue with a single in the bottom of the eighth to break a 9-9 tie.
Landmark Event: None, as of yet. The Reds have not made the playoffs since moving to Great American Ball Park.

Your Great American Ball Park Seating Crib Sheet

Best Sections to View a Game: The best seats are the $200 Diamond seats and the $70 Scout seats, but most fans won't spring for seats at that price point. Great American Ball Park is a fairly intimate venue, and most of the seats provide very good views of the action.

Best Cheap Seats: Sections 401-406 are true bleachers, which means you may be uncomfortable by the end of the fifth inning or so, although the views are adequate. In most ballparks we'd be hesitant in calling $19 seats cheap, but at Great American Ball Park, $19 seems to be the sweet spot where good-to-great views intersect with a decent value. At that price you can sit out in the Sun Deck/Moon Deck seats in right field (which we'll discuss later in this chapter) or Mezzanine Infield seats (sections 415-419), located in the middle deck and fairly close to the field. The two parts of the grandstand don't match up (there's a gap between them allowing a view of downtown Cincinnati from the outfield sections) and the front rows of the Mezzanine Infield seats are in roughly the same level as the Club seating on the opposite side of the gap. If you do sit out in the Sun Deck/Moon Deck, try to get in sections 145-146: you're right in front of the steamboat (we'll explain that later) and part of a very small section.

Seats to Avoid: We don't recommend the $5 Outer View Level seats (sections 509-510 and 536-537): yes, they'll get you into the ballpark, but you'll feel like you're a mile away from the action. Buy those seats, hang out in the concourse areas and then move down to the empty good seats when the ushers quit their patrols.

Most Underrated Sections: We're surprised the Mezzanine Infield seats are priced at $19. Given their location, they should be sold as a premium section. Also a little underrated: anything in the upper deck between the lines.

Great American Ball Park: Rolling on the River

Themed ballparks always seem a little gimmicky. That's why we were a little apprehensive about visiting Great American Ball Park, the home of the Cincinnati Reds. As the home of the first professional baseball team, Cincinnati is a well-known baseball hotbed, and a great area deserves a great ballpark. But the Reds make a big deal about the riverboat theme throughout the ballpark — that made us a bit uneasy.

Is GABP a great baseball venue? At times, yes; at times, no. Despite our misgivings about the theme, in the end the riverboat accoutrements didn't bother us much. The ballpark benefits from a great location and a consistent (though sometimes busy) design. What did bother us, however, was the relatively disjointed nature of the seating; by breaking the ballpark up into so many disparate elements, you don't always get the feeling you're part of a community event. In the end, that kept us from naming Great American Ball Park as one of the best ballparks in the majors, though the many nods to the Reds' rich history makes it a top-notch facility.

First, let's address the themed aspects of the ballpark. Cincinnati is a riverfront city—the ballpark, in fact, sits on the shores of the Ohio River and was threatened with flood damage in the winter of 2004—and as such there are some riverboat elements to the ballpark, particularly in the outfield. In center field the batters eye is decorated to look like the bridge of a steamship, and next to it is the front end of a riverboat. They are not purely decorative: the bridge building contains a group area, while the riverboat is used as a observation deck. In addition, the sponsored

> **INSIDER'S TIP**
>
> Great American Ball Park is notable for one thing: players tend to go out of their way to sign autographs. Sections 111-113 and 133-135 are official autograph areas, but you can usually find Reds players milling around down the right-field line and signing away.

steamboat lights up and spews fireworks when a Reds player hits a home run. In the end, we really didn't see the need for both; the steamboat was borderline cheesy and the bridge superfluous. (The steamboat does have one redeeming factor: it contains misters, which can be refreshing on a hot day.)

The sections next to the steamboat comprise the Sun Deck/Moon Deck, which is designed to be evocative of similar bleacher seats at Crosley Field, the team's former home. (For day games the bleachers were called the Sun Deck; for night games they were called the Moon Deck. Waite Hoyt called those bleachers Burgerville because of the many patrons sipping on a cold Burger Beer.) These are some of the best seats in the house: everything at Great American Ball Park is cozy when it comes to distance from the playing field (much to the consternation of pitchers and the delight of batters), and those outfield bleachers seats are especially so.

In the greater scheme of things, the riverboat elements don't distract too much from what's right with Great American Ball Park—which is a lot.

No, the analog clock at Great American Ball Park looks nothing like the original Longines clock at Crosley Field. The original was black with a white dial done in a Art Moderne style; the new one is white with a black dial. The original clock was in the field of play, sitting atop the scoreboard in left center.

First, there's an agreeable spaciousness to the ballpark. You can walk around the entire place through a 40-foot-wide concourse, with some strategic areas for viewing the field from the outfield and the gap in the grandstand (again, more on that later). The concourse is decorated with famous quotes from Reds notables. The horseshoe design of the grandstand provides great angles for fans and our photos in this chapter are perhaps a bit misleading. In reality, the foul ground isn't as spacious as these photos would indicate, and the folks sitting in the sections down the lines must constantly be on their guard against foul balls.

All seats (save the left-field bleacher seats) have a good view of the large outdoor scoreboard. Its most notable feature is an analog clock designed to evoke memories of the famous Longines clock in Crosley Field. The scoreboard is large and comprises three sections focused on fan information (line score, replays, various stats) sitting above advertising. (If you get a chance, look at the photograph displayed on the back of the scoreboard: it was the bat used by Pete Rose to break Ty Cobb's all-time hit record.) Along the left-field fence is a scoreboard displaying out-of-town scores. Most MLB scoreboards look like huge ad displays with a little section for fan info; Great American Ball Park bucks that trend. That seems to be keeping with the general practice of minimal ad signage at the ballpark.

Our biggest criticism of the ballpark has to do with an intangible: the lack of community within. On one hand, intimacy is a prized commodity at major-league ballparks: you want to feel like you're part of a smaller section and not one small speck in a mob. And groups do like to feel apart from the rest of the

TRIVIA

Many modern ballparks are built on the waterfront, and Great American Ball Park is no exception, sitting on the shores of the Ohio River. When you wander the ballpark, you'll see the riverfront, but you won't see a crowd of fans jostling in small watercraft, hoping to snare a blast from Adam Dunn or Junior Griffey. Even with the presence of many sluggers in the Reds lineup during the first years at Great American Ball Park, it would take a monster shot to reach the river: it's 580 feet from home plate to the Ohio. That would seem to be out of the range of any current major leaguer: remember, accurately measured home runs over 500 feet are few and far between, and although legend has it Mickey Mantle once blasted one over 600 feet, baseball historians have determined the actual distance was only 503 feet— not bad, but not enough to earn a dunk in the river.

crowd. But the Reds take the notion a little too far: some of the group areas (look at the photos in this chapter) feature a poor view of the action and are physically separated from nearby sections. We're all in favor of seating for groups, but the fans buying these seats might as well be watching the game in a sports bar. By breaking the ballpark into many such separate seating areas, there's not much of a community feel during the game.

There are some nice architectural touches, and there's something very unique here: a gap between sections of the grandstand. The point is to give fans sitting in the Sun Deck/Moon Deck a view of downtown Cincinnati, while providing a great vantage point for those standing on the walkway between the sections. This also points out one of the huge advantages of Great American Ball Park: it is outstanding for walking and lounging. The number of places to just stand around and watch the game from a different perspective may be the most we've ever seen in an MLB ballpark: in addition to the aforementioned gap, there are concourses surrounding the entire facility, with standing areas in the outfield that give views both of the ballpark and the riverfront.

Finally, there's one more important aspect worth covering: history. Before you enter, take a moment to walk around the exterior of Great American Ball Park. The original Cincinnati Reds was the first professional team (and reviled by many for that at the time, by the way) and the rich history of Reds baseball is infused in the ballpark. The main entrance, Crosley Terrace, is designed to evoke memories of the Reds' former home, Crosley Field. Statues of former Reds greats Joe Nuxhall, Ted Kluszewski, Frank Robinson, and Ernie Lombardi dominate the area, reached after passing a 167-ton Indiana limestone bas relief entitled "Spirit of Baseball." Outside Crosley Terrace, and along Second Street,

In tribute to Reds stars from the Crosley Field era, catcher Ernie Lombardi receives a pitch from Joe Nuxhall as slugger Frank Robinson swings. On deck nearby is a statue of Ted Kluszewski. The four players designated for Crosley Terrace were selected by Internet and stadium votes from Reds fans.

TRIVIA

The Cincinnati Red Stockings were the first professional baseball team, barnstorming the country in 1869 and 1870, traveling 11,000 miles on the intercontinental railroad, and winning 130 games a row before falling to the Brooklyn Atlantics. The team was formed by Cincinnati attorney Aaron B. Chapman to promote Cincinnati and its businesses, but the lineup was put together by British native Harry Wright, who chose the team uniforms (white flannel shirts, dark shoes and red stockings) and put together the 10-member squad. The payroll for the 1869 team was $9,300—not bad for those days—and the team actually turned a profit of $1.39 after paying salaries and expenses.

Technically, the Cincinnati Red Stockings were not predecessors of the current Cincinnati Reds in anything but name, but there's a tight spiritual connection recognized by Cincinnati baseball fans.

are several banners commemorating important dates in Cincinnati Reds history.

Past the front gates are two large mosaics made of Italian marble honoring the original 1869 Cincinnati Red Stockings and the 1970s Reds of the "Big Red Machine" era. Go out to the children's play area in the northwest corner of the concourse level and you'll see historical displays of prior ballparks in Reds history, including the aforementioned Crosley Field, Riverfront Stadium/Cinergy Park, and the Palace of Fans.

The commitment to commemorating Cincinnati's rich baseball history, quite honestly, is the best thing about the ballpark. Crosley Terrace and the mosaics are just the beginning of the many nods to the past. Take a look at the press box: underneath it are the six players with numbers retired by the Reds (1, Fred Hutchinson; 5, Johnny Bench; 8, Joe Morgan; 18, Ted Kluszewski; 20, Frank Robinson; and 24, Tony Perez). The home plate was transported from Cinergy Field after the last Reds game played there, and the ballpark dimensions are derived from those in Crosley Field and Riverfront Stadium. The left-field-line distance of 328 feet is the same as Crosley Field, while the distance to center field is 404 feet, the same as Riverfront Stadium.

Ballpark Quirks

There are so many. As you can tell, we're not big fans of some of the quirks forced upon the fans of Cincinnati, such as the steamboat theme carried a little too far.

The bullpens are interestingly placed in left-center field and down the right-field line, seeming like afterthoughts in the late stages of design. Fans can get close to the relievers warming up in each bullpen.

One quirk we're not especially fond of is the installation of bleachers in the second deck in left field. Those aluminum seats are pretty open on a summer afternoon; bring your sunscreen. However, the bleachers do offer easy access to the Machine Room Grille and have their own beer garden.

Food and Drink

There are 28 concession stands at Great American Ball Park, not many for such a modern facility. (Chase Field, home of the Arizona Diamondbacks, features 39 fixed and 35 portable concession stands.) Still, we didn't encounter many lines when hitting the concession stands.

There are three local delicacies worth sampling at the ballpark: Big Red Smokies, Montgomery Inn BBQ, and Skyline Chili.

Big Red Smokies are the signature hot dog; basically, they're hot dogs burned to the point where they have a black crust. Some of us grew up on burnt hot dogs and find them tasty. Other people hate burnt foods of all sorts. Your call. For a kick, throw some mustard on the Smokie. Mustard at Reds games is still a novelty: for many years the Reds didn't serve mustard at concession stands, and it wasn't until the move to Great American Ball Park did the team offer Uncle Phil's Dusseldorf Mustard at condiment stands. For many years the Reds offered a hometown mustard, from the Frank Tea & Spice Co., at Crosley Field, but that firm is out of business and the recipe appears to be lost forever.

Montgomery Inn BBQ is served at several stands. Cincinnati isn't regarded as a great barbecue city, but Montgomery Inn prepares some top-notch items.

Cincinnati is a great chili town, however, and Skyline Chili is one of the best offerings. Cincinnati chili is a little on the thin side and meant to be eaten on top of spaghetti, served with cheese. Cincinnati chili also features a touch of cinnamon and chocolate, so we're not talking spicy Texas-style chili here.

The Machine Room brewpub is located in the left-field corner of the ballpark. It honors the 1975-1976 Reds teams—the Big Red Machine—and features the Zamboni (hung over the bar) used to vacuum rainwater from the artificial turf at Riverfront Stadium.

On the Club Level the Fox Sports Net Club 4,192 pays tribute to Pete Rose breaking the career all-time hit record held by Ty Cobb. It's not really a restaurant per se; rather, it's the concession area for those holding Club and Scout seats. You won't find anything offered here you can't find in other concession areas, but you will find a bar where fans (for some reason) decide to watch the game on television rather than in their seats. No, we don't understand, either.

Ballpark Tours

During the season the Reds offer tours of Great American Ball Park Monday through Saturday. Stops on the tour include the seating bowl, a dugout, the broadcast booth, the press box, and the club level.

On game days, tours are offered at 9:00 a.m., 10:30 a.m., noon, and 1:00 p.m. on weekdays, and 10:30 a.m., 11:30 a.m., 12:30 p.m., and 1:30 p.m. on Saturday. (Tours are not offered on Sunday and when a day game is scheduled.) On non-game days, tours are offered at 9:00 a.m., 10:30 a.m., noon, 1:30 p.m. and 3:00 p.m. on weekdays and 10:30 a.m., 11:30 a.m., 12:30 p.m., 1:30 p.m. and 2:30 p.m.

The cost: $5 for adults, 4 for seniors (55+) and $3 for children age 3-12.

Celebrating baseball and the Cincinnati riverfront, the 50-foot-tall "Spirit of Baseball" bas relief greets ballpark visitors.

For the Kids

There is an abundance of activities for kids. Before the game a trip to the Fan Zone is mandatory: kids can participate in a variety of interactive games, including a "Swing Away" batting cage and a "High Heat" pitching game. The Fan Zone is a large open area featuring live music, historical displays, concessions, and a picnic deck.

Two mascots roam the ballpark: the traditional Mr. Red (the original baseball-headed mascot) and Gapper, the newer mascot bearing a distinct resemblance to Montreal's legendary Youppi! and the Phillie Phanatic.

Where to Stay

There are times when you don't feel like you're in downtown Cincinnati when viewing a game at Great American Ball Park, particularly if you're sitting in the grandstand. But you are, and that's a great advantage if you want to stay close to the ballpark.

There are some great hotels close to Great American Ball Park, well within walking distance, including the Westin Cincinnati (21 E. 5th St.; *westin.com*; $250-$350), the Hyatt Regency (151 W. 5th St.; *hyatt.com*; $150-$300), and the Millennium Hotel (150 W. 5th St.; *millennium-hotels.com*; $150-$250). Our personal favorite in downtown Cincinnati hotels is the Hilton Cincinnati Netherland Plaza (35 W. 5th St.; *hilton.com*; $125-$250): built in 1931, the Netherland Plaza is known for its Art Deco stylings and connection to the city's skyway system. Similarly historic is the Cincinnatian Hotel (601 Vine St.; *cincinnatianhotel.com*; $200-$300): built in 1882, it too is on the National

Register of Historic Places and is renowned for its commitment to service. On the northern edge of downtown is the Ramada Inn (800 W. 8th St.; *ramada.com*; $50-$100).

Downtown Cincinnati tends to be a pricy area in terms of hotels, so you may want to look south of the border in Kentucky for cheaper digs. Directly across the Ohio River from downtown is the Comfort Suites Newport (420 Riverboat Row, Newport; *choicehotels.com*; $85-$125), the Radisson Hotel Cincinnati (668 W. 5th St., Covington; *radisson.com*; $150-$200), and the Embassy Suites (10 River Center Blvd., Covington; *hilton.com*; $150-$250). Another popular area for lower priced hotels is close to the Cincinnati/Northern Kentucky Airport in Covington, where you can find the Holiday Inn Cincinnati (600 W. 3rd St., Covington; *holiday-inn.com*; $80-$125) among others.

Local Attractions

The best baseball attraction in Cincinnati is actually part of the ballpark: the Reds Hall of Fame and Museum. It details the history of baseball in Cincinnati from the 1869 Red Stockings (the first professional team) to the present, highlighting the team's many stars and many homes.

The museum's curators weren't afraid to tackle the issue of Pete Rose, properly honoring his accomplishments on the field. The spot where Rose's record-breaking 4,192nd hit landed in Riverfront Stadium is visible from a unique exhibit honoring Rose and other Reds record holders, which includes a 50-foot-high "wall of balls" containing 4,256 baseballs, Rose's career hit record.

Also honored is a unique tradition in Cincinnati: the opening day parade. For many years the first major-league game of the year was played in Cincinnati, and the city took great pride in that honor, throwing a big party highlighted with a parade to the ballpark. MLB lost a little when its leaders decided not to start the

The Wall of Balls commemorating Pete Rose's 4,256 hits, one ball for each hit. (Photo courtesy of the Cincinnati Reds.)

season in Cincinnati, instead letting television programmers decide where the season starts.

You'll also find standard displays honoring great Reds over the years, as well as some unusual items: a dugout bench and seats from Riverfront Stadium, an extensive collection of fan memorabilia set in a recreation of a basement rec room, and historic team documents. There are 64 former Reds in the Hall of Fame, which began in 1958 when Ernie Lombardi, Johnny Vander Meer, Paul Derringer, Bucky Walters and Frank McCormick (all on the 1939-40 championship teams) were inducted. It does not contain Pete Rose, as he is on baseball's ineligible list.

Even if you're not attending a Reds game, we'd recommend a visit, though the schedule can be a little confusing. During the season the Hall of Fame and Museum is open on game days from 10 a.m. to 7 p.m. when there's an afternoon game and 10 a.m. to 8 p.m. when there's a night game. On game days, the hall is open only to fans with tickets to that day's game after 5:40 p.m. The admission fee is $5 if you have a ticket to the game that day. Admission charges on game days before 5:40 p.m.: $8 for adults, $6 for seniors (55+) and $5 for children 3-12.

On non-game days, the Hall of Fame and Museum is open 10 a.m. to 5 p.m. on Monday through Saturday and noon to 5 p.m. on Sunday. Admission charges on non-game days: $8 for adults, $6 for seniors (55+) and $5 for children 3-12.

In the offseason, the Hall of Fame and Museum is open Tuesday through Saturday, 10 a.m. to 5 p.m. Admission charges: $8 for adults, $6 for seniors (55+) and $5 for children 3-12.

Right outside the ballpark, on the Cincinnati Public Landing of the Ohio River, is the National Steamboat Monument, featuring a 60-ton paddlewheel from the American Queen and an interactive whistle grove. At one time this was one the busiest river stops in the country, with an average of 22 steamboats visiting daily.

Getting There

Cincinnati's mass-transit system is not very good. As a result, you'll either need to drive or walk to the game. If you're coming in for the weekend and plan on spending most of your time at the ballpark, stay downtown and walk over to the ballpark: it's the easiest and most convenient way to get there.

If you drive, access to the ballpark is easy and there's an abundance of parking in the area. The ballpark is close to I-71, I-75 and I-471, giving you three easy routes to the ballpark. There are plenty of signs on the freeways pointing you in the right direction to the ballpark.

Once there, you can find plenty of parking within a close walk. The ballpark shares the riverfront with Paul Brown Stadium, home of the NFL's Cincinnati Bengals, and the area between the two facilities is set up for parking. In addition, there's lots of parking to the north and east of the ballpark, as well as more in Newport, on the Kentucky side of the Ohio River. You can park on

Crosley Field in the 1950s, including the famous scoreboard. Note the use of "Redlegs" in the linescore. (Photo courtesy of the Cincinnati Reds.)

the Kentucky side and walk across the Taylor Southgate Bridge or the historic John A. Roebling Suspension Bridge.

Team Ballpark History

The Cincinnati Reds franchise was a charter member of the National League in 1876, but the team was booted from the league in 1880, finding a new home in the American Association. In 1891 the Reds returned to the National League and the first Opening Day parade was organized by team owner John T. Brush (who would later own the New York Giants and build the Polo Grounds).

Since 1884 the Cincinnati Reds played baseball at the intersection of Findlay Street and Western Avenue. League Park was the first to open there and, as happened with most wooden ballparks of the day, it burned to the ground. In 1893, League Park was rebuilt, columned, expanded, and renamed The Palace of the Fans. The Palace of the Fans resembled a Greek temple with an extravagant façade and opera-style private boxes. Alas, it too burned, in 1911, and gave way to Redland (later Crosley) Field.

Redland Field, named to honor the traditional color of Cincinnati baseball teams, opened its gates on April 12, 1912. It was built for $225,000 and was one of the classic steel-and-concrete parks constructed during the first ballpark boom era of 1909-1923. The red brick, boomerang-like edifice was originally built featuring a covered double-deck grandstand that wrapped around home plate and extended about 30 feet past both first and third bases. Single-deck pavilion seating continued into both outfield corners. Total seating capacity was just over 20,000. It was one of the smallest-capacity parks when it was built and remained one of the smallest in the league throughout its six-decade history. The outfield bleachers held only 4,500 fans, all in right field. In fact, permanent seating was never employed in left and center fields.

By 1933 Reds owner Sid Weil lost the team to bankruptcy, and the bank hired Leland Stanford "Larry" MacPhail to look after the Reds. MacPhail, cantankerous and hot-tempered, would prove to be one of baseball's great innovators. His first move was to sell the majority of the club to Powel Crosley, Jr. Crosley was one of the first millionaires whose fortune came from the new medium of direct mail, and he turned that early fortune into a media empire that included 50,000-watt radio station WLW ("the Nation's Station") and the first NBC affiliate. In a way, he was a predecessor of Ted Turner, buying the Cincinnati Reds for $450,000 and using team broadcasts as a way to prop up his radio and television interests. In fact, a Reds TV broadcast became the first sports program ever broadcast in color.

It was said Powel Crosley was not a man of broad interests, and his wife complained that they did little together other than fish and watch baseball. That's a little unfair: Crosley invented the first compact car (sold through department stores, not traditional dealerships), the first car radio (the Roamio), the first refrigerator with door shelving units (the Shelvador), and a bed cooling system (the Koolrest). To his credit, he gave the majority of ownership responsibilities to his younger brother Lewis (Lewis actually ran all the businesses for Powel), changed the name of the park to Crosley Field, and hired Larry MacPhail as general manager.

Many of the major structural renovations at the stadium happened after the new administration took over. Between the 1937-38 seasons, home plate was moved another 20 feet out and, in the middle of their pennant-winning season of 1939, the Reds added roofed upper decks to the left- and right-field pavilions. This gave Crosley Field 5,000 extra seats and the appearance it would retain for the rest of its existence.

The Reds were pioneers in accommodating their opponents. In the 1930s they became the first team to install a clubhouse for the visiting team. And an added bonus for the fans: both team's clubhouses were located behind the left-field stands. Players and coaches had to walk amongst the crowd to enter and leave the playing field.

Perhaps the greatest moment in Crosley Field history came on May 24, 1935 when the Reds defeated Philadelphia 2-1 in the first night game in major-league history. Twenty-six years earlier in 1909, inventor George Cahill had shown off a new portable lighting system. He built five steel towers for The Palace of the Fans and strung lights for an Elks Lodge game between Cincinnati and Newport, Kentucky. In 1931, the Reds shared portable lighting equipment with the touring House of David baseball team for a night exhibition. By the mid-thirties, with one-in-four Americans out of work and the rest employed from nine to five, Larry MacPhail was able to convince Powel Crosley and the minority partners to try night baseball. On that May night, with 20,422 onlookers in eager anticipation, FDR threw a switch 500 miles away in Washington and Crosley Field made history and baseball was changed forever.

By the 1960s, the economic growth Cincinnati was experiencing was all but absent from the warehouses and factories of the west end of town. When the Superior Towel and Linen Service laundry left the area and took with it one of Crosley's hallmarks, it symbolically predicted the Reds' abandonment of the area. The team, playing in the major's smallest stadium, was eager to jump on the multi-purpose stadium bandwagon and flee to the publicly financed Riverfront Stadium downtown on the banks of the Ohio. The final game at Crosley was played on June 24, 1970. Over 28,000 nostalgic fans saw Johnny Bench and Lee May homer to edge Juan Marichal and the Giants, 5-4. After the game, a helicopter transported home plate to the new digs downtown. Crosley would spend the next two years as an auto impound lot and was eventually bulldozed in 1972.

An industrial park now occupies the site. There is a plaque commemorating Crosley Field, along with a ticket booth and a few seats used at the old ballpark.

The Reds moved to Riverfront Stadium (later renamed Cinergy Field) in the middle of the 1970 season. The new home was a round cookie-cutter facility, also home to the NFL's Cincinnati Bengals. Like most multiuse facilities of the era, it featured artificial turf and a hybrid seating scheme that shortchanged both baseball and football fans. There was no public outcry to keep Cinergy Park once the Reds made it clear they wanted a new ballpark. The Reds appropriately commemorated the ballpark by marking the spot of Pete Rose's historic hit breaking the all-time hit record.

Cinergy Field was located right next to GABP—in fact, part of Cinergy Field was torn down to make way for GABP during the team's final year there—and GABP opened partially unfinished when Cinergy Park was demolished.

Local Baseball Attractions

Cincinnati takes its baseball seriously. Between games at Great American Ballpark there are a host of baseball-related diversions.

If you have fond memories of Crosley Field, you can see a reasonable facsimile at the Blue Ash Sports Center (11540 Grooms Road, Blue Ash; *blueash.com*; 513/230-5162) in nearby Blue Ash. Enthusiasts have recreated much of the feel of Crosley Field: the field features the same dimensions as the original ballpark, along with the famous terrace in center field and a scoreboard resembling the one used by the Reds during the last year of pro play at Crosley. Many pieces of old Crosley, including 600 seats and a ticket booth, are installed as well.

There is also plenty of minor-league baseball in the area. The Florence Freedom of the independent Frontier League play at Champion Window Field

(7950 Freedom Way, Florence; *florencefreedom.com*; 859/594-4487), located south of Great American Ball Park on I-71/75. The ballpark is easy to find: just take the freeway south, exit at the Florence/Union exit (#180), and follow the signs.

The Reds have two farm teams within an easy drive of Cincinnati. The Louisville Bats play at Louisville Slugger Field (401 E. Main St., Louisville; *batsbaseball.com*; 502/361-3100), one of the great ballparks of the minors. The Dayton Dragons play at Fifth Third Field (220 N. Patterson, Dayton; *daytondragons.com*; 937/228-BATS), another of our favorite ballparks. Make sure you have a ticket before you head out to the ballpark: the Dragons have sold out games for several years now.

Also within an easy drive: the Lexington Legends, who play at Applebee's Park (207 Legends Lane, Lexington; *lexingtonlegends.com*; 859/252-HITS).

Cleveland Indians
Jacobs Field

Address: 2401 Ontario Street, Cleveland, OH 44115.
Cost: $173 million, although there were later costs combined with the Gund Arena construction.
Architect: HOK Sport.
Owner: Gateway Economic Development Corp.
Capacity: 43,863.
Dimensions: 325L, 370LC, 405C, 375RC, 325R.
Ticket Line: 216/420-HITS.
Home Dugout Location: Third-base side.
Playing Surface: Grass.
Other Tenants: None.
Nickname: The Jake.
First Game: On April 4, 1994 the Cleveland Indians defeated the Seattle Mariners 4-3 in 11 innings, as Wayne Kirby singled in the winning run. President Bill Clinton was on hand to throw out the first pitch.
Landmark Event: The Cleveland Indians made the 1995 and 1997 World Series, but lost both (1995 to Atlanta, 1997 to Florida) away from Cleveland. Between 1995 and 2001 Jacobs Field saw more than its fair share of playoff games, as the Indians won six divisional titles in that span. The American League won the 1997 All-Star Game at Jacobs Field, 3-1, behind local hero Sandy Alomar, whose two-run homer in the seventh inning broke a 1-1 tie. Alomar became the first All-Star MVP to win the award in his home ballpark.

Your Jacobs Field Seating Crib Sheet

Best Sections to View a Game: Almost every seat at Jacobs Field is angled toward the infield, so there are very few bad seats. Generally, ticket prices are on the inexpensive side, giving you more bang for the buck. Field Box seats are only $46, a very cheap seat by MLB standards for a primo location. We're also partial to the left-field bleachers and $18 Upper Box seats: with the steep pitch you feel like you're right on top of the action.

Best Cheap Seats: The Upper Outfield Reserved (sections 507-518) seats are only $7 and provide a pretty good view of the field and the scoreboard.

Most Underrated Sections: Bleacher seats are only $14 and are close to the action, sitting in back of a 19-foot-high fence. Typically there's a rowdy crowd out there as well, making for an entertaining experience. The bad thing about these seats: the impressive scoreboard is at your back.

Seats to Avoid: Sections 119-121 are tucked in the right-field corner. In a ballpark filled with good seats, these stick out like a sore thumb: they present a limited view of the field and are not fully angled toward the infield. Similarly, sections 176 and 177 are tucked into the left-field corner and don't present the best view of the ballpark. Interestingly, these five sections are in the $22 price range and are overpriced; buy seats there only if the rest of the ballpark is sold out. In the upper deck, avoid sections 520 and 521: they are not angled well toward the infield, but are a tolerable buy at $7.

Jacobs Field: An Underrated Masterpiece

If you ever questioned the great and mighty power of karma in our universe, take a visit to gorgeous Jacobs Field in Cleveland. After years of suffering through the cold and damp of Cleveland Municipal Stadium—the original "Mistake on the Lake"—local baseball fans were rewarded with one of the finest facilities in baseball; a downtown ballpark that took the Oriole Park blueprint and refined it further. Retro at its best.

Basically, Jacobs Field is a great baseball experience because it's simply a fun place to be. It's a great ballpark with good front-office management stressing a great ballpark experience. It's easier to get a ticket to an Indians game than it was in the opening years of the Jake, and it's still a must-visit for any baseball fan.

Most people don't remember what a great baseball town Cleveland has been over the years. Despite playing for decades in Municipal Stadium, a cavernous old park, the Cleveland Indians set major-league attendance records when fans showed up in droves to see Bill Veeck's team compete for world championships. But the Muni was also a cold behemoth seating 74,000—the most of any major-league ballpark—and fans suffered through chilly winds coming off the lake, seating so remote the center-field bleacher inhabitants never caught a home-run ball, and management that didn't care much about putting a winning team on the field. You can see why locals were thrilled when Jacobs Field opened in 1994.

Even after 10 years, a night at Jacobs Field is still an event. If you go, head to the ballpark as early as possible and wander through the concourses. For the greatest drama, enter through the left-field gates and take in the crowd that can usually be found gathering two hours before game time. A great advantage to Jacobs Field is the presence of many nooks and crannies where fans are expected to just hang out and watch the ballgame with their friends; the informality afforded by these spaces makes a ballpark the true community builder.

To your left will be the bleachers and a bat-making stand; spend a moment watching a bat being carved on a lathe before heading down the corridor behind the bleachers. Also, take a look at the ballpark from the left-field patio: it's a popular meeting spot before the game and a wonderful vantage point once play begins.

Your next stop is the center-field plaza next to the Batter's Eye Bar: it opens at 4:30 p.m., giving you a chance to unwind while watching batting practice, and on Saturday nights it's a party spot as a live band serenades fans sipping their mixed drinks. The expansive center-field area is also a good spot to grab some food: the pizza is decent, while the Mexican burritos are highly recommended and affordable (by ballpark standards, anyway) to boot. (In general, the food at Jacobs Field is inexpensive; enjoy.) A slew of picnic tables and some bar-style seats overlooking the field make for a nice respite.

Continue your walk through the right-field concourse where you'll pass by a variety of concession stands until you reach the right-field corner. There are

If you're attending a Saturday night game, come early and find a seat on the plaza where you can listen to the band before the first pitch.

three noteworthy features there: a large children's play area, a kid-oriented gift shop, and another smaller patio where standing fans can watch the game.

From this point you'll encounter something fairly unique: dual concourses. Behind the seating you'll find a fairly narrow concourse with its own set of concession stands. Behind that is another wider concourse with yet more concession stands and gathering spaces, such as a picnic area near first base (next to the gift shop) and a food concourse. (Interestingly, the team souvenir shop is on the smaller side, especially for a major-league park.) There's a large-screen television showing the game action for those waiting in line for a beer or a dog. Both the narrow and the wide concourses run from foul line to foul line. As you walk through them, stop to the right of home plate and take in some action from yet another standing area.

As you walk down the third-base line, you'll eventually make your way back to the left-field corner to the aforementioned patio. If you're in a more formal mood, you can dine at the glassed-in restaurant in the left-field corner.

We viewed the ballpark from almost every vantage point; our tickets were for the last row of the left-field bleachers (we would highly recommend sitting out there). Because of a long rain delay we ended up wandering throughout the entire park and spending time in the expensive seating behind home plate and the back of the upper deck. The outfield bleachers are their own world: it's here you find the more rabid fans as well as John Adams playing the Wahoo drum: he purchases two tickets for every game, one for himself and one for his drum. (The big disadvantage: you can't see the scoreboard.)

The upper deck was a pleasant surprise: while they are very high above the diamond, the pitch is quite steep, so you feel like you're looking directly down on the game. (Avoid these seats if you have a touch of vertigo.) And for $5, they may be the best deal in major-league baseball. You also get a good view of the Cleveland skyline, both in front of and behind you.

The Indians used to be the hottest ticket in major-league baseball, at one point selling out 455 straight games and three times selling out entire seasons before opening day. Today it's not as hard to get Indians tickets, though the Indians come close to selling out specific games. In 2006 the Indians drew only 1.998 million fans, less than the total accumulated by Milwaukee, Cincinnati, Minnesota, and Toronto. With the Indians a contender once again, you can expect more competition for seats in future seasons. In the meantime enjoy your visit to the ballpark.

Ballpark Quirks

Jacobs Field features open bullpens, the rage in all the retro ballparks. Interestingly, the bullpens feature three mounds instead of the usual two.

Home plate was originally used at Municipal Stadium and then moved to Jacobs Field when it opened.

The Cleveland Indians have seven retired numbers: 3 (Earl Averill), 5 (Lou Boudreau), 14 (Larry Doby, the first African-American in the American League), 19 (Bob Feller), 18 (Mel Harder), 21 (Bob Lemon), and 455 (the number of consecutive sellouts enjoyed by the team). You can see all the numbers in right field beneath the speed-pitch sign.

Food and Drink

There are 68 concession stands at Jacobs Field, but they are so spread out you don't fight congestion, except perhaps in the right-field food court.

Buy a hot dog for two reasons: they're pretty tasty and they're a good excuse to have some Bertman's Stadium Mustard, a spicy, German-style mustard and a longtime Cleveland delicacy. (In fact, we'd recommend heading to a local grocery store to buy some for home.)

Yes, you can find sushi at the ballpark, but this is Cleveland—you don't go to Cleveland to eat sushi. More remarkable are some of the unique food items found in the Market Pavilion, such as pierogis (Eastern European filled dumplings), garlic fries, knishes, gyros, meatloaf, and the Cuban panini, a grilled sandwich. You can also find Sapporo and Pironi beer out there as well. There are stools and counters for those wanting to watch the game while munching down; there are also plenty of tables if you don't mind missing a half inning or so.

One disappointing aspect to the concessions: the lack of variety among beer offerings. There are only two stands (113 and 552) where there's a decent selection of beer, other than the Market Pavilion stands.

Handicapped-Accessible Seating

The Indians installed 610 handicapped-accessible seats in a variety of configurations. There are accessible seats at the end of a row without an armrest, seating for the visually impaired behind the screened area, and wheelchair seating featuring either an open spot or a pivoting seat for easy access. These seats must be specified when you buy your tickets.

For the Kids

The right-field corner contains a kids play area, a kid-sized concession stand with offerings (like PB&J or hot dog value meals) designed to please the rugrats, and a souvenir store with kid-oriented wares. It's a smaller area and feels cut off from the action, so it's not the greatest place to supervise kids and watch the game. (Be prepared to hunker down at a nearby table and give your kids a good time.) In fact, chances are you'll play the Ms. Pac-Man game instead.

Slider is the Indians mascot, designed along the same lines as Youppi! and the Phillie Phanatic. He's cute, adorable and utterly cloying. Kids will also enjoy building their own Slider at the Build-a-Bear Workshop behind section 142.

One nice touch from the Indians: they offer free ID wristbands personalized with a seat location so lost children can be returned to their seats. Wristbands are available at Guest Service Booths and the Concierge Desk.

Ballpark Tours

Tours of Jacobs Field run between May and the end of the summer, with stops at Kidsland, the press box, a party suite, the club lounge, the Indians dugout, and indoor batting cages. Call 216/420-4385 for more information on dates and times.

Getting There

Jacobs Field is in downtown Cleveland, with an estimated 30,000 parking spots within walking distance. Of course, some of these spots are within a closer walk than others, but we found ramps on the Gund Arena side of the ballpark charging less than $10 for a parking spot.

The ballpark is easy to find if you do drive in. Basically, you'll want to make your way to I-90 (called the Inner Belt), accessible from I-77 and I-71. (Follow the signs to downtown Cleveland.) On I-90, follow the signs to the ballpark, visible from the freeway.

If you're coming in from out of town for a game or series, we recommend staying downtown and avoiding a rental car. Downtown Cleveland is only 12 miles from the airport—which makes for an inexpensive cab ride. There's an abundance of restaurants and attractions in downtown Cleveland, making it the perfect base for a visit.

Where to Stay

An abundance of affordable hotels is within a very, very short walk of Jacobs Field.

We'd recommend starting your housing search with the following four hotels. In the past, visiting teams have been put up at the Radisson Hotel at Gateway (651 Huron Rd.; *radisson.com*; $100-$150), across the street from the sports complex. The Residence Inn Cleveland Downtown (527 Prospect Av.; *marriott.com*; $140-$200) is set in an historic building once housing the Colonial Hotel and still retains a lot of charm. The Wyndham Cleveland at Playhouse Square (1260 Euclid Av.; *wyndham.com*; $85-$150) is a surprisingly affordable and modern hotel. The Hyatt Regency Cleveland at The Arcade (420 Superior Av.; *hyatt.com*; $160-$220) is set in a restored 1890 Victorian-style arcade originally financed by John D. Rockefeller and wealthy Clevelanders. (It's worth a visit even if you don't stay there.)

INSIDER'S TIP

There is one huge disadvantage to staying downtown: you'll be forced to pay for parking, usually between $12 and $22 a night, as street parking in the Gateway area can be difficult. If you're coming in from out of town and just hitting a ballgame or two, we'd recommend taking the short cab ride downtown and staying near the ballpark.

Other hotels within a short walk include the Hilton Garden Inn (1100 Carnegie Av.; *hilton.com*; $100-$150) and the Holiday Inn Express Cleveland Downtown (629 Euclid Av.; *holiday-inn.com*; $89-$125). The Ritz Carlton Cleveland (1515 W. 3rd St.; *ritz-carlton.com*; $185-$225) is considered the city's finest hotel, with views overlooking the waterfront.

While You're There

Downtown Cleveland may not be perceived as the most exciting place on the planet, but there are plenty of bars and restaurants in the area surrounding Jacobs Field. In particular, the Gateway District surrounding the ballpark is a convenient place to grab a beer and a burger before or after the game. The following restaurants are located close to the ballpark.

Alice Coopers'town (2217 Rock and Roll Blvd.; *alicecooperstowncleveland.com*; 216/566-8100) is the Ohio outpost of the popular Phoenix sports bar and restaurant owned by rocker and baseball fan Alice Cooper. The menu stays away from the cutesy item names found at the Phoenix restaurant, thank goodness, and the specialties are some sort of variation on red meat—burgers, ribs, and steaks.

The Winking Lizard is a Ohio chain featuring casual bar food and over 100 beers on tap, and the Jacobs Field location (811 Huron Rd.; *winkinglizard.com*; 216/589-0313) hews to the formula with lizard wings (chicken wings served at a variety of spiciness levels). Don't think too much about it: the place is perfect for kicking back with a beer and some wings.

The Boneyard Beer Farm (748 Prospect Av. E.; 216/575-0226) claims to have Cleveland's largest beer selection, with 40 brews on tap and over 200 available in bottles. The food doesn't rise past your standard bar fare, but with that many beers available, who cares?

Fat Fish Blue (21 Prospect Av.; *fatfishblue.com*; 216/875-6000) combines live jazz and blues with a Creole menu. Local blues legend Robert Lockwood Jr. plays every Wednesday night, with national touring acts in other nights of the week. It's also a good place to head after the game as it's open until 2 a.m. on Friday and Saturday.

Panini's Gateway Bar (840 Huron Rd. E.; 216/522-1510) serves that peculiar Ohio/Pennsylvania delicacy: sandwiches stuffed with French fries. (Check out our chapter on PNC Park for Pittsburgh eateries offering the same sort of thing.) It is the sort of thing you'll groove on after one too many beers. A plus: outdoor seating.

Alesci's Downtown (828 Huron Rd.; *alescis.com*; 216/348-8600) serves a great slice of pizza on a Styrofoam plate.

Nick's Sports Center (612 Prospect Av.; 216/781-0966) is exactly what the name implies: a pure sports bar.

Yes, the House of Blues is a chain restaurant, but it's a fairly decent chain, run by folks who get the blues. The Cleveland outpost (308 Euclid Av.; *hob.com*; 216/523-BLUE) is like all the others, featuring a Sunday gospel brunch, touring musical acts (not all of them bluesmen, alas), and Southern-inspired cuisine.

A mandatory stop for anyone thinking they have led or want to lead the rock-and-roll lifestyle: the Rock and Roll Hall of Fame (1 Key Plaza; *rockhall.com*; 888/764-ROCK), located on the Lake Erie waterfront on the north side of downtown. The glass pyramid does a good job of institutionalizing what began as a rebel music movement. Spend some time listening to the 500 songs that shaped rock and roll (a separate exhibit area with listening kiosks): while you can argue with some of the choices—country, swing, and bluegrass are criminally unrepresented, as is the Velvet Underground—it's a thought-provoking approach to the music that changed the world. Decide early on if you can afford that rock-and-roll lifestyle: tickets are $20 for adults, $14 for seniors, $11 for children between the ages of 9 and 11, and free for kids eight-years-old or younger.

The ballpark and the hotels we list here are also close to the Playhouse Square Center (1501 Euclid Av.; *playhousesquare.com*; 216/771-4444), four restored theaters featuring over 10,000 seats and a plethora of events ranging from touring shows to concerts.

Team Ballpark History

Cincinnati gets the most attention from historians when researching the roots of professional baseball, but there's also a deep tradition of pro baseball in Cleveland as well.

If you go back to the days of the American Association in 1871, Cleveland professional baseball teams have occupied no less than ten ballparks. All had

Jacobs Field has several gathering places for fans, including the standing area in left field offering a good view of the game.

their endearing quirks: for instance, Kennard Street Park, the home of the National League's Cleveland Spiders from 1879 through 1884, was so cozy there were trees in the outfield and the left-field fences were so short any balls clearing them were ruled doubles, not homers. There were also small ballparks occupied by American Association, Negro League, and Players League teams.

The first League Park, featuring a wooden grandstand, was built for the Spiders in 1891 and occupied through the 1899 season before the National League contracted the Spiders out of existence. The American League Indians then played there from 1901 through 1909. A replacement, featuring concrete-and-steel construction, opened for the 1910 season. It was originally known as Dunn Field—so named after Indians owner James Dunn—and also served as the home of the Cleveland Buckeyes of the Negro Leagues.

Many Clevelanders speak nostalgically of League Park, the home of the Indians from 1910 to 1946. (They rarely speak so nostalgically of Municipal Stadium.) It was a small, neighborhood ballpark with a right-field fence originally 290 feet from home plate. Tris Speaker roamed center field and Nap Lajoie patrolled the infield at League Park. Tigers slugger Sam Crawford launched more than a few there before Indians management erected a 40-foot-

TRIVIA
The 1916 Cleveland Indians are regarded as the first team to wear numbers on their uniforms, sporting them on their left sleeves for a June 26, 1916 game. The practice didn't last more than a few months and was attempted again in 1917 before the New York Yankees instituted it permanently in 1929 with numbers on the backs of their jerseys.

TRIVIA
The Indians didn't start life as the Cleveland Indians. When the American League launched in 1901 the team was known as the Blues or the Bluebirds because of their blue uniforms. Players didn't like the name, so the team went by the Bronchos for the 1902 season. That didn't last long: the team underwent another name change to the Cleveland Naps, in honor of the team's most recognizable player, Nap Lajoie. After Lajoie departed for the Philadelphia Athletics for the 1915 season, the team held a name-the-team contest, and the winner was Indians.

tall wire fence; undaunted, Crawford homered over the new fence in his first at-bat. The ballpark dimensions were obviously determined by the size of the rectangular lot: it was 375 feet down the left-field line and 460 feet to center field. Maybe it was the Cleveland water or some deficiencies in the Cleveland pitching staff, but for the most part opposing players hit the most memorable homers at League Park: Ted Williams launched one over the 40-foot-high fence in right-center field, while pitcher Walter Johnson once cleared the whole ballpark with a shot to left-center field.

League Park was also home to two of the more memorable World Series moments: Elmer Smith hit a grand slam (the first in Series history) over the

League Park. The field and part of the ticket office still stand.

Lakefront Stadium, Cleveland, O.

Courtesy of Norbert J. Yassanye — Aero-Ways, Inc. — Cleveland, O.

Municpal Stadium, then known as Lakefront Stadium. The ballpark dimensions were spacious, to say the least; from this angle you can see how far away from home plate the center-field seats were located.

right-field fence in 1920 when the Indians defeated the Brooklyn Robins (the predecessor to the Dodgers) five games to two; and in that same Series, Bill Wambsganss notched an unassisted triple play. It was the only World Series played at League Park.

Bill Veeck made the decision to move the team from League Park for all Indians games, and perhaps it was one of his biggest missteps in a long and mostly distinguished career. Yes, he attracted huge crowds in a short time at Municipal Stadium, but he consigned fans to a miserable existence for decades afterwards and took away what could have become a Wrigley-like ballpark. (League Park held a little less than 22,000.) Cleveland officials didn't have the heart to tear down League Park until 1950 (it was still used for Negro League games up through its final days), and even then left behind some portions of the ballpark. (We discuss where to visit the remnants later in this chapter.)

If League Park was a cozy ballpark, Municipal Stadium was cavernous. Originally named Lakefront Stadium, the ballpark was also known as Cleveland Public Municipal Stadium before the final moniker stuck. For several years the Indians split their time between the two ballparks, playing Sunday and some night games at Municipal Stadium and all other games at League Park. (The reason for the split is simple: on most nights the Indians simply didn't need 70,000 seats.) Originally, center field went back a whopping 470 feet with the left-field power alley a surprising 463 feet. No one ever hit a homer to center field with those dimensions in place; early on both Jimmy Foxx and Wes Ferrell came close, though.

It's easy to see why Veeck wanted the move: he could cram a lot of behinds into the seats. For the first Indians game played at Municipal Stadium, a excess-capacity crowd of 80,284 fans showed up to see the A's edge the hometown heroes 1-0. It was a huge ballpark, holding more than 78,811 fans at its 1953 peak. Lakefront Stadium was originally built to attract the 1932 Summer Olympics, but Los Angeles ended up snaring the games and the city struggled to lure the Indians there.

Despite having the largest capacity in the majors, the Indians never came close to regularly filling the place except for Bill Veeck's stint as Indians owner. It was in Cleveland where Veeck first became known for his outrageous stunts, and he managed to fill the seats regularly with a full set of promotions and gimmicks. In 1946, teepees were constructed in center field, and in 1953 a bandstand was added.

Fans and players alike hated Cleveland Stadium: it was cold most of the year, especially when the winds were whipping off Lake Erie. It took a lot of determination for Cleveland fans to put up with a creaky old ballpark and a losing team—which made it even more rewarding when the Indians turned into winners at Jacobs Field.

Today, most fans erroneously remember Cleveland Stadium from the baseball classic, Major League. Ironically, that movie was shot in Milwaukee's County Stadium, except for some color and exterior shots from Cleveland.

Local Baseball Attractions
You can visit the sites of League Park and Municipal Stadium, discussed in the previous section. In fact, you can walk on the same field where Nap Lajoie and

Jacobs Field

Tris Speaker played if you head to the corner of East 66th Street and Lexington Avenue. Even though the city tore down most of the ballpark after the 1950 season, left intact were the ticket booths/team offices (now housing a youth center), a portion of the left-field stands, and the playing field, still used by youth and community groups. Cleveland officials talk about restoring the ballpark to some extent for minor-league baseball (spurred on by the success of the Sally League's Lake County Captains, which we'll discuss later in this chapter), but budget woes are preventing them from moving forward with a plan any time soon. The site is marked with a plaque from the Ohio Historical Society.

You can also visit the site of Municipal Stadium, but don't look for any similar commemorative markers. Cleveland Browns Stadium, the home of the NFL's Cleveland Browns, was built on the site of Municipal Stadium. (The remains of the stadium were dumped into Lake Erie, forming an artificial reef.) On the outer walls of the new stadium are plaques memorializing great players in Cleveland football history.

There is an abundance of baseball in Ohio if you want to venture outside of downtown Cleveland. The Lake County Captains of the Class A Sally League play in Classic Park (35300 Vine St., Eastlake; *captainsbaseball.com*; 440/954-WINS), located in the suburb of Eastlake. The Captains are one of the successes of minor-league baseball, regularly drawing large crowds to the 7,000-seat ballpark. If you want to drive a little farther, you can catch the Class AA Akron Aeros of the Eastern League, the Class AAA Toledo Mud Hens or the Dayton Dragons of the Class A Midwest League.

Kansas City Royals
Kauffman Stadium

Address: One Royal Way (I-70 and Blue Ridge Cutoff), Kansas City, MO 64129.
Cost: $43 million.
Architect: HNTB.
Owner: Jackson County.
Capacity: 40,793.
Dimensions: 330L, 385LC, 410C, 385RC, 330R.
Ticket Line: 816/504-4474; 800/6ROYALS.
Home Dugout Location: First-base line.
Playing Surface: AstroTurf (1973-1994), grass (1995-present).
Other Names: The ballpark opened as Royals Stadium and was renamed on July 2, 1993 in honor of the late Ewing Kauffman, who owned the Royals.
Other Tenants: None. Arrowhead Stadium, home of the NFL's Kansas City Chiefs, is located next door; together they form the Truman Sports Complex.
First Game: On April 10, 1973, the Royals defeated the Texas Rangers 12-1, with John Mayberry homering and driving in four runs and Paul Splittorff going all the way for the win. By then the core of the Royals had been assembled—Cookie Rojas, Freddie Patek, Amos Otis, Mayberry, Splittorff, and Hal McRae were regulars, while George Brett would be a late-season call up—and the team would finish with an 88-74 record.
Landmark Events: Though the Royals reached the playoffs and World Series several times, the most memorable World Series games held at Royals Stadium (as it was then known) were the final two games of the 1985 World Series—the all-Missouri match (also known as the I-70 Series) when the

Royals took on the St. Louis Cardinals. Down 3-2 in the Series, the Royals needed victories in the final two games of the Series, and one of the most controversial calls in World Series history to gave them omentum. With the Royals down 1-0 in the ninth inning, Jorge Orta was ruled safe at first despite replays showing he was out, and the Cardinals caved. Jack Clark dropped a pop fly and Darrell Porter misplayed a pitch before Hal McRae was intentionally walked, leaving Dane Iorg to single to right and knock in two runs, giving the Royals a 2-1 win. The Cardinals completely collapsed in Game Seven, going down 11-0 and giving the Royals the series victory. The 1973 All-Star Game (won by the National League, 7-1) was played here as well.

Your Kauffman Stadium Seating Crib Sheet

Best Sections to View a Game: Anywhere between the lines is the place to be. The Royals have a fairly unusual pricing strategy: there are lots of seats (like those in sections 125-138) that are fairly mediocre and overpriced at $20. On the other hand, the top ticket price (except for the Crown Club Seats and Dugout Suites) is only $27. The Royals would be smart to raise the prices in the Dugout sections and lower the prices elsewhere.

Best Cheap Seats: The $7 upper-deck seats will get you in the ballpark; from there you can move into better seats in the upper deck or make your way down to the main concourse. The Royals rarely sell out so you will have your run of the place by the third inning.

Most Underrated Sections: All of them. It is sad the Royals don't draw better: with a top ticket price of $27 and a $7 price for much of the upper deck, there's no reason for fans to avoid Kauffman Stadium.

Seats to Avoid: You'll be craning your neck if you sit in sections 125-138, 331-344, or 431-442 (the upper-deck sections down each line): the grandstand and the seats do not angle toward the playing field. Then again, with the Royals charging $7 for sections 331-344 and 431-442, you'll be happy to put up with a sore neck the rest of the evening. Avoid the right-field corner for night games: you'll spend too much time staring into the sun in the early innings.

Kauffman Stadium: Still Ahead of Its Time

When the Truman Sports Complex was designed in the early 1970s, many critics decried it as being wasteful: why build one facility for football (Arrowhead Stadium) and one for baseball (Royals Stadium) when the rest of the world is plugging along with cookie-cutter stadiums like Three Rivers Stadium, Busch Stadium, and Riverfront Stadium?

Today, Three Rivers Stadium, Busch Stadium, and Riverfront Stadium are all gone, while Kauffman Stadium is revered as one of the classic ballparks of baseball. Renamed in 1993 for Ewing Kauffman (who passed away after the rededication ceremonies), the original owner of the Royals, Royals Stadium was decried as wasteful and indulgent, but the dual-facility approach ended up presaging today's ballpark trends by 20 years. Today no one would think of building a multiuse facility for pro football and baseball and only four facilities (McAfee Coliseum, Metrodome, Dolphin Stadium, and Rogers Centre) house both pro baseball and football—and that list may be down to just Rogers Centre in three or four years.

The design of Royals Stadium was also considered revolutionary in its time. Dodger Stadium was the last true MLB baseball-only facility built before Royals Stadium hit the drawing boards, and the designers of Royals Stadium didn't emulate the highly segmented seating areas at that ballpark. Yes, the concourses are small—even with a crowd of 15,000 or so, you're bumping elbows heading to the concessions—but there are plenty of places to stand around in the outfield corners. Alas, Kauffman Stadium comes short of having a concourse wrapping around the entire playing field—a mandatory feature for any minor- or major-league ballpark built in this century.

True, the location is somewhat lacking, and there are parts of the ballpark that could use some TLC. But make no mistake: Kauffman Stadium is one of the best places in the majors to watch a game. That same inconvenient location gives a bucolic quality to the Kauffman experience; on a warm summer night you feel like you're in the middle of nowhere, miles from any sort of civilization, free to focus on the game instead of some distraction right outside the ballpark walls. It's a comfortable place: generations of Royals baseball fans have spent much time here, supporting their team despite living in a small MLB market where few Septembers are spent in contention.

Most of Kauffman Stadium is the same as when it opened in 1973. The 12-story-high center-field scoreboard, complete with crown, 16,320 light bulbs (which dance between innings), and huge logo on the flipside (facing the freeway), is the ballpark's signature item. It's used for a variety of purposes, including the reporting of out-of-town scores. (A large videoboard in left field augments the main scoreboard.) Jackson County has performed minimal upgrades to the ballpark: for instance, there's no race-track displays on the grandstand facades like you see at other ballparks, nor is there a readily apparent pitch-speed display. Sam Beckett, organist for the Royals since 1999, provides most of the between-pitch music.

Still, Kauffman Stadium has changed some with the times. When it opened it featured artificial turf and a rock-hard playing surface. Jackson County and the Royals dumped the artificial turf prior to the 1995 season. Since then the fences have been lowered and moved in, and in 1999 a private club and suites were added.

Kansas City is known as the City of Fountains, dating back to the 1880s when the local Humane Society installed water fountains to ensure horses and dogs had clean drinking water. Today you can find decorative fountains throughout Kansas City, including an elaborate set in center and right-center field at Kauffman. The 322-foot-wide computerized water fountain is one the largest privately financed fountain spectaculars in the world. It still manages to dazzle, especially during an evening when the fountain show runs late in the game.

Yet, not all is perfect with the ballpark. Despite being built for baseball only, not all the seating is perfectly aligned for fans: if you're sitting down the line in either level you'll be craning your neck to watch a batter. A single reversible escalator to the upper deck, and there's a long line for its use when a large crowd is on hand. The outfield area is woefully underutilized: despite how it looks, there's no concourse across the outfield, denying fans a perfect vantage point to watch a game. There is a sponsored group area in the left-field area, complete with a tiny spa, as well as a walkway behind part of the water fountain, but for the most part fans won't be able to watch the action from the outfield.

That will change in the future. The Royals and the local ballpark authority are working on a plan to modernize Kauffman Stadium. The signature fountains will stay and perhaps be expanded, but the area outside the outfield will be enhanced with a new childrens' play, a restaurant, and more.

Kauffman Stadium transcends its age. It doesn't necessarily feel like an old ballpark in most areas, and for both the ballpark enthusiast and the casual baseball fan attending a game, it's a wonderful, bucolic experience.

Ballpark Quirks

There really are none. Kauffman Stadium might need a cleaning here or there, but for the most part it's a very straightforward ballpark, from the symmetrical fences to the ushers who love to chat about baseball.

Food and Drink

Most concessions are located in back of the field-level seating. Generally speaking, the food offerings at Kauffman Stadium are well above regular ballpark standards, with many items produced locally.

We'll discuss Kansas City barbecue later, but junkies can get their quick fix at the Gates BBQ stands located on the main concourse. Barbecue aficionados can debate forever who serves the best barbecue in Kansas City, but the Royals solved the argument for you by handing over the Kauffman Stadium stands to Gates. Beef, turkey, or pork sandwiches sell for $6.50; go for a side of BBQ beans.

Beer fans will be happy to hear Boulevard beers are served at the ballpark: $6 will get you a Boulevard Pale Ale or Wheat. (You'll find Boulevard beers at many local restaurants, and you can tour the brewery on Saturdays. Call 816/474-7095, ext. 7, for information.) If fresh beer is too much for you, Rolling Rock, Labatt Blue, Sam Adams, Corona, and Bud are available by the bottle. Wine and mixed drinks are available for $6.

Another local firm with a reputation for quality is Sheridan's, whose frozen custard is regarded by many as the best in the region. You can find Sheridan's Frozen Custard at dedicated stands; splurge for a sundae.

Finally, there are the hot dogs: the Royals serve Schweigert hot dogs. You don't find Schweigert hot dogs in very many places—basically, they're sold only in Minnesota, Iowa, and Missouri—and for many years Schweigert was the official hot dog of the Minnesota Twins. Today, Schweigert's parent company is located in Springfield, Mo., making it a local choice for the Royals. We'd recommend the tasty quarter-pound hot dog, a steal at $4.25, topped with Boulevard Pale Ale Mustard. Also on the menu: Hebrew National hot dogs and Johnsonville sausages.

Of course, all the usual ballpark foods—candy, popcorn, nachos, pop, plain coffee—are available, as are Dippin' Dots and Krispy Kreme doughnuts. In fact, in recent years Royals' fans reveled in a free doughnut promotion. If the Royals collect 12 hits during a weekday game, fans holding tickets can redeem them for a dozen free Krispy Kreme glazed doughnuts. That's led to more than one crowd chanting "We want doughnuts!" during the late innings of the game when the Royals are closing in on that magic dozen.

Should you prefer sit-down dining, there's an enclosed restaurant in the Stadium Club down the left-field line.

For the Kids

Behind the right-field corner there is a diamond—the Little K—where children can play wiffle ball. There's a lot of space out there, so parents can let kids run around while keeping an eye on both the game and the children. Next to the Little K is a four-hole mini-golf range.

Also, a Fun Zone behind Section 118 features speed guns, player cutouts, and more.

Ballpark Tours

The Royals offer tours of Kauffman Stadium from June 1 through Aug. 31 daily except for Sunday; the tour includes stops at the Royals Hall of Fame, press box and interview room, Royals Wall of Fame, the home dugout, the visitors clubhouse (when available), and the Royals gift shop. The price is $6 for adults, $4 for children and seniors, with a discount for groups. Tours depart every hour beginning at 9:30 a.m., with the last one scheduled for 11:30 a.m. on Saturday and 2:30 p.m. on weekdays. Call 816/504-422 for more information.

Getting There

Though the local bus line serves the ballpark, almost all Royals fans drive to the game. The ballpark is located on Interstate 70 (which runs east-west through downtown Kansas City) at the Blue Ridge Cutoff, which makes getting to the game very convenient.

By major-league standards, parking at Kauffman Stadium is fairly reasonable: $9 for cars, $11 for oversized vehicles. Since the parking is so spread out, you're never too far from a ballpark entrance unless there's a huge crowd on hand. The spacious parking lots also allow for tailgating (a popular pre- and post-game activity no matter the size of the crowd). You can, in theory, park at a local hotel and walk in, but it's quite a hike.

Despite the suburban location, there's a good mass-transit alternative to driving: the Kansas City Area Transportation Authority runs the Royals Express from downtown Kansas City to the ballpark. The bus picks up and drops off at the Plaza and Crown Center (look for the red Stadium Express sign) beginning two hours before game time and up until 50 minutes before game time. The price is $5 but you receive $5 off a single game ticket. Call 816/346-0348 for more information.

If you want to catch a taxi after the game, they line up outside the right-field corner entrance.

Where to Stay

Two hotels are within walking distance of Kauffman Stadium: the Drury Inn and Suites (3830 Blue Ridge Cutoff; *druryhotels.com*; $100) and the Clarion Hotel Sports Complex (9103 E. 39th St.; *choicehotels.com*; $65-$100). Truth is, we've never stayed at either, though reports from others are none too encouraging. Given the easy freeway access to the ballpark, there's no logistical reason to stay so close to the ballpark: we'd recommend staying in town and driving out to the game. (If you do want to stay close to the ballpark, look for hotels in the Independence/Blue Springs/Lee's Summit areas. Many are geared toward families and are five miles or so from the sports complex.)

Hotels in downtown Kansas City are geared toward business travelers, but most do offer weekend rates and parking downtown is never a problem on Saturdays and Sundays. One unique downtown hotel is the Hotel Savoy (219 W. 9th St.; *www.bbonline.com/mo/hotelsavoy*; $89-$120), a turn-of-the-century businessman's hotel converted into a boutique hotel.

The J.C. Nichols Country Club Plaza (47th and Broadway; 816/753-0100; *countryclubplaza.com*) is home to several upscale and moderately priced hotels. The Intercontinental Kansas City at the Plaza (401 Ward Pkwy.; *ichotelsgroup.com*; $125-$300) is a fairly typical entry in the high-end chain: the rooms are comfy and well-appointed. The Hotel Raphael (325 Ward Parkway; *raphaelkc.com*; $130-$175) is a quaint, European-style hotel with moderate rates. The rooms are a little smaller, but they're well-appointed, and the staff is very attentive. Nearby is the Hyatt Regency Crown Center (2345 McGee St.; *hyatt.com*; $140-$250).

Several hotels are located near the airport on the far north side. We don't especially recommend them: you're out quite a ways from both downtown Kansas City and the ballpark.

While You're There

You are not near a lot in suburban Jackson County. The development local officials expected after the sports complex opened never occurred, and there's very little close to the ballpark unless your idea of fun is slammin' down a burrito at the gas station.

We'd recommend heading back into Kansas City when you're not at a game. Kansas City may have a rep as a little cowtown on the prairie, but there are definitely enough attractions to keep you busy. The city is best known for two things: ribs and jazz. If you do some planning you can combine them into a single trip.

On the food front, when you talk Kansas City you're talking barbecue. No getting around it. The locals debate who has the best barbecue in the city, with special points awarded the best 'Q served in the tackiest of circumstances. They even debate which is better: beef brisket or pork ribs. Eating barbecue in Kansas City is a rite of passage.

If the locals can't decide on who has the best barbecue in the city, we're certainly not going to have the final say. Here are the leading contenders for best barbecue in Kansas City. It's definitely not a complete list—we're probably missing some hole-in-the-wall joint where the ribs are so succulent the mere scent of them will send you into ecstasy—but you can't go wrong eating at any of these places. All are located near the downtown area.

Arthur Bryant's BBQ (1727 Brooklyn; *arthurbryantsbbq.com*; 812/231-1123) is perhaps the most famous barbecue joint in Kansas City, and rightly so: the beef brisket is renowned far and wide. It's man-styled sloppy food, with the brisket piled on white bread and smothered in vinegary sauce. Everyone is treated the same: you wait in line for your order and pray there's an empty table. Arthur Bryant started selling barbecue in 1946 and his place hasn't changed much.

Fiorella's Jack Stack Barbecue (101 W. 22nd St.; 816/941-4309; *jackstackbbq.com*) is a little more elegant, setting up shop in a former freight house, making it a little more presentable for tourists. The food is presented in a more refined way, though at its heart this is still a Kansas City barbecue joint. Try the lamb ribs for something different.

Gates Barbecue (1221 Brooklyn; *gatesbbq.com*; 816/483-3380) is where out-of-towners will be startled by shouts of "Hi! May I help you?" when they walk through the door. The barbecue here is truly great: the ribs are meaty, the chicken is smoky, and the sandwiches are piled high. The Brooklyn address is the flagship shop; there are other Gates locations throughout the Kansas City area and, as we noted earlier, inside Kauffman Stadium.

Smokin' Joe's Bar-B-Q (101 Southwest Blvd.; 816/421-2282) is a Western-style barbecue, but it's unique in that its sauce seems to be based on a sweeter cinnamon recipe.

B.B.'s Lawnside Barbecue (1205 E. 85th St.; 816/822-7427) is a combination rib joint and night club, excelling at both. You won't find white table linens here—the food is served on Styrofoam plates or plastic baskets lined with wax paper. Go for the ribs: they're a little sweeter than the normal Kansas City version, with a sauce based in brown sugar and apple sauce. There is live music most evenings.

Oklahoma Joe's Barbecue (3002 W. 47th Av.; 913/722-3366; *oklahomajoesbbq.com*) is attached to a gas station and liquor store, winning brownie points among barbecue aficionados. The barbecue isn't your traditional version—the sauce has more of a Carolina twang, and the pulled pork sandwich (topped with cole slaw) is the house specialty.

Winslow's (5th and Walnut; *kc-bbq.com*; 816/471-RIBS) is a relative newcomer to Kansas City, opening in 1971. It follows the standard Kansas City rib formula: huge slabs dripping in sauce.

Danny Edwards Famous Kansas City's Barbecue (1227 Grand Blvd.; 816/283-0880) is known for its beef brisket: Danny Edwards himself smokes 200 pounds of brisket a day. If you ask a local for directions, they'll probably know it as Lil' Jake's Eat It and Beat It.

If barbecue doesn't float your boat there's Kansas City's other red meat: steak. You'd expect great steak in Kansas City and these places won't disappoint. Again, they're located in or near downtown unless otherwise noted.

Hereford House (20th and Main; *herefordhouse.com*; 816/842-1080) is a relative newcomer to the Kansas City steak scene, opening in 1957, but it has the formula down: great steaks (the filet mignon is particularly revered) and prime rib. You can get fish, but it's fried, and a great steak beats fried fish any day of the week. You could go to one of the four other Hereford House locations in the area, but the downtown location is the flagship.

The Majestic Steakhouse (931 Broadway; *majesticsteakhouse.com*; 816/471-8484) has been around since the turn of the century, but the basic offerings haven't changed: huge steaks and thick chops, It's one of the more expensive steakhouses in town, so it's definitely a splurge. A downstairs jazz club features live music and cocktails.

Plaza III, The Steakhouse (4749 Pennsylvania; *plazaiiisteakhouse.com*; 816/753-000) is regarded by many as the best steakhouse in a city known for them. The atmosphere is straight out of a private club, and the offerings are on the simple side: steak or fresh seafood and sides served ala carte. Be prepared to spend several hours dining.

If you're taking our recommendation to stay near the Country Club Plaza area of the city, you'll be within walking distance of some very fine restaurants. Skip the chain restaurants in the area (Cheesecake Factory, P.F. Chang's) and head for these local favorites:

George Brett's (210 W. 47th St.; *georgebretts.com*; 816/561-6565) is a sports bar in a town short on them. The bar features several flat-screen TVs broadcasting games of all kinds, while the menu takes the classic sports-bar offerings (burgers, sandwiches, steaks, pizza) and applies an upscale twist. You'll find the standard sports memorabilia here, but it doesn't overwhelm the modern design.

O'Dowd's Little Dublin (4742 Pennsylvania; *odowdslittledublin.com*; 816/561-2700) may seem out of place as an authentic Irish bar—the bar and fixtures were imported from Ireland—in the middle of Kansas City, but the formula works. Live music is scheduled regularly.

Eden Alley (707 W. 47th Street; *edenalley.com*; 816/561-5415) is located in the basement of Unity Temple and features healthy vegetarian fare. Head there the morning after you've put back way too much beer and ribs the night before; a little cleansing is good for the soul.

The Classic Cup Plaza (301 W. 47th St.; *classiccup.com*; 816/753-1840) features upscale bistro food (Thai chicken pizza, asparagus-and-brie salad) on a lovely patio.

Bo Ling's (4800 Main Street; *bolings.com*; 816/753-1718) is the place for Chinese food in Kansas City. Strictly speaking, it's off the main Plaza area and can be a little hard to find, but it's worth the search. The dim sum weekend brunch is particularly noteworthy.

The Country Club Plaza area is also home to upscale shopping. The plaza area opened in 1922 and at that time was considered suburbia. The 14-square-block development was the brainchild of local developer J.C. Nichols, who kept the project going when the Great Depression threatened to shut him down. Even if you're not a shopping fanatic, it's worth walking around the area to see how well the architecture has fared since the 1920s.

Union Station (30 W. Pershing Rd.; 816/460-2020; *unionstation.org*), located south of downtown, is worth a stop. When Kansas City was at the crossroads of the nation, Union Station was the center of action. It's still the second-largest passenger station in the country (only New York City's Grand Central Terminal is larger) with a 400-by-800-foot Grand Hall that's been fully restored. Today the Amtrak trains still stop in Kansas City, but the station is known more for its added attractions—theater, museums, restaurants, and restored interior—than for its role as a transit hub. The best way to learn about the station is to head to the second-floor exhibit area, which presents the history of the station and shows how bad it had deteriorated before restoration efforts were launched. Be sure to walk outside and watch the Henry Wollman Bloch Fountain on the south side of the station; its 232 jets put on quite the water show. Connected to the station is Crown Center, headquarters for Hallmark, which features shopping and hotels.

Kauffman Stadium is located on the east side of Kansas City, on the way to city of Independence, best known as the home of President Harry S. Truman. The Truman Presidential Library (500 W. U.S. Hwy. 24, Independence; 800/833-1225; *trumanlibrary.org*) honors one of the more unique presidents in American history: he followed a truly great president in Franklin Delano Roosevelt and managed to end World War II while achieving unexpected popularity with his plain-spoken manner. He retired to Independence after his second term; the library honors his tenure as president and features visiting historic exhibitions. Alternately, you may choose a quick, interesting tour of the

Truman home (219 Delaware St., Independence; 816/254-9929; *trumanlibrary.org/trivia/tours.org.*)

Team Ballpark History

The expansion Kansas City Royals began play in 1969 at Municipal Stadium, the former home of the Kansas City Athletics.

Before the Royals and the Athletics, however, there was already was a rich baseball tradition in Kansas City. Municipal Stadium was originally known as Muehlebach Field, which opened on July 3, 1923 as the home of the Kansas City Blues (American Association). Like many owners of the era, George Muehlebach named the grand new home southeast of downtown Kansas City after himself. Muehlebach was a Kansas City hotelier and brewer—the Muehlebach Hotel at 12th and Baltimore was a landmark in downtown Kansas City and is now a Marriott—and he bought the team in 1918, yet another American brewer who entered the baseball business.

The Kansas City Blues were a mainstay of the old American Association, a circuit just below the major leagues operating in Midwest cities such as Minneapolis, Columbus, St. Paul, Milwaukee, and Toledo. The core of the American Association was stable throughout most of that league's history, and Kansas City was regularly among the league leaders in attendance, attracting 425,000 fans in 1923.

Muehlebach Stadium was also the home of the Kansas City Monarchs, an original member of the Negro National League, formed in 1920 in Kansas City. The Monarchs were a huge draw in Kansas City: Opening Day for the Monarchs was filled with pageantry, the Fashion Parade featuring the well-dressed African-Americans of Kansas City making their way to the ballpark. At Kauffman Stadium there is a small display honoring the Monarchs.

The New York Yankees bought the Blues from Muehlebach in 1937 and renamed the ballpark Ruppert Stadium. (Ruppert had a history of buying ballparks and renaming them Ruppert Stadium: the home of the International League's Newark Bears was also named Ruppert Stadium when the Yankees owned the team.) That name lasted until 1943 when the ballpark was renamed Blues Stadium. Until the Athletics moved to town, the Blues remained a top farm team of the Yankees; Mickey Mantle played there in 1951.

The ballpark's original configuration featured a single, partially covered grandstand and no outfield seating. It remained relatively unchanged until 1954 when Arnold Johnson announced a move of his Philadelphia Athletics to Kansas City and the city agreed on an expanded ballpark for the team, paying $2.5 million from the proceeds of a bond issue. Muehlebach Field then became Municipal Stadium, a 30,296-seat ballpark that opened on April 12, 1955. The seating capacity was expanded with the addition of a covered second deck, while bleachers were temporarily moved into the right-field area to accommodate large crowds. (Also part of the renovation: the scoreboard from Braves Field in Boston was purchased and moved to Kansas City.) It served as the home of the A's until owner Charlie Finley moved the team to Oakland after the 1967 season.

A display at 22nd Street and Brooklyn Avenue commemorates the ballpark's site.

Local Baseball Attractions

At the game you'll want to visit the Royals Hall of Fame, located behind Section 107 (shown below). It's not very large, but it does highlight many of the great players who wore Royal blue; the 1985 World Series trophy is on display as well.

Kansas City has been a hotbed of professional baseball since the turn of the century, both in terms of minor-league baseball and Negro League baseball.

A mandatory stop for baseball fans is the Negro Leagues Baseball Museum (1616 E. 18th St.; 816/221-1920; *nlbm.com*), located at 18th and Vine, the historic heart of the Kansas City African-American community. The Negro Leagues (there were several leagues across the country, though many fans tend to lump them together) featured some of the best baseball of its era—many claim Josh Gibson was the greatest player who ever lived—and the Kansas City Monarchs were the royal team of the era when Satchel Paige, Buck O'Neil, and Gibson played at Muehlebach Field (mentioned in the previous section). The Negro National League was formed in Kansas City in 1920, but the museum honors all of the Negro leagues as well as the first African-American players with each major-league team. Begin your tour by watching a film showing the stars of the era in action, followed by memorabilia, uniforms, advertising, and other artifacts from the era. The centerpiece of the museum's design is a diamond honoring the nine best Negro Leagues players.

Though the Negro Leagues existed from 1920 through a last gasp in 1960,

their real heyday came in the 1930s and 1940s when stars like Gibson and Paige drew large crowds to major-league ballparks (Griffith Stadium, the home of the Washington Senators, sometimes drew larger crowds for Homestead Grays games than for Sens matches). Ironically, integration killed the Negro Leagues when Jackie Robinson (who started in the Negro Leagues), Larry Doby, Satchel Paige, and other luminaries jumped to the major leagues, leaving the Negro Leagues without many box-office draws. Admission for the Negro Leagues Baseball Museum is $6 for adults, $2.50 for children.

The same complex houses the American Jazz Museum (1616 E. 18th St.; 816/474-8463; *americanjazzmuseum.com*). Between the 1920s and the 1940s, Kansas City was the crossroads of the American music world, with local musicians like Charlie Parker swapping chops with nationally known greats like Duke Ellington, Count Basie, and Louis Armstrong. The jazz played in Kansas City was party jazz: heavy on the beat and designed for dancing, though the museum commemorates all types of American jazz. The Blue Room attached to the museum books live music. Admission for the American Jazz Museum is $6 for adults and $2.50 for children, but you can buy a joint pass covering both museums: $8 for adults, $4 for children under 12.

The Kansas City T-Bones (1800 Village West Pkwy.; Kansas City, KS; *tbonesbaseball.com;* 913/328-BALL) of the independent Northern League play at CommunityAmerica Ballpark in Kansas City, Kansas.

St. Joseph, located 56 miles north of Kansas City, is known as the gateway to the west, but it's also the home of Phil Welch Stadium. Today, the ballpark is used by the St. Joseph Blacksnakes of the independent American Association, but in the 1930s and 1940s it was home to various minor-league Western Association teams and a regular stop for the Kansas City Monarchs, according to Buck O'Neil: "We used to play here, and this place used to be packed," O'Neil told the St. Joseph News-Press in 2005. "We'd play a doubleheader in Kansas City on Sunday, a night game Monday, Tuesday we were in St. Joe, Wednesday in Omaha and Thursday in Des Moines." Phil Welch Stadium is well worth a drive these days. If you go, take note: the light stanchions in the outfield are all in play.

Oakland Athletics
McAfee Coliseum

Address: 7000 Coliseum Way, Oakland, CA 94621.
Cost: $25.5 million (original construction), $200 million (1996 expansion).
Architect: Skidmore, Owings & Merrill (original 1966 design); HNTB (1996 expansion).
Owner: City of Oakland and Alameda County.
Capacity: 34,077.
Dimensions: 330L, 367LC, 362LC, 400C, 362RC, 388RC, 330R.
Ticket Line: 510/762-BALL.
Playing Surface: Grass.
Home Dugout Location: Third-base side.
Other Tenants: The NFL's Oakland Raiders played here from 1966 to 1981 and moved back in 1994.
Previous Names: Oakland-Alameda County Coliseum (1966-1998), Network Associates Coliseum (1998-2004), also called "The Net." During all this time the prevailing nickname for the stadium has been the Coliseum.
First Game: On April 17, 1968, the Oakland Athletics lost to the Baltimore Orioles 4-2 before a crowd of 50,164. Boog Powell, Mark Belanger, and Brooks Robinson all homered off losing pitcher Lew Krausse, while Dave McNally went the distance for the O's.
Landmark Event: The Oakland A's ended 40 years of playoff futility by winning the American League West Division in 1971, but that appearance ended in a playoff sweep at the hands of the Baltimore Orioles (adding insult to injury, the Orioles clinched a trip to the World Series in the first playoff game ever played at Oakland-Alameda County Coliseum). In 1972, the A's found the

formula and won the franchise's first World Series since 1930 (four games to three over the Cincinnati Reds), repeating in 1973 and 1974. The A's claimed a World Series victory again in 1989, sweeping the San Francisco Giants 4-0. After the A's won the first two games in Oakland, the third game at Candlestick Park was halted by an earthquake and ultimately delayed for 10 days while the Bay Area recovered from the destruction. The A's won the next two games at Candlestick Park.

Your McAfee Coliseum Seating Crib Sheet

Best Sections to View a Game: Technically speaking, all the seats in the circular McAfee Coliseum face the infield. The issue, really, is how far away you are sitting from said infield. There are two very good sections in the ballpark: the outfield bleachers and the Field Level Seats near the foul lines. The cheapest seats in the ballpark are the bleacher seats, and you don't need to worry about ushers preventing access. The Field Level seats are zealously guarded by ushers no matter how small the crowd.

Best Cheap Seats: The bleachers. At $10 a pop, you'll have a good view of the action and be joined by the most interesting fans in the ballpark. The bleachers are where the hardcore, passionate A's fans sit, and chances are good they'll be as entertaining as what's going on in the game.

Most Underrated Sections: Though they're a little pricey at $30, the Field Level seats in Sections 103-106 and 128-130 afford great views of the action.

Seats to Avoid: Truthfully, the Oakland A's did everyone a favor by blocking off the upper deck of McAfee Coliseum at the beginning of the 2006 season: the upper-deck seats were among some of the worst in baseball, even in back of home plate. Thanks to the circular grandstand, most seats face the infield—but the sections past the bases are set off quite a ways from the action, as the circular football/baseball design dictates there being a sea of foul space.

McAfee Coliseum: A Concrete Doughnut

Walk around the stadium concourse and you can tell once upon a time McAfee Coliseum was a pretty nice sporting facility. But while time marched on and change came to the rest of baseball, things stood still in Oakland. McAfee Coliseum is now one of the oldest facilities in the American League and the oldest multiuse facility (only Fenway Park and Kauffman Stadium are older; Angel Stadium, too, opened in 1966 but was extensively renovated in 1996). Today, the home of the Oakland Athletics is an acceptable but hardly outstanding major-league facility, with baseball clearly playing second fiddle to the NFL's Oakland Raiders.

Too bad: Oakland is a better baseball community than people assume, but the powers-that-be have done their best to snuff out interest in baseball in the East Bay. It's clear there's not much of a future for professional baseball in McAfee Coliseum, making the team's search for a new ballpark such an imperative.

McAfee Coliseum is a multiuse facility, typical of its era (think Minneapolis's Metropolitan Stadium, Philadelphia's Veterans Stadium, et al) that's managed to exist in suburbia when single-use downtown facilities are the rage. On one hand, the location does make access easy, and the presence of a Bay Area Rapid Transit (BART) station to the east of the ballpark makes access even easier for those who want to avoid the $14 parking fee. But on the other hand, the majority of seats are geared toward watching a football game, with the newest and spiffiest facilities—contained in the center-field monstrosity built to lure the Raiders back from Los Angeles—farthest from the playing field.

The Coliseum won't impress you as you approach from the freeway. It's not an especially pleasing exterior, made less so by a sea of concrete and asphalt. And you're probably not going to get chills down your spine when entering the ballpark unless you're a hardcore fan summoning the ghosts of Charlie O. Finley and Athletics teams of the past.

Once inside, the ballpark layout is fairly standard: a concourse sits in back of the seating areas and rings the ballpark. The concourse is fairly narrow so you'll be fighting traffic in any popular area, and for some reason the concourse is sheltered from the field at spots, so you can't watch the action while heading for a beer. The circular shape of the bowl means there are some awkwardly configured seats (like the left-field bleacher seats) and a huge foul area, which places fans even farther away from the field. Too bad the configuration is horrible for bleacher fans: both right-field and left-field bleachers feature some rabid and passionate A's fans, complete with banners and clappers. If they're indicative of the potential passion of baseball fans in Oakland, we imagine management is right to continue seeking a new ballpark in the area.

While there were always bleachers in center field, the monstrosity featuring suites and additional seating was added in 1996 when the Raiders were lured back to Oakland from Los Angeles. (Before the addition, the ballpark featured a lovely view of the California countryside.) The lower bleachers and club area

are sold for Athletics games, but the upper bleachers are not, making for a more intimate feel at Athletics games.

That looming center-field section may make sense for football (the football field is laid out parallel) but adds little for baseball. It also eliminated some views of the California foothills and created an insular environment.

If that's not enough, there's one more fatal flaw with the ballpark: the vast majority of the seating is set far, far away from the action. Pitchers may love the wide expanses of foul space, but fans don't. The Athletics added some big-buck seats closer to the playing field, but that doesn't really help most fans. The second-level club section is set way back from the playing field.

TRIVIA

Oakland uses a white elephant as a marketing symbol—a symbol for the team since its earliest days. New York Giants manager John McGraw derisively dismissed the Athletics franchise as a "white elephant"—that is, a rare object expensive to maintain—for spending too much money after he raided the incumbent Phillies for several players. Athletics owner Ben Shibe and manager Connie Mack seized on the image and marketed the team around a white elephant, at one point placing an elephant logo on the jersey front. (Ironically, later in his career Mack became known as tight with the pursestrings.)

Charlie O. Finley dumped the elephant when he bought the Kansas City Athletics, replacing it with a mule (Finley had a thing for mules, as you'll see later in the chapter). The Oakland Athletics resuscitated the white elephant in 1988 and it's been a central part of the team's marketing efforts ever since.

The spread-out design also ensures there are virtually no seats in the shade for an afternoon game, except the last 12 rows in the lower level.

In the end, you've got to feel a little sorry for Oakland A's fans. They remain passionate in the face of high prices and a fairly lousy ballpark desecrated to attract a football team. The future of baseball in the Bay Area won't be with McAfee Coliseum, and that's a good thing.

Ballpark Quirks

The biggest quirk is the vast amount of real estate between the foul lines and the grandstand. You can be sitting in the front row behind home plate and still feel remote from the action. Interestingly, the most intimate seats in the ballpark are down the lines where the grandstand circles back to the playing field. The bullpens are located down each line where the grandstand curve is most pronounced; sit in back of them and you can see how cheaply the plywood bullpen roofs were constructed.

Food and Drink

There is an abundance of concession stands ringing the concourse with a wide variety of offerings. The beer selection is impressive if not a little spendy ($7.50 for a premium brew): Widmer, Gordon Biersch, Sierra Nevada, Pyramid, Stella Artois, Red Hook, and Tecate. Of course, you can also drink Bud, Bud Light, MGD, Lite, and Coors Light.

The Grilled Coliseum Dog ($4.50), made by Miller's, is tasty; there are also tofu dogs for the meatless crowd. Other stands feature excellent BBQ (don't forget the sweet-potato pie), Saag's Sausages, fish and chips, and vegetarian offerings (outside section 109). Speaking of Biersch: You can find their legendary garlic fries at a few stands, but it will take some work (try outside section 116).

If you want to eat at a picnic table overlooking the field, BBQ terraces are located down each line.

Other premium areas include The Field, an Irish pub featuring Guinness, Bass and Harp on tap, and Irish whiskies by the glass. Also, the suite-level club is open to anyone; it features table service, a Mexican booth (with Cuervo margs for $10), and a bar.

The best food in the house, however, is tucked away at the Black Muslim Bakery, which features a fine bean pie, veggie burgers and hot dogs (which are also available at many other concession booths), and ginger lemonade.

Oakland runs perhaps the most egalitarian ballpark in the majors. Some of the concessions in the center-field section—mainly given over to suites—are open to all (making it a convenient beer stop if you're sitting in the bleachers), while the West Side Club is accessible as well. It features several concession stands (including a panini stand and a Mexican eatery) and sitdown service.

For the Kids

With the emphasis on beer and food, we didn't feel McAfee Coliseum was a very kid-friendly place. The Stomper Zone, located outside the ballpark behind Section 220, features batting cages, pitching games, and a playground, but a parent will sacrifice watching part of the game in order to entertain the kids.

Ballpark Tours

The Athletics offer weekly tours every Thursday at 11 a.m. and 2 p.m. The cost is $8 and tour stops include the A's dugout, the visitors' clubhouse, a batting cage, and the press box. Reservations are required; call 510/563-2230.

Local Baseball Attractions

The biggest baseball attraction in the Bay Area is AT&T Park, the home of the San Francisco Giants. We cover it in its own chapter.

Several minor-league teams play in the region. Worth a drive is Raley Field (400 Ballpark Dr., West Sacramento; *rivercats.com*; 916/376-4700), home of the Sacramento River Cats, the Triple-A affiliate of the Athletics. Raley Field is not the flashiest of ballparks, lacking the sort of signature item found in most top-tier ballparks, but it is certainly one of the most beloved ballparks in the minors. During the night of our most recent visit the temperature was over 100 degrees, yet the ballpark was packed, with an actual crowd over 10,000. (It was the eighth consecutive crowd of over 10,000, including the Triple-A All-Star Game and All-Star Monday.) Any ballpark drawing these sorts of numbers is doing something right; Raley Field has been the most popular new minor-league ballpark built in the last 10 years.

Also worth a drive, albeit a longer one: Banner Island Ballpark (404 W. Fremont St., Stockton; *stocktonports.com*; 209/644-1900), home of the Stockton Ports of the Class A California League. Banner Island Ballpark is quite a pleasant ballpark sitting on the edge of downtown Stockton. The model is basic: there a single level of seating with a concourse wrapping the entire ballpark. Though the effect comes off a little sparse—the 4,200 fixed seats are between the foul poles, while there's additional berm and patio seating in the outfield—the end result is most fans will have a good view of the game without feeling too confined.

With such a large concourse, there's plenty of room to stand around and watch a game. During our visit—when the temperature had already hit 100 degrees before an early-afternoon gametime—fans were taking advantage of the many shaded areas for a good chunk of the game.

Getting There

The Coliseum complex is located next to I-880. If you're coming in from downtown Oakland or San Francisco, take the 66th Avenue exit and follow the signs; if you're coming in from the south, you can either take the 66th Avenue exit or the Hegenberger Road exit, where you'll turn left onto Coliseum Way after leaving the freeway.

Parking is a steep $14 (season-ticket holders pay half price) but there is a ton of it surrounding the ballpark. Because of the abundance of room to spread out, a parking lot is a popular spot for tailgating before and after games. The only restriction on tailgating: no kegs allowed.

Oddly enough, despite the sea of parking (9,600 spots), it's a cumbersome process to get in and out of the ballpark. There are only two entrances off I-880—on the north and south sides of the complex—and the south entrance to the complex is unmarked. You can expect to wait a line a while before paying your $14 for parking, which seems a little insulting.

If you want to avoid parking, the Bay Area Rapid Transit (BART) Fremont/Richmond line has a stop at the Coliseum. You can take the BART all the way from San Francisco International Airport; it takes about one hour and requires one transfer. BART trains run until midnight. Call 510/464-6000 or visit bart.gov for more information.

Handicapped-Accessible Seating
Fewer than 125 handicapped-accessible seats are available in the stadium, and those are contained in a small number of areas.

Where to Stay
The Coliseum area is set in an industrial park, so don't expect a lot of charm if you want to stay close to the complex. Most of the closest hotels are clustered south of the complex, off I-880 and Hegenberger Road: the Days Inn Oakland Airport Coliseum (8350 Edes Av.; *daysinn.com*; $60-$75), the Clarion Hotel Oakland Airport (500 Hegenberger Rd.; *choicehotels.com*; $75-$100), the La Quinta Inn Oakland Airport (8465 Enterprise Way; *lq.com*; $70-$100), the Quality Inn Oakland Airport (8471 Enterprise Hwy.; *choicehotels.com*; $70-$90), the Fairfield Inn Oakland Airport (8452 Edes Av.; *marriott.com*; $65-$75), and the Courtyard by Marriott (350 Hegenberger Rd.; *marriott.com*; $99-$129). Be warned you won't be strolling through a charming neighborhood to get to the stadium from these fine establishments; you'll be lucky if you have a sidewalk.

If you're driving anyway, there are a number of nicer hotels closer to the airport, down Hegenberger Road, including the Hilton Oakland Airport (1 Hegenberger Rd.; *hilton.com*; $100-$150) and the Holiday Inn Express Suites Airport (66 Airport Access Rd.; *holiday-inn.com*; $95-$125).

We mention Oakland's Jack London Square elsewhere in this chapter, where there is a hotel worth checking out: the upscale Waterfront Plaza Hotel (10 Washington St.; *waterfrontplaza.com*; $125-$175).

Local Attractions
If you love being in an industrial park, you'll love hanging around the McAfee Coliseum area. There is nothing else in the area: no hotels, no restaurants, no bars, nada.

You'll need to look elsewhere for entertainment. Oakland is only 10 miles away from San Francisco and many baseball fans will stay there or somewhere on the west side of the Bay. It's easy enough to get to Oakland from San Francisco (just avoid the rush hour) by taking the Bay Bridge (I-580) to Oakland and then heading south on I-880 to the Coliseum complex.

Those more interested in a relaxing weekend will want to check out Oakland's Jack London Square (*jacklondonsquare.com*) as a base of operations. Originally developed as a tourist trap a la Ghirardelli Square in San Francisco, Jack London Square has evolved into an appealing mix of mellow businesses (i.e. coffeehouses galore), some curious attractions (like FDR's yacht), chain stores, bars, and restaurants. You'll also find a small section of an Alaskan cabin once occupied by author Jack London—who also spent more than his fair share of time in the shacks along the waterfront—there as well. Worth a visit: the small Heinold's First and Last Chance Saloon (48 Webster Street in Jack London Square; 510/839-6761; *heinoldsfirstandlastchance.com*), a bar where London actually spent time; the charmingly retro Oyster Bar (1000 Embarcadero; 510/836-2519; *oyster-reef.com*); the upscale Soizic Bistro (300 Broadway; 510/251-8100; *soizicbistro.com*); and the museum and gift shop at Peerless Coffee & Tea (260 Oak St.; 800/310-KONA; *peerlesscoffee.com*), supplier of fine coffees and teas to the entire Bay Area.

Another option—and one we highly recommend—is spending a lot of time in Berkeley on your baseball trip. Berkeley is best known for the liberal environs of the University of California-Berkeley, but aside from academia, Berkeley is a charming small town, filled with great restaurants. (It's also filled with mediocre hotels. Stay there at your own risk.) The place to go is Telegraph Avenue where you'll find a host of small shops, coffeehouses (like Peet's), and restaurants.

Team Ballpark History

The Philadelphia Athletics franchise was an original member of the American League, beginning play in 1901. There had been several amateur teams and a National Association team called the Philadelphia Athletics in the late 1880s, and minority owner Cornelius MacGillicuddy was wise enough to co-opt that name recognition when he formed his team. He certainly knew a thing or two about name recognition: we know him as Connie Mack, one of the major baseball figures of the 20th Century.

Mack was no stranger to baseball before arriving in Philadelphia, playing for the Washington Nationals and the Pittsburgh Pirates before arriving in Milwaukee for a four-year stint as manager of the Western League's Milwaukee Brewers. There he met up with Ban Johnson, Charles Comiskey, and the other founders of the American League, securing a spot with the Philadelphia franchise in the fledgling venture in partnership with Ben Shibe.

Mack became synonymous with Philadelphia baseball, serving as manager and eventually owning the A's until his retirement after the 1950 season. At the end he was regarded as a quaint curiosity because he never donned a uniform in the dugout while managing, but he had an impressive record as a manager,

Shibe Park circa 1913. In the chapter on the Citizens Bank Park we show how Shibe Park—then known as Connie Mack Stadium—looked after the Phillies moved out. You can see many differences. (Courtesy Library of Congress, LOT 11147-3 [P&P].)

winning 3,731 games and losing 3,948 in his 7,755-game managerial career (all three are MLB records unlikely to be broken). He also won nine pennants and five World Series during that stretch, with his 1929 team considered one the best in baseball history, featuring the likes of Jimmie Foxx, Mickey Cochrane, Al Simmons, Mule Haas, Bing Miller, Lefty Grove, George Earnshaw, Rube Walberg, and Jack Quinn.

The Athletics' first home was Columbia Park, a 9,500-seat ballpark at 29th and Columbia in Brewerytown. It was a simple wooden ballpark with a covered grandstand between the bases and open bleachers down each line. It never featured dugouts so players sat on an open bench. Despite the limited seating, the Athletics drew well and packed the ballpark often past posted capacity. Based on the team's following and the promise of financial windfall, Shibe and Mack planned a grand new palace of baseball to open for the 1909 season.

Indeed, the Philadelphia Athletics are most closely associated with Shibe Park, the team's home from 1909 through 1954. Located at 21st Street and Lehigh Avenue north of downtown Philadelphia, that part of Philly—dubbed Swampoodle—was farmland when Benjamin Shibe built a 23,000-seat, $315,248 ballpark on a 5.75-acre site. After years of battling fires in wooden facilities, the baseball industry was moving to a concrete-and-steel phase of construction (Wrigley Field, Forbes Field, Fenway Park, Ebbets Field, and Cleveland's League Park were all built in the same era), and Shibe Park was considered one of the finest ballparks of that era. The signature item at Shibe Park was the domed tower and cupola (housing team offices) at the main entrance, but there were decorative elements throughout the stadium: ornamental scrollwork decorated the exterior while arched windows allowed plenty of light into the grandstand. The Swampoodle area of Philadelphia was not exactly attractive when Shibe bought the former site of the Philadelphia Hospital for Contagious Diseases, and it would take a flashy facility to attract hordes of fans to the new ballpark. It also acknowledged the future with parking under the bleachers for 200 cars.

The Athletics were highly successful at Shibe Park. In the early days, excess crowds could be accommodated with standing-room-only space behind a rope in the outfield (though the Athletics added outfield bleachers in 1915 to address this need), but eventually the Athletics faced the same problem suffered by other successful teams: ballpark neighbors would erect stands on their houses and sell tickets. In Chicago this ended up being an endearing and colorful addition to Wrigleyville, but other owners saw it as money taken from their pockets. Mack ended up erecting a 34-foot-high fence across the right-field wall to deter crowds from gathering outside the ballpark.

Shibe Park was the sporting center of Philadelphia: the Philadelphia Phillies moved there from Baker Bowl in 1938 and the NFL's Philadelphia Eagles played there from 1940 to 1957.

Cornelius MacGillicuddy, better known as Connie Mack. (Courtesy Library of Congress, LC-B2- 2315-4[P&P].)

In the final year of the Athletics' stay the ballpark was renamed Connie Mack Stadium. The Phillies played at Connie Mack until 1970 when Veterans Stadium opened. The ballpark was torn down in 1976; today there is an evangelical church on the site with the pulpit positioned where home plate once laid.

The next home of the Athletics was Kansas City's Municipal Stadium after owner Arnold Johnson and the city agreed on an expanded ballpark for the team, paying $2.5 million from the proceeds of a bond issue. Muehlebach Field was formerly the home of the American Association's Kansas City Blues and the Kansas City Monarchs of the Negro Leagues, but after the renovation it became known as Municipal Stadium, a 30,296-seat ballpark opening on April 12, 1955. The seating capacity was expanded with the addition of a covered second deck, while bleachers were moved temporarily into the right-field area to accommodate large crowds. (Also part of the renovation: the scoreboard from Braves Field in Boston was purchased and moved to Kansas City.) It served as the home of the A's until owner Charlie Finley moved the team to Oakland after the 1967 season.

It was at Municipal Stadium where Finley first began his outrageous promotional antics. He installed a petting zoo down the left-field line, complete with monkeys, pheasants, goats, and Charlie O, a mule that became a Finley trademark. It was also at Municipal Stadium where Finley first ran

The east entrance to the Shibe Park grandstand. (Courtesy Library of Congress, HABS PA,51-PHILA,683-5.)

The Complete Guide to Big League Ballparks

The crowd gathers at Shibe Park for the opening game of the World Series on October 9, 1914. The Athletics were swept by the Braves. (Courtesy Library of Congress, LC-B2-3260-9[P&P].)

afoul of baseball's powers-that-be when he installed a 296-foot home-run "Pennant Porch" down the right-field line in 1965; Commissioner Ford Frick ordered it be removed, even though Finley argueg it was the same distance as the famous right-field porch in Yankee Stadium. Finley then built a fence 325 feet from home plate—the minimum allowed at the time under MLB rules—and called it the "One-Half Pennant Porch." (He was a constant tinkerer with the ballpark's dimensions; in 1967 the height of the right-field fence was raised to 40 feet.) And we can't forget Finley's love of mechanical gimmicks: "Harvey," a mechanical rabbit, rose out of the ground with new baseballs for the home-plate umpire, and a compressed-air device blew dirt off the plate.

The expansion Kansas City Royals played at Municipal Stadium until 1973 when Royals Stadium opened. After the Royals moved, Municipal Stadium was torn down in 1976 and a community garden now stands on the site.

The Complete Guide to Big League Ballparks

Minnesota Twins
Hubert H. Humphrey Metrodome

Address: 34 Kirby Puckett Place, Minneapolis, MN 55415
Cost: $55 million.
Architect: Skidmore, Owings and Merrill.
Owner: Metropolitan Sports Facilities Commission.
Capacity: 48,678.
Dimensions: 343L, 385LC, 408C, 367RC, 327R.
Ticket Lines: 612/33-TWINS or 800/ 33-TWINS.
Home Dugout Location: Third-base line.
Playing Surface: Sports Turf (1982-1987), Astroturf (1987-2003), AstroPlay (2004-present)
Other Tenants: Minnesota Vikings (NFL), University of Minnesota Golden Gophers (NCAA football). The Metrodome also was the inaugural home of the NBA's Minnesota Timberwolves.
First Game: On April 6, 1982, the Twins drew 52,279 fans for the first regular-season game at the Dome. The Seattle Mariners defeated the Twins 11-7 despite a 4-for-4 effort from rookie 3B Gary Gaetti, who slammed two homers and almost had a third when he tried to stretch a triple into an inside-the-park homer.
Landmark Events: 1985 All-Star Game (won by the National League 6-1), 1987 World Series (won by the Twins over the St. Louis Cardinals, 4-3), and the 1991 World Series (won by the Twins over the Atlanta Braves, 4-3). The Metrodome is also the only facility to play host to the World Series, All-Star Game, Super Bowl (1992), and NCAA Final Four Basketball Tournament.

Your Metrodome Seating Crib Sheet

The Twins now offer variable pricing after raising ticket prices for "premium" games—the matches likely to attract the largest crowds. These are baseline prices.

Best Sections to View a Game: Sections 119-131, particularly in the first 15 rows. At $44, these are reasonably priced ducats. Past that you're fairly distant from the action and might as well be sitting in the upper deck for half the price.

Best Cheap Seats: These would be some, but not all, of the $7 Cheap Seats section. Our favorite sections are 210-212. The chief drawback is you'll miss some plays in deep right field, but otherwise you'll be pretty close to the action. Avoid sections 203-234: you're high up *and* remote from the action. (In a ballpark quirk, the sections in the Upper Deck aren't arranged numerically. So watch the section numbers closely.)

Most Underrated Sections: Section 221-228, particularly in the first 7 rows. They're so good the Twins boosted ticket prices significantly for these seats in 2006; they now go for $22 per game. We remember when they were $10.

Seats to Avoid: More than half the seats in the Metrodome are terrible. The worst offenders are sections 113-117 and 133-139 (these sections face center field and require you to crane your neck toward home plate to see the action); they're also overpriced at $29. The reserved Home Run Porch seats in left field (sections 100-106, 140-141) are way overpriced at $19; since the better outfield seats are held by season-ticket holders (yes, they're all assigned), you have virtually no chance at catching a homer and are too far from the action. (To make things worse, the front row of that section is blocked off.) It's not worth paying $12 to sit in the "family" non-alcoholic sections (215-216); most Minnesotans handle their expensive stadium beers with kid gloves and rarely get out of hand so there's little reason to sequester your family in some horrible corner seats.

Metrodome: Coasting on Memories

When it first opened, the Hubert H. Humphrey Metrodome was hailed by many as a ballpark of the future, a refinement on earlier domes that allowed for more flexibility and a better atmosphere. With a slightly translucent roof, you could tell when the sun was out. With retractable seats and a pitching mound that lowers to ground level, the Metrodome could host a Twins game beginning in the late morning and have the field converted in time for an evening Vikings or Gophers football game. And since it is climate-controlled, those farmers from North Dakota making their yearly pilgrimage to Minneapolis would be assured of a Twins game no matter how bad the weather is outside.

Why, it even came in under budget.

Today the Metrodome is reviled by almost everyone involved with it; the only variance seems to be how much people hate it. (Confession time: we complain incessantly about the Hump, yet we manage to fork over our bucks for partial season tickets each year.) It's sterile, say longtime Twins fans, especially on one of those glorious June Minnesota nights. In fact, many Twins fans actively avoid going to games at the Dome, preferring instead to follow their Twinkies on the road in Milwaukee, Chicago, and Kansas City.

Is the Metrodome that unlovable? For the most part, yes. The concourses are cramped, monotonous in their sterile concrete sheen, and poorly lit. The concessions are limited and the amenities are few. Since a bureaucratic sports commission owns and runs the place, there's little stress on customer service and little thought given to fan comfort. You have no spots to stand around and just watch the game, making it impossible to move around during a game and view the action from a few different viewpoints. Unless your seat is between the bases or in the outfield bleachers, be prepared to crane your neck for most of a game.

It's just not a very good place to view a game unless you're in the ballpark's few sweet spots. The Metrodome was designed for football and the sightlines show it. Overall the Metrodome has a rectangular configuration ideal for football, and one side of the seats retract to provide enough space for a baseball diamond and full outfield. It's a pretty compact playing field: the right-field foul pole is only 327 feet from home plate and the 23-foot-high "baggie" out in right field makes the Metrodome semi-respectable as a baseball facility while also covering up most of the 7,600 retracted seats. (It also gives opposing outfielders fits: while Fenway Park's Green Monster is solid, the baggie has so much slack many balls slide directly down to the warning track.)

The many quirks lead to the most interesting thing about the Metrodome: it is the MLB ballpark where ground rules and odd dimensions impact a game the most, giving the Twins a definite home-field advantage. If you look at the stats, there were years when a lot of home runs were hit in the Metrodome, attributed by many to the cozy dimensions of the Dome. This led the Twins to install Plexiglas windows on top of the left-field wall. Today, the windows are gone and fewer homers fly to the stands.

The ballpark hasn't changed, so what's the deal? In the Homerdome days, the Twins had plenty of players (Kent Hrbek, Tom Brunansky, Kirby Puckett, Gary Gaetti) capable of hitting 30+ homers in a season, while the pitching staffs were fairly weak. In 1999-2001, the Dome became the fifth-stingiest ballpark for homers (behind Oakland, Seattle, Boston, and Detroit), and the Twins hit more homers on the road than in the Dome. Today, the Twins have strong pitching staffs (Johan Santana won the 2004 and 2006 American League Cy Young Awards) and a roster made up mostly of utility infielders, and the homer rate is down dramatically.

The stats may be a little misleading in this instance.

Still, the Twins do use the Metrodome to their advantage. For instance, much of the outfield "wall" has a good amount of give, which allowed Kirby Puckett and Torii Hunter to wow crowds with their leaping grabs of balls seemingly destined to be hit beyond their reach. The center field fence technically is 408 feet from home plate, but realistically it's at least three or four feet more than that when you consider the give. Puckett and Hunter used that give to their advantage, being two of the best outfielders ever to use a defensive play to turn a game around.

The backstop is oddly offset in the corner of the rectangle, making seats in the immediate ball diamond corner pretty decent for baseball, but leaving almost every other seat in the place awkwardly situated for that game. The angled backstop also leads to some weird caroms on wild pitches and passed balls.

And then there's the roof. Opposing players hate the roof, especially on a summer afternoon when the sun is high and enough light comes through to brighten it. You can count on five or six visiting players per season losing fly balls, which is pretty entertaining. Sadly, the lives of opposing outfielders became easier when AstroPlay was installed at the Dome: it's less bouncy than AstroTurf, so it's now rare for a ball to bounce over the head of a rapidly charging outfielder.

TRIVIA

The Metrodome roof has never totally collapsed, although it's come close a few times. The most memorable time came during the seventh inning of an April 26, 1986 game between the Twins and the California Angels. A heavy storm tore a hole in the outer skin of the roof, causing it to sag and leak rainwater onto the playing surface. The roof was designed to be self-healing in such an instance, however, and although the roof sagged enough to lower the lights almost to the upper-deck seats, the healing mechanism kicked in and the roof reinflated. Two of the authors of this book were at that game and had the indescribable pleasure of hearing longtime Twins announcer Bob Casey ask folks—in an agitated voice—to calmly evacuate to the concourses. Nine minutes after the roof started sagging, the turf was vacuumed and the game resumed. By the way, the home team was deflated far more than the roof that day. The Twins lost 7-6 after the Angels rallied for six runs in the ninth inning.

On April 14, 1983, a scheduled game against the California Angels was postponed after the roof was torn by the weight of heavy snow. It is the only postponed game in Metrodome history.

Even though we mock the Metrodome roof, it actually was an engineering marvel when first constructed. Despite the appearance it's not a cloth-based roof: instead, it's 10 acres of Teflon-coated fiberglass in two layers. And it's not as light as it appears, weighing 580,000 pounds. The air in the Metrodome must be constantly pressurized in order to keep the roof inflated. This accounts for the constant breezes flowing through the Dome.

It also accounts for the stories of the Metrodome fans being turned on and off to supposedly benefit the home team. Yes, the air movement is usually pronounced at the end of a game, but that's also the time when fans are leaving the Dome, causing a drop in air pressure. Have the Twins manipulated the air conditioning? We don't know. Do rumors of air-conditioning shenanigans play mind games on opposing players? That's for sure.

Outfielders may hate the roof, but batters aren't always thrilled with the ground rules at the Metrodome, either. There's a lot of stuff hanging from the Metrodome roof—lights, speakers, a catwalk, some lighting grids for concerts—and occasionally a home run will turn into a double, a foul ball, or an out after striking a cable or another fixture. Several players have hit balls off the roof: the Twins' Randy Bush did so in 1983 (it was caught in foul ground by the Blue Jays' Buck Martinez for an out), while the Tigers' Rob Deer bounced

TRIVIA

Only one batter has hit the ball out of the Metrodome. On May 4, 1984, Dave Kingman, then with the Oakland A's, hit a popup through one of the many ventilation holes in the Metrodome roof. He was awarded a ground-rule double for his troubles, despite loud complaints from the A's coaching staff.

two off the roof on May 30, 1992, with Twins shortstop Greg Gagne catching both. That same season Chili Davis hit a blast to right field that struck a speaker and caromed to Orioles second baseman Mark McLemore, who caught it for an out. (The ground rules are not very clear. If a ball hits a speaker or roof in fair territory, the final landing point for the ball determines whether it's fair or foul. So let's say Joe Mauer really gets his back into one and launches a mammoth shot down the right-field line, but it hits a speaker. If the ball heads into the stands, it's a foul ball. If it lands somewhere in center field, it's a fair ball. If it's caught by a fielder, it's an out. However, if Mauer pops one and it hits a speaker in foul territory, it will forever be a foul ball—and an out if caught by a fielder.)

Despite all the quirks, the Metrodome has been home to many of the most memorable World Series games in history. The Twins have never lost a World Series game at the Metrodome, winning all eight home games in the 1987 and 1991 Series without garnering a single road victory either year. Nary will a Twins fan forget Dan Gladden's dramatic grand-slam homer against the St. Louis Cardinals in 1987 in the first World Series game played indoors. The 1991 World Series against the Atlanta Braves was even more memorable for its dramatics. Wrestling fan Kent Hrbek put a hold on Atlanta outfield Ron Gant and forced him off first base while tagging him out, preserving a Twins victory in Game 2. Kirby Puckett single-handedly willed the Twins to a seventh game with a 3-for-4 performance in Game Six, including a dramatic 11th-inning homer that won the game. And then there was the greatest game in World Series history: Game Seven, when local hero Jack Morris threw a shutout over 10 innings before Gene Larkin's single drove in the winning run in a 1-0 win.

Today, attending a Minnesota Twins baseball game is sort of an oddball experience. A taped announcement from the late Bob Casey telling fans there's

no smoking in the Metrodome (smoking was once allowed in the underventilated concourses; Lord, that was nasty) gets a round of cheers from many in the Minnesota sporting audience. The big between-innings entertainment is watching someone in the second deck try to throw a baseball into the bed of a truck. And you never really get used to the smell of the place; think plastic and you get an approximate scent. A ballpark should smell like a ballpark with hamburgers on the grill and popcorn in the popper. None of the sensual pleasures of baseball—mown grass, a cool breeze, that gentle transition from day to night—are present in the Metrodome. And we are all the worse for it.

Ballpark Quirks

There are a slew of them, most of which we've already discussed. Also notable: the curtain in center/right-center field added prior to the 1996 season. It does give the Metrodome a cozier feel while giving the Twins space to display banners celebrating retired greats Harmon Killebrew, Tony Oliva, Kirby Puckett, and Kent Hrbek.

When the Metrodome opened it lacked air conditioning; the thinking was the air constantly moving throughout the stadium would keep indoor temperatures cool. But put 30,000+ fans into a confined space and there's no way circulating air would be enough. Metrodome management finally relented and installed air conditioning in the midst of the 1983 season.

Food and Drink

The Twins have very little say over concessions at the Metrodome, so we don't hold them responsible for the rather limited fare. Now, having said that, things are better on the food and drink front at the Metrodome than in past seasons, and the prices are middling for a major-league facility. If you hunt, you can find a few stands featuring exotic fare like Philly cheese steaks, Famous Dave's BBQ, and one-pound hot dogs.

The Dome Dogs, made by Minnesota firm Hormel, are a little overpriced at $4, but the hamburgers located at several grills are top-notch. Thanks to a state law mandating a certain percentage of beer sold at the Metrodome be Minnesota-brewed, you can find a decent beer apart from the likes of Bud and MGD. You can usually find Gluek's, James Page, or Summit at several concession stands, while Leinenkugel is available on the main concourse.

For the Kids

Very few attractions cater to children at the Metrodome. There's no play area and about the only activity geared toward kids involves face-painting. On Sundays, kids and their parents can go down to the field after the game and run the bases.

Ballpark Tours

Tours of the Metrodome are presented on Wednesday, Thursday, and Saturday between April and November at 11 a.m., beginning from outside Gate F. (As you might expect, there are no tours when an event is scheduled.) Cost is $3. In addition, groups can schedule private tours, with a minimum of 23 participants. Call 612/335-3309 for more information.

Local Baseball Attractions

When the Metrodome was sold to a skeptical Minnesota public in the late 1970s, revitalization of the western part of downtown Minneapolis was a core argument. That revitalization never really took root so there are only a few attractions within a short walk (two blocks) of the Metrodome.

One is Hubert's (601 Chicago Av.), across the street from Gate F. It's a standard sports bar with decent food. Because it's the only bar close to the Dome, it does a healthy amount of business on game days and is pretty deserted the rest of the time. You can sip a Summit Pale Ale and spend a good half hour looking at the sports memorabilia posted on the walls, including programs from the 1965 World Series and the early days of the Minnesota Vikings, as well as team photos from the days when the University of Minnesota Golden Gophers were a national football powerhouse.

The other attraction serves no alcohol. Ray Crump's Baseball Museum is located a block from the Metrodome at 910 S. 3rd St., near Gate A. Founded by Ray Crump, longtime equipment manager of the Twins, the museum features lots of sports-related odds and ends: World Series bats, autographed baseballs and bats, and more. It won't take you long to peruse the offerings, but if you're a Twins fan you'll probably have a good memory or two revived.

Getting There

The Metrodome is located at the edge of downtown Minneapolis, which presents some good points and bad points in terms of access. On the plus side, mass transit options abound. The most popular mass transit to the Metrodome is the Hiawatha Line, the light-rail system running from downtown Minneapolis out to Minneapolis-St. Paul International Airport and the Mall of America. The fares are reasonable ($1.50 during nonpeak hours, $2 during peak hours) and there's a stop right next to the Metrodome. Many fans choose to park along the line in south Minneapolis and then take the train into the game.

Metro Transit oversees the bus system as well as the Hiawatha Line. For more information visit *metrotransit.org* or call 612-373-3333.

INSIDER'S TIP

The only free parking in the area is under some limited circumstances: you can park in loading zones after 6 p.m. These spots are located at the ends of blocks and alley entrances. Read the posted signs closely, however; some loading areas are restricted until 10 p.m.

The meters are enforced between 8 a.m. and 10 p.m. seven days a week, but the meters closest to the Dome (on south 3rd, 4th and 5th streets from the Dome west to 5th Avenue South, as well as meters on Chicago, Park, Portland, and Fifth avenues between Washington Avenue and South 7th Street) offer an eight-hour maximum, at $.50/hour, but meters farther away have a two-hour limit. The traffic patrols are out when the Twins are playing, so don't even think about being a scofflaw.

Parking at surface lots ranges from $5 to $12, but the best bargain is the parking ramp located to the west of the Metrodome at 425 Park Av. S. (beneath the light-rail station); it costs only $5 during Twins games. You could park on the West Bank (the neighborhood directly east of the Metrodome, across I-35) and walk over to the ballpark or take light rail (there's a Cedar-Riverside stop), but there are a limited number of free parking spots in the area. There's a decent nightlife still to be found on the West Bank, once frequented by a young Bob Dylan: the 400 Bar is for the musically adventurous and Palmer's is for the generally adventurous.

The freeway system in Minneapolis offers easy access to the Dome. From I-94 westbound, take the 5th Street exit; you'll drive right next to the Dome. From I-394 eastbound, take the 4th Street exit and drive through downtown Minneapolis to the Dome. From northbound I-35, take the 4th Street exit and head west to the north side of the Dome. From southbound I-35, take the Washington Avenue exit and hang a right; the ballpark will be to your left.

Most Minnesotans don't take cabs anywhere other than the airport. If you want to catch a cab after the game, they're located at the corner of 6th Street and Kirby Puckett Place, across from the large Metrodome sign at the southwest corner of the Dome footprint (kitty-corner from Hubert's).

Metrodome

Taking the Train

Jesse Ventura may not have been the best governor in Minnesota history, but he'll be remembered for one amazing instance of pure pig-headedness that actually made for good public policy: he fought hard for light rail in the Twin Cities. When the Hiawatha Line opened in the summer of 2004, the Minnesota Twins were an unlikely beneficiary of Ventura's gubernatorial largesse as thousands of Twins fans took advantage of convenient mass transit offered before and after games. The train line could not be handier for baseball fans: the Hiawatha Line runs from the Mall of America to downtown via Hiawatha Avenue, stopping at the Metrodome and then ending at the city's trendy Warehouse District.

That means you can board the line after a cocktail or two before the game at the Loon Café or Gluek's and then rendezvous after the game for a nightcap. Or you can spend the day shopping at the Mall of America and then take the train down to the ballgame. Or you can park your car at one of the many free park-and-ride lots along the route and then taking the train downtown, saving money on parking.

Here are some worthy watering holes on the train line, before or after the game:

Cardinal Tavern (38th Street stop; 2920 E. 38th St.): Burgers and cheap beer are the reason to hit the Cardinal before or after a game. It is the prototypical neighborhood tavern (if you're lucky you can buy into a meat raffle) so leave the little kids at home.

The Loon Café (Warehouse District/Hennepin Avenue stop; 500 1st Av. N.): Located at the northern terminus of the light-rail line, the Loon was a sports bar before sports bars became trendy. It's one of the most popular places in the Warehouse District; be prepared for crowds before and after games, and

it's a place where local movers and shakers come to see and be seen. The chili is great.

Gluek's (Warehouse District/Hennepin Avenue stop; 16 N. 6th St.): Established in 1902, Gluek's has been serving German-style beer in a Bavarian-style beer hall to generations of Twin Citians. The current Gluek's isn't really the same as the old one—it was destroyed in a 1989 fire—but it certainly captures the spirit of Gottlieb Gluek's original beer hall.

Mall of America (Mall of America stop): Yes, it's big, and it contains every chain store you can imagine. We'll be honest: we don't spend a lot of time perusing the shops and restaurants of MOA. But that doesn't mean hundreds of folks won't be spending the day shopping and then heading to the ballgame on the train. Be warned: most of the popular bars on the fourth floor of the mall closed down in mid-2005, and as of this writing there was little nightlife left there.

Where to Stay

As the Metrodome is in downtown Minneapolis, a number of hotels are within walking distance. The closest hotel is the Embassy Suites Hotel Minneapolis-Downtown (425 S. 7th St.; *hilton.com*; $125-$150), but there's not much nightlife within a short walk of this hotel. Instead, we'd recommend one of the two hotels at the Depot (225 3rd Av. S.; *marriott.com*): a Courtyard by Marriott ($99-$125) and a Residence Inn ($125-$150). The old Milwaukee Road Depot, originally built in 1899 for passengers, is one of the great historic reclamation projects of the Twin Cities area. Abandoned for many years, the old depot was finally developed into a hotel complex featuring a seasonal ice-skating rink, meeting spaces, and an indoor water park.

Pretty much any downtown hotel will do, however, and these are all within a mile of the Metrodome. There's always the charmingly retro Best Western Normandy Inn (405 S. 8th St.; *bestwestern.com*; $90), a funky two-story motor hotel that amazes all Minneapolis residents by remaining open. The Grand Hotel (615 2nd Av. S.; *grandhotelminneapolis.com*; $175-$200) bucks the chain mold and presents upscale rooms in a historic atmosphere, complete with a hip nightclub (Martini Blu) and trendy sushi bar with plenty of televisions for tracking the action. The Crowne Plaza Minneapolis (618 2nd Av. S.; *crowneplaza.com*; $100-$125) is a mainstay among downtown hotels, as are the Hilton (1001 Marquette Av., *hilton.com*; $200-$225), the Marriott Minneapolis City Center (30 S. 7th St.; *marriott.com*; $125-$150), the Marquette (710 Marquette Av.; *hilton.com*; $100-$125), the Hyatt Regency (1300 Nicollet Mall; *hyatt.com*; $125-$175), and the Radisson Plaza Hotel (35 S. 7th St.; *radisson.com*; $150-$200), all of which place you a block from trendy Nicollet Mall and its many attractions (which we'll discuss a little later). The Graves 601 Hotel (601 1st Av. N.; *graves601hotel.com*; $160-$200) is the hippest of all downtown hotels, with a funky lounge and a modern décor; it's also about as far away as you'll want to get from the Metrodome and still be within walking distance. The Holiday Inn Express (225 11th St. S.; *ichotelsgroup.com*; $75-

$99) isn't really close to other downtown attractions, but it is clean and cheap. (Beware of the misleadingly named Radisson Metrodome: it's actually across the Mississippi River, far from downtown Minneapolis and squarely in the midst of the University of Minnesota campus.)

For a slightly different orientation, there's the Holiday Inn Metrodome (1500 Washington Av. S.; *metrodome.com*; $125-$150), which doesn't feel as close to the Metrodome as other downtown hotels but does place you in Minneapolis's Seven Corners area, where the city meets the University of Minnesota.

Local Attractions

Downtown Minneapolis does have its charms. Much of the city's trendy restaurants and nightlife is on Nicollet Avenue, which runs north-south through downtown. We'll guide you though the best downtown bars and restaurants, beginning on 6th Street and ending south on 13th Street.

Going to **Murray's** (26 S. 6th St.) is like walking into a movie set; you expect Fred and Ginger to emerge from behind the curtains and glide through the room. Many of the servers have been at Murray's since the days of Fred and Ginger and the best items on the menu, like the butter-knife steak (so tender you can cut it with a butter knife), have been around a lot longer than many readers of this book. The powers that be lunch at Murray's; venerable *Star Tribune* columnist Sid Hartman is a regular.

The Oak Grill (700 Nicollet Mall), located in the 12th floor of Macy's, is the sort of old-fashioned, clubby place you don't find much anymore. It used to be one of the gathering spots for the powerful in the city, but today you're more likely to find casual shoppers looking for a place to decamp. It's open for lunch and dinner through 7 p.m.

McCormick & Schmick's (800 Nicollet Mall) is the local outpost of the esteemed seafood restaurant. The quality among the restaurants in this chain is uniformly good, and the outdoor seating is essential for those warm Minnesota evenings.

Zelo (831 Nicollet Mall) may be the best restaurant on Nicollet Mall for people-watching, as crowds gather there to see and be seen. The food's not bad, either, and the outdoor patio is preferable when weather allows. Indoor seating is extremely pleasant, as well.

The Local (931 Nicollet Mall) has an Irish heritage, but it's more than just whiskey and Harp. The menu features several twists on Irish fare, including an Irish reuben.

The Newsroom (990 Nicollet Mall) is a sprawling bar/restaurant with an inviting outdoor patio. The many, many flat-screen televisions are always displaying sports of some sort or another. Beware of the restrooms; they're outfitted with one-way mirrors that allow you to sneak a peek at the opposite sex's wash basin.

The Dakota Bar and Grill (1010 Nicollet Mall) is a jazz institution where you're likely to find the stars of tomorrow performing today. The food is good, though not great; the Apple and Brie soup is a Minneapolis tradition, while the French fries with Béarnaise sauce or the mac and cheese are great after a few cocktails.

Vincent (1100 Nicollet Mall) is sleek and filled with beautiful people, featuring Vincent Francoual's takes on classic rustic recipes.

Brit's Pub (1110 Nicollet Mall) is a casual British-themed restaurant with a great selection of whiskies and one of the best Cosmopolitans in town. The food isn't that great (reflecting the British heritage); stick with the fish and chips. The rooftop terrace is great fun and even includes lawn bowling.

Team Ballpark History

When the Washington Senators moved to Minnesota in 1961, the team's initial home was Metropolitan Stadium, first built in 1955-1956 to attract a major-league franchise. In the mid-1950s, the Twin Cities civic leaders considered themselves ready to enter the "big leagues" and launched a pursuit of major-league football and baseball teams. To further these efforts, the Baseball Committee of the Minneapolis Chamber of Commerce paid $478,899 for 164 acres of farmland in rural Bloomington to be used to build a baseball stadium for a major-league ball team. Before the Twins arrived, the Met was home to

The Minneapolis Millers of the American Association opened an unfinished Metropolitan Stadium in 1957. (Photo courtesy of the Hennepin County Historical Society and the Minneapolis Star Tribune.)

the American Association's Minneapolis Millers.

Meanwhile, Twin Cities leaders targeted several owners, with Bill Veeck and Horace Stoneham expressing interest in the Twin Cities. Stoneham—who by that time owned the Millers and had real-estate investments in suburban Minneapolis—came the closest to moving his New York Giants to the Met before Walter O'Malley convinced him to move to California along with his Brooklyn Dodgers.

After Branch Rickey's Continental League agreed to place a team in Minneapolis, MLB officials countered with expansion (Washington and Los Angeles in 1961, New York and Houston in 1962) and allowed Washington owner Calvin Griffith to move his Senators to Minneapolis-St. Paul. The original name of the team was the Twin Cities Twins (hence the TC on the team's original cap logo), but before the first pitch Griffith was persuaded by local businessmen to use the broader Minnesota name instead.

During the team's time in Washington, the home of the Nationals/Senators was first American League Park (1901-1910) and then Griffith Stadium (1911-1960).

Local Baseball Attractions

Most folks will want to visit the Mall of America during a stay in Minneapolis. The Mall of America was built on the former site of Metropolitan Stadium, and there's a curious memorial to the Met in the amusement park in the middle of the mall. Head to the Ghost Blaster ride in the northwest corner of the Park at MOA. Near the ride is a bronze home plate commemorating the location of the original home plate at the Met.

Stand at the plate as though you're a right-handed slugger—say, Harmon Killebrew—and look up into what would be the upper deck of the outfield On the wall you'll see a lone red seat 520 feet from home plate. That seat marks the final resting place of the longest home run hit in Met Stadium history, by Killebrew in 1967.

The St. Paul Saints of the independent American Association play across town at another rather unlovable ballpark, Midway Stadium. The Saints are one of the top-drawing teams in independent baseball, but it's not because Midway is such a great facility; it's because the Saints put on a great show. Many games do sell out, but there are always a few scalpers right outside the gate and the Saints run a ticket exchange for season-ticket holders, so anyone who really wants to get into a game can find a way. *Midway Stadium, 1771 Energy Park Dr., St. Paul; spsaints.com; 651/644-6659.*

The summer collegiate Northwoods League has several teams within a two-hour drive of Minneapolis. The Eau Claire Express play at historic Carson Park, where Hank Aaron played his professional season in the old Class D Northern League. (*One Carson Park Dr., Eau Claire, WI; eauclaireexpress.com; 715/839-7788.*) The Mankato MoonDogs play at cozy Franklin Rogers Field, home to a Mets farm team in the late 1960s. (*Hope Street and Caledonia Street, Mankato; mankatomoondogs.com; 507/625-7047.*)

At Midway Stadium you're never far from the action.

If you're up for a longer drive, the Duluth Huskies play at the WPA-era Wade Stadium (*132 N. 34th Av. W., Duluth; duluthhuskies.com; 218/786-9909*), and the La Crosse Loggers play at cozy Copeland Park (*1223 Caledonia, La Crosse, WI; lacrosseloggers.com; 608/796-9553*) near the Mississippi River waterfront.

The NWL's Rochester Honkers play at historic Mayo Field (*403 E. Center Street, Rochester; rochesterhonkers.com; 507/289-1170*). It's mostly known as the home of semipro and amateur baseball in the area: Swede Risberg spent a few seasons here after being booted from the Chicago White Sox for his participation in the 1919 Black Sox gambling scandal and later ended up farming in a local community. Rochester is also known as the final resting place of Archie "Moonlight" Graham, forever memorialized in W.P. Kinsella's *Field of Dreams*. For baseball fans, Graham is known as a minor-league ballplayer finally called to the big leagues on June 29, 1905, playing right field for the New York Giants for one inning. He didn't see any real action—that day's opponent, the Brooklyn Dodgers, went down one-two-three without hitting the ball out of the infield—and that same day he retired from professional baseball, deciding instead to pursue a medical degree first at the University of Minnesota and later at Johns Hopkins. He spent 50 years practicing medicine in Chisholm on Minnesota's Iron Range, the last 44 as the school physician for the Chisholm schools. He gained attention from his peers for his studies of children's blood pressure. He died at age 89 and was buried in 1965 at Rochester's Calvary Cemetery (*215 8th Av. NW.*) in Section 9, Lot 4, 1E.

If you're a real baseball geek, you can head to the former locations of two legendary minor-league ballparks, Nicollet Park in Minneapolis and Lexington Park in St. Paul. Nicollet Park (31st St. and Nicollet Avenue) was the home of the Minneapolis Millers for 54 years. The Millers were the class of the minors, continually leading the way in attendance and winning percentage, and grooming future stars like Willie Mays, Ted Williams, and Carl Yastrzemski. A marker commemorates the location of the old ballpark.

Across town the rival St. Paul Saints played at Lexington Park, located at the southwest corner of Lexington and University avenues in the city's Midway district. The Saints were a worthy competitor to the Millers: the teams would play day-night doubleheaders in both cities and fill trolley cars with fans commuting between the games. There currently is no marker commemorating Lexington Park; a development formerly occupying the site contained a bronzed home plate marking the location of the ballpark.

Milwaukee Brewers
Miller Park

Address: One Brewers Way, Milwaukee, WI 53214.
Cost: $400 million.
Architect: HKS.
Owner: Miller Park Stadium District.
Capacity: 42,400.
Dimensions: 344L, 370LC, 400C, 374RC, 345R.
Ticket Lines: 414/902-4000 or 800/933-7890.
Home Dugout Location: First-base line.
Playing Surface: Grass.
Other Tenants: None.
First Game: On April 6, 2001, a sellout crowd was on hand to see President
    George W. Bush throw out the first pitch at Miller Park. Outside the
    temperature was 43 degrees, so the game began with the roof closed. The
    Brewers defeated the Reds, 5-4.
Landmark Events: The infamous 2002 All-Star Game was played at Miller
    Park—infamous because both managers burned through their pitching staffs
    and the game was declared a 7-7 draw after 11 innings by Commissioner
    Bud Selig, who announced his decision to jeers and boos from the
    audience. That game led Selig and baseball officials to look to inject new
    meaning into what had become a very tired exhibition match, as well as
    structure rosters so an emergency pitcher would always be available.
    Starting with the next season, the winning league in the All-Star Game was
    also awarded home-field advantage for the World Series.

Your Miller Park Seating Crib Sheet

Best Sections to View a Game: There simply aren't many bad seats at Miller Park. We're fans of the outfield bleachers and anything between the foul lines.

Best Cheap Seats: The Uecker seats are only $1 and sold only at the gate on the day of the game. They're actually quite good, located on the Terrace Level behind home plate; many teams relegate the cheap seats to the most distant sections of the ballpark. You can always buy better seats at the gate (let's face it, the Brewers aren't exactly selling out Miller Park aside from Cubs games) if you can't score a Uecker seat.

Most Underrated Sections: The outfield bleachers (101-105, 201-205, 233-238). The Field Bleachers are a steal: you're close to the right-field action and have access to a large grouping of concessions. The loge bleachers sit higher up, but they provide a great view of the park at a low price.

Seats to Avoid: Sections 217, 238, and 417 are the family seating areas—no beer allowed. As you might expect, they're not that popular with the general Brewer fan base and are usually occupied by church groups. Also, the Terrace Reserved sections down each line are a ways from the action, as Miller Park has a pretty severe vertical orientation. We'd avoid sections 404-411 and 435-442. You might be fighting the overhang in sections 106 and 131. We'd recommend you skip the Club Level, which is overrated and overpriced. Normally, we're fans of a Club Level if you're not a regular or are an out-of-towner and want to see the best of the ballpark (the Club Level at AT&T Park, for instance, is spectacular), but the Club Level at Miller Park is a drag. The centerpiece is a bar and four small concession stands, each offering the same limited menu. Want ice cream? Forget it. We sat on the Club Level and ended up hoofing it down to the main concourse to buy fun items.

Miller Park: Love Among the Cheeseheads

You know you're in for a uniquely Wisconsin experience when, upon entering the parking lots at Miller Park, your biggest concern is avoiding the concrete containers used by tailgaters for charcoal disposal. On a sunny weeknight, you can count on hundreds of folks tailgating: drinking beer and standing around whilst the brats burn on the grill. On a nice weekend, the number reaches the thousands.

This relaxed carpe diem attitude toward life and partying is why Miller Park is such a great place to attend a baseball game. So what if the Brewers suck? After a few Hubers in the parking lot, it really doesn't matter.

The Miller Park experience starts in the parking lot where you're expected to tailgate. Wisconsinites are masters at tailgating, which involves some sort of meat grilled over charcoal, accompanied by a beer or perhaps a wine cooler. This isn't done to avoid eating in the ballpark; think of those brats as an appetizer.

The Brewers were smart to embrace this tailgating tradition and extend it in the Miller Park parking lot with the aforementioned concrete containers for charcoal. Didn't bring a grill? No problem. You can buy brats and beer at the Klement's Sausage Haus, located in the east parking lot, before you enter the ballpark.

That attitude carries over to the ballpark itself. With plenty of beer on tap and brats on the grill, Miller Park is one big party most nights. The designers of Miller Park were shrewd about a design featuring wide concourses and places to just stand around and watch a ballgame. Despite their laid-back nature, most Wisconsinites have a hard time sitting in one place and actually watching a ballgame from beginning to end (something about attention deficit is at play, obviously), so the good fans can head to the outfield and just watch the game from the concourse.

We kid our neighbors to the east, mainly because we're really jealous of Miller Park. It is a fine facility, so fine that most fans don't miss County Stadium, a classic ballpark from the 1950s.

Because of the way Miller Park is constructed, it doesn't feel necessarily like an outdoor ballpark in the seating areas. And when the roof is closed, there's plenty of light coming in from outside, thanks to the huge banks of windows rising far beyond the last row of seats. These windows also flood the playing field with light on a sunny day, but provide some sorely needed contrast to the sea of bricks used on the ballpark's inner and outer walls.

The tall walls are topped by what appears to be a sea of girders extended from behind home plate and going down each line—it's the retractable roof, folded up. This roof uses a unique clamshell design where three panels of the roof retract over a fixed panel down the third-base line. The roof is an engineering marvel, weighing 12,129 tons and covering 10.5 acres. The ballpark was designed so the roof would not be a focal point (unlike, say Rogers Centre or Minute Maid Park). When it's open, you don't feel like you're sitting in a big box with the top off. Yes, there have been plenty of mechanical

problems with the roof since the ballpark opened: for years the panels didn't seal properly (so during some heavy rainstorms water leaked onto the playing field), and it also made a huge noise while closing—imagine the sound of 10,000 fingernails being dragged across a giant chalkboard and you have an idea of how bad it sounded. These issues were addressed in the 2006 offseason when the bearings and the seals in the roof were replaced. The roof is closed immediately after a game and the Brewers invite fans to stick around and watch it happen.

This feeling of the great outdoors is lost in the huge concourses. Miller Park has an extremely large footprint thanks to these large areas. It can take you quite a bit of time to traverse the ballpark and even longer to move from level to level on the three sets of escalators.

The big event of the game: the sausage race at the end of the sixth inning. It is all you would imagine as tens of thousands of fans cheer on their favorite stuffed meat product. It's always worth watching. Players have been known to don the royal sausage garb and participate in the race, including Pat Meares, Hideo Nomo, and Geoff Jenkins. And it was during a sausage race that Randall Simon of the Pittsburgh Pirates knocked over the Italian sausage mascot with his bat, causing the woman in the costume slight injuries. Simon, on the other hand, was arrested and jailed, and later suspended by Major League Baseball.

One nice touch: before every Friday home game (at least through 2006) the Brewers hold autograph sessions with six to 10 players and coaches. Don't bother bringing your memorabilia: the team provides the signature cards as part of the promotion. Still, it's a fairly impressive promotion, putting you so close to the players and coaches.

The Brewers don't have an stellar history (post-Seattle and pre-Yount, the Brewers were a pretty lousy team), but the Brewers Walk of Fame on the Home Plate Plaza at the front entrance of the ballpark honors great Brewers of the past: Henry Aaron, Cecil Cooper, Rollie Fingers, Jim Gantner, Paul Molitor, Allan H. (Bud) Selig, Gorman Thomas, Robin Yount, Harry Dalton, Bob Uecker, Don Money, and Harvey Kuenn. In that same area are statues of Aaron and Yount.

Be forewarned, the Brewers have a particularly obnoxious variable-pricing model that basically taxes Chicago Cubs fans who drive up for the game. The difference between the pricing for regular and "marquee" games can be as high as $20 per ducat, so don't be shocked when you order a ticket and the end price is much more than you anticipated.

For those not wanting to hang around the riff-raff, there's the obligatory Club Level. We don't recommend paying the extra money to sit there. The reason why major-league teams institute a club level is purely economic: seats with middling views can be sold at a premium because a whole slew of services are added. Curiously, the concessions on the Club Level—the most expensive individual-game seats in the ballpark—are incredibly weak. At Miller Park there are only a few concession stands serving the entire level and the offerings there are amazingly limited: burgers, brats, hot dogs, beer, and pop. Waiters will serve you at your seat, but the menu there isn't much better. We ended up heading down to the main concourse to pick up staples like ice cream for the kids. Of course, most folks don't come to the Club Level (which also contains the luxury suites) for the food: during the course of the game the Home Plate Bar was filled with folks ordering mixed drinks and watching the game on the tube.

Ballpark Quirks
Anything quirky in a ballpark this new would have been purposely designed as a quirk, which makes it uninteresting.

Food and Drink
Beer and brats: what more could you want? The Miller Brewery is in clear view from the Miller Park parking lots and, as you'd expect, Miller brews are readily available on tap and in the bottle. It would be a mistake to pass up a chance to quaff a Miller High Life at Miller Park: the Champagne of Beers is still the same as when your old man had a couple after his Friday afternoon factory shift. Of course, other Miller beers are available, including Miller Lite and Miller MGD. The beer selections at the main concession stands are limited to Miller brands, though the Beer Haus stands do feature a wider selection, including Leinenkugel Red and New Glarus (brewed at an extremely trendy microbrewery in New Glarus, Wis.) and local microbrews from Sprecher. If

beer is too tame for you, the Third Base Bar (opposite Section 129) and the Terrace Beer Garden (opposite Section 405) sell mixed drinks and frozen margaritas.

The perfect pose at Miller Park is beer in left hand, brat in right. Huge curved concession stands are located throughout the ballpark on each level, and here is where you'll find your ballpark staples: Klement's brats, Italian sausages (with onions and peppers, if you hit the right stand), grilled hot dogs, Polish sausages, butter burgers (a uniquely Wisconsin treat, where the buns are slathered in butter before they're grilled—as if there wasn't enough fat in a normal hamburger), hot dogs, pizza, popcorn, and more. The prices are fairly reasonable: $4 for a brat and $2.75 for a hot dog. If you like, you can ask for your brat to be dipped in Secret Stadium Sauce before it's served, or you can apply it yourself. We're not quite sure what's contained in the Secret Stadium Sauce: it tastes like barbecue sauce watered down with sauerkraut juice. At County Stadium they sold bottles of it at every concession stand; they're not so eager to to do so at Miller Park, but you can find it in the Brewers team store.

Besides the large concession stands, a sea of specialty stands feature the likes of smoothies, soy dogs, kosher dogs, Italian beef sandwiches, pork tenderloin sandwiches, ice cream, and more. If you really want to eat a submarine sandwich at a ballgame, the Brewers offer both ham and cheese and turkey subs. Gorman's (so named after former Brewers great Gorman Thomas) Corner BBQ stand opposite Section 103 offers Klement BBQ sandwiches, while the Brushback BBQ offers pork or chicken nachos as well as BBQ pizza. And there's the requisite $9 fish fry at several stands on the first two levels.

For the Kids

Two areas appeal to the younger set. Smaller kids—up to 48 inches tall—will delight in Bernie's Clubhouse on the Terrace Level behind home plate featuring an interactive playground, Kids Zone store, and concession stand with kid-sized treats. Older kids will want to hit the Big League Blast on the Loge Level in the leftfield corner where they can participate in a number of interactive games, an ESPN SportsCenter announcing area, and races with the sausages. In addition, the area near T.G.I. Friday's features video games of all sorts.

During the game, kids will want to keep their eyes on Bernie's Dugout. One of the biggest mistakes the Milwaukee Brewers made when moving from County Stadium was not bringing Bernie Brewer's digs to the new park. At County Stadium, Bernie occupied a chalet next to a huge beer keg and slid into a giant beer stein whenever the Brewers hit a home run, but the Brewers decided to scrap the chalet and the beer stein at Miller Park, going instead for a new Bernie's Dugout in left field. (It wasn't the first time: in a rather mystifying move, the Brewers scrapped Bernie's chalet for 10 seasons, deciding in 1993 to bring it back. When the Brewers have a choice between pleasing fans and alienating them, there's a rich tradition of the latter. Way to go, Bud.)

The new Bernie's Dugout immortalizes broadcaster Bob Uecker's home-run phrase—"Get up, get up, get outta here! Gone!"—and lights up after a homer. Now Bernie just slides to a platform. It's like watching a water-park slide without any water; really dry. If you want to see Bernie's original chalet, it's now displayed at the Lakefront Brewery (1872 N. Commerce St.; *lakefrontbrewery.com*).

Ballpark Tours

The Brewers offer tours of Miller Park during the baseball season. They're conducted seven days a week at 10:30 a.m., noon, 1:30 p.m. and 3:00 p.m., but some tours may be scratched if there's an afternoon game. Stops include the dugout, luxury suites, clubhouse, Bob Uecker's broadcast booth, and more. The price is $6 for adults, $3 for children and seniors. Call 414/902-4005 for more information.

Local Baseball Attractions

The former site of County Stadium is commemorated on the Miller Park grounds in the form of Helfaer Field, a smaller ballpark built for youth baseball and softball. County Stadium was the home of the Milwaukee Braves from 1953 through 1965 and the Milwaukee Brewers from 1970 through 2000. County Stadium was a grand old ballpark with a high-ceilinged grandstand and real box seats.

Several features at Halfaer Field memorialize County Stadium. A display honoring the 192 men who played for the Milwaukee Braves is installed down the third-base line; close by is a bronze plaque marking the original home plate for County Stadium.

Alas, there is no tribute to Borchert Field, for many years the home of the

American Association's Milwaukee Brewers. It occupied a city block bounded by West Chambers and Burleigh streets, and north 7th and 8th streets; the location is now basically covered by Interstate 43.

If you're tooling around downtown Milwaukee, stop at the corner of 3rd and Kilbourn, the former location of the Republican Hotel. This landmark hotel was home to an historic meeting on March 5, 1900 when five owners in the minor Western League decided to challenge the National League and establish their own major league. The American League was born that day in room 185. Two of the attendees ended up in the Hall of Fame: Ban Johnson, president of the new league, and Charles Comiskey, who moved his St. Paul, Minn. franchise to Chicago, setting up shop as the White Sox. There's a plaque commemorating the historic meeting.

There is minor-league and summer collegiate baseball played within an easy drive of Milwaukee. The Beloit Snappers of the Class A Midwest League play in quaint, old Pohlman Field (2301 Skyline Dr.; *snappersbaseball.com*). The Snappers was for decades a Brewers farm team, but now they are affiliated with the Minnesota Twins. For slightly larger crowds, Madison's Warner Park houses the Madison Mallards of the summer-collegiate Northwoods League (2920 N. Sherman Av.; *mallardsbaseball.com*). A Mallards game is a great experience for the whole family and well worth the drive.

Getting There

You could take the bus to the ballpark. But you won't. Miller Park is set up so it's difficult to attend a game without driving there. County Stadium was designed for easy freeway access (just hop on I-43 and get off at Miller Park Way) and descendent Miller Park likewise. It's also virtually impossible to park outside the Miller Park grounds and walk to the game, so you're forced to drive. You'll be forced to pay the fairly obscene—and mandatory—parking fees: $6 to park in a remote lot and $12 to park nearer the ballpark.

If you insist on mass transit, Route 90 on the Milwaukee County Transit System (MCTS) runs out to the ballpark from stops along downtown's Wisconsin Avenue. You can get specific schedules by calling 414/344-6711 or visiting *ridemcts.com*.

Where to Stay

There's no hotel directly adjacent to Miller Park, so throw away any notion of walking to the ballpark directly from your hotel and stumbling home after the game. Miller Park is located right off the freeway about three miles from downtown Milwaukee, so you can stay downtown (particularly on a cheap weekend rate) and drive to the park.

The historic Pfister Hotel (424 E. Wisconsin Av.; *thepfisterhotel.com*; $175-$250) is the crown jewel of downtown Milwaukee, opening in 1893 to wide acclaim and costing over a million dollars. It was last renovated in 1993 with the grand lobby still the most elegant place to meet in Milwaukee. The ghost of Charles Pfister is said to wander the corridors of his hotel.

Most large chains have a presence in downtown, including Courtyard by Marriott (300 W. Michigan St.; *marriott.com*; $80-$100), Ramada Inn (633 W. Michigan Av.; *ramada.com*; $80-$100), Holiday Inn (611 W. Wisconsin Av.; *holiday-inn.com*; $80-$100), the recently renovated Hilton (509 W. Wisconsin Av.; *hilton.com*; $110-$150), Hyatt Regency (333 W. Kilbourn Av.; *hyatt.com*; $100-$175), Residence Inn (648 N. Plankinton Av.; *marriott.com*; $90-$125), and Wyndham (139 E. Kilbourn Av.; *wyndham.com*; $125-$175).

Alas, the Republican Hotel—where the American League was formed in 1901—was torn down years ago. A plaque at 3rd and Kilbourn honors the site and the history.

A cluster of hotels, such as the Extended Stay America, are located west of the ballpark in Wauwatosa and Brookfield. In addition, most of the hotels near the Mitchell Airport are within five miles or so of the ballpark and easily accessible via the freeway.

You should also consider staying in Madison and driving in for a game. Madison has a slew of affordable hotels next to the freeway, and it takes about an hour to get from Madison to Milwaukee. This gives you a chance to check out the Madison Mallards, the attendance leader in all of summer-collegiate baseball.

INSIDER'S TIP

If the idea of staying at a chain hotel is anathema to you, some smaller places in downtown may be a little more unique but a bit more rundown as well.

Irish-music fans will want to check out the 30-room County Clare (1234 N. Astor St.; *countyclare.com*; $75-$125), which features a popular Irish bar in the lobby.

The Ambassador Hotel (2308 W. Wisconsin Av.; *ambasshotel.com*; $99-$150) was renovated in 2005 with the boutique-hotel treatment. Built in 1923, the Ambassador is an Art Deco gem that had fallen on bad times.

Also dating from the 1920s is the Astor Hotel (924 E. Juneau Av.; *theastorhotel.com*; $100-$200). It began life as an extended-stay hotel for businessmen and politicians.

Local Attractions

You may head to Milwaukee with the best of intentions, not meaning to spend the weekend pleasantly buzzed, counting the minutes between beers.

Don't bother.

Milwaukee's DNA is wired for beer consumption. All roads lead to a bar of some sort and, on a good day, the smell of malted barley is thick in the air. (It used to be thicker before the Pabst and Blatz breweries closed down; such is progress in the modern world.) Off Brady Street—especially in the area north of Brady, south of North and east of Humboldt—are a number of neighborhood bars. On a cold winter's night, several years ago a group of us attempted to hit as many bars as we could within walking distance of an apartment off Brady

Street. To this day none of us can remember the exact number of bars we visited (at least nine or ten) or how many beers were consumed. We ended the night at Wolski's Tavern (1836 Pulaski), which is legendary among Milwaukee bar fans for ownership with an utter disdain for local bar-closing times. We wandered out of Wolski's at 2:30 a.m. and the place was still rocking. If you are there at whatever time Wolski's closes, you receive a treasured "I closed down Wolski's" bumper sticker.

Though most of the breweries that made Milwaukee famous are gone (like the original Pabst, Schlitz, and Blatz breweries), a few remain. The largest is the Miller Brewery (4251 W. State St.; *millerbrewing.com*; 800/944-LITE) and tours run between 10:30 a.m. and 3:30 p.m. At first you might think the location a little odd—nestled in a residential neighborhood, built into the side of a hill—until you realize the brewery dates from the days when beer kegs were stored in caves to keep them cool. You can see these caves, as well as the packing area and the brewhouse, on an hour-long guided tour.

Beer is brewed on a smaller scale at the Sprecher Brewing brewery (701 W. Glendale Av., Glendale; *sprecherbrewery.com*). It dates back to 1985 when Randal Sprecher left Pabst Brewing and launched his own microbrewery, specializing in German and Belgium brews and gourmet sodas. (Our fave is the Black Bavarian, but the Triple Abbey has a wide following.) Reservations are required for the tour; call 414/964-2739.

If you're in Milwaukee for a limited time, we recommend you stick to three areas: the Brady Street area, the Farwell/North area, and the Water Street area. All three are directly north of downtown and can be covered in a day.

The Water Street area is on the edge of the original Blatz Brewery site (indeed, many of the old Blatz buildings have been adapted to other uses, including apartments and office spaces). It's not a big area—really, only two blocks by two blocks—but at least 13 bars and restaurants dot the area. On a weekend night the area is crammed with bar hoppers. A favorite among the beer cognoscenti is the Water Street Brewery (1101 N. Water St.; *waterstreetbrewery.com*) serving an array of tasty beers brewed on the premises.

In a city full of bars, it does take some sort of gimmick to cut through the clutter. Kids will love International Exports Ltd. (779 N. Front St.; *safehouse.com*), known by the more familiar Safe House moniker. The gimmick here: behind the exports façade is a haven for international spies of intrigue to relax. It opened in 1966 at the height of the British spy mania (James Bond, The Avengers, The Saint). Look for the red door with the International Exports Ltd. and expect to be debriefed as you enter. Yes, the martinis are shaken, not stirred.

The Farwell/North area is the trendy center of youth-oriented nightlife in Milwaukee. The Oriental Landmark Theater (2230 N. Farwell Av.; *landmarktheatres.com*) shows first-run artsy movies, while the next-door Landmark Lanes (2220 N. Farwell Av.) offers bowling, live music, and cheap beer by the pitcher. Across the street, Von Trier's (2235 N. Farwell Av.) serves a wide variety of beers—both domestic and imported—in a German-themed space. Shank Hall (1434 N. Farwell; *shankhall.com*) attracts national and local bands.

Brady Street runs through the heart of an old Italian neighborhood, with trendy restaurants and bars popping up alongside Italian markets and bakeries. If nothing else, drop by the Peter Sciortino Bakery (corner of Humboldt and Brady) for some outstanding cannoli.

One other dining recommendation: the Historic Turner Hall Restaurant (1034 N. 4th St.) Friday night fish fry. Turner Halls were once found anyplace

Germans congregated: they were essentially gymnasiums and social halls that promoted healthier living through gymnastics. Turner Halls remain scattered across the Midwest; in Milwaukee, the Turner Hall is a grand old building that encompasses a gym and large dining hall. The fish is served in many different styles (fried, broiled), accompanied by a buffet line of side dishes, including coleslaws and breads. The walls are festooned with trophies and pictures of old Turner athletic teams. Contrary to public perception, Friday night fish fries did not originate because of any link with Lenten Catholicism—they popped up during the Depression as a marketing gimmick to draw folks out at the end of the week and payday, which is why you can find fish fries year-round in Wisconsin. Many other fish fries are offered in Milwaukee, but none as grand as Turner Hall's.

Also unique to Milwaukee—and Wisconsin as a whole—is the ubiquitous frozen-custard stand. Only in Wisconsin will you find such an abundance of frozen custard—ice cream fortified with extra eggs and cream to make it an especially smooth and rich diet-buster. With three locations, Kopps (*kopps.net*) is the leader for the frozen delicacy in Milwaukee, though many are fans of Leon's (3131 S. 27th St.) with its classic 1950s drive-in decor.

Team Ballpark History

The Milwaukee Brewers began life in 1969 as the Seattle Pilots expansion franchise. The Pilots spent only a year in Seattle before Allan "Bud" Selig and a group of investors bought the team out of bankruptcy court (while the Pilots were in spring training, no less) and moved it to Milwaukee. That single year in Seattle, however, is one of the most storied seasons in baseball, mainly due to Jim Bouton's endearing baseball memoir, *Ball Four*, chronicling his comeback attempt with the Pilots and giving fans a real sense of life behind clubhouse doors.

The Pilots' home was Sick's Seattle Stadium—a showcase for minor-league baseball when first constructed in 1938—rundown by the time the Pilots entered the American League. The scoreboard from Sicks' Stadium remains in use at Vancouver's Nat Bailey Stadium, home of the minor-league Vancouver Canadians. (See our chapter on the Seattle Mariners for a discussion of professional baseball post-Pilots.)

When Selig and his investment group moved the Pilots to Milwaukee, they had a ready-made major-league ballpark: County Stadium, previously the home of the Milwaukee Braves of the National League. When County Stadium opened in 1953, it was considered state of the art and fans flocked to see their championship Braves. It also was a pioneer in another way: County Stadium was the first municipally financed ballpark, paving the way for decades of debate over the appropriate level of public subsidies for major-league baseball teams.

But over time the Braves lost their appeal and left for Atlanta in 1966. During the time the Brewers were the main occupant, the ballpark deteriorated and there was never a serious attempt at renovation. In the end, County Stadium

ended being a shrine to corrugated sheet metal, distinctive more for the
memories of Hank Aaron slamming a homer or Robin Yount flawlessly diving
to prevent a sure hit up the middle.

Houston Astros
Minute Maid Park

Address: 501 Crawford Street, Houston, TX 77002.
Cost: $248 million.
Architect: HOK Sport.
Owner: Houston-Harris County Stadium Authority.
Capacity: 40,950.
Dimensions: 315L, 362LC, 435C, 436RC, 373RC, 326R.
Home Dugout Location: First-base side.
Ticket Line: 713/259-8000.
Playing Surface: Grass.
Previous Ballpark Names: Enron Field (2000-2001), Minute Maid Park (2002-present).
First Game: The Houston Astros opened Enron Field with a pair of exhibition games against the New York Yankees, winning the first 6-5. The regular-season opener took place on April 7, 2000, with the Philadelphia Phillies defeating the new-look Astros 4-1. Randy Wolf shut down the Astros on five hits in seven innings of work, while Scott Rolen and Ron Gant homered for the Phillies. Richard Hidalgo homered for the Astros' only run.
Landmark Events: The first World Series games in Houston history were played at Minute Maid Park in 2005. Alas, the Astros didn't win either game played there, with the Chicago White Sox clinching the Series sweep in Houston. The 2004 All-Star Game was played at Minute Maid Park, with the American League defeating the National League 9-4 behind homers by Manny Ramirez, MVP Alfonso Soriano, and David Ortiz. Astro and National League starter Roger Clemens was rocked for six runs (three earned) in his only inning of work.

Your Minute Maid Park Park Seating Crib Sheet

Best Sections to View a Game: The $44 Dugout Box seats are located directly behind home plate and afford the best view of the game, particularly those on the third-base side. Interestingly, they are not the most expensive seats in the house. In general, sit on the third-base side as opposed to the first-base side: you'll have a better view of the impressive scoreboards in right field.

Best Cheap Seats: It's hard to imagine, but the $27 Crawford Box seats are relatively cheap when compared to other seats in Minute Maid Park. These seats sit high (there's a scoreboard beneath), but they are so close to the action you won't mind. The $12 Tier I View Deck seats, located behind home plate, are a good choice for those who like a panoramic view above the action. The best thing about the $5 Outfield Deck tickets are they'll get you in the ballpark, allowing you to head to the concourses to watch the game.

Most Underrated Sections: The Bullpen Box seats don't get the attention the Crawford Box seats do, but they provide a good view of the action. The biggest drawback is the scoreboards in right field are to your back. The same goes for the $15 Mezzanine seats: with a full set of concessions serving a relatively limited area, you won't miss much of the game when heading back for a beer.

Seats to Avoid: The $35 Field Boxes are situated down the line, past the infield. While they are not bad seats per se, they are overpriced relative to other seats in the ballpark. The Club Level seating is divided into two areas: the $45 Tier I seats are great, but the $38 Tier II seats are farther down the line and not really worth the money.

Minute Maid Park: Thinking Big in Texas

The folks in Houston aren't afraid to think big. The original home of the Houston Astros, the Astrodome, was hailed a modern wonder of the world.

Curiously, Minute Maid Park doesn't seem to be quite as impressive an undertaking as the Astrodome, at least when you approach it from downtown Houston. True, the place is immense, even when the roof is closed. But when compared to other mega-ballparks built in the last 10 years, it's definitely on a human scale from the outside. There's really no theme to the exterior besides brickwork and corporate logos, and the most notable feature is a 135-foot-high clock tower. (The height makes the tower a convenient meeting place before and after games.) Form follows function in that the exterior serves as a support for the huge retractable roof.

The signature architectural element of Minute Maid Park is the 242-foot-high retractable roof. Houstonians like to block out the elements (with the elements as they are in Houston it's understandable) and the roof keeps it cool in summer. Early in the season the roof is left open as the lovely spring weather makes for a perfect outdoor ballpark experience. The roof does dominate the proceedings at Minute Maid Park. After awhile you get used to its rather massive presence (and these photos tend to minimize its impact, as opposed to in person), but everything is larger than life in Texas. Minute Maid Park is no exception.

One negative to our visit: because the weather was so gorgeous, the roof was open when we arrived at the ballpark so we couldn't judge how it felt when closed. However, we did talk to some season-ticket holders who said the ballpark feels fairly open even with the roof closed. Because the wall in back of the railroad track is made of three huge glass panels, you can see the downtown Houston skyline and feel the sunlight pouring in. It takes less than 20 minutes for the roof to open.

Aside from the roof, the ballpark is curiously understated when it comes to bells and whistles, though the curvilinear look to the grandstand is a little more reminiscent of European sports facilities than ballparks. In fact, one of the coolest things about the ballpark is the interplay between the sensually curved elements (the roofline down the third-base line and the retracted roof) and the rigid straight lines of the diamond, the foul poles, and the adjoining train station. In that sense there's a somewhat European feel to Minute Maid Park— and Houston would be one of the last places you'd expect it.

In most other ways Minute Maid Park follows the physical and financial model of new downtown MLB ballparks built in the last 10 years. The location is decent: it's easily accessible from the entire Houston area thanks to the freeways close to the ballpark, and there's plenty of parking thanks to a next-door convention center and Toyota Center down the way. There is a variety of seat price points, ranging from the pricey lower-level seats and the obligatory club-levels seats to midrange bleacher seats and very cheap seats ($1!) in right field. With a concourse ringing the ballpark, there are plenty of places to stand around and watch the action. And the concessions are plentiful, though there are

some Texas touches (which we'll discuss later).

Besides the roof, there are a few signature elements to the ballpark. One of the main entrances to the ballpark—and the one used by most fans—is Union Station, the city's former train station. Opened in 1911, Union Station was the main entry to Houston for three generations of Texans. You must enter Minute Maid Park through Union Station, even if you parked on the other side of the ballpark. The restoration job is stunning and the historic atmosphere sets the mood for the entire ballpark experience.

As far as former train stations go, Union Station is on the smaller side, but it suits the scale of the ballpark perfectly.

You walk through the former station and encounter left field as seen through a series of arches designed to evoke a rail bridge. (The station is also functional: it contains the Astros team offices and the roof features a group party space.) This part of the concourse actually extends over the field of play, giving you a unique view of a left fielder when he scrambles to chase a ball rolling to the fence. The concourse under the arches is a popular place to gather and watch the game.

The railroad theme is extended from the Union Station entrances. Concession booths are built like cabooses, and a locomotive dating back to 1860 runs along the track above the left-field concourse. (This is a real train, by the way, weighing over 500,000 pounds. In theory, it could reach a speed of 10 miles per hour. However, it's been extensively modernized—costing $1.2 million—with computerized controls, and both the smoke and whistle are fake.) When the Astros hit a homer, the engineer climbs aboard and the train chugs a little way down the track. We've expressed some displeasure before with overly themed ballparks (see our chapter on Great American Ball Park for an example), but here the elements are appropriate and not overdone.

Left field is also home to some of the coolest bleachers in the majors, the Crawford bleachers. At $27, the Crawford Box seats are fairly spendy for left-field bleachers, but at only 315 feet from home plate, they're an intimate set of bleachers and also an inviting target for sluggers. There are a few drawbacks—fans sitting there can't see the train or the old-fashioned hand-operated

TRIVIA

Could someone hit the ball completely out of Minute Maid Park? It's possible. The top of the train track is only 373 feet from home plate, but the top of the track is 61 feet high. It would take a mighty shot to make it out. Similarly, the roof is only 386 feet from home plate—but it's also 164 feet high.

scoreboard beneath them—nevertheless most fans seemed happy to be there.

Also intimate: the positioning of the backstop. The front row of seats are only 49 feet from home plate, putting them closer to the catcher than the pitcher.

The bleachers in right field are a completely different beast. On the bottom level are bullpen box seats, which are farther away from the infield than the left-field bleachers but offer an intimate view of the home bullpen.

On the second level of right field are the cheap, cheap seats: $5 for adults and $1 for kids. For the money, these are pretty decent seats. The view is distant and you can't see the mondo scoreboards at your back, but you get plenty of concessions and a price suitable for a family.

Speaking of the right-field scoreboards: they display pretty much any sort of stat you can imagine, while the large videoboard shows replays. Unique is a closed-caption display dedicated to those hard of hearing.

All the seats we viewed are generally skewed toward the playing field, though some may be slanted more toward the outfield than the pitchers' mound. However, the grandstand down each line was curved in toward the infield, making them decent places to watch the game.

Minute Maid Park

One thing about Minute Maid Park: this is a ballpark where the suites do not dominate the action. In a state and a city where excess is all, it's somewhat surprising to see such a subtle approach to the most expensive seats in the house. Overall, this sums up the ballpark: despite the tendency toward gaudiness and excess in Houston, Minute Maid Park is fairly understated and refined, and a great place to watch a game.

Ballpark Quirks

"Tal's Hill," a slope in the deepest part of center field. Named for Astros President Tal Smith, the 90-foot-wide slope rises 20 degrees behind the warning track and contains a flagpole in play. It presents a definite home-field advantage: more than one visiting center fielder has paused before following a fly ball up the slope. The flagpole in play is an homage to Tiger Stadium, which also featured a flagpole in play. Interestingly, there was a similar hill in Crosley Field's center field, but it was not recreated in Great American Ball Park—though Albuquerque's Isotopes Park contains a center-field hill as well.

The bullpens are in two separate locations: the visitors' bullpen is located under the left-field concourse—fully sheltered—and the home bullpen is located in right-center field, out in the open.

Speaking of the left-field concourse: in addition to the Crawford Box seats jutting out, the Conoco Home Run Porch extends over the field of play. The gas pump installed there tracks the number of home runs hit by the Astros at Minute Maid Park.

Food and Drink

Texas is beef country, and the best food at Minute Maid Park comes off the hoof—or at least processed from something coming off a hoof.

The thing with Minute Maid Park food: there is a lot of good stuff available, but it does require some searching. There are 35 concession stands scattered throughout the park and most sell the same sort of ballpark staples. For instance, the hot dogs come in a number of sizes—$5.25 for a foot long, $4 for a Super Star Dog—and you can find them everywhere. Also abundant are concession stands offering Mexican food and BBQ (we must admit the brisket was decent). There's also an emphasis on national brands as opposed to local delicacies: the pizza comes from DiGiorno and the ice cream comes from Dreyer's. (In the defense of concessionaire Aramark, most of the stands feature Nolan Ryan hamburgers. The former Astro great is now in the cattle business, among other things.)

Virtually every unique food item is sold on the main level: the half-pound Steak Dog and a foot-long Jalapeno sausage are sold at Blaylock's Grill behind section 104, while the signature food item of the visiting team city is offered at the All Aboard For... booth at Section 109. And, of course, the main activity at the Build Your Own Burrito stand at section 119 is pretty self-explanatory.

The selection of beverages for grownups is mixed. Most concession stands feature the old warhorses—Miller Lite, Bud Light, Bud, Coors Light—while a few feature Shiner Bock in bottles and on tap. If you care at all about beer, take the extra time to seek out a Shiner Bock (we saw only one Shiner Bock tap on the main concourse); it's what the enlightened locals drink, even though it costs a whopping $8.75 for a 24-ounce cup. You can find liquor on the Club Level and in the ballpark restaurants, but the margaritas sold in the main concourses do not have real tequila.

If sit-down fare is your preference, there are a few places to dine at the ballpark. The Mexican restaurant located down the right-field line, 9 Amigos, is huge, and there was a fairly long line of folks waiting to get in before the first pitch during our visit. In addition, Larry's Big Bamboo is located behind home plate and serves Caribbean-tinged bar food (chicken tenders, Nolan Ryan burgers, etc.). It's named for Astros broadcaster (and former manager and pitcher) Larry Dierker. Shiner Bock is on tap and it features a full bar as well. As a plus (or a minus, depending on your point of view), it's one of the few places in the ballpark where smoking is allowed.

Ballpark Tours

The Astros offer daily tours of Minute Maid Park year-round. The tours last an hour and hit Union Station, the press box or a broadcast booth, a dugout, a luxury suite, and more. The price: $7 for adults, $5 for seniors, and $3 for children between 3 and 14 years old.

The tours depart at 10 a.m., noon, and 2 p.m.; on game days there's also an Early Bird tour scheduled one hour before gates open, limited to those holding ticket for that game. Call 713/259-TOUR for more information.

Handicapped Accessibility

Minute Maid Park features 412 spaces for wheelchair-bound fans. In addition, hearing aids for fans are available behind sections 112 and 323. Also, the right-field scoreboards feature a closed-caption display dedicated to those hard of hearing. This is very unique for a ballpark; we didn't see it anywhere else in our travels.

For the Kids

The Minute Maid "Squeeze Play" is nirvana for both kids and parents. The huge entertainment center, located near section 133 and the Right Field Entrance, features interactive games (speed guns measure pitch velocity, while kids can get their cuts in at a batting cage) and a kid-sized concession stand. Best of all, there are television screens so adults don't miss any action.

Where to Stay

You can find a wide variety of hotel types across Houston, but the establishments closest to the ballpark are mostly of the upscale variety, including several in converted office buildings. In other words, they won't be the cheapest hotels in town, but for the most part they're well worth a splurge.

Directly across from Minute Maid Park is the Inn at the Ballpark (1520

Texas Av.; *innattheballpark.com*; $250-$350), a high-end hotel done up with a baseball theme and stocked with the luxuries: flat-screen televisions, high-thread-count sheets, and free wireless Internet. It's not cheap, but if you're indulging yourself for a weekend series, this is the best home base possible.

Similarly upscale is the Alden-Houston (1117 Prairie St.; *aldenhotels.com*; $250-$350). The Sam Houston Hotel opened in 1924 and reopened in 2002 as an upscale boutique hotel, complete with DVD players, 400-thread-count sheets, and free wireless Internet. Another restoration effort is the Lancaster Hotel (701 Texas Av.; *lancaster.com*; $300-$350).

The Hotel Icon (220 Main St.; *hotelicon.com*; $179-$300) is housed in a converted 1911 bank building and is all glitz and gold filigree plus furnishings that borders on the bordello—a décor that has served Houston well over the years. The Magnolia Houston (1100 Texas Av.; *magnoliahotels.com*; $125-$250) is positioned as a boutique hotel, but the rates tend to be lower, especially on weekends. The Magnolia chain takes old office buildings—in this case, the 1920s-era *Houston Post Dispatch* building—and converts them into hotels with a formula that includes modern furnishings, a club complete with billiards and a library, and heated rooftop pool.

The newish Hilton Americas (1600 Lamar St.; *hilton.com*; $100-$250) is billed as Houston's largest convention hotel, which means you can usually find cheap rates during the weekend. The hotel is modern and well-appointed, connected by skyway to the adjoining convention center.

If you want a safe, traditional upscale hotel close to the ballpark, there's always the Four Seasons (1300 Lamar St.; *fourseasons.com*; $175-$450). For a Four Seasons, it's not that nice, but that still puts it beyond most hotels.

Not every hotel in a restored property is upscale. Bucking the trend are the Residence Inn and the Courtyard by Marriott (916 Dallas St.; *marriott.com*; $99-$200), both located in the former Humble Oil Building.

You can, of course, stay elsewhere in the city. The Galleria defines upscale shopping, and there are a number of luxury hotels, such as the InterContinental, in the city's Uptown area.

INSIDER'S TIP

Most upscale Houston hotels have cars that will take you to and pick you up from destinations within the downtown area. If you're coming into town to watch some baseball and want to grab a bite elsewhere in the city, chances are good your hotel has a car and driver on call. Considering most downtown hotels charge for parking—between $10 and $30—it can be cheaper to rely on hotel cars.

Local Attractions

If you stay downtown near the ballpark and want something nearby, Bayou Place (500 Texas Av.; 713/230-1600) is the first place to check out. The 130,000-square-foot Bayou Place is the city's former convention center, now converted to theaters, restaurants, and bars. There's a Hard Rock Café there, as well as blues and billiards clubs.

Kids will enjoy the Downtown Aquarium (410 Bagby St.; *aquariumrestaurants.com*; $16), which features a large shark tank (which you tour while riding a miniature train), smaller tanks, special exhibits, rides, and a restaurant.

Otherwise, there aren't a ton of downtown attractions or in the general vicinity. There's the aforementioned Galleria as a shopping attraction, of course, but Astroworld—the theme park located next to the Astrodome, a short drive from downtown—was closed by Six Flags in summer 2005. Space Center Houston (*spacecenter.org*), the visitor center for NASA's Johnson Space Center, is located 25 miles south of downtown Houston on the Gulf Freeway.

Getting There

Most everyone drives to Astros games unless they're staying at a hotel close to the ballpark. There is an abundance of parking within a close walk of the ballpark. The Astros say there are 25,000 parking spots in area surface lots and ramps, with additional street parking available as well. The city's convention center is a few blocks from the ballpark, adding to the parking pool.

And the ballpark is easy to find. For starters, it's hard to miss even from a good distance, and we saw plenty of street signs pointing the way. If you take any freeway to downtown Houston and follow the signs to Downtown Attractions or to the ballpark (U.S. Hwy. 59, Texas Avenue, Crawford Street, and Congress Street comprise the main streets surrounding the ballpark), you'll be in fine shape.

Alas, mass-transit options for reaching the ballpark are limited after the local bus line eliminated special service via the Homerun Express and Shortstop Shuttle lines. You can find taxis on the west side of the ballpark, on La Branch.

Team Ballpark History

The Houston Astros entered the National League in 1962 as the Houston Colt .45s. The Astros play homage to the Colt .45s era with an exhibit on team history in the left-field concourse. The team's first home was Colt Stadium, a single-level temporary facility best known for muggy nights and monstrous mosquitoes.

The design of Colt Stadium was on the simple side: a single-tier grandstand went from foul pole to foul pole, with half of the seating flamingo-colored seats and the other half bleachers. There were additional bleachers in both left and right field, while the scoreboard was located in center field (which didn't do a lot of good for those sitting in the outfield bleachers). Because the entire stadium was a single deck there was no second deck to provide any shade. (No wonder the first-aid room was visited regularly by those suffering from heat exhaustion—almost 80 people sought medical attention during one memorable 1962 doubleheader.) The infield was rock-hard and hot, and players took salt tablets during the game. Major League Baseball suspended a rule prohibiting

The history of the franchise, which includes beginnings as the Houston Colt .45s, is detailed in the left-field concourse.

Sunday night games so Colt .45s and visiting players could avoid the hot midday sun.

If the sun didn't get you the bugs did, although insect repellant was available at the concession stands. The scoreboard itself was an oddity when the ballpark opened, as it displayed hits ahead of runs in the line score.

The Colt .45s lasted three seasons (1962-1964) at Colt Stadium before moving into the Astrodome and changing the team name to the Astros. Hailed as the eighth wonder of the world, the Astrodome was the first domed ballpark in MLB history and the first to feature air conditioning.

It was also the first to feature artificial turf. When the Astrodome opened in 1965, the plan was to use a specially bred Bermuda grass which, in theory, would receive enough light through the glass panels on the roof to grow. However, the Astros fielders complained about the glare when fielding fly balls, so two of the panels were painted white. The grass made it through most of the season before dying completely in the offseason after the paint job, leading the Astros to commit to a new artificial turf. AstroTurf changed the way pro sports was played for the next 40 years. It was durable and predictable and, more importantly, it could be easily moved and reconfigured in facilities hosting baseball and football.

The Astrodome still stands next to Reliant Field, the home of the NFL's Houston Texans. It's still used for various events—car and boat shows, the Governor's Ball during rodeo time—and the residents of Houston have made it clear they don't want to see it torn down. It was most recently put to use as a temporary home for Hurricane Katrina refugees.

Let's give the Astrodome a little credit. Indoor baseball was not unheard of right after the turn of the century: go to any historical society in any large city and you'll see accounts of indoor baseball in the newspaper clippings. And the Astros were not the first organization to propose a domed stadium: Brooklyn Dodgers owner Walter O'Malley commissioned geodesic-dome pioneer Buckminister Fuller to draw up plans for a domed stadium to replace Ebbets Field, but he dropped the plan after Robert Moses and New York City refused to let the team acquire land on Flatbush Avenue. The Astrodome was rightly dubbed the Eighth Wonder of the World when it opened and, although it could be viewed as a transitioning technology (retractable roofs give us the best of all worlds), it should not be blamed for the domed stadia that followed. The Astrodome had the sass and brashness that makes Texans so endearing.

Other Baseball Attractions
The Houston Buffaloes were a mainstay of the old Texas League, and the team's home was Buff Stadium (4001 Gulf Freeway). Built in 1928, Buff Stadium featured a low-slung, Spanish-style architecture and was home to many future St. Louis Cardinals stars moving up the farm system. Buff Stadium was damaged by Hurricane Carla in 1961, sold later that year at auction for $20,000, and eventually torn down in 1963. The Finger Furniture Mart was built on the site and the owners installed a small display commemorating the Buffs, complete with a marker on the original location of home plate.

Baltimore Orioles
Oriole Park at Camden Yards

Address: 333 W. Camden St., Baltimore, MD 21201.
Cost: $110 million.
Architect: HOK Sport.
Owner: Maryland Stadium Authority.
Capacity: 48.876.
Dimensions: 333L, 364LC, 410C, 400RC, 373RC, 318R.
Ticket Line: 888/848-BIRD.
Home Dugout Location: First-base side.
Playing Surface: Grass.
Other Tenants: None.
First Game: On April 6, 1992, the Baltimore Orioles inaugurated Oriole Park
with a 2-0 win over the Cleveland Indians. Rick Sutcliffe threw a complete-
game shutout for the win, striking out six. Chris Hoiles drove in Sam Horn
with the eventual winning run.
Landmark Event: The Orioles have reached the playoffs twice in Oriole Park
history: 1996 and 1997, in each case losing in the American League
Championship Series. The 1993 All-Star Game was played at Oriole Park,
with the American League winning 9-3 behind a double and homer from
MVP Kirby Puckett. The most notable event, however, came on Sept. 6,
1995 when Cal Ripken Jr. played in his 2,131st consecutive game, breaking
Lou Gehrig's record. The record, once assumed to be unbreakable, was set
the year after the World Series was cancelled and is widely credited with
helping save baseball.

Your Oriole Park Seating Crib Sheet

Best Sections to View a Game: Many of the better seats in Oriole Park are either sold out or part of a season ticket, so forget about sitting in most of the Field Box and Club Box sections. One issue with the ballpark: many sections are close to the action because of the small foul area, but the ballpark was not built with a vertical emphasis, which puts the outfield sections relatively far from the action. There's nothing wrong with that if you want the wider vantage point, but just be warned the much-touted intimacy of Oriole Park doesn't extend to all the seating. Having said all that, the best seats are between the bases, all the way up to the upper deck: you have a great view of the game and the scoreboard, with the B&O Warehouse providing a scenic backdrop. In general, it's better to sit down the third-base line than the first-base line, both because of the scoreboard and the orientation of the seats to the infield. If you do pay extra for premium seating—like in sections 62-66—you'll be happy to see the seats are angled toward the infield.

Best Cheap Seats: The Left Field Upper Reserved seats—particularly in sections 382-388—are a steal at $9. Yes, you're a ways from the action, but you do have a clear vantage point. The $15 Outfield Bleachers may not be the most comfortable seats in the park, but they provide an intimate experience. (Except for Section 98, which faces the outfield.) The problem with these recommendations: none of these sections provide a good view of the scoreboard.

Most Underrated Sections: Oriole Park sports an asymmetric design, and the three-level grandstand begins in the right-field corner and wraps around the ballpark to left field. Those left-field seats—particularly in the Lower Box and Lower Reserved sections—are close to the outfielders and the bullpens. The problem, of course, is that you don't get a good view of the scoreboard, and views from the rear of these sections can be obstructed by the overhang.

Seats to Avoid: Despite what proponents claim, Oriole Park is not a perfect ballpark and there are some sections to avoid. The Terrace Box seats in sections 1-17 are positioned toward center field (despite what ballpark seating diagrams may show), and sitting in Section 1 can be like sitting on your own island. You'll spend most of the game craning your neck toward home plate, regretting you spent $27 on these seats.

Oriole Park: Old is New is Old

Aficionados refer to the retro trend in ballparks: facilities designed to look old, typically with a brick exterior and lots of exposed steel and brick inside. Add a configuration designed solely for baseball (the heck with football), wide concourses, and some decorative touches evoking baseball's rich past, and you have the perfect retro formula.

It's a formula that's been played out many times in the last ten years, ranging from Philadelphia to Seattle. Fans like it, teams like it, and while some decry it as becoming clichéd, the retro style is closely associated with the renaissance of baseball over the past decade.

Oriole Park at Camden Yards is correctly hailed as a trendsetter in ballpark design, the first retro ballpark in the major leagues. (The trend actually began in the minor leagues: Dunn Tire Park, the home of the International League's Buffalo Bisons, predates Oriole Park with its retro design and downtown location.) The retro look is perfectly aligned with the surrounding Baltimore neighborhood—a warehouse and historic train station on one side, a residential neighborhood on the other—making Oriole Park a must-visit for anyone who loves baseball and ballparks.

If you visit, be sure to take your time and get to know both the ballpark and the surrounding neighborhood. Oriole Park is located between downtown Baltimore and an old neighborhood made up mostly of low-slung row houses, fitting comfortably within both.

We unwittingly hit upon the perfect itinerary for experiencing the best of Oriole Park and the surrounding area during our first visit to the ballpark. First, we arrived early on a Sunday and scored free street parking. (Not all the parking in the area is free on Sundays, but the meters are, and you can find

Oriole Park at Camden Yards

other clearly marked free street parking as well.)

Among the row houses: the house where George Herman Ruth was born, now a museum and memorial to the Babe. Our primo parking spot was a scant two blocks from the Babe Ruth Museum (216 Emory St.; *sportslegendsatcamdenyards.com*; 410/727-1539), an appealing pit stop on the way to the ballpark. (We'll explain why later, but when you pony up admission, buy the joint ticket that includes admission to Sports Legends at Camden Yards.)

The museum is small. Don't expect to see a detailed description of Ruth's early years—he came from a rough background and was sent to reform school by the time he was seven—but there is enough historical information to make you appreciate the impact he made on the game of baseball and popular culture.

The museum is three blocks from Oriole Park; follow the 61 baseballs painted on the sidewalk to guide your way. We had plenty of time before the game, so we used the second half of our admission ticket to peruse the larger Sports Legends at Camden Yard, a companion museum to the Babe Ruth Museum. This two-story museum is built in Camden Station, the former Baltimore and Ohio Railroad terminal. It's an historically significant building: the Civil War began nearby and Abraham Lincoln passed through there several times, once on his way to deliver the famous Gettysburg Address. The building had been closed down for many years (though the exterior was renovated when Oriole Park opened) before the Babe Ruth Museum embarked on a renovation fundraising drive.

Saving the museum was well worth the years of fundraising. It encompasses the general history of Baltimore sports, ranging from the original International League Baltimore Orioles to Johnny Unitas' Colts. Baseball fans will want to check out the exhibit on the Negro Leagues' Baltimore Black Sox and the Baltimore Elite Giants (for whom Roy Campanella, Joe Black, and Junior Gilliam all played) and an in-depth look at the life of Babe Ruth. The museum experience begins with a walk through a simulated B&O Railroad car. For much of Baltimore's history the train was the preferred method of travel, and many professional teams arrived in Baltimore in that very train terminal before airline travel became the prevalent mode of transportation.

Baseball fans will be fascinated by the nine-inning tribute to Baltimore baseball: the city hosted major-league baseball at the turn of the century before the International League's Baltimore Orioles dominated minor-league baseball. It was the Orioles' legendary owner Jack Dunn who found Babe Ruth and signed him to a contract; in those days it was the role of the minor leagues to find talent and then sell contracts to the majors. Dunn also deserves credit for developing the game of baseball as we know it today, stressing defense and

INSIDER'S TIP
Alhough it's not marked at the ballpark, the center-field area was once home to Ruth's Cafe, a saloon operated by Babe Ruth's father.

speed. (His great-grandson, Jack Dunn IV, is a minority owner of today's Orioles.) You'll also find a complete history of the Orioles after the team moved from St. Louis, highlighting the many great players and managers in the Orioles Hall of Fame (Frank Robinson, Brooks Robinson, Jim Palmer, Paul Richards, Jim Gentile, Earl Weaver, Cal Ripken Jr.).

Following all this history and immersion in Baltimoriana, it's time to actually stroll over to the ballpark. After heading out of the museum, walk by the Babe Ruth statue (take a close look at it, reminding yourself Babe really was a lefty) and the aluminum monuments honoring retired Orioles numbers before entering the ballpark at the Eutaw Street entrance, Gate H. (If you take the train to the ballpark, Gate H will be the closest entrance.) To your right is the scoreboard and the playing field; to your left are the warehouses formerly used to store goods transported on the B&O Railroad line. These warehouses have been converted to restaurants, bars, and offices.

As you walk along the concourse, take a close look at the cement underfoot and the walls of the warehouse. Embedded in the cement are markers commemorating where homers landed, listing the player, the team, the date, and the distance of the homer. Only one player has hit the warehouses on the fly: Seattle's Ken Griffey Jr. did it during the Home Run Derby held before the 1993 All-Star Game with a 445-foot shot. (You can find the marker below the Warehouse C sign.) True, it's a tad contrived to count what is basically a batting-practice blast, but stand where the ball landed and you'll be mightily impressed at Junior's power. Also in the concourse: plaques honoring members of the Orioles Hall of Fame.

In the same general vicinity: Boog's BBQ, shown above. It's now *de rigueur* for former ballplayers to put their name to barbecue stands in new ballparks (i.e., Randy Jones, Greg Luzinski, Gorman Thomas, and Orlando Cepeda), but former Oriole John "Boog" Powell was the first, and he knows something about real barbecue, or at least what passes for barbecue in Maryland. (Indeed, Powell also runs a barbecue joint in nearby Ocean City.) You'll find brisket, pulled pork, ribs, and turkey at Boog's, served either as part of a platter or on a sandwich. Expect a long line, but you can also expect to see Boog interacting with fans and signing autographs.

In general, that corner of the ballpark is a popular gathering spot. One trait shared by retro ballparks—a trait that isn't actually rooted in anything historical, by the way—is the emphasis on open spaces throughout the ballpark. At Oriole Park, there's a huge standing-room area in right field: fans claim their turf and then camp out for the entire game. It's actually not a great area for camping out—the wall is rather high—but that doesn't seem to diminish the area's popularity. Technically, the Orioles call this the Flag Court, with flags representing each American League team, arranged in the order of the standings.

This is also a good place to take stock of the ballpark. The influence of this ballpark cannot be understated. There were 14 classic ballparks built between 1909 and 1923—Wrigley Field, Fenway Park, Ebbets Field, Shibe Park, and Forbes Field all fall within this group—and Oriole Park hearkens back to all of them to some degree. Look at the outfield fence. It's not just an outfield fence: it's made up of straight wall segments, the first ballpark since Ebbets Field to feature such an arrangement. (Think about it. Most ballparks feature curved outfield fences.) Concrete has been the construction material of choice for most 1950s and 1960s ballparks (the exception being County Stadium in Milwaukee), but Oriole Park is reminiscent of the classics by stressing steel as a structural material.

Also located in center field: the main scoreboard. The scoreboard is a rather modest affair, with a videoboard and a matrix display featuring in-game information. The more noteworthy things about the scoreboard are the decorative elements mounted on top. The double-sided analog clock, built in Maryland, can be viewed both inside and outside the ballpark, while the two weathervane Orioles show which way and to what degree the wind is blowing.

Be warned Maryland is a state with loose smoking laws. If you walk around the ballpark, you'll need to run the line of smokers lighting up heaters on the outer concourses.

Our perfect day ended with a walk back to the car and a short drive over to Harborplace, the shopping and dining experience near Oriole Park on the city's waterfront.

INSIDER'S TIP
Another great area to stand and watch the game is the center-field terrace, complete with picnic tables. This area is often closed to groups for pregame parties, but it is sometimes opened at the start of the game. It's worth a look.

Going to Oriole Park for a weekend series and staying downtown is perhaps the perfect ballpark vacation for families. There are plenty of attractions in downtown and Inner Harbor to fill the time, and kids of all ages will love a game at Oriole Park. The ballpark may be retro, but the experience is decidedly modern—and mandatory for anyone who loves baseball and ballparks.

Ballpark Quirks

The biggest quirk—if you count something that didn't turn out as originally intended—would be the statue of Babe Ruth outside the Eutaw Street entrance.

Babe, of course, was a lefty, but you wouldn't know it from the statue. It caused quite a stir among locals when unveiled (although some insist gloves for lefties were rare when Babe Ruth was a youth, therefore making the sculpture historically accurate), and eventually the decision was made to leave the statue as is.

This isn't a ballpark quirk, but rather a franchise quirk: Orioles fans have unusual attitudes toward music. During the singing of the National Anthem, fans loudly emphasize the "O" in "O, say does that Star-Spangled Banner..." in some sort of musical homage to the O's. In the seventh inning the locals stand and sing to John Denver's "Thank God I'm a Country Boy." We can't explain it, either.

Food and Drink

We would recommend visiting the aforementioned Boog's BBQ. You can get a BBQ beef or pork sandwich for under $8—a bargain. You should also seek out a concession stand selling Maryland crab cakes, although it appears Philly cheesesteaks are also popular among Orioles fans.

The basic ballpark fare is pretty decent: the Orioles serve both Esskay and Hebrew National hot dogs, with the best selection at Hot Dogs Plus. Also available: chicken tenders, Italian sausage, pizza, and everything else you'd expect. The Uncle Teddy's Soft Pretzels stand in the main concourse serves a mean pretzel. (Yes, there really is an Uncle Teddy.)

In most stands the beer selection is ordinary—mostly corporate brews, with Yuengling being the exception. (Sadly, we must now count Rolling Rock among the corporate beers after brewing was moved away from Latrobe. Pa., by Anheuser-Busch.) If you walk around you can find microbrew stands featuring local beers: Wild Goose India Pale Ale (brewed in Frederick), Bad Moon Porter (brewed in Abingdon), and a Clipper City lager brewed in Baltimore. On Eutaw Street you can find an Irish stand featuring Guinness, Harp, and Smithwick's beers for $6.75—a relative bargain. For those craving something a little stronger, mixed drinks can be consumed at one of several Pinch Hitter Pubs.

For the Kids

There is a Rainbow playground and merchandise booth deep in the right-field corner, near Gate C. When larger crowds are expected this area is manned with Orioles personnel and vendors.

Ballpark Tours

The Orioles offer tours of Oriole Park daily, even in the offseason. Stops include the Orioles dugout, the press box, the scoreboard/JumboTron control room, and the suite level.

On weekdays, tours start at 11:30 a.m. and 1:30 p.m. On Saturdays tours are offered at 11 a.m., noon, 1 p.m., and 2 p.m.; on Sundays, tours run at 12:30 p.m., 1 p.m., 2 p.m., and 3 p.m. Prices are $7 for adults and $5 for seniors and children aged 12 and under. Call 410/547-6234 for more information; you can also buy tickets online at the Orioles Web site.

Getting There
Oriole Park at Camden Yards is easily accessible via freeway, with routes clearly marked. There are a multitude of freeways and highways leading to Oriole Park and we won't pretend to offer insightful advice as to the best routes. Let's just say we found the ballpark ridiculously easy to find.

Many fans find the train an easier way to make it to the ballpark, but do some planning before relying on mass transit. MTA trains stop next to Oriole Park at Camden, but specific times depend on the day of the week. For instance, the Camden Line running between Washington's Union Station and Baltimore's Camden Stadium runs only during the week. (You can find more information at *mtamaryland.com*.) Alas, the Amtrak service to Baltimore isn't totally convenient for those staying downtown. The Baltimore station is a couple miles from the Inner Harbor and the ballpark, requiring a short cab ride.

Once there, you'll need to address the issue of parking. On Sundays, it's not an issue so long as you are willing to walk as there's free street parking in the area. Otherwise, it's an issue. Oriole Park is located directly north of M&T Bank Stadium, the home of the NFL's Baltimore Ravens, and there are several parking lots located between the two facilities. These parking lots are accessible from the local freeway exits (just follow the signs). Private parking lots are also available close to the ballpark. Still, parking in the general vicinity is about average for a major-league facility, with most lots and ramps charging between $7 and $10.

The major airport serving Baltimore is Baltimore-Washington International (BWI). It's only 10 miles south of downtown Baltimore and served by all the major airlines.

Where to Stay
An abundance of hotels in downtown Baltimore's Inner Harbor area are close to the ballpark. Be warned: pricing for these hotels ranges all over the map, but in general staying in the Inner Harbor area can be spendy any day of the week. You'll also need to spring for parking ($15 a night and more) should you drive. Most of these hotels cater to the business traveler, so don't expect too many family-friendly amenities.

Those heading in for a weekend visit should consider the Wyndham Baltimore (101 W. Fayette St.; *wyndham.com*; $130-$300). It's the largest hotel

INSIDER'S TIP
If you're staying downtown and need to get there from the airport, don't bother with cabs. The SuperShuttle runs between BWI and the downtown Inner Harbor hotels every 30 minutes and the price is a reasonable $12 each way (or $23 round trip).

in Maryland (707 rooms), which means there's usually an abundance of open rooms on weekends. It's not the closest hotel to Oriole Park, but it is usually one of the better-priced alternatives in the area. Located in the Wyndham Baltimore is Shula's Steak House (*donshula.com*), appealing to sports fans— remember, football coach Don Shula's first success came as coach of the NFL's Baltimore Colts—as the menus are hand-painted on NFL footballs personally signed by Shula.

Close to both the ballpark and Inner Harbor is the Hyatt Regency Baltimore (300 Light St.; *hyatt.com*; $150-$250). Insiders say the views from this glass-clad hotel are the best on the waterfront, and it has a selection of suites for traveling families.

The Marriott Baltimore Inner Harbor at Camden Yards (110 S. Eutaw St.; *marriott.com*; $190-$300) is less than two blocks from the ballpark. Again, you're looking at basic business accommodations here; you're paying for location, not for total comfort. Similarly close to the ballpark is the Holiday Inn Inner Harbor (301 W. Lombard St.; *holiday-inn.com*; $150-$200). Again, you're talking about a hotel geared to business travelers with nothing flashy for the leisure traveler.

Those looking for a bargain should seek out the Days Inn Inner Harbor (100 Hopkins Place; *daysinn.com*; $90-$160). The room arrangements are more suited for business travelers, complete with oversized desks.

The Sheraton Inner Harbor (300 S. Charles St.; *sheraton.com*; $120-$300) is one block away from Inner Harbor and two blocks from Oriole Park.

All of these hotels are on the newer side (built within the last 20 years), but there are a few oldtimers worth seeking out. The Harbor Court Hotel (550 Light St.; *harborcourt.com*; $285-$360) is a small European-style hotel heavy on the amenities: rooftop terrace, clubby cocktail lounge with live music, and canopy beds. The Radisson Plaza Lord Baltimore (20 W. Baltimore St.; *radisson.com*; $150-$279) has been around since 1928, and the lobby decorations represent the French Renaissance style of the time; , while the rooms have been renovated in recent years.

While You're There

The many attractions near the ballpark makes Oriole Park the perfect weekend destination for families. We've already mentioned the baseball museums close to the ballpark, but there are plenty of other historical attractions nearby.

The Baltimore & Ohio Railroad Museum is regarded as the top facility of its kind in the nation. America's railroad system began here: the B&O Railroad featured the first commercial long-distance track and the first terminal station. The collection in this museum has been around awhile: it was collected for display at the 1892-1893 World's Columbian Exposition in Chicago and expanded for the 1904 Louisiana Purchase Exposition in New Orleans. Everything associated with the golden age of railroading is here, ranging from the big (steam locomotives) to the small (pocket watches, china), all set in the historic Mt. Clare roundhouse, where the first locomotive, the Tom Thumb, was built. *The Baltimore & Ohio Railroad Museum, 901 W. Pratt St., Baltimore; borail.org; 410/752-2490. Adults, $14; seniors (60+), $12; children (ages 2-12), $8; children under 2 years of age, free.*

The Inner Harbor waterfront is still a working port, but it's known now as home to a host of attractions, retail, and restaurants. Located five minutes away from Oriole Park, it's a natural place to head before or after the game.

The National Aquarium, located on the harbor, features the obligatory shark and dolphin tanks as well as exhibits on local critters, a coral reef, and the Amazon rainforest. *The National Aquarium, 501 E. Pratt St.; aqua.org; 410/576-3800. Adults, $21.95; seniors (60+), $20.05; children (ages 3 to 11), $14.95; children under three, free.*

The Maryland Science Center features exhibits both local and out of this world—from nearby blue crabs in the bay to the Hubble Space Telescope National Visitor Center, focusing on the orbiting telescope. *Maryland Science Center, 601 Light St., Baltimore; mdsci.org; 410/685-5225. Pricing varies based on attractions.*

The Inner Harbor is also home to shopping and dining, and three places are worth noting for baseball fans. ESPN Zone (601 E. Pratt St.; *espnzone.com/baltimore*; 410/685-2776) is the Baltimore outpost of the popular chain of sports bars: adults will like the bar and the abundance of big-screen televisions showing popular games, while kids will enjoy the games in the Sports Arena. The British-themed Wharf Rat (206 W. Pratt St., *thewharfrat.com*; 410/255-8900) is a popular brewpub and restaurant. During our most recent visit the Wharf Rat had 17 ales on tap brewed on the premises, ranging from brewpub staples like bitter and stout to sweetened ales. A popular brewpub chain, Capitol City Brewing Company, has a local outpost (301 S. Light St.; *capcitybrew.com*; 410/539-PINT;) with a great view of the Inner Harbor.

Earlier in this chapter we discussed the historical significance of the Camden Yards area as the place where the Civil War started. That event is marked by the Baltimore Civil War Museum, housed in the former train terminal where the Sixth Massachusetts Volunteer Militia Regiment arrived on April 19, 1861, and was attacked by Southern sympathizers. The small museum, located near the Marriott Inner Harbor, recounts the Civil War battles and Baltimore's important position straddling the North and the South. *Baltimore Civil War Museum, 601 President St., Baltimore; mdhs.org; 410/385-5188. Adults, $4; children 13-17 years, students with ID and seniors, $3.*

INSIDER'S TIP

If you plan on hitting more than one attraction, consider buying the Harbor Pass, which includes admission to the National Aquarium, Maryland Science Center, Port Discovery, and more, as well as $5 off the price of an Orioles ticket. The price is $46 for adults, $30 for children.

Team Ballpark History

The Baltimore Orioles began play as the Milwaukee Brewers, a charter member of the American League. That team played at the Lloyd Street Grounds located near downtown Milwaukee. Hugh Duffy, who later achieved fame as a outstanding outfielder in the American Association and immortality as a BoSox coach for tutoring a young hitter named Ted Williams, was on that team.

That original Brewers team lasted only a season before alighting for St. Louis and taking on the St. Louis Browns moniker in 1902. That took some guts: the St. Louis Cardinals were originally named by owner Chris von der Ahe the St. Louis Brown Stockings (shortened to Browns by most), and were wildly popular between 1882 to 1898. Many St. Louis baseball fans would have had fond memories of original Browns like "Buttermilk" Tommy Dowd, "Sleeper" Sullivan, "Klondike" Douglass—and a certain first baseman named Charlie Comiskey, who helped found the American League and achieved fame as the owner of the Chicago White Sox. These days, of course, that sort of market confusion would bring on a lawsuit.

There were three St. Louis ballparks called Sportsman's Park built on the same site, and the Browns played at the second and third iterations. The second version wasn't very interesting, seating only 18,000.

The third version of Sportsman's Park is the one most St. Louis fans remember fondly, but unfortunately it's remembered more as the home of the St. Louis Cardinals, not the Brownies. This is the ballpark where St. Louis Browns owner Bill Veeck, who lived in an apartment in the ballpark, sent midget Eddie Gaedel up to bat in one of baseball's greatest stunts. In the end, Veeck's shenanigans couldn't draw enough fans to the park to see a losing team. Under pressure from his fellow owners, Veeck sold the ballpark to Gussie Busch and the team to Baltimore brewery interests, who moved the Browns to Maryland after reaching a territorial settlement with the owners of the Washington Senators. (We cover Sportsman's Park more in depth in the St. Louis Cardinals chapter.)

When the Browns moved to Baltimore in the 1954 season, the team's home was Memorial Stadium, originally named Babe Ruth Stadium and renamed in December 1949. It was designed mainly for football and adapted first for the International League's Baltimore Orioles and then the relocated St. Louis Browns. Most of Baltimore's professional baseball teams have gone by the Orioles moniker since before the turn of the century, so it was only natural the new American League team would be named the Orioles as well.

Memorial Stadium wasn't an ideal baseball facility. It sported an oval

TRIVIA

Memorial Stadium was built to replace Oriole Park, the former home of the International League's Baltimore Orioles, destroyed by fire in 1944. The current Oriole Park is really the sixth ballpark in Baltimore baseball history to go by that name.

shape with the diamond located in one end of the oval. The seats perfectly positioned for the 50-yard line at Colts games faced center field for Orioles games, and outfield seats were poorly positioned for baseball. In addition, Memorial Stadium was awkwardly constructed in two phases (a second deck was added when the Browns moved to town), with the result being an abundance of support poles in the lower level. (Interestingly, one reason the many poles were needed was because the ballpark was built entirely of heavy reinforced concrete—a far cry from the newest Oriole Park.)

In fact, those support poles were about the only things completed for the first Orioles game on April 15, 1954. There was no outfield fence, so hedges marked the edge of play. (Later on a mesh-wire fence was added.) The lights weren't operational for the afternoon game, and the brick on the exterior of the stadium was not completed.

The brick exterior and large concrete plaque honoring veterans were the most notable architectural elements of the stadium. The words on the plaque read, "Dedicated as a memorial to all who so valiantly fought in the world wars with eternal gratitude to those who made the supreme sacrifice to preserve equality and freedom throughout the world—time will not dim the glory of their deeds."

Despite the many problems, Orioles fans developed a fondness for Memorial Stadium and the team developed a passionate following. They were led by Wild Bill Hagy, the mad "Roar from 34," so named because his seats were in Section 34. True, the team never drew exceptionally well there until the late 1970s (those great Orioles teams of the early 1970s barely drew a million fans eacg season), and only when Oriole Park at Camden Yards was under

construction did the Orioles draw
two million fans in a season.
After the Orioles moved to
Oriole Park, the Bowie BaySox of
the Class AA Eastern League played
at Memorial Stadium until Prince
George's Stadium was completed. It
was torn down in 2001 and 2002,
with much of the concrete dumped in Chesapeake Bay to form an oyster reef.

INSIDER'S TIP
The Sports Legends at Camden Yard
museum features several exhibits
highlighting Memorial Stadium;
check out the Orioles and Colts
sections there for more information.

Local Baseball Attractions

We've already discussed the two major local baseball attractions: the Babe Ruth
Museum and the Sports Legends at Camden Yards.

You can also hit a minor-league park within an easy drive of Baltimore,
and all of the teams listed here are Orioles affiliates as well. We've already
mentioned Cal Ripken Jr. and his importance to America's Pastime, and these
days Cal is a minor-league entrepreneur, owning two lower-level teams. His
Aberdeen IronBirds of the short-season New York-Penn League play at Ripken
Stadium (located right next to the Aberdeen exit on I-95; you can't miss it). As
of this writing, the Ripken Museum was closed to the public, but there's a small
exhibit honoring Ripken on the club level of the ballpark. *Ripken Stadium, 873
Long Dr., Aberdeen; ironbirdsbaseball.com.*

The Delmarva Shorebirds of the Class A South Atlantic (Sally) League play
at Arthur W. Perdue Stadium (6400 Hobbs Rd., Salisbury, MD;
theshorebirds.com; 410/219-3112), which also features the Eastern Shore
Baseball Hall of Fame Museum honoring local players (such as Jimmie Foxx)
and their impact on the game.

Also playing in the region: the Bowie BaySox of the Class AA Eastern
League play at Prince George's Stadium (4101 NE. Crain Hwy., Bowie, MD;
baysox.com; 301/805-6000) and the Frederick Keys of the Class A Carolina
League play at Harry Grove Stadium (21 Stadium Dr., Frederick, MD;
frederickkeys.com; 877/8-GO-KEYS).

And, of course, the District of Columbia is only a short drive or train ride
away. We cover RFK Stadium and the Washington Nationals in a separate
chapter.

San Diego Padres
Petco Park

Address: 100 Park Boulevard, San Diego, CA 92101.
Cost: $494 million.
Architect: HOK Sport.
Owner: JMI Realty and City of San Diego.
Capacity: 42,455 (plus about 2,500 Park at the Park standing room).
Dimensions: 334L, 367LC, 396C, 382RC, 322R.
Ticket Line: 877/374-2784.
Home Dugout Location: First-base side.
Playing Surface: Grass.
Other Tenants: None. Few events are planned beyond the 81-game Padres schedule.
First Game: On April 8, 2004, the Padres battled in 10 innings to a 4-3 victory over the San Francisco Giants before 41,400 (just short of a sellout). Sean Burroughs was the unlikely hero, driving in the winning run after Trevor Hoffman blew the save. Even more unlikely, the victory went to reliever Eddie Oropesa. As for the first event at the ballpark, the San Diego State University Aztecs defeated the University of Houston Cougars 4-0 on March 11, 2004; the 40,106 attendance was the largest crowd in college-baseball history.
Landmark Event: The Padres gained their first National League West Division title in seven years by defeating their closest pursuer, the San Francisco Giants, 9-1, on Sept. 28, 2005. With 33,992 in attendance, veteran starter Pedro Astacio picked up the win and the Padres evened their season record at 79-79. Since then, the Padres have made the playoffs again, but there's nothing like clinching in your home park for the first time.

Your Petco Park Seating Crib Sheet

Best Sections to View a Game: Virtually every seat in Petco Park is a winner, but some locations are especially desirable. If you can find them available and are willing to pay, the top-shelf Terrace Infield seats are the best in the house—sections 202-210. However, Terrace Reserved farther down each line might be somewhat overpriced at $45. For $5 less, Field Boxes put you closest to the action—especially sections 101-112.

Best Cheap Seats: Petco Park is cheap-seat Nirvana. Take your pick—Upper Reserved down either line, Left Field Reserved—all excellent $12 seats, and the beach-side bleachers at $8. For day games, you will want to make a key decision between sun and shade. Pick the bleachers or Upper Reserved down the right field line—especially sections 315, 317 and 323 if you worship the sun. If you want shade, go with the Left Field Reserved (section 226 is best) or Upper Reserved down the left field line—especially sections 316, 318 and 324.

Most Underrated Sections: In a venue clearly designed to give virtually every fan a good view, it is difficult to deem particular seats underrated. Every seat inside the two Tower Lofts is superb and fairly priced ($18-55). Particularly good values are available in the $12 Upper Reserved (especially sections 315-318 and 323-324), as well as Left Field Reserved section 226 located next to the funky Western Metal Supply Party Suites. Truly the most underrated seats, though, are the $8 bleachers flanked by the sandy beach beyond the center field fence and the Park at the Park. This is the place to come if you have young children who enjoy playing in the sand, or if you crave going shoeless with soft grass cushioning your feet between the bleacher rows. Come with a group of friends and have the ultimate San Diego lawn and beach party. Truly the most underrated seats, though, are those $8 bleachers flanked by the sandy beach beyond the right-center field fence and the Park at the Park. This is the place to come if you have young children who enjoy playing in the sand or if you crave going shoeless with soft grass cushioning your feet between the bleacher rows. Even the seats are very good as bleachers go. Despite no backs, they are pretty comfortable individual seats—slightly sculpted to conform to your posterior.

Seats to Avoid: To be precise, the worst place to sit is in an area with no seats. You can gain entrance to the Park at the Park for $5 and plop down your blanket on the grassy knoll. This is hardly a good deal when you consider that for $3 more you can get comfortably formed bleacher seats near the sandy beach play area, as well as access to the ballpark's many outstanding common areas. In addition, the Party Suites in the Western Metal Supply Co. Building are fine for partying but somewhat isolated for watching the actual game; and these are the only seats in the ballpark requiring rigorous head-craning to watch the infield action.

Petco Park: Welcome to the Neighborhood

Considering Petco Park nearly failed to reach construction due to strong community opposition and scandal, the ballpark has overcome some significant challenges to achieve success, although promised development surrounding the ballpark remains something of an uncertainty.

The project had been rocked by court challenges, a city council scandal, and a two-year completion delay. This isn't surprising considering the unprecedented scale of redevelopment associated with the Petco Park project. When San Diego voters overwhelmingly approved the ballpark plan in 1998, they endorsed creation of an ambitious 26-block Ballpark Redevelopment District near the city convention center and an already resurgent Gaslamp Quarter. The referendum approval cemented a long-term, large-scale development partnership between the City of San Diego and JMI Realty—the development arm of Padres owner John Moores.

It is hard to argue with the clear evidence of success. During our late-summer 2005 visit, we saw no less than five super-sized cranes operating within two blocks of the ballpark. We were told that at other times even more construction activity can be seen in the ballpark district. In fact, city redevelopment officials expect the "ancillary development" around Petco Park to produce no less than $1.4 billion in investments involving more than 30 projects within the ballpark's large redevelopment zone.

These massive efforts will take many years and the transitional impact in the immediate area surrounding Petco has been less than overwhelming so far. The ultimate key to overall success will be added housing. Ambitiously projected at more than 4,000 units, the housing proposal has been scaled back significantly. Still, the entire area historically known as East Village is clearly on the upswing, with several new projects under construction or in the planning stages.

As for the ballpark itself, few complaints from the ballplayers were heard at Petco when the Padres clinched their fourth-ever NL West title in 2005. A year earlier, though, San Diego amassed the best away record in the senior circuit's West Division but failed to reach the playoffs due to an anemic 42-39 home record. Notwithstanding the middling home performance, the Padres set an all-time attendance record of 3,040,046 in 2004. Despite the small market, San Diego remains in the top half of MLB attendance.

Padre sluggers are not particularly enamored with Petco Park's dimensions, especially when they glance at the extreme power allies. While straight-away center is a reachable 396 feet, the power alleys extend to 402 in left and right (with right field brought in from a whopping 411 feet prior to the 2006 season) and a whopping 411 in right. These are challenging distances for a near sea-level ballpark.

Not surprisingly, Padres hitters argue for bringing in the fences, but pitchers (not surprisingly) argue to keep the status quo—and the pitchers have prevailed, as team management smartly realizes the ballpark contributes to the team's winning ways. There have been some minor changes since the ballpark

opened—the center-field batter's eye has been changed, while some minor viewing obstructions in the cheap seats were also removed—but overall the park is a haven for pitchers.

While the ballpark has more than its fair share of questionable quirks (see below), its most distinctive and enduring qualities far outnumber them. Few could argue that Petco Park does not pamper its visitors.

Perhaps most noteworthy is the grouping of the Park at the Park and beach-party bleachers already mentioned. The uniqueness of these design elements has drawn some criticism, mostly coming from crustier baseball enthusiasts unwilling to embrace bold, new innovations. Most critics and fans view the ambitious overall design as a grand success. Albuquerque design architect Antoine Predock combined San Diego and some subtle Southwestern design elements into a sociable neighborhood feel throughout the facility. The seating patterns are distinct due to the intelligent use of sectional angles and the two massive Tower Lofts near first and third bases. On a large scale, attempts to create "neighborhoods" can unintentionally result in a sense of isolation apparent in some newer ballparks. This is not the case at Petco Park.

One unifying design factor is the well-conceived, over-sized concourses filled with concessions that draw fans to the Petco Park early and often. No fewer than seven restaurants are present, but don't plan on visiting all of them (most are in the restricted Terrace seating areas). Petco invites fans to stroll around the spacious concourses and a quick tour of Western Metal Supply is a must-see. Nearby is the well-designed left field standing area where socializing with a beer and some baseball cuisine come naturally.

During our visit we did not get an opportunity to try out the Terrace seats. Fewer than 5,000 seats are located within this exclusive intermediate level, served by no fewer than four private restaurants/lounges. Ticket pricing for the privilege is reasonable, but you are clearly isolated from the rest of the ballpark experience. Given you have so much to explore at Petco and you're virtually guaranteed wonderful weather in San Diego, skipping the Terrace scene won't be a tremendous setback. Besides, the better seats between first and third base (Terrace Infield) typically are pretty scarce.

The ballpark includes three outlets for Guest Services/Box Office: outside the Home Plate Gate (south-southwest side), Main Concourse—Third Base side (Sec. 108), and Upper Concourse—First Base side (Sec. 313). The team does not heavily promote ticket sales inside the facility, and frankly the tellers aren't fully trained—check your tickets closely before leaving the window. Most likely you won't be rushed, as these ticket offices aren't often busy (especially in the upper deck).

Perhaps the most interesting aspect of Petco Park is the ambitious incorporation of the Western Metal Supply Co. building. For the most part, this preservation effort works well. A team store is located here and the excellent display area on the main level features an interesting history of San Diego baseball and neighborhood archeological finds. Turn around and you even find a bit of whimsy attached to a structural support in the middle of the

concourse—an old cast iron steam radiator apparently preserved from the 1909 building's original infrastructure. As with any daring design element, the Western Metal Supply Co. incorporation has its proponents and its detractors. Overall, we have a favorable impression of the design—even though the premium seating in the old building falls short of the high standards achieved in the other "neighborhoods" of Petco Park.

As is so often the case with newer ballparks, some sense of team history seems lacking. About all you find as a tribute to Tony Gwynn and the retirement of his #19 displayed in the outfield, as well as a somewhat obscure gesture in naming one of the stadium watering holes—Club 19. Who knows, maybe the 19 really stands for the 19 consecutive years Tony hit at least .300 right up to the end of his career in 2001. Actually, in those 19 years after his rookie season, Gwynn never batted lower than .309—a particularly impressive feat when you consider that early in his career the major leagues were considered pitcher dominated. Assuredly, the lack of recognition afforded Gwynn at Petco will all change as he enters the Hall of Fame in 2006. For the foreseeable future, "Mr. Padre" may well be the last Hall of Famer to play for only one Major League team.

Prior to Gwynn, the only player to enter the Hall of Fame as a Padre was Dave Winfield, who now serves as Vice President and Senior Advisor to the team. Although he spent more years with the Yankees, Winfield chose to be enshrined as a Padre. He had always maintained a good relationship with his very first professional team, and Winfield's high-profile feud with Yankee owner George Steinbrenner probably made the decision that much easier.

Four other Hall of Famers spent time with the Padres—albeit for abbreviated periods: Rollie Fingers, Willie McCovey, Gaylord Perry, and Ozzie Smith. As for Padres retired numbers other than Gwynn (19) and Winfield (31), the team has also honored Steve Garvey (6) and Randy Jones (35). Missing from that list: San Diego native Ted Williams, the last major leaguer to hit .400 in a season. Williams started his career as a San Diego Padre. In 1937, the 18-year-old Williams led the second-year team to a league title—in the Pacific Coast League (PCL). The National League Padres didn't begin play until 1969 when Williams was 50 years old and managing the Washington Senators.

Although it is somewhat obscured in a long hallway leading to the Pacific Coast League Bar & Grill near Section 103, an impressive display of early PCL history includes more than 30 league Hall of Fame plaques. A bust of Johnny Richey proclaims him the "Jackie Robinson of the Pacific Coast League" for breaking the league color barrier.

Ultimately, Petco Park manages to accomplish the rare feat of catering not only to the fan focused entirely on the game, but also the visitor interested in the overall experience.

Ballpark Quirks

It would be hard not to notice Petco Park has a boatload of quirks, and for some visitors this will be a turnoff. In our view, we found more quirky perks than Petco peeves. The outfield fence has a large number of jogs and its height fluctuates nearly as much as the Dow Jones industrials. The fence line starts at only 4 feet in the left-field corner, rises to 7 feet in left center, climbs to 12 feet in right, and drops to 10 feet in the extended right porch area in foul territory near the right-field foul pole. The visitor's bullpen is squeezed into right-field foul territory, but home relievers can stretch out in their roominess beyond the left-field fence. The right field porch area is not a popular seating location (for good reason—the view is poor), and the extent of restriction to the visitor's bullpen is not at all worth the contrivance. These quirks are relatively minor in the whole scheme of things.

The incorporation of the Western Metal Supply Co. building is Petco's signature element and in most respects it works very well. This ballpark certainly would be far less distinctive without it. At least designers are taking some risks nowadays and in this instance the gamble pays off. Ultimately, the ballpark has proven to a popular destination based on significantly higher attendance over the first three years. For the lone game that Petco hosted post-season play so far, the "Metal Supply Co." portion of the building façade label that follows "Western" was supplanted by a "Division Champs" banner. If you think that looked a little tacky, you're quite right.

The winningest quirk at Petco is the unique Bleachers setup complete with beach area next to the fence. Even if you have one of the best Terrace seats in the house, you would be missing the full flavor of the venue if you failed to spend an inning or two in the Bleachers as well as checking out the adjacent Park at the Park. This is essential San Diego.

Food and Drink

Going to Petco Park is meant to be far more than a chance to watch a ballgame, and the concessions are a big part of the value-added experience. No fewer than seven restaurants are offered, but don't plan on visiting all of them (four are in the restricted Terrace seating areas). You have a lot of cuisine choices here—at a price. To give you a good idea, a Hebrew National kosher dog fetches $5.50 (this might even be enough to get the Yankees thinking of a move to San Diego). You have some fairly good deals on food if you look closely—$3.50 for a tasty "world famous" fish taco at Rubio's Fresh Mexican, and you can look for a Tastee-Freez soft serve dessert at $3.75. Out in the Park at the Park, you can sample Randy Jones' BBQ, including ribs or chicken for $11.50, barbecue pork or beef sandwiches with chips for $8.50, or a half-pound slugger (hamburger) for $6.50.

The best part of the concessions is the wide-open dining area overlooking the bay. Finding a seat near the closed-circuit TV might prove challenging. Another option is to dine in the left-field standing area (as mentioned earlier). You can go upscale in your food selection; for instance, Anthony's Fish Grotto

offers a Shrimp Avocado Salad for $12 or a bowl of clam chowder for $6.50—and you rarely have to wait long in line.

As for beverages, you can find a very wide array of beers—domestic and imported. Possibly the most interesting is San Diego's Stone Pale Ale ($7.75) served in only one location—near the left field corner standing area (mentioned above). Also available: a yard glass of margarita ($8) and white wine ($9).

Finer, sit-down dining in the nonexclusive part of Petco is available at the PCL Bar & Grill. Although it has an unusually isolated feel to it, you can get a great harbor view. The ala carte menu accompanies a full bar with beer, wine and extensive liquor selections. Another option is the Padres Hall of Fame restaurant featuring a buffet, located on the fourth floor of the Western Building Supply Co.

For the Kids

Children are not exactly spoiled at Petco Park. The kids' amusement area in the 2.8-acre Park at the Park is located as far away from any bustling baseball activity as you can get. Not surprisingly, this area is virtually ignored most of the time. On the other hand, the Little League infield next to the ballpark provides youngsters with batting practice fun well-staffed by the Padres. In addition, the beach area is a big draw for younger children when visiting the bleachers. An entertainment area, the Padres Power Alley, includes 12 PlayStation consoles, and a batting cage is located near Section 131.

Ballpark Tours

Individuals, families, and groups smaller than 25 can join walk-up tours offered six days a week. Tour times are as follows: Tuesday-Friday at 10:30 a.m. and 12:45 p.m.; Saturday-Sunday at 10:30 a.m., 12:30 p.m., and 2:30 p.m. Note no 2:30 p.m. tour is offered on days with evening home games, and no scheduled tours are conducted on Mondays nor days with afternoon home games. Prices are $9 for adults, $8 for military, $6 for seniors, $5 for children. Off-season tours are available. Tickets are available online at *padres.com* (see the Petco Park tours section) or at any Petco Park box office location 30 minutes in advance of each tour time.

Local Baseball Attractions

The San Diego Hall of Champions (south side of Balboa Park; 2131 Pan American Plaza; 619/234-2544) has its share of baseball memories, but also pays tribute to San Diego notables in more than 40 sports. Located within the Federal Building, the large exhibition area can be toured in under an hour—especially if you want to focus primarily on baseball exhibits. Admission: $6—adults; $4—military/seniors; $3—ages 6-17; no charge—age 6 and under; free admission for all every fourth Tuesday of the month.

If you're hoping for a glimpse of Tony Gwynn or some Surf Dawgs, you'll be visiting the campus of San Diego State University. At Tony Gwynn Stadium (5500 Campanile Drive) constructed in 1997, you can see the ballpark's

Only in San Diego can you spend time visiting the "Beach" just beyond the right-center field fence or sitting in the Bleachers with grass beneath your feet.

namesake and SDSU alum at the managerial helm for the Aztecs (619/283-7378 for tickets), or catch a Golden Baseball League game during the summer hosted by the San Diego Surf Dawgs (*sdsurfdawgs.com*; 619/282-4487). The stadium seats 3,000 and a new museum at the stadium features SDSU Aztec baseball highlights and memorabilia.

Point Loma Nazarene College (3900 Lomaland Drive) features Carroll B. Land Stadium, situated on a seaside cliff with a great view of the Pacific Ocean beyond the outfield fence. Home to the Sea Lions, the team claimed third place in the NAIA World Series in 2004.

Getting There

Fans have a choice when it comes to the price and location of parking, but the limited locations between Petco Park and the popular Gaslamp Quarter tend to be pricey. More than 27,000 parking spaces are available in the general area with 11,000 designated specifically for Petco Park fans at prices from $3, $5, $8, and $10, depending on proximity to the ballpark. Most of these lots are fairly remote—at least eight blocks from the gates. Premium parking is available directly adjacent to the ballpark for $17. Other unofficial lots near the ballpark charge up to $20. Fans who drive should choose a parking location based upon the direction they'll be heading after the game. Public transportation at Petco (several bus lines and the trolley) is readily available and encouraged, but San Diego fans have been slow to embrace alternatives.

One of the most consistent complaints heard from San Diego fans is directed at the limited, high-priced parking in proximity to the ballpark. Of course, most of the natives aren't nearly as enamored with the novelty of the Red Trolley as tourists.

Whether you choose to use a taxicab, pedicab, or a bus, you are likely to end up at the designated transportation hub located beyond right-center field on K Street between 10th and 11th avenues. The *padres.com* web site can be very helpful with all transportation options and interactive parking map, but getting to "Petco Park Access" can be a bit tricky. Under Petco Park in the drop down listing, go to the "About Petco Park" page, where you will find "Petco Park Access" in the listing on the left side.

Where to Stay

A wide range of good lodging options is available close to the ballpark and throughout the Gaslamp Quarter. The heart of the district is Market and Fifth, four blocks from Petco. Some of the nicest hotels are located in downtown's main financial district, about a mile from the ballpark.

Clearly, the best bet for die-hard ballpark fans is the baseball-themed Omni Hotel San Diego (675 L St., *omnihotels.com*, $209-$349) directly linked to the Main Concourse of Petco Park via a fourth-floor "skybridge"; you might even opt for one of the dozen rooms that provide a view of the field. If you opt for San Diego Marriott Gaslamp Quarter (660 K Av.; *marriott.com*; $199-$299), you're only steps away from the ballpark. Two other nicer properties nearby are the trendy, 2005-completed Hotel Solamar (435 6th St., *hotelsolamar.com*, $169-$329)—one of the Kimpton hotels that provides some rooms for pets; and the highly regarded Hilton San Diego Gaslamp Quarter (401 K St., *hilton.com*, $149-$359). If you want the utmost in latter 20th Century hotel elegance, you will want to stay in the heart of downtown at The Westgate (1055 Second Av.; *westgatehotel.com*, $149-$399).

Several older Gaslamp district hotels compete for value-minded customers. Three of the more highly recommended options are: the cozy Victorian-style Horton Grand (311 Island Ave, *hortongrand.com*, $149-$225); the classic, time-worn Gaslamp Plaza Suites (520 E St., *gaslampplaza.com*, $90-$250); and the tidy, well-kept Ramada Inn-Hotel St.

INSIDER'S TIP

The hotels closest to Petco Park are price sensitive to the baseball season with discounts generally available in off-season—especially when no major convention is in town. Off season, you are likely to find specials listed on the hotel websites.

James (830 Sixth Av.; *stjameshotel.com*, $119-$250), featuring some nicer touches and quiet rooms on the smallish side. As you might imagine, resorts are very popular in the San Diego area and you have many choices. If you are seeking the ultimate golf resort experience, try the highly regarded Lodge at Torrey Pines located north of the city (11400 N. Torrey Pines Rd.; *lodgetorreypines.com*; $450-$600).

Local Attractions

Unless you're somewhat of a homebody staying at the Omni Hotel connected to the ballpark, you will want to venture out at least a few blocks from Petco Park to check out the dining, bar scene and shopping located in the Gaslamp Quarter. Most of the activity is centered along Fifth Avenue extending several blocks from busy Market Street. Your best bet for a drink and quick bite near the ballpark is Trophy's Restaurant (570 K St., 619/237-9700), a small local chain with reasonable prices. You can always find good seafood in San Diego and

The Tin Fish (170 Sixth Av., 619/283-8100) is a good lunch choice with quick service at reasonable prices (sometimes closed for dinner on weekdays); the outdoor-only seating is rarely unavailable in San Diego. Although you can find many fine-dining experiences in the Gaslamp Quarter, the place to go for cutting-edge, global-fusion cuisine is Chive (558 Fourth Ave., 619/232-4483). On the opposite side of the scale with old neighborhood dive-bar authenticity is Tivoli (505 Sixth Av., 619/232-6754). Exploring further from the ballpark will bring you to the heart of the Gaslamp Quarter, where almost every possible palate can be satisfied. If you're a fan of the late singer-songwriter Jim Croce, you'll want to seek out the fine dining at Croce's (802 Fifth Ave., 619/233-4355)—owned by Ingrid Croce in tribute to her late husband. One of your best bets for a simple meal is a fine old deli plainly named the Cheese Shop (627 Fourth Ave., 619/232-2303 or 619/232-0302); superb sandwiches, good beer, friendly service, reasonably priced.

Team Ballpark History

Drawing directly from the San Diego Padres franchise of the Pacific Coast League that had served the community for the previous 33 baseball seasons, the National League expansion team came to life (to put it generously) at San Diego Stadium in 1969. (The early Padres were the poster-child definition of an expansion baseball team, finishing 52-110 and failing to climb out of last place through their first six seasons.) At least the team was playing in a modern new venue, albeit primarily a football stadium built in 1967 for the American Football League (AFL) Chargers.

Six years earlier, team owner Barron Hilton was persuaded by San Diego Union sports writer Jack Murphy to move his team from the L.A. Coliseum to San Diego. Murphy's next challenge was to convince the city to build a stadium for their team. This was accomplished when a ballot measure passed in 1965 with better than 72 percent of voters approving, authorizing $27.75 million to build a new multipurpose stadium in Mission Valley. Hard hats were donned on Christmas Eve of the same year for the groundbreaking of the 53,000-seat stadium.

After Jack Murphy died of cancer in 1980, then-Mayor Pete Wilson and the city council voted to rename the venue San Diego Jack Murphy Stadium. Some citizens were opposed to the renaming, so in 1984 the issue was put before the voters who approved keeping the name. In 1984, the stadium was expanded to nearly 61,000 and 50 suites were added at a cost of $9.1 million. In 1997, a $78-million expansion added 10,500 seats, bringing the total seating capacity to 71,500; added 34 suites for a total of 113; installed Club Level seating with four lounges; upgraded food service; and added two new video screens and a practice facility for the Chargers. At this time, San Diego telecommunications company Qualcomm agreed to pay the city $18 million for naming rights over the next 20 years and provide the final financing piece for completion of the expansion project.

While You're There

Of all the big-league cities, San Diego might win the award for achieving a sense of "human scale." Many of the key attractions and facilities are fairly close together and easy to navigate.

Balboa Park (*balboapark.org*, 619/239-0512) comprises a 1,400-acre area between downtown and Mission Valley, containing the world-renowned San Diego Zoo, 13 major museums, beautiful gardens, and noteworthy Spanish Colonial architecture. To truly enjoy the park, you should set aside no less than the better part of a full day.

Other good options for exercise and seeing the sights include a visit to Tijuana, Mexico, right across the border, and walks along Mission Bay, Coast Walk near La Jolla Cove, and numerous other beach areas along the coast.

Along with the zoo, two other leading wildlife attractions bring acclaim and crowds. SeaWorld San Diego (*seaworld.com*, 800/380-3203, 619/226-3901) has evolved over four decades from primarily an educational experience to an "adventure park" with an emphasis on entertainment. Perhaps lesser known but certainly no less interesting is the three-square mile San Diego Wild Animal Park (*wildanimalpark.org*, 760/747-8702) featuring an estimated 3,500 animals—many endangered—located 35 miles north of the San Diego off of the Via Rancho Pkwy exit from I-15.

Families considering a drive between San Diego and Los Angeles might look at visiting Legoland California (*lego.com/legoland/california*, 760/918-5346) located in Carlsbad, about 30 minutes north of San Diego.

Pittsburgh Pirates
PNC Park

Address: 115 Federal St., Pittsburgh, PA 15212.
Cost: $262 million total ($216 million plus land acquisition and site-preparation costs).
Architect: L.D. Astorino.
Design Architect: HOK Sport.
Owner: City of Pittsburgh Sports & Exhibition Authority.
Capacity: 38,496.
Dimensions: 325L, 389LC, 410CLC, 399C, 375RC, 320R.
Ticket Line: 800/BUY-BUCS (800/289-2827).
Home Dugout Location: Third-base side.
Playing Surface: Grass.
Other Tenants: None.
First Game: On April 9, 2001, the Pirates fell 8-2 to the Cincinnati Reds before a crowd of 36,954. The game was played only hours after the death of Pirate Hall of Famer Willie Stargell. Pittsburgh native Sean Casey hit a two-run homer off Todd Ritchie in the first inning to put the Reds in front. The first Pirates run came in the seventh inning on an Aaron Boone error; Aramis Ramirez scored on the misplayed John Vander Wal grounder.
Landmark Event: If you're looking for a meaningful late-season game in Pittsburgh with playoff implications, keep in mind the Pirates haven't recorded a winning season since Dan Quayle was Vice President. Outside of the Pirates' 81-game home season schedule, PNC Park has hosted only a handful of major events in the ballpark's first five years, including the 2006 All-Star Game.

Your PNC Park Seating Crib Sheet

Best Sections to View a Game: You don't have to worry about ending up with a bad seat at PNC Park. It is hard to argue against the exclusive Home Plate Club seats directly behind the plate, where you are pampered in every possible way, including a pregame buffet, a private luxury lounge and in-seat wait service. All of this comes at a steep price—$160-$210 for individual tickets (a whopping $50 hike compared to season tickets). You still get pampered premium seats if you choose to go with Pittsburgh Baseball Club seating priced at $37-$42. Although these seats are located upstairs in the lowest rows of the second deck, they provide an excellent close-in view of the action and access to three highly rated club areas. If you are seeking shade for a day game, you will want a location along the right field line with sections 109-114 most preferred. When inclement weather threatens, look for main concourse rows T or higher, affording you overhang protection.

Best Cheap Seats: Depending on your definition of cheap seats, you have several choices. The PNC Grandstand seats, at $16, are probably among the best under-$20 seats you can find in Major League Baseball. In particular, look for sections 313-320 for short rows and terrific views of the downtown skyline. Another good option is Outfield Reserved at $17 with sections 142-144 your best bets. Although you lose the skyline view, these seats are especially desirable if you are likely to spend a lot of time roaming the ballpark. If you wish to economize further, choose Left/Right Field Grand Reserved; your best bets are short-rowed Section 301 near the right field foul pole, or Section 327 beyond third base—both sections allow for good views of the crystal clear scoreboard and the downtown skyline (albeit over your right shoulder in 301).

Most Underrated Sections: Nearly every seat provides a good view at PNC Park, so it is hard to say any of the seats are underrated. All the cheap seats mentioned in the previous section qualify as a good deal. In the middle price range, you should consider going with Infield Box seats priced very reasonably at $27. These seats have you close to the action because PNC Park keeps foul territory to a minimum. Look for the best seats in sections 114-119 (between the dugouts). Often overlooked are the intimate left-field seats located in sections 30-32 priced at $26 in the Baseline Boxes, as well as the Outfield Boxes at $20 in sections 130-131 directly behind them.

Seats to Avoid: Probably none of the seats at PNC qualify as those to avoid, but some sections would qualify as least desirable. In particular, the $26 Baseline Boxes, along the right-field line, offer a somewhat awkward perspective and virtually no view of the skyline. In addition, the $9 general-admission bleachers in left field feel somewhat isolated from the rest of the ballpark.

PNC Park: Good Things Come in Small Packages

What happens when a small-market MLB baseball team decides to build a ballpark requiring an especially tight budget, an unusually short timetable, and yet demanding copious façade materials mined from halfway across the continent—all drawn together into unique design specifications?

In the case of the Pittsburgh Pirates, you reach your goals on time and within budget while achieving widespread acclaim and enhanced community support. In fact, baseball insiders universally agree that PNC Park is now the model for any small-market team in need of a new ballpark.

Several political careers were cut short when city and county officials opted for "Plan B" public financing after voters in 11 counties decisively turned down a massive $800 million-plus proposal to construct two new stadiums to replace Three Rivers Stadium and expand Pittsburgh's convention center. Oddly enough, the most visible proponent of the Plan B's diversion of county sales-tax dollars, Pittsburgh Mayor Tom Murphy, survived for one more four-year term in 2001; the national acclaim accorded PNC Park that year most certainly boosted his political fortunes. (Murphy wisely chose not to run in 2005 after the Pittsburgh financial outlook sunk to junk-bond status.)

The first model of PNC Park was unveiled in August 1998 and demolition to prepare the site began the next month. The ceremonial groundbreaking took place on April 7, 1999, and the first (exhibition) game was played a week shy of two years later. Despite relying on a fast-track design-build approach, the ballpark was remarkably prepared to impress the baseball world in time for the first pitch of the 2001 season. The process was smooth. All 23 labor unions involved in the construction signed a no-strike pact. Despite unusual conditions that required Steelworkers' manipulation of uniquely formulated steel beams and scuba divers who modified the 1,100 foot Allegheny River bulkhead wall, no workers sustained serious injury throughout the expedited construction process. Much of the streamlined process was accomplished by feeding plans through special fabricating computers—sometimes operating 24 hours a day.

"Intimate" is the word most often used to describe this ballpark. With a capacity under 38,500, it's is even smaller than Wrigley Field. In fact, PNC Park has the stingiest seating capacity in the National League; only Fenway is slightly smaller among all Major League venues.

For fans who have a fear of heights or vertigo, the number 88 has special meaning at PNC Park: the highest seats are located only 88 feet above the playing field. To give you an idea of how low that is, if you extended the distance from home plate to second base straight up, you'd still have to look upward 39 feet to see the base from your lofty perch. As the only modern MLB ballpark limited to two decks, some ingenious engineering and design ideas were essential to accomplishing this task. PNC's Upper Concourse contains the luxury suite level, club level seats and upper-level seating. The 69 luxury boxes are tucked under the club level but are contiguous with it in the upper tier. All the upper-level pre-cast components rest on massive steel frames. This emerging design-build process using pre-cast single, double and triple risers largely explains how the two-deck layout was accomplished, as well as achieving remarkable timetable and materials cost efficiencies.

By employing engineering and sizing efficiencies, the project gained leeway to spend more on distinctive, quality finishing materials. The PNC Park look is anything but cheap. While the vast majority of newer ballparks feature some sort of firebrick appearance, PNC Park's facade is distinguished by the generous use of golden Kasota limestone shipped from a Minnesota river valley. The massive steel beams and ballpark seats are painted a lustrously deep blue in strikingly handsome contrast to the brightly toned limestone. Typically, the reaction to this color combination from first-time PNC Park visitors is nothing short of awe and admiration.

From an urban planner's perspective, by all accounts PNC Park hit a home run. The ballpark is consistently praised for fitting in perfectly with the North Shore street grid and blending in well with existing architecture. In a smaller market you can achieve a sense of human scale, and PNC Park accomplishes this feat in many ways. Perhaps the most stunning example of this is the excellent framing of the city skyline across the Allegheny River from so many seating perspectives; it gives you a sense that you're in a city substantially larger than it truly is.

Given Pittsburgh has hosted baseball since 1876, you would expect a new millennium ballpark to reflect heavily on Pirates history. This goal is accomplished in subtle and pleasing ways, thankfully avoiding the temptation to inundate fans with an overly heavy dose of reminiscence. The stadium itself only subtly hearkens to the Forbes Field era—61 years encompassing the early and mid-20th century. The nostalgic touch recalling Forbes is seen in the exterior masonry, archways and engaging decorative terra cotta pilasters. Still, PNC Park does not shout "retro" first and foremost, and most baseball aficionados rightfully view this reality as refreshing.

Another subtle touch is the silent tribute to Hall of Famer Roberto Clemente, who roamed right field in Pittsburgh for 18 seasons, winning 12 Gold Gloves. In his honor the right field fence at PNC Park is 21 feet high, matching his retired #21. Clemente batted .317 for his career, claiming four National League batting crowns and winning the 1971 World Series MVP with a .414 batting average. In the twilight of his playing career, Clemente died in an airplane crash in his native Puerto Rico on New Year's Eve 1972. The disaster-relief flight was headed for earthquake-stricken Nicaragua to deliver supplies.

Other Hall of Fame players honored with retired Pirates numbers are Ralph Kiner (4), Willie Stargell (8), Bill Mazeroski (9), Pie Traynor (20), and Honus Wagner (33). The numbers of managers Bill Meyer (1) and Danny Murtaugh (40) are also retired. In Pittsburgh, Hall of Fame credentials don't necessarily get your number retired. The other Pirate players who have reached the hallowed Hall without getting their numbers retired are Max Carey, Fred Clarke, Kiki Cuyler, Joe "Arky" Vaughn, and brothers Paul "Big Poison" Waner and Lloyd "Little Poison" Waner.

Of the three exquisite statues erected outside of PNC, the ultimate place of

honor was reserved for Honus Wagner near the home-plate main gate. With a plaque simply stating he was "the greatest shortstop in baseball history," Wagner was one of five original Hall of Fame inductees in 1936—named on the exact same number of ballots as Babe Ruth. The life-size statue mounted atop a marble stand honoring "The Flying Dutchman" is well traveled—placed originally at Forbes Field with an intermediate stop at Three Rivers Stadium. "Hans" Wagner was born in Carnegie, Penn., only a short distance from Pittsburgh. He remained active with the Pirates as a coach until 1951—more than a half century after he came to the team as a player.

The Roberto Clemente statute traveled the short distance from Three Rivers Stadium to the gateway area between the Roberto Clemente Bridge (formerly known as the Sixth Street Bridge) and the center-field entrance. Only two days before his death and the first regular-season game at PNC, the Willie Stargell statue was unveiled in front of the left-field gate. Taken together, these three statues rate among the finest baseball sculptures you are likely to find. Once again at PNC, you find quality over quantity.

The two rotundas linking the Main Concourse to Grandstand Level are easy to navigate. The large display lining the home-plate rotunda chronicles many great Steel City sports moments in history—although it can be frustrating to get close to portions of the display while navigating the spiral path.

It is possible to go overboard with praise for this ballpark and gloss over its faults. In fact, several characteristics of PNC Park will clearly remind you this facility was built on a tight budget. Intimate describes both favorable and disappointing facets of the place. Other than the Riverwalk area beyond the right-field stands, the concourses are somewhat cozy for a modern ballpark and that presents a problem when attendance swells past 25,000. This wasn't a concern on our late-season visit for two games—the Pirates had already

The statue of Roberto Clemente stands in front of the bridge named in his honor, just outside of PNC's centerfield entrance.

unluckily clinched their 13th straight losing season in 2005.

So you can imagine a large share of the visitors might be interested in the other Major League games on any given evening. The Pirates are very accommodating. Along the tall wall in right field you'll see a comprehensive real-time listing of not only the score and inning, but also number of outs and runners-on-base visuals.

While most every vantage point at PNC Park gives you a sense of harmony with your surroundings, this is less so in the left-field stands where you might feel somewhat isolated. One of the more expansive standing areas to watch the game is located in left field, but the overall design is somewhat uninviting with very limited space to place your food and beverage. Most of the concourses away from field views are attractive and feature spectacular views. However, one would think a few more of the 645 television monitors in the ballpark could have been placed in these locations away from the field. The three restaurants/bars serving Club Seats patrons are a bit cramped.

Perhaps the single most disappointing aspect of PNC Park is the Spartan arrangement of the bathrooms. Absolutely none of the features—from the faucets to flushing fixtures and towel dispensers—are of the modern automatic variety found in most newer, large public facilities. While the bathrooms are large enough, the doors to them are inexplicably small.

Of course, these problems are what you should expect from a ballpark built on an austere budget. The niggles are minor and the important decisions on how to make PNC as pleasant as possible for fans primarily interested in watching the baseball game were right on the mark.

Ballpark Quirks

Consistent with the overall authentic initial impression of this ballpark, you will find virtually no bothersome quirks at PNC Park. The irregularity of the fence dimensions, reaching 410 feet in left-center, is vaguely reminiscent of the 457-foot mark similarly located at Forbes Field. Another gentle reminder of Forbes is the location of the press box above the highest row of seats—hardly a quirk.

Food and Drink

As Major League Baseball concessions go, what is offered at PNC Park is consistently better than average food at fairly reasonable prices. All in all it's a better deal than you find at the majority of ballparks, and you can pick from a wide variety of selections.

In the first few years at PNC, the Pirates objected to fans bringing in bottles of water. More recently, clear water bottles up to 24 ounces have been allowed through the gate. That's good because $3 for a bottle of water is a bit steep. If you only want a pickle at Primanti Brothers, they'll charge you $1.50—that's one expensive pickle. But the typically long lines at this stand are really there for the most famous deli sandwich in western Pennsylvania; priced at $6 neither your stomach nor pocketbook will complain. Another quality concessionaire is Benkovitz Seafoods, where you can pick up a very tasty fresh fish sandwich for $5.75 or a fish and chips basket for $6.75 (shrimp is also available for the same price). This is one of those ballparks where you recognize that alternatives to the standard hot dog are probably your best option. For instance, the grilled Polish Kielbasa ($5) is more appealing than the foot-long hot dog ($5.50) at Federal Street Grille locations. This is Pittsburgh, after all.

Your beer selection at PNC is also better than average, especially if you are

PNC Park

looking for the notable regional brews—Iron City, various Penn brews and
Yuengling (prices vary depending on size, bottle or draft). Iron City is a quality
beer but comes from the deeply financially troubled Pittsburgh Brewing
Company—so sample it soon while you still have the chance.

If you decide to buy Pittsburgh Baseball Club seats, you will likely want to
seek out the highly touted Carvery for superb sandwiches ($9). The only
complaint here is the line moves slowly. Even at an afternoon game with fewer
than 13,000 fans in attendance, it took the better part of two innings to go
through the line.

For the Kids

You can have a good time with your kids around PNC both inside and outside
the ballpark. The river walk along the North Shore provides constant
entertainment that's fascinating for all ages. Not only do you get the downtown
skyline and view of the bridges, you'll see a wide variety of boats. Once inside
the ballpark head for the Kids Play Land located at the Right Field Gate,
featuring a miniature PNC Park configuration as well as a multi-purpose play
set. Accompanied by an adult, children ages 5-10 are encouraged to participate
from the time the gates open until the 8th inning. Pirates' event staff may close
the area in the event of inclement weather. Before Sunday afternoon home
games, you have an added block party-type attraction along Federal Street near
the Roberto Clemente Bridge from 11 a.m. until the 1:35 p.m. game time. The
Kids Fun Zone is free to all fans and offers a variety of kids-oriented games,
activities, giveaways, and entertainment for Pirates fans ages 12 and under.

Ballpark Tours

PNC Park tours are offered from mid-April through mid-October, Monday-Friday. A limited number of Saturday tour days are scheduled throughout the year. Tours begin promptly at both 10 a.m. and at noon on days when the Pirates schedule an evening game. An additional 2 p.m. tour will be given on dates when no home game is scheduled. No tours are available on dates when a day game is scheduled or on holidays.

Tour ticket prices for adults are $6, or $4 for seniors (55+) and children/students. From 9 a.m. to 2 p.m. each weekday, tour tickets are available at the left-field-side Pirates ticket window along General Robinson Street.

Local Baseball Attractions

Interesting bits of Forbes Field history are preserved in what is now the east side of the University of Pittsburgh campus. A small commemorative area that includes Forbes Field's home plate embedded under glass is located in Posvar Hall at the corner of Roberto Clemente Drive and S. Bouquet Street (a right turn off of Forbes Avenue when heading east from downtown). Marking the former location of the left-center field wall, a plaque in the sidewalk indicates where the most-famous homerun in Pirates history exited Forbes—the 1960 World Series game-seven walk-off shot slugged by Bill Mazeroski. Across the street in a park area is the main attraction—a large intact portion of the red-brick center field wall including the 457-foot sign and the flagpole.

Perhaps the most exciting recent development for sports fans visiting the

Right-center field at Forbes Field was marked at "only" 436 feet compared to the 457-foot left-center corner marker in front of the flagpole. The well-preserved ivy-covered wall is now part of the University of Pittsburgh campus.

area is the Western Pennsylvania Sports Museum, located in the Smithsonian Institute-affiliated Senator John Heinz Pittsburgh Regional History Center (1212 Smallman St., 412/454-6000). With 70 interactive displays housed in 20,000 square feet of exhibition space, the new museum features a wide array of both amateur and pro sports memorabilia. Included are a baseball glove worn by Satchel Paige, a tribute to the 1960 Mazeroski blast, and a visual of Roberto Clemente rounding the bases. (Don't be put off by the historically named location of the museum in the "Strip District"—this is a bustling family-oriented waterfront market area that draws local shoppers and tourists alike.)

The Pirates' closest affiliate is the Class AA Altoona Curve of the Eastern League playing at Blair County Ballpark (1000 Park Ave.; *altoonacurve.com*; 814-943-9050). The 7,200-seat facility opened in 1999 was also designed by PNC Park architectural partner LD Astorino of Pittsburgh. Although Altoona is less than 100 miles east of Pittsburgh, the trip on U.S. 22 varies between two and four lanes, and likely will take at least two hours. One possible side trip to the south—visiting the temporary memorial of the Sept. 11 Flight 93 crash site—takes you a little out of the way but allows you to travel mostly on interstate highways I-70 and I-99. The memorial gathering place is 500 yards from the actual crash site that is remotely located near Shanksville. A permanent U.S. Park Service memorial will not be completed until at least a decade after the 9/11/01 event.

If you're interested in attending an ballgame closer than Altoona, suburban Pittsburgh has the Washington Wild Things, named appropriately based on their reputation for wacky between-innings antics. This independent Frontier League team plays at Falconi Field (1500 Chestnut St.; *washingtonwildthings.com*; 866/456-9453).

PNC Park 325

Getting There

If you are coming from downtown or the North Shore, it is strongly advised you map your route ahead of time as signage directing you to PNC Park is minimal. If coming by car, you will want to find parking on the North Shore if you're coming from the north. If you are arriving from the south, east, or west, parking downtown is preferable; cross the river on the Roberto Clemente Bridge which is restricted to pedestrians on game days. Parking is generally considered a pretty good deal in Pittsburgh, especially if you locate a garage a few blocks away from the ballpark.

From the north: Via southbound I-279 take either exit 8B to the Allegheny Center garage or the new North Shore garage, or exit 7A to Red Lots 7A, 7B, 7C, or 7D. Via southbound Route 28 take either the East Ohio Street Exit to Allegheny Center garage or the Lacock Street exit to North Shore garage. Via southbound 65 take the North Shore ramp to Gold Lots 1 or 2.

From the west and wouth: Via I-279/Route 19 through the Pitt Tunnel, take exit 6B to the Boulevard of the Allies, or take exit 6A to I-376 East exit 1C onto Grant St. Via northbound Route 51 through the Liberty Tunnel to 6th Avenue, take Forbes St., 5th Avenue or 6th Avenue for various downtown garage locations.

From the East: Via westbound I-376, take exits 2B, 1D, 1C, or 1B to various downtown garage locations. North Shore parking is also available by taking southbound Route 28 to the East Ohio Street Exit to Allegheny Center garage or the Lacock Street exit to North Shore garage.

If you are interested in riding light rail, Pittsburgh has a small system known at the "T," linking only the South Hills neighborhood with downtown. The odd thing you wouldn't want to discover by mistake is the fact that (much

Willie Stargell primarily played in left field, leading the Pirates all-time in home runs (475) and runs batted in (1540) over the 21 seasons he played exclusively for the Bucs.

like a bus) the T will not automatically stop at a station unless a passenger requests it. Plenty of parking is available at the South Hills T stations. You can get off the T at either the Wood St. or Gateway Center station in downtown.

Of course, numerous bus routes also provide service into downtown.

Where to Stay

Pittsburgh has an amazingly complete and competitive set of major, quality downtown hotels, as well a few distinctive smaller properties.

The hotels closest to PNC Ballpark offer you easy walking to the game and great river views, yet are relatively close to the center of downtown. If you prefer a quieter, economical area just outside of downtown, you will want to opt for a more-intimate North Shore hotel near the ballpark.

Possibly the grandest restored hotel in Pittsburgh is also the closest downtown hotel to PNC Park, just across the bridge—the Renaissance Pittsburgh Hotel (107 Sixth St.; *renaissaincehotels.com/pitbr*; $139-$209), fully renovated in 2001. In the heart of downtown, you have the ornate historic landmark Omni William Penn (530 William Penn Place, *omniwilliampenn.com*, $105-209). Another conveniently located and well-appointed option is the Hilton Pittsburgh (600 Commonwealth Place, *hilton.com*; $94-$239)—the largest hotel in town with 719 rooms. The two large hotels next to the convention center are also relatively close to the ballpark—Courtyard by Marriott Downtown (945 Penn Av.; *courtyardpittsburghdowntown.com*; $99-$289) and Westin Convention Center (1000 Penn Av.; *westin.com*; $149-$229).

Opting for a North Shore location is logical, but be aware this is a transitional area and not a destination neighborhood for much more than the ballpark and football stadium. By far the newest and closest property is the SpringHill Suites Pittsburgh North Shore (223 Federal St.; *marriott.com*; $99-$179)—just north of the ballpark. Further north you have distinctive choices of a Euro-style boutique—The Priory Hotel (614 Pressley St.; *thepriory.com*; $119-$155), or the grandly gothic mansion Inn of the Mexican War Streets (604 W. North Av.; $99-$199). We stayed at The Priory on our 2005 visit and found the place interesting, spacious and accommodating with a good continental breakfast.

Local Attractions

Although you can skip the Primanti Brothers offerings at PNC, you will want to visit the original Pittsburgh institution open 24/7 (46 18th St., 412/263-2142); visitor comments about this deli often come out something like, "people from Pittsburgh are the luckiest people on earth." Of course, if you find a sandwich with coleslaw, French fries, meat, and cheese between the buns a little too messy, you might decide to pass.

The tavern-restaurant choices near PNC are all within a block of the ballpark, located on Federal Street or General Robinson Street. Among the bars located within the ballpark structure beyond the left-field wall, Atria's (103 Federal St., 412/322-1850) and Vincent's Pizza (101 Federal St., 412/325-4485) draw the liveliest crowds before night games.

PNC Park and the Pirates offer ballgame packages with the 10,000-square-foot Outback Steakhouse (109 Federal St., 412/321-9003) with game views behind glass in left field. Best views are from the tables ($52 per person) near the windows, and booth seating ($43 per person) is also offered; the price includes a $25 food and beverage credit. The Outback deal is something you might want to try for an alternative experience, but it is not a good idea if your primary goal is to see the game or get to know the ballpark.

A good, informal dining and drinking option if you choose to stay on the North Shore is Max's Allegheny Tavern (537 Suisman St., 412/231-1899). Several highly regarded downtown restaurants are within walking distance of PNC Park, including: The Carlton, located in One Mellon Center (500 Grant St., 412/391-4152); a fine Italian bistro, F. Tambellini Ristorante (139 7th St., 412/391-1091); the nearby Grille on Seventh Street (130 7th St., 412/391-1004); or the upscale small-scale chain Palomino (4 Gateway Center, 412/642-7711).

You might want to check out the offerings on the south side just across the Monongahela River from downtown, including: the Grand Concourse/Gandy Saloon, giving you an option for more formal or lighter fare (1 W. Station Square, 412/261-1717) or Café Allegro (515 S. 12th St., 412/481-7788).

For good reason, many of the destination restaurants in Pittsburgh require a hike to Mt. Washington where you'll find breathtaking views of downtown and the Golden Triangle (where the rivers converge). Here you will find "Restaurant

The exterior of Forbes Field, circa 1909. (Courtesy Library of Congress, LC-USZ62-113335.)

Row" along Grandview Avenue. Some of the more highly regarded restaurants include: Cliffside (1248 Grandview Ave., 412/431-6996); Monterey Bay Fish Grotto (1411 Grandview Ave., 412/481-4414); and Tin Angel (1200 Grandview Ave., 4112/381-1919).

The Tin Angel hosted President Bill Clinton and British Prime Minister John Major in 1994. From the bottom of the small mountain, they took a ride up on the Duquesne Incline (1197 W. Carson St., 412/381-1943). Parking at the base of the ride is free.

Team Ballpark History

Although it has nothing to do with actual ballpark history, you will better appreciate the Pirate heritage if you know how the name came about. In its earliest years, the team was known as the Pittsburgh Alleghenies. However, in 1891 the Players League folded after its lone season and a scramble for the league's better players ensued. While it was assumed veteran players would return to their former teams, second baseman Louis Bierbauer signed with the Alleghenies. Rather than return to the American Association's Philadelphia Athletics, his signing with Pittsburgh prompted accusations of "pirating." Bierbauer stayed in Pittsburgh and so did the Pirates name.

Prior to National League affiliation as the Pirates, the Alleghenies

815   Forbes Field, Pittsburgh, Pa.

1B-H2202

originally began as a pro team in 1876 at Union Park (later known as
Recreation Park) and disbanded after playing in the minor-league International
Association the following year. Continuous operations started in 1882 in the
American Association. The team was accepted into the National League for the
1987 season and began league play as the Pirates at Recreation Park, located
near the northeast corner of North Avenue and Allegheny Avenue, about a mile
northwest of PNC Park. With a capacity of around 17,000, the stadium was also
used for bicycle racing and by University of Pittsburgh football team.

In its second year after substantial renovation, Exposition Park became
home to the Pirates starting in 1891. (The Players League Burghers had
occupied the ballpark the previous year before the league folded.) Probably the
most notable Exposition Park event was the hosting of the first-ever World
Series in 1903. As host team, the Pirates claimed only one win in four against
the Boston Americans, despite managing a 2-2 record in Boston (Americans
won the series, 5-3). A year earlier, Exposition Park hosted an unusual 4th of
July event. River flooding resulted in deep outfield water so modified ground
rules dictated that all outfield hits would be ruled singles; the Pirates swept
Brooklyn that Independence Day. For much of the time spent at Exposition
Park after the turn of the century, the Honus Wagner-led Pirates dominated the
National League and claimed pennants in 1901, 1902, and 1903, then took
second place in three of the next five seasons. Exposition was located on the
north shore of the convergence of the Allegheny, Monongahela, and Ohio rivers
immediately east of what is now Heinz Stadium.

In what would become a miniature tradition, the team relocated in midseason 1909. In the midst of one of the most dominating Major League seasons
of all time, the Pirates moved from Exposition Park to a spacious modern

wonder, Forbes Field. The first concrete and steel ballpark in the National League drew some initial ridicule for its remote location in the Oakland neighborhood. Not surprisingly, the Bucs drew over a half-million fans for the first time in 1925 on their way to a 110-42 record and 4-3 World Series championship over the Detroit Tigers, capped by an 8-0 victory away.

Another 4-3 World Series championship came in 1925 over the Washington Senators with the 9-7 finale coming at Forbes Field. By this time, capacity at Forbes had increased from 25,000 to 35,545; the 1925 World Series games drew far more than capacity—well over 40,000 for each of the four games. Arguably the greatest post-season game of all time took place on Oct. 13, 1960 at Forbes Field when Mazeroski claimed the 4-3 World Series championship for the Pirates over the New York Yankees with the first-and-only walk-off Series-ending homer. The see-saw game ended with a 9-8 Pittsburgh win. Forbes hosted one other World Series in 1927 when the Yankees swept the Pirates in four games. Two All-Star games were hosted at Forbes Field, with the National League winning both times, in 1944 and 1959. Although memories of Forbes are typically romanticized, by the 1960s the ballpark had fallen into disrepair and its odd dimensions, outfield impediments (flagpole, light tower cages), rock-hard infield, and severely obstructed view seats were annoyances—not mere quirks. The contending Bucs gave Forbes Field a proper send off on June 28, 1970 with doubleheader sweep of the Chicago Cubs.

After more than six decades at Forbes Field, the Pirates made another midseason transition during a victorious season. The first game at Three Rivers Stadium was a 3-2 loss to the Cincinnati Reds on July 16, 1970, part of a long series of interesting coincidences. The Reds also made a midseason transition in 1970 from Crosley Field to Riverfront Stadium. As West Division winners that year, the Reds defeated the East Division champion Pirates 3-0 in the National League Championship Series. The only game of that series played at Three Rivers Stadium was the 3-2 Reds clincher—exactly the same result as the inaugural game earlier in the season.

In the first full season at Three Rivers the following year, the Pirates claimed the World Championship with a 4-3 series victory over the Baltimore Orioles. Steve Blass pitched a masterful three-hit complete game victory over Mike Cuellar in the first World Series game at Three Rivers. In Game 4 the following day, Three Rivers hosted the first World Series night game—a 4-3 Bucs win. In fact, the home team won the first six games of the 1971 Series, but it was Blass who broke that streak with another complete game—this time a four-hitter on the road—to secure the 2-1 win and the 4-3 Series match. The same two teams faced off again in the 1979 World Series with the same result—Pittsburgh claiming a 4-3 Series victory over the Orioles. This time around the Pirates lost two of three at home but once again claimed Game 7 at Memorial Stadium, 4-1. Bucs manager Chuck Tanner used five different starting pitchers over the seven games. The Pirates' theme that year will be forever remembered as "We Are Family"—the popular Sister Sledge song of the era.

Divisional titles were claimed by the Pirates in three straight years, 1990-

92, but the National League pennants in those years went to Cincinnati and then Atlanta twice. By most accounts, Three Rivers Stadium's greatest attribute was its location along the North Shore (in the same place as old Exposition Park, just east of the current Heinz Stadium). Its $35 million final cost was nearly double the original estimate. As was typical of those times, Three Rivers was a carpeted, uniform, oval multi-purpose facility. Capacity for baseball was 48,000; for the football Steelers it was 61,000. In 19 seconds and at a cost of $5.1 million, Three Rivers Stadium was imploded on Feb. 11, 2001. You get unlimited bonus points if you can name the third professional team to call Three Rivers Stadium home (the USFL's Pittsburgh Maulers in 1984).

While You're There

Close to the ballpark, you have some good options both on the North Shore and on the downtown side of the Allegheny River. One block northeast of PNC you will find the Andy Warhol Museum (*warhol.org*, 412/237-8300) at Sandusky and General Robinson streets, one of four Carnegie Museums of Pittsburgh. In general, the museums of Pittsburgh are considered at least one cut above the typical. On the downtown side of the river, you can head for the three rivers' point of convergence where you will find Pittsburgh's landmark 150-foot tall fountain and Fort Pitt located in Point State Park (*dcnr.state.pa.us/stateparks/parks/point.aspx*; 412/471-0235). No admission is charged at Point State Park, nor the adjoining Allegheny Riverfront Park.

Certainly any of the four Carnegie museums (*carnegiemuseums.org*) are good options, but you might want to consider the diverse experiences available at the Frick Art and Historical Center (*frickart.org*, 412/371-0600) about nine miles east of downtown Pittsburgh. Along with a quality fine art collection, the six-acre property features Clayton—the 19th century Italianate-style mansion home of Henry Clay Frick and his wife Adelaide Howard Childs, an antique car and carriage collection, and an impressive floral conservatory.

Another entertaining option for the family is the Pittsburgh Zoo and Aquarium (*pittsburghzoo.com*, 412/665-3640 or 800/474-4966) located seven miles northeast of downtown. Among the attractions are a large children's zoo ("Kids Kingdom"), a Komodo dragon, a walk-through bat flyway and a 45,000 square-foot saltwater aquarium.

Toronto Blue Jays
Rogers Centre

Address: One Blue Jays Way, Toronto, ON M5V-1J3.
Cost: C$600 million.
Architects: Rod Robbie and Michael Allen.
Owner: Rogers Communications.
Capacity: 50,516.
Dimensions: 328L, 375LC, 400C, 375RC, 328R.
Ticket Lines: 416/341-1234 or 1-888/OK-GO-JAY.
Home Dugout Location: Third-base side.
Other tenants: Toronto Argonauts (CFL). The SkyDome was also the original
    home of the NBA's Toronto Raptors.
Playing Surface: AstroGrass (1989-2004) FieldTurf (2005-present).
First Game: On June 5, 1989, the Milwaukee Brewers defeated the Blue Jays
    5-3 before a full house as the team moved midseason from Exhibition
    Stadium. Paul Molitor, who later starred for the Blue Jays, got the first hit in
    the new ballpark with a leadoff double off Jimmy Key and scored the first
    run.
Landmark Events: 1991 All-Star Game (won by the American League, 4-2),
    1992 World Series (Toronto defeated the Atlanta Braves, four games to
    two), and the 1993 World Series (Toronto defeated the Philadelphia Phillies,
    four games to two). In addition, two Grey Cup games (the Canadian
    equivalent of the Super Bowl, where the Canadian Football League crowns
    a champion) have been played at Rogers Centre.

Your Rogers Centre Seating Crib Sheet

Best Sections to View a Game: The seating at Rogers Centre is a bowl, but it's not a symmetrical bowl: the bottom of the oval is squished, meaning seats directly in back of home plate (both in the lower sections and in the upper deck) are fairly close to the action.

Best Cheap Seats: Sections 504-507 are $9. (All prices in this chapter are in Canadian dollars.) If you look at a diagram of Rogers Centre seating, you'll think we're nuts for recommending these seats, but they're great. You're in the upper deck, but you can see almost all the action—including the massive center-field scoreboard—and you're in the shade in sections 504-507 during an afternoon game. Devoid of bleachers, at Rogers Centre you're always assured of having a theater-style seat.

Seats to Avoid: The oval shape of Rogers Centre means some of the seats, particularly in sections 113-115 and 127-130, are set back from the action, as are 513-517 and 532-537. Though Rogers Centre is a multiuse facility, the seats in those sections are angled quite nicely for baseball. The outfield seats offer great views, but they are overpriced at $26. If you're there for an afternoon game, be sure to sit down the first-base line and not in the sun field down the third-base line.

Underrated Seats: The aforementioned sections 504-507.

Rogers Centre: Still an Engineering Marvel

Most people forget the first two MLB ballparks with retractable roofs were in Canada: Montreal's Olympic Stadium featured a funky Kevlar-coated retractable cover that finally became operational in 1987, and Toronto's SkyDome—now Rogers Centre—pioneered a "hard" retractable roof, proposed by two Canadian architects, Rod Robbie and Michael Allen.

It was a real roof made up of PVC membranes attached to a steel deck, not a flimsy fabric cover (a setup so flimsy in Montreal that it was later left permanently in the "closed" position). The 11,000-ton roof is made up of three sections: two slide over the outfield and a third rotates over home plate and underneath the other two. The roof needed a solid construction to withstand the extreme climate of Toronto—heat in the summer and lots of snow in the winter—and so far it's held up splendidly. However, the touted roof did not begin under auspicious circumstances: during the first series played at SkyDome in June 1989, the roof would not close all the way, leaving a center open spot with rain falling down on the pitchers' mound and home plate. The game was postponed.

And there was more to SkyDome than just the roof: the grandstand parts, the dugouts descend, and whole sections move when the facility's use shifts from baseball to football. At 310 feet high (or 31 stories), it's the tallest ballpark in the majors, but it's still dwarfed by the landmark CN Tower next door, giving some proportion to the landscape.

When SkyDome opened in 1989, it was rightly hailed as a

Rogers Centre

wondrous step forward in the engineering of massive sports facilities. Robbie and Allen solved many problems ballpark architects today still struggle to solve; then again, spend enough money and you can solve most engineering problems. When it opened, SkyDome was by far the most expensive stadium ever built at over $600 million. SkyDome was also a giant step forward in anticipating what fans would expect from a ballpark: complete with a hotel and restaurant, SkyDome was a year-round destination years before other baseball officials realized the financial appeal of loading up a ballpark with additional attractions. (Compare what Toronto carried out against what the White Sox settled at U.S. Cellular Field, even though SkyDome opened two years earlier. U.S Cellular Field is a basic ballpark with few amenities or the qualities necessary to bring in fans when there's not a game. The ballparks are contemporaries, but they are galaxies apart in almost every other way.)

Today, Rogers Centre is still quite the engineering feat. Its creators rightly anticipated baseball fans would want to be outside on a sunny day and indoors on a cold, wet April night (it takes only 20 minutes to close or open the roof), but they failed to anticipate one thing: the human factor. With lots of exposed concrete and a sterile artificial-turf playing surface, Rogers Centre is hardly an inviting facility. The current Blue Jays ownership has spiffed up the place, but there's a long way to go before Rogers Centre can be called a warm venue.

It might be the Blue Jays front office got so spoiled after the opening of SkyDome—setting American League attendance records and regularly selling out the house—that the fine art of customer relations never became part of the team's DNA. Or it could be the Blue Jays had been owned for years by mega-corporation Labatt Breweries, and running the baseball team was not emphasized. Or, most likely, the absentee private corporation that ended up owning SkyDome had little incentive to squeeze more out of the place. Rogers Communications, owners of both the team and Rogers Centre, has shown a commitment to enhancing the fan experience, and interest in the Blue Jays is now higher than it has been in years.

Still, ownership of the SkyDome has been spotty, to say the least. It was built with funding from the Ontario provincial government, the city of Toronto and over 30 Canadian corporations. This entity was not financially solid, however, and was granted one large government grant before declaring bankruptcy. Sportsco bought the SkyDome out of bankruptcy court for $85 million; Rogers Communications bought the SkyDome after the 2004 season for $25 million and renamed it Rogers Centre. Pretty shrewd investment, actually.

To their credit, the Toronto Blue Jays and Rogers are trying to spice up and humanize the ballpark experience. Some of the problems with Rogers Centre simply can't be changed to make it a great baseball venue. From the way it was explained to us, the engineering used to convert the facility from baseball to football also makes it virtually impossible to install real grass and replace the FieldTurf. Still, it's a good place to take in a game.

Before the 2005 and 2006 seasons, Rogers did made some changes to the

ballpark, first changing the name from SkyDome to Rogers Centre (dumb move; SkyDome is a great name and Rogers SkyDome would have been a terrific compromise), but more importantly Ted Rogers (finally, both the team and the ballpark have an engaged owner) announced a multi-million project to upgrade the facility. The most notable change before the 2005 season was the installation of a new Jumbotron in center field: the crystal-clear display is 33 feet tall by 110 feet wide. Also added were new video boards on the outfield walls and a racetrack scoreboard between sections. The effect of these changes is stunning, adding some sorely needed color to a bland Rogers Centre décor.

Still, there's something missing at Rogers Centre. The layout is a little too perfect, an oval that unfortunately evokes visions of cookie-cutter stadiums past. Or perhaps it's all that exposed concrete, the most characterless stadium building material on the planet. The sound system is outstanding, but it fails to excite the polite Canadian crowd.

Perhaps the most egregious shortcoming is the inability to move around freely at a game. Rogers Centre was designed before the retro craze popularized open areas where fans can just stand around and watch a game, so forget about grabbing a beer and stretching your legs while viewing the game from a different vantage point. There are no escalators between the sections, so be prepared for a really, really long hike if you've purchased seats in the upper deck.

There's a lot to like about Rogers Centre. The new ownership is clearly committed to improving the fan experience. The ballpark location is the most perfectly situated in major-league baseball: there's just no way you can go to Toronto for a weekend series and not have a great time. And, although the Blue Jays cannot change all the shortcomings at the ballpark, early signs indicate they are working hard at fan-oriented improvements.

Ballpark Quirks

The roof seems to be central to most of the ballpark's quirks. For starters, the vast majority of the ballpark's ground rules concern the roof. It's up to the Blue Jays front office whether the roof is open, though the crew chief is consulted on the decision. The crew chief informs the visiting team of the decision; the opposing manager has the power to challenge the decision if he feels it gives the Blue Jays a competitive advantage. Once the game starts, the roof can be closed, but not opened. To avoid problems during the 1992 and 1993 postseason, the American League ordered the roof shut for the duration of the playoffs.

The roof does affect the game, but to a lesser degree than the playing conditions at Tropicana Field or Metrodome. When the roof is closed, the ballpark is neutral. When the roof is open, breezes coming off Lake Ontario create a wind tunnel in the ballpark that tends to hold back potential homers.

Though the Blue Jays suffered through plenty of quirky game delays and forfeits at their former home, Exhibition Stadium, the ultimate in unique game delays for the Toronto Blue Jays came on Aug. 27, 1990. The roof was open for

Rogers Centre

a lovely Ontario evening, but more than fans were attracted to the ballpark:
huge swarms of gnats descended upon the players, forcing home-plate umpire
Don Denkinger to order the roof closed. The Milwaukee Brewers ended up
winning the game 4-2.

Food and Drink

When Exhibition Stadium opened for Blue Jays baseball in 1977, it had limited
concessions and no beer. No beer! One's mind boggles at the thought of
attending a Canadian baseball game without a Labatt Blue in hand. Then again,
it took a while for Toronto to really get baseball: when SkyDome opened,
McDonald's controlled the concessions, so the food choices were extremely
limited and extremely fattening.

Today the concessions are more varied, with new owners Rogers
Communications promising to make more changes. The most unique food items
are sold on the main level where you can find back-bacon sandwiches ($8.50,
which seems a little spendy for back bacon) or kosher hot dogs for $4.25 with a
potato latke ($3.75) on the side. The majority of concession stands sell the same
things: hot dogs (which are quite good), Pizza Pizza pizza, and Mr. Sub subs.
Specialty offerings include Philly cheesesteaks (which seemed popular even at a
price of $8.25), Icees, deli sandwiches, and veggie dogs. The beer selection
includes some corporate brews (Bud, Bud Light) and local heroes (Labatt Blue,
Alexander Keith's, Moosehead).

Be forewarned, the concessions are not uniformly distributed. Practically
no concessions can be found behind the center-field stands so you'll need to
walk a ways should you buy seats there.

There are also a number of restaurants with views of the action. The largest is Home Plate Bar & Grill in center field on the 200 level (which features a 300-foot-long bar), while the attached Renaissance Hotel features two restaurants with ballpark views, and the attached Hard Rock Café has a limited view of the action.

Speaking of the 200 level: the Blue Jays added a formal Club 200 area to the ballpark. It's pitched by the club as an exclusive, service-driven area, much like other club-level areas in big-league ballparks.

For the Kids
A new play area was added behind sections 116-117 before the 2006 season. In addition, the Blue Jays added a slew of entertainers outside the ballpark before many games. For selected Saturday games, kids and parents can go down to the field after the game and run the bases.

Ballpark Tours
The Blue Jays offer hour-long tours of the ballpark. The cost is pretty spendy: $13.50 for adults, $9.50 for seniors and youth (12-17), and $8 for children aged 5-11. Call 416/341-2770 for information.

Local Attractions
Even though we're baseball fanatics, we were particularly impressed with the Hockey Hall of Fame. Hockey is to Canada as baseball is to America: a sport filled with sentimentality and nostalgia, used as a starting point when discussing national traits and tendencies. Canadians love their hockey and it's the dream of every Canadian schoolkid to play for their national team and in the National Hockey League. The Hockey Hall of Fame is a fascinating tribute to the many ways hockey permeates Canadian life, ranging from youth and junior hockey to the many pro leagues over the years. It's also participatory: fans can face off as a goalie or a scorer in simulation games, while would-be broadcasters can hone their craft in a mock play-by-play booth. All in all, this is clearly the best sports hall of fame on the planet. Sorry, Cooperstown. *Hockey Hall of Fame, BCE Place, 30 Yonge St., Toronto; hhof.org; 416/360-7765. Adults, $12; youth (4-13), $8; seniors, $8.*

You will not go hungry or thirsty while staying near the ballpark in Toronto. We won't give you a long list of potential places to eat and drink; we'll just pass along some favorites.

Anyone serious enough about hockey to visit the Hockey Hall of Fame will be absolutely ecstatic at the notion of eating at Wayne Gretzky's, located just north of the ballpark. Some of the Great One's memorabilia is on display and supposedly some of his favorite foods are on the menu. Normally we're not fans of celebrity restaurants, but, geez, we're talking about Gretzky here. *Wayne Gretzky's, 99 Blue Jays Way; gretzkys.com; 416/979-7825.*

Go another block north (past Mercer) and you'll hit Toronto's entertainment district, as well as the row of restaurants and bars on King Street. They all follow a similar formula: clever name (Kit Kat Italian Bar, Fred's Not

Here, Hey Lucy), casual food, outdoor dining in the summer, and lots of liquor. A personal favorite is just off King: the Duke of Argyle (86 John St.), billed as a Nova Scotia-style pub in the heart of Toronto.

You can also go a little farther a field to find some restaurants and bars suitable for baseball fans.

C'est What Brew/Vin Pub Restaurant is renowned for its locally brewed beer and wine as well as a menu stressing comfort food. They're not afraid to take chances on the brewing side; recent selections have included a hemp ale, chocolate ale, and a coffee porter. If one of the microbrews doesn't strike your fancy, 28 other beers are on tap, and chances are pretty good you've never heard of—never mind tasted—most of them. The wine comes from grapes grown in Niagara and is served in four varieties: two whites (Riesling and Seyval Blanc) and two reds (Baco Noir and Gamay Noir). For those wanting something more robust, there's a full selection of whiskies and bourbons (curiously, though, selection is small when it comes to the new breed of Canadian whiskies on the market). *C'est What, 67 Front St. E. (corner of Front and Church); cestwhat.com; 416/867-9499.*

In the same neighborhood, beer lovers will also find another great watering hole: Beer Bistro, where it's beer, beer, beer: beers on tap, beer in the appetizers, beer in the entrees, beer in the pizza dough, mussels steamed in beer, beer in the ice cream, beer in the chocolate fondue. We kid you not: it's a bistro devoted to showing the many flavors of beer. And it's open until 2 a.m. on Fridays and Saturdays. *Beer Bistro, 18 King St. E.; beerbistro.com; 416/861-9872.*

Along the same vein: the Esplanade Bier Markt, where over 100 beers are on tap. The Esplanade Bier Markt doesn't go quite as far as the Beer Bistro when it comes to food (beer is not an ingredient in most of the entrees), but they do pair beer with some odd ingredients to create some funky cocktails. *Esplanade Bier Markt, 58 The Esplanade; thebiermarkt.com; 416/862-7575.*

Getting There

You can get to Rogers Centre easily by plane, train, and automobile.

Most fans attending games will be driving in. There are a ton of parking spots in surface lots and ramps within six blocks of the ballpark, as well as a Rogers Centre parking ramp and a CN Tower ramp. During the day the area surrounding the ballpark is a business district, and as those spots are vacated they are replaced by game attendees. Some prices for lots are as high as $10, but if you look around a little you can find parking ramps like the Simcoe ramp on Front Street for as low as $5. The lots immediately east of the ballpark north of Bremner Boulevard and west of York Street are convenient and inexpensive as well.

If you drive, Rogers Centre is ridiculously easy to find. If in doubt, head toward the next-door CN Tower, by far the tallest structure in downtown Toronto. Because the ballpark is 31 stories high it's also easy to see from a distance. Most visitors will come in on the Queen Elizabeth Way (QEW) freeway from the east (the same route from Pearson International Airport as well). At one point the QEW splits into Gardiner Expressway and Lakeshore Boulevard; both will bring you to the ballpark. From Gardiner or the QEW, take the Spadina Avenue exit north; from Lakeshore Boulevard take the Rees Street exit and head north. In all cases the route to Rogers Centre is clearly marked, although in some cases it's still designated as SkyDome.

Pearson International Airport is the larger of the two Toronto airports. It's a big three-terminal airport about 20 minutes from downtown Toronto. If you're coming from out of town and flying in, our recommendation is to avoid a car: you simply won't need it. By staying close to the ballpark (we list nearby hotels in the next section) and walking over, you'll see the best of a great international city. For a reasonable $26.75 you can take a round-trip shuttle bus, Airport Express (*torontoaurportexpress.com*), from any of the three terminals to one of eight downtown hotels. They take credit cards.

The closest subway stops are at Union Station and St. Andrews Station. From Union Station: If the weather is bad you can use the Skywalk from the station to the base of CN Tower. If the weather is good just walk down Front Street to the ballpark. For more information on subways, contact the TTC (Toronto Transit Commission) at 416/393-INFO or check out the TTC web site at *city.toronto.on.ca/ttc*. For more information on Toronto buses and light rail, check out the GO transit web site at *gotransit.com*.

And then there's always the train. Rogers Centre is located three blocks from the aforementioned Union Station, a grand old railroad terminal dating back to the days when train travel was the only way to get from point A to point B in a reasonable amount of time. Both Via Rail Canada and GO serve Union Station. It's not exactly in pristine shape (picture a run-down Penn Station with a underused main hall) but it's still convenient, particularly if you're coming in from another Canadian city or an U.S. city with Amtrak connections.

Where to Stay

With a host of hotels at a variety of price points within walking distance of the ballpark, the most obvious place to stay is downtown Toronto. Be warned the hotels closest to Rogers Centre are not the cheapest, but they are the most luxurious.

The most convenient place to stay is the Renaissance Toronto Downtown (One Blue Jays Way; *marriott.com*; $200-$300) located within the ballpark. It's a luxury hotel with 70 rooms overlooking the action in center field. Be prepared to pay a premium to stay there during the season, although you can probably avoid the price of a ticket if you're content to sit in your hotel chair and glance at the TV for the replays. (With cable rights, Rogers Cable, Rogers Sports Net and TSN provide the feed for all Blue Jays games—home and away.)

We're partial to grand old hotels, which is why our favorite place to stay in downtown Toronto is the Fairmont Royal York (100 Front St. W.; *fairmont.com*; $200-$300), the flagship of the old Canadian Pacific hotel chain. The Canadian equivalent of New York City's Waldorf=Astoria, the Royal York features a majestic lobby and an emphasis on luxury. Many of the rooms have been recently remodeled. It's a splurge, but a wonderful splurge.

Similar splurges, albeit in newer packaging, are the InterContinental Toronto Centre (225 Front St. W.; *torontocentre.intercontinental.com*; $200-$300) and Westin Harbour Castle (1 Harbour Square; *westin.com*; $200-$300). Across the street from Rogers Centre, the InterContinental has also been recently renovated with an emphasis on the business traveler. The Westin is located south of the ballpark on the waterfront.

We've stayed at the Hilton Toronto (145 Richmond St. W.; *hilton.com*; $250-$325) and were underwhelmed; for the money you can do a lot better. There's also a cluster of hotels north of the ballpark near Eaton Place (a major shopping center in downtown Toronto), including the majestic Le Royal Meridien King Edward (37 King St. E.; *toronto.lemeridien.com*; $300-$400), Marriott Downtown Toronto (525 Bay St.; *marriott.com*; $200-$250), Delta Chelsea (33 Gerrard St. E.; *deltahotels.com*; $150-$225), Courtyard by Marriott (475 Yonge St.; *marriott.com*; $150-$200), Ramada Hotel Suites Downtown (300 Jarvis St.; *ramada.com*; $100-$150), and the Comfort Suites City Centre (200 Dundas St. E.; *choicehotels.com*; $100-$125).

Two other local hotels we can recommend don't require a luxury payment. The Holiday Inn Toronto on King Street (370 King St. W.; *holiday-inn.com*; $125-$175), three blocks from the ballpark, is in the midst of a funky neighborhood with great bars and restaurants. The Holiday Inn Express Downtown Toronto (111 Lombard St.; *holiday-inn.com*; $100-$150) is inexpensive.

Local Attractions

Proximity to the action is where Rogers Centre shines. It is perhaps the most perfectly situated ballpark in major-league baseball (apologies to AT&T Park). Downtown Toronto is a beautiful, historic area and, with a wealth of mass-transit and hotel options, there's little reason to stay and play anywhere but close to the ballpark.

A ride to the top of CN Tower (301 Front St. W.; *cntower.ca*; adults, $19.99; children, $13.99) next door is a mandatory stop for families. At 1,815 feet, 5 inches high, it's billed as the tallest building in the world (though it's truly a tower, technically speaking). Each year, two million people visit the world's highest observation tower, the SkyPod, at 1,465 feet above sea level; another attraction is the rotating 360 Restaurant which sits 1,150 feet above sea level. And it's so doggone Canadian: even though building a big tower for the sake of building a big tower is instinctually inbred in every man on the planet, the CN Tower web site rationalizes the construction as being practical because it gave locals better wireless reception. As if they needed to build the world's largest tower to enable better reception—maybe, eh, all the way to Thunder Bay.

Next door to the ballpark is the Steam Whistle Brewery (*steamwhistle.ca*), housed in a 1929 Canadian Pacific Rail steam locomotive repair facility.

Brewery tours run on the hour, complete with samples of the brewery's sole brew, a Canadian Pilsner. If you're with a group of friends and it's a nice day, buy a six-pack and put back a few at one of the picnic tables outside the brewery. Don't forget a bottle opener: these aren't twist-offs.

Team Ballpark History

The first home of the Blue Jays was Exhibition Stadium, where Toronto played from April 7, 1977 to May 28, 1989. Never a stellar baseball facility, it was built in 1959 for the Toronto Argonauts of the Canadian Football League. Exhibition Stadium was revamped in 1975-1977 for the expansion Blue Jays. The football grandstand was converted into the left-field bleachers, while a new grandstand and bleachers were added down each line, bringing the capacity to 38,522 in 1977 and 43,272 in 1978.

The configuration made for some rather awkward situations. Because the Canadian Football League playing field is wider and longer than American football fields, fans sitting in seats down each line were facing center field quite a ways from the action, and a plastic fence in right field blocked off the rest of the football field. (Due to the large football field and the Blue Jays' needs, the Astroturf surface was the largest ever installed at 160,000 square feet.) The only covered seats in the whole facility were in the outfield bleachers. At least it was cheap: the cost of converting Exhibition Stadium to a baseball facility was $17.6 million.

Exhibition Stadium was so named because of its location at Exhibition Place near downtown Toronto. It's home to the Canadian National Exhibition, a yearly celebration of all things Canadian. After the Blue Jays and the Argonauts moved to SkyDome in 1989, there was really no use for Exhibition Stadium past the occasional concert, and so the entire facility was torn down in 1999; the site is now a parking lot.

Despite the stadium's relatively short history, it was home to some quirky baseball moments. The first game at Exhibition Stadium on April 7, 1977 was played with snow covering the artificial turf, despite attempts by the groundskeepers to clear the field with a Zamboni ice resurfacer borrowed from the Toronto Maple Leafs. An April 30, 1984 game was postponed due to high winds, the only time that's happened in major-league baseball. And a September 15, 1977 game against the Baltimore Orioles was forfeited after Earl Weaver withdrew his team from the contest, claiming the exposed field-side tarps were hazardous. The umps agreed.

On Aug, 4, 1983, Exhibition Stadium was also home to one of the strangest happenings in pro-baseball history. Warming up before the bottom of the fifth inning, Yankees right-fielder Dave Winfield threw the ball toward the Yankees dugout and struck a sea gull on the head, killing it instantly. Following the game—won by the Yankees 3-1, with Winfield driving in two of the three runs—Winfield was arrested by Ontario Provincial Police and charged with cruelty to animals. After posting $500 bond he was released.

"They say he hit the gull on purpose," acerbic Yankees manager Billy

Martin said to the press. "They wouldn't say that if they'd seen the throws he'd been making all year. It's the first time he's hit the cutoff man."

Charges were dropped the following day.

The Blue Jays were not the start of professional baseball in Toronto. The Toronto Maple Leafs were a mainstay of the original International League and Maple Leaf Stadium was regarded as one of the palaces of the league. Located on the waterfront at the foot of Bathurst Street, on Lakeshore Drive and Stadium Drive, the $300,000 ballpark opened in 1928. The distinctive two-story grandstand seated 20,000 and over the years many greats played there, either with International League teams or on barnstorming tours. After World War II the Maple Leafs were a major draw—under owner Jack Kent Cooke (later owner of the NBA's Los Angeles Lakers and the NFL's Washington Redskins) the team drew 440,000 a year for several years—and Toronto was heavily considered by major-league baseball as the future home of the St. Louis Browns, Washington Senators or Philadelphia Athletics. But a relocation never materialized and the Maple Leafs fell on hard times, finally moving in 1967.

Maple Leaf Stadium wasn't located too far from Rogers Centre; a marker commemorates the old ballpark at 0 Bathurst Street.

Before Maple Leaf Stadium was Maple Leaf Park. Located on Hanlan's Point, a popular summer recreation spot, Maple Leaf Park was a concrete ballpark holding 18,000 fans. It was a large ballpark for its day, and it's notable for one historic event: Babe Ruth hit his first home run there as a professional in 1914. The 19-year-old Ruth was a member of the International League's Providence Grays, sent to the minors by parent Boston Red Sox. In those days Ruth was projected as a pitcher, but he showed all aspects to his talent on a September 14 doubleheader. In the first game Ruth threw a one-hit shutout. In the nightcap, Ruth blasted a three-run shot in the sixth inning—the only homer he hit in the minors, by the way. There's some dispute as to where the ball landed: some eyewitnesses say it cleared the fence and landed just beyond on a strip of land, while others say it made a splash in Lake Ontario.

In either case, there's now a pair of commemorative markers on Hanlan's Point, marking the spot where Ruth hit his first professional home run.

Washington Nationals
RFK Stadium

Address: 2400 E. Capitol St., Washington, DC 20003.
Cost: $24 million.
Architect: George A. Dahl and Osborn Engineering.
Owner: The Government of the District of Columbia, under the auspices of the
    D.C. Sports & Entertainment Commission.
Capacity: 56,000.
Dimensions: 335L, 385LC, 410C, 385RC, 335R.
Home Dugout Location: Third-base side.
Ticket Line: 202/397-SEAT (7328).
Playing Surface: Grass.
Other Tenants: Pro soccer's D.C. United has played here since 1996. The
    second Washington Senators played here from 1962 through 1971, while
    the NFL's Washington Redskins played here from 1961 to 1996.
Previous Names: District of Columbia Stadium (1961 to 1969), usually
    shortened to DC Stadium.
First Game: The Washington Senators defeated the Detroit Tigers, 4-1, on April
    9, 1962. Mickey Vernon was the manager, and that day the second-year
    Sens were led by shortstop Bob Johnson (3-for-4, 2 RBI) and pitcher
    Bennie Daniels, who shut down a potent Tigers offense (Al Kaline, Rocky
    Calavito, and Norm Cash were in the middle of the batting order) with a
    complete-game five-hitter. (This wasn't the first sporting event at the
    stadium: the NFL's Washington Redskins played their 1961 season at RFK,
    opening the facility on October 1 with a 24-21 loss to the New York Giants
    before a crowd of 36,767.) MLB returned to Washington on April 14, 2005,

when former Senators reliever Joe Grzenda handed a ball used in the last Washington Nationals game in 1971 to President George W. Bush, who threw out the ceremonial first pitch. The Nationals defeated the Arizona Diamondbacks, 5-3, with Livan Hernandez earning the win and Chad Cordero notching the save. Third baseman Vinny Castilla went 3-for-3 and drove in four runs with a double, triple, and home run.

Landmark Event: RFK Stadium is one of the few major-league parks to host more than one All-Star Game, as the 1962 and second 1969 games were played there. (For several seasons MLB played two All-Star Games.) The second Senators never made the playoffs, so the most notable game may be the last Sens game played at RFK Stadium. On Sept. 30, 1971, the Senators were leading the New York Yankees 7-5 with two outs in the ninth inning when fans rushed onto the field to protest the team's impending move to Texas. The umpires called the game and awarded a 9-0 forfeit win to the Yankees.

Your RFK Stadium Seating Crib Sheet

Best Sections to View a Game: Though the pricing is a little steep at $45, the Infield Box seats are pretty good. If you're going to RFK Stadium for a single game, splurge. It's not that hard to nab good seats to Nationals game: after the initial pent-up demand was sated by the end of the 2005 season—with the D.C. punditocracy openly whining about their seat placement at times—the novelty wore off, and average crowds settled in by April 2006.

Best Cheap Seats: The $7 Outfield Upper Reserved seats are surprisingly fine. You can see the entire field and not feel like you're a mile away from the action. (As a bonus, these seats are wooden and original to the ballpark.) Buy these seats and move down to the Outfield Lower Reserved seats if there's not a big crowd on hand, as there are relatively few ushers patrolling the outfield seats.

Most Underrated Sections: Sections 444 through 469 in the outfield (the Outfield Lower Reserved sections): you're perched above the action and can see the whole field. Sit in the left-field area if possible; sitting in right field obstructs your view of the videoboard.

Seats to Avoid: The Infield Terrace Box Rear seats in sections 307 to 323. The large press box—built to accommodate the hordes of press covering the Washington Redskins in the 1980s—hangs from the second deck and limits the view from these seats. The Baseline Boxes (201-206, 223-228) are not great, either, with an orientation toward the outfield.

RFK Stadium: Baseball is Back in the Capital

There may be no second acts in American life, but there are second chances galore, and Washington's RFK Stadium has a second life as the home of the Washington Nationals. Built in 1961 as the home of the second Washington Senators and the NFL's Washington Redskins, RFK Stadium has been infused with new life as millions of fans passed through the turnstiles in 2005 and 2006 to cheer on the relocated Montreal Expos.

In retrospect, RFK Stadium was the only logical destination for the Expos. It was designed for major-league baseball. The infrastructure for handling large crowds—freeway and mass-transit access, concessions, a wealth of luxury boxes—was in place, and the District of Columbia was hungry for major-league baseball. RFK today is a place where Republicans and Democrats can coexist. America's pastime in America's capital is a match made in heaven.

RFK was one of the original cookie-cutter stadiums: circular facilities designed to host both pro football and baseball, with the fences and stands reconfigured depending on the use. At RFK, the transition between football and baseball originally took several hours to complete, with an entire set of seats (now located down the third-base line) rolling on a curved train track to open the end of the football field and add seats to the sidelines. When RFK was being readied for baseball before the 2005 season opener, crews from Turner Construction were nervous about whether the track would work, as it had not been used in years. It did.

The traditional definition of a cookie-cutter stadium involves a circular design, but nothing about RFK Stadium is circular. Instead, the design features a few different ovals that intersect. The stadium isn't a perfect circle and neither is the seating bowl for baseball. You can sit in the outfield looking directly down the middle of the plate and be a little disoriented because what's behind it isn't a perfect semicircle. This leads to a few other quirks as well; for example, there's a lot of foul territory.

There aren't many cookie-cutter stadiums left: Cincinnati dumped Riverfront Stadium, St. Louis left the second Busch Stadium, and when a new D.C. ballpark in completed, the Nationals will be leaving RFK Stadium as well.

What happens then is anyone's guess. RFK Stadium was given up for dead several years ago when the Washington Redskins flew to the suburbs, and only the lack of a game plan for the area saved the stadium from the wrecking ball.

Until then, RFK Stadium will serve admirably as the home of the Nationals. For a 40-year-old-plus cookie-cutter stadium, RFK Stadium is in better shape that you'd expect. Yes, it's definitely frayed around the edges, but it received a good power washing and some badly needed concession upgrades during the 2006 season. Overall, it's got more charm than you'd expect in such an old and disused facility.

Just remember: it's old. RFK Stadium is the second-oldest ballpark in the National League, with only Wrigley Field opening before RFK. DC Stadium (as it was originally named) opened for baseball on April 9, 1962, while Dodger Stadium opened on April 10. Much of its layout reflects that age: the

concourses are cramped, no escalators move between levels, and the outfield sections rise a full level above the playing field. Luckily, the ballpark was designed before the rise of artificial turf.

The expansion Senators team playing at RFK was never very good: the team never won a division and approached .500 only under the underrated tutelage of Ted Williams. For many years Frank Howard was the box-office draw at RFK, with his mammoth homers regularly reaching the upper deck. The Senators marked the seats where Howard's shots finally came out of orbit; alas, these seats were painted over with Redskin gold and burgundy after the Senators fled, a color scheme that still stands. One thing missing at RFK Stadium is an homage to baseball's rich history. Other than a marker commemorating Clark Griffith outside the ballpark, ther are no displays honoring the original or expansion Senators, the Homestead Grays, other Negro League teams, or great players like Walter Johnson (save a perfunctory listing on the Washington Hall of Fame) and Josh Gibson. You wouldn't know Washington had a colorful baseball past after visiting RFK Stadium.

Part of the reason why RFK is interesting is its architectural flourishes. The roller-coaster roof is recognizable from a distance (you always knew the Redskins were in town when CBS would flash an exterior shot), and the waves soften the edges of the ballpark. They aren't symmetrical throughout the park and exist only behind home plate.

Baseball changed greatly between the last days of the Senators and the beginning of the Nationals. Fans aren't expected to spend nine innings planted in their seats with the occasional bathroom and concession break, and RFK Stadium is ill-suited to fans who want to wander the ballpark and watch the action from multiple vantage points. The Nationals don't prevent you from wandering; it's just that there aren't many places to stand and watch the game past the main-level concourses down each line. The aisles and rows between are narrow, and the angle of seating differs. It's a steep climb between rows in the upper deck, but the angle is so slight on the grandstand it's sometimes hard for shorter fans to see the action. On the bright side, the seats are wide, so once you're sitting you'll be comfortable.

Major League Baseball did mandate some improvements to RFK Stadium upon the arrival of the Nats. A new videoboard in right field provides replays, scores, and other game information. Concessions were upgraded during the 2006 season after fans complained of long lines and poor food selection (a problem that seems to have been addressed by new team owners). The funky closed-circuit TV displays dating to the Redskins days are still scattered through the concourses, their picture quality as fuzzy as ever. For anyone who spent a lot of time at Washington Redskins games, the memories will come back quickly.

Otherwise, there's little in the way of interesting décor at the ballpark. The most noteworthy flourish is a huge clock in the outfield sporting a Nationals logo. A Washington Hall of Fame board in right field honors great athletes and sports figures of the past.

More interesting décor may be the faces in the stands, as Washington's political pundits—Bob Novak, Fred Barnes, David Brooks—queued up for season tickets. (Alas, one of the problems faced by the Nats is the large number of people buying season tickets and not showing up for games, as the punditry class and others abandoned the team at the end of 2005.) During our initial visit to a Nats game, Fox News anchor Brit Hume threw out the first pitch: predictably, it sailed to the right of center.

RFK Stadium is a temporary home for the Nationals, as a new ballpark in Southeast D.C. is scheduled to open for the 2008 season. Considering the franchise has spent much of its history in "temporary" facilities—Jarry Park, Hiram Bithorn Stadium, even the final days at Olympic Stadium—the Nationals and their fans could do a lot worst than biding time at RFK Stadium.

Ballpark Quirks

The curved section of seats down the left-field line are the movable seats discussed earlier (they move along a track when the facility converts from baseball to football). This section is original to RFK Stadium and isn't the most stable of platforms: when enough fans coordinate their efforts, the stands bounce up and down—which happened often early in the 2005 season when the Nationals were drawing large, excited crowds.

Smoking is allowed in the concourses. Clean-air laws have not yet reached the District, so be prepared to walk through a phalanx of smokers as you hit the restrooms and concession stands.

Food and Drink

Concessions at RFK Stadium are considerably better now than they were when the Nationals moved from Montreal. Our first trip to RFK Stadium yielded the same limited menu at most concessions stand: $4 hot dogs (avoid; ours were cold and bland), nachos, popcorn, chicken tenders, candy, and fries. Sausages and brats are sold at Dominic's of New York stands (despite the name, Dominic's is a Virginia firm).

The new Washington Nationals ownership (the Theodore Lerner family bought the team in mid-2006) upgraded concessions considerably. Available now are crab cakes, barbeque (briskets and riblets), Texas sausage, kosher knishes, and more. The Burrito Brothers burritos stand behind section 109 is a reliable source of good Mexican fare, and the beer selections include Heineken, Dos Equis, Red Hook, Guinness, Harp, and Killians.

Behind section 116 there's the Foggy Bottom Brewpub, serving beers from the Olde Heurich Brewing Company. Heurich is a traditional name in Washington brewing: the Christian Heurich brewery was a D.C. landmark for decades (torn down to make way for the John F. Kennedy Center for the Performing Arts), and grandson Gary Heurich carries on the family tradition. Alas, Foggy Bottom beers are contract-brewed in upstate New York. A special pilsner is brewed for consumption at RFK. Since the smoking regulations in D.C. are on the liberal side, this is a popular gathering spot for smokers. Mixed drinks are also on the menu.

For the Kids

Parents can amuse their children at a new play area outside the north side of the ballpark.

We're not sure kids will be entertained by the Nationals' mascot, Screech. Screech is a bad, bad mascot, resembling the pompous Muppet, Sam the Eagle.

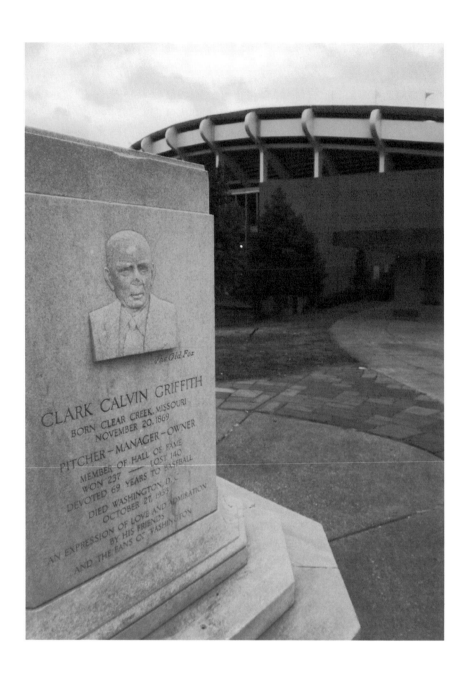

THE OLD FOX

CLARK CALVIN GRIFFITH
BORN CLEAR CREEK, MISSOURI
NOVEMBER 20, 1869

PITCHER – MANAGER – OWNER
MEMBER OF HALL OF FAME
WON 237 — LOST 140
DEVOTED 69 YEARS TO BASEBALL
DIED WASHINGTON, D.C.
OCTOBER 27, 1955

AN EXPRESSION OF LOVE AND ADMIRATION
BY HIS FRIENDS
AND THE FANS OF WASHINGTON

President Calvin Coolidge shaking hands with Walter Johnson at Griffith Stadium, circa 1923-1927. (Library of Congress LC-USZ62-32732.)

Ballpark Tours

The D.C. Sports & Entertainment Commission does not offer tours of RFK Stadium.

Local Baseball Attractions

Before you enter the ballpark, head to the main entrance on the south side to admire the tribute to Clark Griffith. (Also take a peek at the two ancient Redskins helmets, a reminder of better times in the stadium's history.) Griffith was the longtime owner of the Washington Senators, but his baseball pedigree is much more extensive. One of the first National League stars to jump over to the upstart American League in 1901, Griffith compiled a 24-7 mark for Charlie Comiskey's Chicago White Stockings, as well as managing the team to the pennant.

He then managed the New York Highlanders (the predecessor to the Yankees) and the Cincinnati Reds before managing the Washington Nationals in 1912. The Nationals (also popularly known as the Senators) played at National Park. After mortgaging his farm to buy a chunk of the team, Griffith kept adding to his ownership stake until he controlled the franchise with the aid of minority owners, eventually renaming National Park to Griffith Stadium.

Under his ownership, the Senators weren't quite as bad as legend has it: in

American League Park on May 6, 1905: Washington vs. Philadelphia. The attendance was 9,300. (LC-USZ62-88346, LC-USZ62-88347)

the early days the Sens were quite competitive and won a World Series in 1924 behind Walter "Big Train" Johnson, one of the most dominant pitchers ever to play the game. Players like Joe Cronin, Sam Rice, Sam West, Heinie Manush, Buddy Myer, Joe Judge, and Ossie Bluege kept the Senators in contention.

After 1945, Griffith lost control of the talent side of the equation, leaving onlookers to mock the team and leading a pundit to give the franchise the ultimate in putdowns: First in war, first in peace, and last in the American League. Musicals were written about the team's futility.

Griffith also had a more dubious legacy: he was one of the major-league owners who most stubbornly resisted integration. Griffith Stadium was a popular locale for Negro League games; large crowds were common, and the popular Homestead Grays ended up moving most of their games there. Griffith told legendary sportswriter Sam Lacy it would kill the Negro Leagues for MLB to sign black ballplayers (he was right), and in that instance Griffith chose the sure paycheck from the Grays over the chance to be a pioneering team owner— a reversal of the pioneering spirit he showed when jumping to the nascent

American League. Lacy and others insisted a black star would have eventually saved the Senators, but that's debatable: the Dodgers did indeed move out of Brooklyn despite the signing of Jackie Robinson, so attracting a racially integrated clientele was not an assurance of business success. (Though, in Lacy's defense, D.C. had a thriving minority middle class that looked to baseball for entertainment.) It took Griffith a few years after the integration of baseball to sign a black ballplayer, and in tempo with his timid nature, the first black player for the Senators was a Cuban, Carlos Paula, not one of the Negro Leagues stars who drew large crowds to Griffith Stadium. Paula didn't make his Senators debut until September 6, 1954, long after most MLB teams had racially integrated. (Interestingly enough, the Senators were integrated before the New York Yankees and the Philadelphia Phillies.)

Still, Griffith was a beloved owner until his death, known for his emphasis on family (he adopted nephew Calvin Griffith and niece Thelma Haynes, leaving them the team). You can check out the tribute on the marker for more details.

An overhead shot of Griffith Stadium. Notice the jog in center field.

Griffith Stadium was one of the more unusual ballparks in major-league history. Baseball was a popular game in D.C. before the turn of the century, as the Washington Monument was built on the site of a well-used baseball ground near the White House. Professional baseball was played by the Washington Nationals of the American Association in 1901 and the National League

The demolition of Griffith Stadium—a sad end to a historic venue.

Washington Senators from 1892 through 1899, who played in the all-wood National Park (also called Boundary Field). The upstart American League saw the opportunity to place a team in Washington, and the Nationals were born in 1901.

The Nationals (who were sometimes called the Senators; team names were a much more fluid notion in those days) played in their own ballpark a few blocks from American League Park, and then moved onto the National Park site after the 1903 season, bringing wooden bleachers from their old ballpark. In 1911 American League Park burned down, but a new ballpark was ready to open three weeks later as reconstruction commenced with a steel and concrete structure. This new ballpark was more permanent, serving as the home of the Nationals/Senators through 1960 and the expansion Senators in 1961.

One of the most noticeable characteristics of Griffith Stadium was its asymmetry. The distances from home plate to the foul poles changed often over the years, but for most of the park's existence, the left-field fence was about 100 feet further away than the right-field fence (LF 410', CF 420', RF 320'). The outfield zigged and zagged. Just beyond the center field wall stood five residential duplexes and a massive oak tree. The owner of the property would not sell, so the center-field fence had to jut in and form a 90-degree angle to accommodate the buildings. The oak tree, visible to all watching and playing the game, became one of the hallmarks of Griffith Stadium.

Griffith Stadium was also the birthplace of one of the more enduring traditions in baseball: the ceremonial first pitch delivered by the President. President William Howard Taft threw out the ceremonial first pitch of the 1910 season—a toss apparently performed spur-of-the-moment by the portly Taft, a huge baseball fan. (Another tradition attributed to Taft at Griffith is apparently an urban folk tale: the seventh-inning stretch did not originate when Taft stood up to stretch at a Nationals game and the crowd rose in response. Others have documented the roots of this fine baseball tradition further back in history than the Taft presidency.)

Griffith Stadium was demolished in 1965. Howard University Hospital stands in its place today, and there is no public marker denoting the location.

Getting There

One of the big advantages of the Expos moving to RFK Stadium: an infrastructure capable of handling tens of thousands of fans daily was in place, thanks to the enormous popularity of the Redskins in the 1980s and 1990s. The infrastructure routes people around the surrounding neighborhood. There's not much of note in the area: it's mostly rundown residential with no restaurants or bars catering to sports fans. There is no reason for you to spend any time in the area around the ballpark.

(This saddens us. A ballpark has the potential to become an integral part of the fabric of an urban neighborhood, but D.C. officials never attempted to integrate RFK Stadium into the nearby disadvantaged neighborhood. Since it looks as though RFK Stadium will be torn down after the Nationals and D.C. United move into new facilities, the neighborhood will have never benefited from its presence.)

Two routes to the ballpark are popular: driving and the Metro. Taking the Metro is the cheaper and easier method. D.C.'s subway system is among the best in the world: it's clean, safe, and serves every important part of town, including surrounding communities like Alexandria and Arlington. (Based on the Metro service to the ballpark and the condition of the surrounding area, we'd recommend you stay elsewhere in D.C.) The Blue-Orange Line stops at the Stadium-Armory station at 19th and East Capitol Street; just walk two blocks from there to the ballpark.

Driving is almost as easy, and there are 10,000 parking spots onsite. The ballpark is located next to I-395 on the east side of the District. If you're coming from the south, watch for the RFK Stadium exits on the left side of the freeway past the Maine Avenue exit. Follow those signs off the freeway and onto a regular highway leading directly into the ballpark's No. 8 parking lot. The charge for parking is only $10—a bargain by big-league standards—and you're just a short walk from the ballpark. If you're driving through the city, take Massachusetts Avenue east until you hit Lincoln Park at 12th Street; go around the park and look for East Capitol Street. Take that street directly to the ballpark.

Where to Stay

You won't want to stay near the ballpark. For starters, there's nothing (hotels, restaurants, attractions) within walking distance of the ballpark, and secondly the surrounding area is in pretty rough shape. Plus, given the excellent mass-transit and freeway access to the stadium, there's no reason to stay nearby.

INSIDER'S TIP
The budget-conscious will want to check out D.C. hotels run by Kimpton, which specializes in taking older properties and upgrading them as boutique hotels. In the Dupont Circle area, check out the Topaz Hotel (1733 N St. NW.; *topazhotel.com*; $140-$200) or the Hotel Madera (1310 New Hampshire Av. NW.; *hotelmarera.com*; $140-$200) for a stylish stay.

That leaves the greater District of Columbia area as a potential home base. We're not going to highlight all of the great hotels in the area, but we will pass along a few neighborhoods with plenty of hotels and easy access to the ballpark. Be warned staying in Washington is not cheap; it used to be you could find deals in late July through Labor Day, but a rise in the area's popularity means you could pay $200 or so a night for a hotel, especially if you want to stay at a location close to a Metro stop.

The Dupont Circle neighborhood is a popular area close to downtown Washington. It's home to Embassy Row, giving it a certain international feel while offering easy access to the rest of Washington through the Dupont Circle Metro stop. Right on the circle is the popular Jurys Washington Hotel (1500 New Hampshire Av.; *jurys-washingtondc-hotels.com*; $175-$275), and close by are the Hilton Washington Embassy Row (2015 Massachusetts Av. NW.; *hilton.com*; $200-$300), the Westin Embassy Row (2100 Massachusetts Av. NW.; *westin.com*; $200-$300), and the Residence Inn Washington Dupont Circle (2120 P St. NW; *mariott.com*; $250-$300).

Downtown Washington is once again a popular destination. The areas near the White House and the Mall have been gentrified and cleaned up. This is where you'll find the old, historic hotels of D.C.:

The **Capital Hilton** (1001 16th St. NW.; *hilton.com*; $120-$300) is huge and a centerpiece of government tradition, hosting every president since Franklin Delano Roosevelt.

The **Hay-Adams** (One Lafayette Square; *hayadams.com*; $275-$500) is definitely a splurge. Built in the 1920s and extensively renovated in 2002, the Hay-Adams has always been a preferred address of the elite.

The **Renaissance Mayflower** (1127 Connecticut Av. NW.; *marriott.com*; $125-$400) sits at the crossroads of downtown Washington. Franklin Delano Roosevelt lived here while waiting to move into the White House, and Harry S. Truman once said he preferred staying here over the White House.

The **Jefferson** (1200 16th St. NW.; $200-$1,500) may be best known as the home for political consultant Dick Morris's foot-fetish trysts, but that's unfortunate: it's a small Beaux Arts classic with a great bar.

The **Madison** (15th and M streets NW.; *themadisondc.com*; $400-$500) is small, exclusive, and private.

The **St. Regis** (923 16th St. NW.; *stregis.com*; $200-$600) stays to the same high level of luxury as the rest of the chain.

INSIDER'S TIP
Staying downtown doesn't have to cost an arm and a leg. The Lincoln Suites Downtown (1823 L. St. NW.; *lincolnhotels.com*; $125-$225) isn't especially old or historic, but it's a great choice for families who would prefer to stay in for some meals and schedule naps between an afternoon of sightseeing and the evening meal. The Hotel Monaco (700 F. St. NW.; *monaco-dc.com*; $150-$350) is another in the outstanding Kimpton chain. Occupying the former Tariff Building — the first all-marble building in D.C. — the Hotel Monaco features spacious rooms and a location near the Smithsonian's National Gallery of Art. The Four Points Sheraton (1201 K St. NW.; *sheraton.com*; $100-$200) is safe, reliable, and inexpensive. And the newly remodeled Embassy Suites Hotel Downtown (1250 22nd St. NW.; *hilton.com*; $150-$300) is a good bet for families, although it's really on the edge of downtown and requires a short Metro trip to the Smithsonian museums and the mall.

The **Willard Inter-Continental Washington** (1401 Pennsylvania Av. NW.; *intercontinental.com*; $200-$4,800) is home to many visiting foreign dignitaries and is considered by many as the classiest hotel in the District.

While You're There

Your biggest problem during your visit won't be finding enough things to do—it will be trying to fit everything into a limited schedule.

Take the Smithsonian Institution. You could easily spend three or four days going through all the excellent Smithsonian museums on the National Mall and still feel as though you rushed through things.

We're not going to tell you to rush from attraction to attraction just so you can say you saw Judy Garland's slippers from *The Wizard of Oz* or a famous Gilbert Stuart painting. Instead, put some thought into what you want to see and then spend the time to get the most out of your visit. The centerpiece of your visit should be the National Mall, easily accessible via several Metro lines and within walking distance of downtown Washington. Here are some recommendations as a starting point; all are free except where noted.

The **Smithsonian Institution** comprises several museums, most located on the National Mall. A mandatory stop is the National Museum of American History, a sprawling collection of artifacts important to understanding the United States. Some of the permanent exhibitions are very serious—like the display of dresses worn by First Ladies and a history of the American Presidency—while others are purely whimsical, like the recreation of Julia Child's Cambridge, Mass., kitchen. The third-floor Popular Culture exhibit includes one of the pairs of ruby slippers worn by Judy Garland in *The Wizard of Oz*, as well as an original Kermit the Frog and the puffy shirt made famous by Jerry Seinfeld. The transportation exhibit is surprisingly engrossing, with items ranging from antique automobiles to a Southern

Railway locomotive. The original Star Spangled Banner—yes, the one that inspired our National Anthem—is the centerpiece of a renovated museum. Stay for lunch: the Palm Court serves sandwiches and ice cream among the interior of Stohlman's Confectionery Shop as it appeared around 1900.

Kids will enjoy the **National Museum of Natural History**: who can resist a hall full of dinosaurs? Some of the academic stuff can be boring, but there's nothing like watching your child awed by a full-scale wooly mammoth. Stay for lunch: the Atrium Café is excellent.

Kids will also enjoy the popular **National Air and Space Museum**. The collection ranges from Charles Lindbergh's Spirit of St. Louis to a collection of spacecraft, including a Mercury orbiter, a walk-through Skylab orbital workshop, and an Apollo lunar module. You could easily spend an entire day here, walking through spacecraft, airplanes, and battleships to your heart's content. Alas, the only food option here is a restaurant with three fast-food offerings. (Smithsonian museums are open every day but Christmas Day, 10 a.m.-5:30 p.m.)

The **National Gallery of Art** is also located on the National Mall and is assumed to be a Smithsonian museum, though it's not. It's not among the great art museums of the world, but it features the works of important American artists. The café on the ground level between the old and new buildings is worth a visit. (Open Monday-Saturday from 10 a.m.-5 p.m. and Sunday from 11 a.m.-6 p.m.)

The **National Archives** building is a block off the National Mall (700 Pennsylvania Av. NW.) and displays the most important American documents: the Declaration of Independence, the Constitution of the United States, and the Bill of Rights. The experience has been enhanced by a remodel in the last few years. but kids who lack knowledge of their American roots may find the whole thing a little boring.

You'll need to plan for a tour of the **White House**: they are limited to groups of 10 or more, conducted only during the morning and must be arranged a month or more in advance. Requests must be submitted through your member of Congress and are accepted up to six months in advance. The **White House Visitor Center** (at the corner of 15th and E streets) showcases the White House through several exhibits.

Many of the same rules apply to the **Capitol**: if you want to be assured a tour you need to put together a group of 40 and schedule a tour at least one month in advance. Otherwise, plan on arriving at 7:30 a.m. to score a ticket for a tour later in the day. Security dictates the scheduling: it used to be you could just wander into the Capitol and poke around, but post-9/11 it's difficult to see some of our nation's treasures. The exceptions are the Senate and House chambers: you can see the House chambers at any time or the Senate chambers when the Senate is in session, provided you have a pass issued by your member of Congress.

The **Lincoln Memorial** stands at the end of the National Mall and is the most impressive and moving of the presidential memorials. Honoring former

President Abraham Lincoln, the memorial includes inscriptions from the Gettysburg Address and his Second Inaugural Address, as well as murals commemorating his greatest accomplishments: abolishing slavery and keeping the union intact through the Civil War.

In the midst of the National Mall is the **Washington Monument**, the tallest structure in the area. Take the elevator to the top in the morning: you'll see all the landmarks mentioned here and you'll beat the daily rush. The Washington Monument is one of the most popular sites in D.C. Going to the top of the monument is free, but tickets go fast so prepare to wait in line for a ticket, then wait to actually go to the top. (As a baseball fan, you'll have another reason to visit: the monument was built on what were popular baseball grounds before the turn of the century.)

The **Library of Congress** is off the beaten path (1st St. SE.), but it's worth the walk. The original building has been restored, and the permanent collections encompass some of the most important American documents aside from those stored in the National Archives. On display are Thomas Jefferson's rough draft of the Declaration of Independence, pages from Larry David's script for the final Seinfeld episode, and a lock of Walt Whitman's hair. The majority of the book collection is stored on 532 miles of shelves across three buildings.

Arlington National Cemetery (across the river from Washington) is easily accessible via Metro and noteworthy for three memorials. The Tomb of the Unknowns contains the remains of unidentified soldiers from both World Wars and the Korean War. John F. Kennedy is buried in Arlington, along with his wife Jacqueline Kennedy Onassis and his brother Robert Kennedy. (This is the most visited destination; be prepared for some company when you make your pilgrimage.) The Women in Military Service for America Memorial is a fairly new addition to the cemetery, honoring the 1.8 million women serving in the Armed Forces from the Revolutionary War to the present.

Ford's Theatre (517 10th St. NW., between E and F streets)—still a working live theater—was where Lincoln was assassinated by John Wilkes Booth. Lincoln was carried across the street to the nearby Petersen house (which is open as well), where he died. You can visit the presidential box and then head downstairs to a small museum honoring Lincoln and his legacy; fans of the macabre can see the pistol used by Booth to kill Lincoln, some bedding stained with Lincoln's blood, and a diary kept by Booth.

The **International Spy Museum** (800 F St. NW.; *spymuseum.org*; $13 adults, $12 seniors, $10 children 5-11) isn't nearly as hokey as the name implies: while it's not exactly an academic look at the world of spies, it's immensely engrossing. You'll see the tools of the trade in the shadowy world of espionage—like a single-shot pistol disguised as a lipstick tube and tiny radio transmitters. You'll learn about the history of espionage, starting with the biblical era and running to the present. The International Spy Museum is amazingly popular despite the high price of admission; call

202/432-SEAT for advanced tickets or you stand in line. Across the street is the excellent Gordon Biersch Brewery Restaurant, located in an historic bank building.

Team Ballpark History

The Montreal Expos entered the National League as an expansion franchise in 1969. The team's first home was Jarry Park, a small, single-deck ballpark originally constructed as a temporary stadium. It was the site of the first MLB regular-season game played outside of the United States: on April 14, 1969, the Expos won 8-7 over the St. Louis Cardinals. It was a great beginning to big-league baseball in Montreal: over 29,000 eager fans crammed into a stadium that held only 28,000, oblivious to the fact that the ballpark wasn't completed—folding chairs were used instead of bleacher seats, which were still on their way. Fans stood on big piles of snow outside the second eight-foot right-field outfield fence and watched the game for free.

As a "temporary" facility, Jarry Park had few amenities. The only covered seating was in the press box, and the climes of Montreal frequently meant that games were played in cold and damp conditions. There was a single set of bleachers in left field. It didn't matter to Montreal fans: despite having the smallest stadium in the majors, the Expos drew 1.2 million fans their inaugural season.

Today there's still a Parc Jarry in Montreal, but it bears little resemblance to the original Expos ballpark. The site is now under the control of Tennis Canada and is used for professional and amateur tennis events, as well as concerts, exhibitions, and other sporting events.

In 1976 the Expos moved to Olympic Stadium, built for the 1976 Summer Olympics and designed as the original retractable-roof stadium. It was a facility where seemingly nothing went right: it opened late and way over budget, and the funky Kevlar retractable roof was not operational until 1987.

The design was groundbreaking. The Kevlar roof was attached to a series of cables and could be placed on and off the concrete bowl; at the end of the cables was a tower that also served as an observation deck. But the Kevlar was never up to the stress of repeated openings and closings, so the roof was affixed in a permanently closed position.

The Expos were one of the most popular teams in the mid-1980s. The team attracted 2.3 million fans in both 1982 and 1983, drawing 1.6 million fans as late as 1996. But things went downhill quickly under absentee owners and, in February 2002, Major League Baseball bought the Expos from Jeffrey Loria (who then purchased the Florida Marlins). Under MLB's oversight the Expos played several series in the 2003 and 2004 seasons in San Juan's Hiram Bithorn Stadium. Despite having no owner in place MLB moved the team to Washington, D.C. before the 2005 season.

Seattle Mariners
Safeco Field

Address: 1250 First Av. S., Seattle, WA 98134.
Cost: $517 million.
Architect: NBBJ Architecture.
Owner: King County.
Capacity: 47,447.
Dimensions: 331L, 390LC, 405C, 387RC, 326R.
Home Dugout Location: First-base side.
Ticket Line: 206/622-HITS.
Playing Surface: Grass.
Other Tenants: A variety of soccer and football games, including the Seattle Bowl, have been played at Safeco Field.
First Game: The Mariners moved into Safeco Field in the midst of the 1999 season. On July 15, 1999, the Seattle Mariners lost to the San Diego Padres, 3-2. The Padres scored two runs in the top of the ninth inning off Jose Mesa (who walked four in his one-third inning of work) for the win, ruining a strong eight-inning performance by M's starter Jamie Moyer, who allowed just one run and struck out nine in eight innings of work. Longtime Mariners broadcaster Dave Niehaus threw out the first pitch.
Landmark Events: The Seattle Mariners, under the guidance of Lou Piniella, reached two AL Championship Series in 2000 and 2001, losing to the New York Yankees both seasons. The 2001 All-Star Game was played at Safeco Field, with the home American League winning 4-1 behind MVP Cal Ripken Jr., playing in his final All-Star Game. Finally, Rafael Palmiero notched his 3,000th hit as a member of the Baltimore Orioles in a game at Safeco Field.

Your Safeco Field Seating Crib Sheet

Best Sections to View a Game: There are few truly really great seats at Safeco Field, and we say this as huge fans of the ballpark. Unlike the newer ballparks built with a vertical orientation, Safeco Field sprawls, and if you're in the back of a section or in the upper deck you are a good distance from the playing field. Of course, the best seats are between the bases behind home plate, but those seats can be hard to snare unless you're a single. If you want to experience the best in Seattle ambiance, sit a little farther up along the first-base line: you'll have the downtown Seattle skyline in front of you. If it's a clear evening, you'll be dazzled by the changing colors as downtown and its skyscrapers transition from day to night.

Best Cheap Seats: A center-field-bleacher seat goes for $7. Go this route and wander the ballpark: you'll feel like you're sitting about a mile away from home plate. We're fans of View Reserved ($18): the upper-deck seats are pretty choice and you can see the action on the field and the drama of the downtown Seattle skyline if you sit to the right of home plate near the top. Be warned, you'll be a little more exposed to the elements up there if the roof is opened. Also, make sure you're not sitting too far down either line.

Most Underrated Sections: The Lower Outfield Reserved seats in right field are $25. While you won't get any great views of the skyline, you will get some intimate views of the playing field and easy access to concessions and the center-field kids' area. There are also two Lower Outfield Reserved sections, 151 and 152, in left field. The best place to see a gorgeous sunset over Puget Sound is in the right-field upper deck.

Seats to Avoid: We're not fans of the $38 Field Level seats down each line. Even though the seats are angled toward the infield, you'll still be craning your neck to see most of the action. Be warned, sections 103 and 342 are family (i.e., non-alcoholic) sections.

Safeco Field: Third Time's the Charm

The easiest way to raise the hackles of a Seattle resident is to paint the local weather as predominantly rainy. No, they will patiently explain, it doesn't rain an unusual amount in Seattle—in fact, it rains more in Boston on a yearly basis than Seattle.

Technically, that's true. But the issue isn't necessarily the amount of rain, it's how it comes down. In Boston, when it rains, it *rains*. In Seattle, locals suffer through 240 totally overcast days a year, many involving some sort of precipitation.

Which is why a covered ballpark—as opposed to a domed, fully enclosed facility—made so much sense for the Seattle Mariners. Safeco Field is a perfect match for Seattle residents who combine the best of urban living with a keen appreciation of the outdoors. At Safeco Field, the roof is merely a umbrella-like cover: even when closed there are gaps between the ballpark and the roof, allowing the elements in and never cutting fans off from the outdoors. The lack of any climate control also means you should dress for the elements at all times: if it's cool outside (as it frequently is after dark), it will be cool in the ballpark.

This blending of the urban with the outdoors is one of the many reasons why Safeco Field presents one of the best baseball experiences in the majors— nay, the planet. The ballpark itself is gorgeous, perfectly integrated with the Seattle skyline, and worth a visit if you're at all a fan of ballparks.

For the best effect, enter the ballpark at the southwest corner's Home Plate Gate (shown below). There you'll see much of the "Art in the Park" installed under King County's public-art guidelines. The most impressive works: a stunning circular baseball chandelier featuring 1,000 translucent bats (somewhat reminiscent of the famous bat chandelier gracing the entrance to Ebbets Field, but on an entirely different level), and a gorgeous baseball-themed terrazzo floor.

From there you can head to your seat. No one at a Mariners game seems in

a hurry to get to theirs, but Seattle fans do like to show up early and mill around before the game, so be prepared to fight the crowds. Most evenings you'll find concourses jammed as fans hit a concession stand or two before settling in for the evening. Having open concourses and multiple places to view a game encourages interaction among fans, and Safeco Field has a very social atmosphere. During our most recent visit we met two elderly tourists from the Netherlands attending their first baseball game (they were enthralled with the Kidd Valley hamburgers), a family with season tickets who made a point of arriving early at the park so the kids romp in the playground area, and a former colleague now running a coffeehouse—and all of this was in the center-field concourse area.

If this is your first time to the ballpark, walk the main concourse and take in the ballpark from all angles. Head to center field to peruse the kids' play area before heading to the left-field corner. From there, descend the stairs to a lower concourse and can watch the starting pitchers warm up. (You'll also want to head back there in later innings when relievers are warming up.) That lower concourse, the Bullpen Market, is one of the more popular spots in the ballpark for fans who like to stand around and view a game.

It is, however, not a good place to watch the roof open, so head back upstairs when it starts to move. Unlike the Diamondbacks or the Brewers, the Mariners don't make a huge fuss when the roof opens, and chances are good it will start inching open without you realizing. The roof also moves very slowly, taking up to 20 minutes to open, so watching it is like watching a tortoise crawl toward a pond.

The retractable roof is more a cover than a real roof: the three panels cover the ballpark, but they don't seal the inside, letting fans view the outside through openings below the roof when closed. It is also shockproof in case of an earthquake or windstorm.

Safeco Field features a subtle signage system: even though there are 11 electronic displays and a old-fashioned hand-operated scoreboard in left field you don't feel overwhelmed by electronics.

INSIDER'S TIP
The orientation of Safeco Field allows for great views of the downtown skyline and the port, even when the roof is closed. You can get the best views of the skyline from the upper deck and Lookout Landing, located at the end of the left-field line in the upper deck.

Growing grass is an issue in covered ballparks, especially for one in the Northwest, but the Mariners manage to produce a good playing surface early in the season with the help of an underground watering system made up of plastic hose buried under the field distributing warm water to the turf, coaxing it out of dormancy.

Regarding the Seattle weather: no matter how warm the day has been, be prepared to bring something warm to wear at the game. When the wind comes in off Puget Sound, the temperature can drop in a hurry, bringing with it a few raindrops. There's a reason why the locals dress in layers: by the end of the evening, you'll probably want them all.

Ome bad aspect to Safeco Field is the ballpark sprawling with its horizontal design, keeping most fans far from the action. (Ironically, fans were closer to the action in the much-maligned Kingdome.) If you're sitting in the back of a section or in the upper deck, you are farther away from the playing field than in most newer ballparks. Perhaps that's why we've not experienced Safeco Field really rocking like Minute Maid Park. It never seems like the crowd noise reaches critical mass, especially when the roof is open.

Still, Safeco Field is one of our favorite ballparks in the majors. The social atmosphere is great for fans, the food is top-notch, the integration with the best of the Puget Sound area is unique, and Seattle fans love their Mariners. What more could we want?

Ballpark Quirks

Like most covered ballparks, the Mariners have a policy covering balls hitting trusses. A ball hitting a truss in fair territory shall be judged fair or foul based on where it lands or is touched by an infielder. If it hits a truss in fair territory and is caught in foul territory, it's an out. If it lands in fair territory, it's in play. If a hit ball touches a truss in foul territory, it's immediately ruled a foul ball and out of play.

The Mariners also have a slightly unusual policy regarding roof closings and openings. The Mariners reserve the right to open or close the roof at any point during a game, based on fan comfort, but the umpiring crew must be notified and the visiting manager has the power to appeal the decision, with the crew chief holding the final power of decision.

Food and Drink

Local is the way to go when dining at Safeco Field. Sure, you can buy generic ballpark food from any number of concession stands, but the best food is served up by local vendors, all imparting a Seattle twist to the cuisine.

Ivar's Acres of Clams, the notable local seafood-restaurant chain, has two outposts at Safeco Field. The clam chowder is a must on a cold evening, but the better and tastier alternative is the Ivar Dog, fried fish on a hot-dog bun, slathered with tartar sauce. Also served by Ivar's: a decent salmon sandwich.

The best hamburgers at Safeco Field—and perhaps in the majors—are served by the Kidd Valley concession stands. Kidd Valley is another Seattle institution, starting out in 1975 as a hamburger and shake emporium in the city's University district. The burgers are fresh, the fries are hot, and the shakes are thick. (Also going well with the burgers: Grounders garlic fries.) You can find the Kidd Valley stands near the left-field corner in the main concourse and behind first base in the upper concourse.

When Safeco Field opened, sushi was a novelty at ballparks and in the general populace, and the sushi stand wasn't exactly crowded. The debut of Ichiro Suzuki and the growing popularity of sushi made sushi a hot commodity at Safeco, and today you'll find long lines of people waiting to buy an Ichi-roll (a spicy tuna roll) and other sushi. (The Japanese influence at Safeco Field goes beyond sushi: a portion of the program is presented in Japanese, and Japanese-language schedules are available. The team is owned by a Japanese corporation, Nintendo.) Similarly, you'll find long lines at the International Wok concession stand, where food is made to order.

Wash down the Ichi-roll with any number of beverages. On a cold night, there's nothing like an espresso or latte to take off the edge. While the beer is expensive, the selection is spectacular. Besides the standard corporate swill, you can find Pyramid, Red Hook, Fat Tire, Alaskan Amber, Mac & Jack's, and Pabst on tap and in the bottle.

The Bullpen Market is one of the most unique public places in the majors. Located below the left-field concourse, the Bullpen Market features several concession stands. More importantly, it provides a unique up-close access to the bullpens. At the beginning of the game this area is filled with fans watching starting pitchers warm up, and later on the space is filled with other fans perusing relievers as they prepare for an appearance.

Close by is the Bullpen Pub, a sports bar providing a view of the bullpen as well as the manually operated scoreboard. It's a sitdown place with a full bar (kids are not allowed) and a regular menu. Try the renowned sliced-pork sandwich or the hot wings.

A Ben & Jerry's store serves ice cream year around. You can access the shop from the street near the left-field entrance before entering the ballpark, or you can head to a window next to the Mariners Team Store within the ballpark to score some Chunky Monkey.

The Hit It Here Café is located in the right-field corner and features both indoor and outdoor reserved sitdown dining. The cost in 2006 was $43 for a

seat, with an $18 food voucher.

Finally, head to the Alaska's Gourmet Subs stand for a reindeer-sausage sandwich, or any of the other quirky items on the menu. The reindeer sausage is smothered in barbecue sauce and served on a 10-inch roll.

For the Kids

The Children's Hospital Playground in the center-field concourse features a slew of baseball-themed games and activities suited to the younger set. The Moose's Munchies concession stand offers kid-oriented and -sized foodstuffs. You can spend innings watching the kids out there: strategically placed televisions broadcast game action.

Most kids get a kick out of being close to players. Take them down to the Bullpen Market and let them get close to a reliever or two.

Handicapped Access

Safeco Field features 450 wheelchair-accessible seats. In addition, there is reservable handicapped parking in the Safeco Field ramp.

Ballpark Tours

The Mariners offer tours year-round, but the schedule depends on whether you want to go during the season or offseason.

During the season, tours are offered at 10:30 a.m. and 12:30 p.m. on game days; on nongame days a 2:30 p.m. tour is added. During the offseason, tours are offered at 12:30 p.m. and 2:30 p.m. on Tuesdays through Sundays, but the schedule can vary.

The price: $7 for adults, $6 for seniors, and $5 for children ages 3-12. You

can order tickets through Ticketmaster, but it seems obscene to pay a surcharge in this instance. We'd recommend calling the team for more information and to verify whether tours are still being offered.

Getting There

Safeco Field is located near the intersection of I-5 and I-90, south of downtown Seattle. From either direction on I-5, the ballpark and neighboring Qwest Field are easy to find; just follow the signs. The same goes for I-90: take the Fourth Avenue exit and follow the signs.

It's hard to find a free parking spot close to the ballpark unless you arrive ridiculously early or are prepared to walk a good distance. We'd recommend you pay to park close to the ballpark.

Four ramps and surface lots simplify that task. The ramp combining accessibility (across the street from the ballpark) and price ($15) is the Qwest Field and Event Center Garage, located across the street from the ballpark (to the north) on Royal Brougham Way between 1st Avenue and 4th Avenue. The Union Station Parking Ramp (820 4th Av. S.) is a little farther away, as is the North Lot (2nd Av. S. and S. King St.); both are also priced at $15.

The Safeco Field Garage (Edgar Martinez Drive at 1st Avenue) costs $22 and is often filled by season-ticket holders and those with single-game reservations. We don't recommend parking there unless the Qwest Field garage is filled.

Mass transit is promoted in Seattle, but the bus system will be in flux for two years while a new light-rail system is built. Unless you know the area and the layout of the park-and-ride locations (check out *transit.metrokc.gov* for details), we'd recommend driving.

Where to Stay

There's no reason not to stay in a hotel close to the ballpark, as downtown Seattle is about a mile north, with Pioneer Square located between. Downtown Seattle is filled with great independent boutique hotels, so it's a great chance to eschew the chains and go for something unique.

The hotel closest to the ballpark is directly across the street from Safeco Field: the Silver Cloud Hotel Stadium (1046 1st Av. S.; *silvercloud.com*). Many baseball fans were dismayed when the city approved the hotel's location, as it blocks the Seattle skyline for fans sitting in the Safeco Field grandstand. But the hotel met all zoning requirements and the city's only choice was to approve the project.

Also within walking distance of the ballpark: the Best Western Pioneer Square (77 Yesler Way; *pioneersquare.com*; $125-$225). Pioneer Square is one of Seattle's more notable party spots, but it's not regarded as the safest of neighborhoods after dark. The Best Western is in a restored Victorian-style building, which leads to some unique room configurations. We wouldn't recommend it for families, but for younger singles who want to take advantage of the Pioneer Square nightlife after an M's game, it's perfect.

The Alexis Hotel (1007 1st Av.; *alexishotel.com*; $225-$300) is also within walking distance of the ballpark, located north of Pioneer Square. It's a high-end establishment, situated in a century-old building listed on the National Registry of Historic Places. The emphasis here is on art: there's a huge Dale Chihuly chandelier in the lobby and some of the themed rooms feature art from the likes of Miles Davis and John Lennon.

Otherwise, a slew of downtown hotels are within a mile of the ballpark as the crow flies, although there are some convoluted paths from downtown hotels to the ballpark. We're fond of the Inn at Harbor Steps (1221 1st Av.; *innatharborsteps.com*; $165-$250). Part of a small 10-hotel chain in the western United States, the Inn at Harbor Steps features homey rooms (each has a gas fireplace) and teddy bears.

If you've read other chapters in this book, you'll know we're big fans of the Kimpton hotel chain. The chain's flagship (of sorts) is the Hotel Monaco (1101 4th Av.; *monaco-seattle.com*; $299-$329), and it features all the quirky charm you'd expect from a Kimpton hotel: evening wine reception, yoga equipment delivered to rooms, a pet-friendly environment, and pet goldfish available. Three rooms provide views of Mount Rainier (on a clear day, anyway): 1019, 1119, and 1219.

A great bargain is the Executive Plaza Pacific Hotel (400 Spring St.; *pacificplazahotel.com*; $110-$260), which dates to 1928 but has been renovated in recent years. The rooms are small and lack air conditioning, but the location is ideal for those attending ballgames.

The Hotel Vintage Park (1100 5th Av.; *hotelvintagepark.com*; $139-$475) may not appeal to hardcore baseball fans: the emphasis is on the romantic, with rooms named after Washington wineries and a port tasting later in the evening. Finally, the grande dame of downtown Seattle hotels is the Sorrento Hotel (900

Madison St.; *hotelsorrento.com*; $220-$340), which opened in 1909 as the city's most elegant address and still retains that atmosphere.

You'll also find the usual chains represented in downtown Seattle: Fairmont, Grand Hyatt, Hilton, W, Sheraton, Crowne Plaza, Wyndham, Westin, Marriott, and Red Lion.

While You're There

Seattle is one of the great travel destinations in baseball. It combines the best of urban living— coffeehouses, fine dining, and plenty of culture—with easy access to nature and vibrant scenery. Many national trends, like modern coffeehouse culture, have their roots in Seattle. So plan on spending a lot of time away from the ballpark during your visit, and bring your walking shoes. Seattle is best seen from street level, by foot.

A few attractions are within a short walk, two with particular appeal to beer fans. Across the street from Safeco Field, on Royal Brougham Way and First Avenue, is the Seattle outpost of the Pyramid Alehouse (Pyramid Alehouse, Brewery & Restaurant, 1201 First Av. S.; *pyramidbrew.com*; 206/682-3377) chain. You'll find beers from the popular microbrewery in many ballparks. With 15 great beers on tap, a large beer garden, and an extensive menu, the large Pyramid Alehouse is a popular gathering place before and after games. Elysian Fields (Elysian Fields, 542 1st Av. S., *elysianbrewing.com*; 206/382-4498) has been a noteworthy Seattle brewpub for years, and now open is a Safeco Field/Qwest Field outpost. It's not a sports bar, though baseball fans are welcome.

Easterners may not recognize the name, but those from the West know the C.C. Filson brand as a top-notch clothing line. Filson's main store and manufacturing facility is south of Safeco Field, done up in a lodge-style décor. Filson clothing is expensive, but it's designed and created to last forever, and on a gloomy, drizzly day it's appropriate to pop in and enjoy the fireplace before heading to the game. *C.C. Filson Building, 1555 4th Av. S., Seattle; filson.com; 206/622-3147.*

If you don't want to spring for an Ichi-roll there are several eateries witin walking distance of the ballpark. Many Mariners fans stop by Saigon Gourmet (502 S. King St.; 206/624-2611) for a homemade sandwich on their way to the

---

INSIDER'S TIP

There's one issue when staying downtown: it can be very expensive. If you have a car at your disposal, there are two areas featuring less expensive family-oriented hotels: the Seattle Center area and near Sea-Tac Airport. There are several affordable hotels, such as the Comfort Suites or the MarQueen, in the Seattle Center area (which we discuss in the next section), and the many family-oriented attractions in that area makes for an active vacation. Also, there are many affordable hotels near Sea-Tac airport, located 12 miles south of downtown Seattle. The location makes for a good center of operations for a Seattle tourist, particularly if you follow our advice and attend a Tacoma Rainiers game during your visit (as we detail later in this chapter).

game. These aren't ordinary sandwiches: these are Vietnamese *banh mis*, filled with ingredients like deep-fried tofu, fried eggs, pickled carrots, various meats, soy sauce, and cilantro. They cost $2 or less, to boot.

Two rib joints stand out: Jones Barbeque (2454 Occidental Av., Suite 3A; *jonesbarbeque.net*; 206/625-1339) is said by many to be the best place for barbecue in Seattle, while Mac's Smokehouse (1760 1st Av. S.; 206/628-0880) offers cheap smoked-meat sandwiches (pork, Texas-style brisket). Have a real turkey sandwich—none of that pressed-loaf stuff—at Bakeman's Restaurant (122 Cherry St.; 206/622-3375). We're also partial to Andy's Diner, an old railroad diner that hearkens back to Seattle's more colorful days. The menu looks to be unchanged for decades, and the prices are ridiculously low. *Andy's Diner, 2963 4th Av. S., Seattle; 206/624-4097.*

First Avenue runs north-south from Safeco Field through downtown to the edge of Seattle Center. Staying near First Avenue will provide enough attractions to keep you busy during your trip to Seattle.

North of the ballpark is the Pioneer Square District, Seattle's original business district and the initial Skid Row. (In Seattle's early days logs were skidded down Yesler Way to a waterfront mill. Over time, though, the term came to refer to an area occupied by dead enders, gin joints, and flophouses.) There's still a Skid Row edge to Pioneer Square, as the panhandlers can be aggressive and the partiers can be obnoxious, but it certainly is a lively place. The actual Pioneer Square at First Avenue and Yesler Way is rather small, and the nearby Occidental Park is usually occupied mainly by the homeless. The most amazing things about Pioneer Square is the juxtaposition between the longtime street culture of the area (typified by the storefront missions serving the homeless) and the gentrified restaurants and art galleries. Despite decades of gentrification, the two forces seem to be at a standoff. To see the best and the worst of Pioneer Square, take Bill Speidel's Underground Tour (608 1st Av.; *undergroundtour.com*; 206/682-4646), where you'll see why the area was called Skid Row.

Downtown Seattle is home to a slew of outstanding attractions and restaurants, so many that we cannot possibly name them all. In recent years downtown has blossomed as a shopping mecca, anchored by Nordstrom and the snazzy Pacific Place mall. The best attractions are the old ones, however, so we'd recommend a visit to the Pike Place Market (*pikeplacemarket.org*) at Pike Street and First Avenue. Yeah, you've seen the vendors at Pike Place Fish throwing fresh catch about, but there's much more to the market than flying fish. Besides the selection of local delicacies, Pike Place Market is home to local craftspeople and artists, the best doughnuts in the universe at Daily Dozen Doughnut, and perhaps the quintessential Seattle restaurant in Etta's Seafood (2020 Western Av.; *tomdouglas.com*; 206/443-6000), celebrity chef Tom Douglas's casual establishment. Reservations are mandatory, so call ahead. Next door you'll find the Pike Brewery (1415 1st Av.; *merchantduvin.com/pages/3_pike_brewing*; 206/622-6044), a microbrewery and restaurant specializing in ales.

You can buy Ivar's products at Safeco Field, but you'll want to visit the original Ivar's Acres of Clams (Pier 54 on Alaskan Way, Seattle; *ivars.net*; 206/624-6852), located since 1938 on the city's waterfront, a short distance from the ballpark. The emphasis is on fresh Northwest seafood (though, to be honest, the fried fish tastes the best, especially after a few Rainiers), while the clam chowder is a local delicacy.

Also on Pier 54: Ye Olde Curiosity Shop (1001 Alaskan Way, Seattle; *yeoldecuriosityshop.com*; 206/682-5844), the very definition of a kitschy tourist trap. The collection of shrunken heads lures you in and soon you'll start debating whether to bring home that shark in a jar. Bring kids here at your own peril.

Stay on First Avenue long enough and you'll end up at Seattle Center, the 74-acre 1962 World's Fair site now host to several museums and attractions. Its most recognizable attraction is also a symbol of sorts for Seattle: the Space Needle (400 Broad St.; *spaceneedle.com*; 800/937-9582), which features an observation deck and a very good restaurant.

Kids will love the Space Needle, but there are plenty of other attractions at Seattle Center to occupy their time. Fun Forest (305 Harrison St.; *funforest.com*; 206/728-1586) is a collection of 19 rides and minigolf. Older kids will appreciate the Experience Music Project (325 5th Av. N.; *emplive.com*; 877/EMPLIVE), gazillionaire Paul Allen's shrine to the music of his youth. It's not really a museum, but rather an eclectic collection of memorabilia highlighting the history of rock in Seattle and a series of interactive exhibitions. There are usually long waits for those wanting to play instruments, so head to the displays covering the history of grunge and guitars. It is a tad spendy—$20 for adults, $15 for children—but worth it for music fans. Also located in the same building: the Science Fiction Museum and Hall of Fame, which requires an additional admission fee. Key Arena, the home of the NBA's Seattle Sonics, is located on the Seattle Center grounds.

If you stay downtown, you can get to Seattle Center via the Seattle Monorail. It links Seattle Center to downtown and its many shopping delights, including an opulent

INSIDER'S TIP

You've undoubtedly seen the Space Needle on television, and it's as impressive in person as you'd expect. It is a mandatory stop for any visitor to Seattle, as you'll be able to see the entire city and region—and Mount Rainier—from the observation deck on a clear day.

However, we're here to tell you not to go to the observation deck, which costs $13 for adults and $6 for children. Instead, have lunch at SkyCity, the revolving restaurant within the observation deck. Prices at lunch are fairly high, but when you factor in the admission to the observation deck as part of the meal, it becomes a more palatable proposition. Plus, the skies tend to be a little clearer at noon, giving you a better chance to view the landscape and Mount Rainier.

Emil Sicks (in the middle) outside Sick's Seattle Stadium during the heyday of the Rainiers and Pacific Coast League baseball in Seattle.

Nordstrom. The Seattle Monorail was build in 1962 for the World's Fair and still runs every 10 minutes between Westlake Center Mall (at Fifth and Pine Street) and the Seattle Center station. Round-trip fares are $3.50 for adults, $1.50 for youth (5-12) and $1.50 for seniors.

There is much, much more to downtown Seattle than we can present in this short overview. But this should be enough to whet your appetite for more.

Team Ballpark History

Though Safeco Field opened in 1999, the groundwork for it was laid in the 1960s.

The Seattle Pilots entered the American League in 1969, joining the NBA's Seattle SuperSonics and firmly establishing Seattle's credentials as a big-league city. Baseball officials were nervous about the entry of the Pilots: like fellow expansion team Montreal, the Pilots lacked a major-league-quality facility, and Dewey and Max Soriano—both important figures in the history of baseball in the Northwest—assured baseball officials the city was poised to build a domed stadium a la the Astrodome.

In the meantime, the Pilots would play in Sick's Seattle Stadium, the first major-league facility in Seattle, before being plucked out of bankruptcy by Allan "Bud" Selig Jr. and moving to County Stadium, becoming the Milwaukee Brewers. Though the Mariners never played in Sick's Stadium, this is the perfect place to discuss the venerable old facility, as it is an important part of Seattle baseball history.

Built in 1938 to house the Seattle Rainiers of the Pacific Coast League,

Sick's Stadium had clearly seen better days by the time the American League expanded to Seattle. It was originally envisioned as a temporary home for major-league baseball: when Dewey and Max Soriano were awarded the rights to an American League franchise in 1967, league officials made it clear they expected to see a new domed stadium in Seattle to someday house the Pilots. Baseball legends such as Joe DiMaggio made the pilgrimage to Seattle to solicit public support of the project.

In the end the domed stadium did materialize—it would later open as the Kingdome—but not in time to save the Pilots. Indeed, it was clear on Opening Day 1969 that Sick's Stadium was wholly unsuited for major-league baseball. As a minor-league ballpark, Sick's Stadium seated 12,000, and the Pilots planned for an expansion to 25,000. But construction of new left-field bleachers ran late, and on Opening Day fans showed up with tickets for nonexistent seats. (The construction work also delayed the start of the game.) The Pilots never really recovered from that opening day *faux pas*. Then again, it was probably a good thing the Pilots didn't draw bigger crowds. Water pressure was a huge problem. Visiting teams showered in their hotels, while toilets throughout the ballpark couldn't refill with fresh water fast enough when there were crowds of over 10,000.

TRIVIA

Both Safeco Field and the Kingdome were on Royal Brougham Way, named for longtime Seattle sportswriter Royal Brougham, who championed baseball in the Rainiers era and was key in drumming up public support for the Pilots, Mariners, and Seahawks. Fittingly—or ironically, depending one's viewpoint—Brougham's last day on the job was spent covering a Seahawks game at the Kingdome. He suffered a heart attack in the press box and was carried out of a 1978 exhibition game, passing away a short time later. He worked 68 years at the Seattle Post-Intelligencer, rubbing elbows with the likes of Babe Ruth, William Randolph Hearst, and Jack Dempsey.

Initially, Sick's Stadium was a showcase of the Pacific Coast League. Because a previous ballpark (Dugdale Park) located on the site had burned down due to the work of an industrious arsonist, Sick's Stadium, with its steel-and-concrete construction, was designed to be a more permanent home for baseball. The ballpark was built and funded by Emil Sick, a German-born brewer who learned the trade at his fathers' Canadian brewery. When the Eighteenth Amendment was repealed—ending Prohibition in the United States—Sick came to Washington State to pursue the family trade. His original brewery, Sick's Century Brewery, was a success, even more so when he merged operations with the Rainier Brewery, whose roots in the Northwest went back to 1883.

Sick had no interest in baseball, but when the Seattle Indians of the Pacific Coast League were on the verge of leaving town after Dugdale Park burned down, friends and business associates convinced him to put up the $100,000 for the franchise and turn the team into a tool for selling more beer.

Sick followed up with a $350,000 investment in a new ballpark in Rainier Valley, at the intersection of Rainier Avenue and McClelland Street. The team and the ballpark were an instant hit. On the field, the team was a consistent winner, as Sick did not hesitate to buy the best talent and management he could find. And there certainly were spectacles at the ballpark. Announcer Leo Lassen, also known as "The Great Gabbo," became a fixture in Seattle thanks to his colorful descriptions and astute ways of working product promotions into his between-inning and between-pitch patter. Between 1938 and 1952 the Seattle Rainiers were the best-drawing team in minor-league baseball.

After the Pilots were moved to Milwaukee, local baseball proponents continued their pursuit of a domed stadium. It came to fruition in 1976 when the Kingdome opened, with the expansion Seattle Mariners beginning play in 1977.

The Kingdome was the second domed stadium in the majors—the Astrodome was the first, and the Metrodome didn't open until 1981. It was never truly loved as a ballpark, with lots of concrete and small crowds dominating the ballpark history. At one time the Kingdome hosted the Mariners, the NFL's Seattle Seahawks and the NBA's Seattle Supersonics, with no one truly satisfied with the aesthetics and atmosphere in the place. The Mariners did attempt to make the ballpark warmer, with a blue wall in right field reminiscent

Cheney Stadium under construction in 1960. (Courtesy of the Tacoma Public Library.)

of the Green Monster, dubbed the Walla Walla, and the USS Mariner in center field, with cannon blasts celebrating Mariners homers. (The Mariner theme was much more pronounced when the stadium opened: distances down each foul pole were marked in feet and fathoms.)

The Kingdome rocked when the Mariners became competitive under manager Lou Piniella, knocking the Yankees out of the playoffs in a huge 1995 upset. Still, by then it was clear the Kingdome was not a long-term solution: the much-ballyhooed roof leaked and, in 1994, four ceiling tiles crashed into the stands before a Mariners game. The threat of more tiles possibly falling on fans led the team to postpone the game and forced them to play 15 games on the road before the season was ended by a strike.

The final Mariners game in the Kingdome came on June 27, 1999 when a sellout crowd watched Seattle down the Texas Rangers 5-2. Cory Segui, the grandson of former Mariner (and Pilot) Diego Segui, threw the final ceremonial pitch at the Kingdome to Bob Stinson. Diego Segui and Stinson was the battery at the beginning of the first Mariners game in 1977. It was imploded on March 26, 2000, and Qwest Field, the home of the NFL's Seattle Seahawks, was built on the site. The Kingdome was sometimes called the Concrete Cupcake, so it's only fitting much it ended up recycled for use in Qwest Field construction.

Local Baseball Attractions

You can visit the former location of Sick's Seattle Stadium, the longtime home of professional baseball in Seattle, at 2700 Rainier Av. S. A Lowe's home-improvement store now stands on the site, but a sign marks where the ballpark stood (look for it on McLellan Street, east of Rainier). A display case inside the front entrance contains memorabilia from both the Pilots and the Rainiers, while a bronze home plate is installed outside the front door.

Rainier is a somewhat

The statue of Ben Cheney is permanently affixed to a seat in Cheney Stadium. That same section features old-style seating from Seals Stadium.

Nat Bailey Stadium in Vancouver: one of the great old ballparks of baseball. It's worth the drive from Seattle.

sacred term in the Northwest, thanks to the iconic presence of Mount Rainier on a clear day. Today, the Seattle Rainiers are no more, and Rainier Beer is brewed in Texas. But you can find a modern version in nearby Tacoma, as the Tacoma Rainiers of the Class AAA Pacific Coast League play at venerable Cheney Stadium (2502 S. Tyler St., Tacoma; *tacomarainiers.com*; 253/752-7700), built in 1960 and one of the more charming ballparks in the minors. Cheney Stadium began as a labor of love for a local businessman, Ben Cheney, who wanted a showcase for baseball in Tacoma. Today, Cheney (pronounced *chee-ney*) Stadium is still a beloved part of the fabric of life in Tacoma, largely unchanged from the original design laid out by Ben Cheney in the early 1960s.

Ben Cheney still presides over the ballpark—or a representation of him, at least. As Tacoma officials oversaw the installation of new seating in sections B-P before the 2005 season, they left intact part of one section (Section K) with old seats originally installed in Seals Stadium during the final days of the PCL's Seals and the earliest days of the San Francisco Giants. The light stanchions, still standing, also came from Seals Stadium. Go to Section K, Row 1, Seat 1 and you'll find a statue of Ben Cheney, peanuts in hand, wearing a blazer with a Cheney Studs patch (as shown to the right). Cheney will go down in history as the inventor of the 2x4 stud cut down to eight feet—quite the innovator in his day—but he was also a fan, sponsoring Cheney Studs with 5,000 kids playing on Cheney Studs teams over the years in different sports. Thanks to the bronze statue he's forever the fan, enthralled with the action on the field.

Tacoma is an easy drive from Seattle: just head south on I-5. Once you're in Tacoma, take Exit 132 (Hwy. 16) west and then take the 19th Street exit going east (to the right). Once on 19th, turn right on Cheyenne. If you're staying near Sea-Tac Airport, you're already halfway there.

The Everett AquaSox play to large crowds at Everett Memorial Stadium (3900 Broadway, Everett; *aquasox.com*; 425/258-3673). Everett is about 30 miles north of Seattle, right on I-5.

If you're up for a 140-mile drive, head north to Vancouver and its scenic ballpark, Nat Bailey Stadium, home to the Vancouver Canadians (4601 Ontario St. [next to Queen Elizabeth Park], Vancouver; *canadiansbaseball.com*; 604/872-5232) of the short-season Northwest League. The ballpark opened in 1951 as Capilano Stadium, the home of the Pacific Coast League Vancouver Capilanos. It's been changed several times since it first opened, mostly to increase and decrease capacity over the years. While it was far too small for the PCL Canadians (who ended up moving to Sacramento), it's one of the larger ballparks in the short-season Northwest League, and one of the most scenic. The scoreboard in right-center field was originally used at Sick's Seattle Stadium.

New York Mets
Shea Stadium

Address: 123-01 Roosevelt Av., Flushing, NY 11368.
Cost: $25.5 million.
Architect: Praeger-Kavanaugh-Waterbury.
Owner: City of New York.
Capacity: 57,369.
Dimensions: 338L, 378LC, 410C, 378RC, 338R.
Home Dugout Location: First-base side.
Ticket Line: 718/507-8599.
Playing Surface: Grass.
Previous Names: In its planning stages the ballpark was called Flushing
   Meadows Park.
Other Tenants: No other stadium in history can lay claim to hosting two Major
   League Baseball teams and two National Football League teams all in the
   same year, 1975. The Yankees played in Shea for the 1974 and 1975
   seasons while Yankee Stadium was under reconstruction, plus one day
   game on April 15, 1998. It was followed in the evening by a Mets game after
   concrete chunks had fallen off Yankee Stadium, raising safety concerns.
   The New York Jets called Shea Stadium home for two full decades, from
   1964 to 1983. The New York Giants played at Shea for one season, 1975,
   after two seasons at the Yale Bowl and just prior to their relocation to East
   Rutherford, N.J.
First Game: On April 17, 1964, Bill Mazeroski of the Pittsburgh Pirates singled
   off Mets reliever Ed Bauta in the ninth inning to drive in the go-ahead run in
   a 4-3 Pirates win. It was a typical Mets result, dropping the team's record to
   0-3 on the season. The Mets were on the way to a 52-109 record (the one

remaining game ended in a tie and was not completed).

Landmark Event: Many important events have been held at Shea Stadium. For instance, the Beatles played Shea in a landmark 1965 concert, and virtually every important rock band, from The Who to Bruce Springsteen, has played to tens of thousands at Shea. Throw in a papal visit and the use of the ballpark as a landing area after 9/11 and you've got a lot of New York City cultural history wrapped up in Shea Stadium.

Your Shea Stadium Seating Crib Sheet

A word of caution is necessary about the Mets' complex pricing scheme. Not only are there 11 seat categories at Shea, you have five possible prices depending on game desirability. All quoted prices in this section of the book assume "Bronze" games—the second lowest tier. Roughly 40 percent of the games are priced in the Bronze category, far more than any of the other price categories.

Best Sections to View a Game: By far the best seats at Shea Stadium are the Inner Field Box ($45), but relatively few are available in these sections and they are priced accordingly, based on supply and demand. It is unlikely that you will be able to obtain seats in sections X1, X2, 1, and 2 directly behind the plate. The best views from Inner Field boxes come in sections 47, 48, 63, 64, 217, 218, 225, and 226. If you are a sun worshipper attending a day game, be sure to pick a section on the third-base side. If it's a hot day and you want the sun at your back, select seats on the first-base side.

Best Cheap Seats: Overall, it is difficult to recommend the best "cheap" seats because you are picking from 55 price points largely determined by the potential draw of a particular game. You will notice a swing of more than three-fold for the lowest-priced seats ($5-18) in Loge Reserved-Back Rows, Mezzanine Reserved-Back Rows, or Upper Reserved. While it is tempting to try to get closest to the field in this favorable price range, anything higher than Row H in Loge Reserved-Back Rows ($12) could cause viewing problems (see next section). You are far more likely to get a good, unobstructed view if you choose Mezzanine Reserved-Back Rows, with especially good seats available in Sections 1-15. If you are willing to move up by purchasing seats in a middle price range ($19-29, Bronze games— $23), the best deals will be found in Mezzanine Reserved Sections 1-12. These are especially desirable because of the relatively small number of seats in Rows A-G.

Seats to Avoid: Unfortunately, the list of seats to avoid at Shea is quite long. The row number often is more important than the section assignment. In our most recent visit, we grabbed a cheap seat (we weren't planning to sit much) in Loge Reserved-Back Rows ($12) Row L—as in "Last" row or "Loser." You basically have obstructed view in the last two or three rows of these field level seats due to the severe mezzanine overhang. So, just a few rows will make a huge difference in visibility. You are much better off sitting two sections further down the line in Row H than requesting the infield area in Row K or L. As you look at the seating chart, be aware seating views are linear, so sections angled away from the infield will force you to crane your neck. Even Sections 17 and 18 in the highest priced category (Inner Field Boxes, $45) direct your view outside the foul line. Most of the Outer Field Box seats ($35) are also directed away from the infield action. If you are attending a night game, the seats near the right-field flagpole can be a problem due to the angle of light from behind home plate before sunset.

Shea Stadium: Last of a Breed

By any measure, Shea Stadium is the ultimate testament to 1960s stadium architecture. Its unyielding symmetry elevates form over function. The outside view of Shea Stadium is very attractive with a circular layout and an open center field. It looks like a unique abstract sculpture from a distance, as anyone who has flown in or out of LaGuardia Airport can tell you.

In a day and age when naming rights are a lucrative source of income, Shea Stadium retains its original moniker. It was named after William Shea, an attorney who worked to bring National League baseball back to New York City after the Giants and Dodgers fled for the West Coast. To be precise, Shea appeared destined to be a founder of the fledging Continental League (along with Branch Rickey), which looked to put a team in the Polo Grounds and cities lacking major-league baseball (Dallas, Houston, Minneapolis-St. Paul, Toronto, Denver) but the seriousness of the competitive threat was enough to propel expansion plans forward in order to thwart the upstart movement. It worked, and the Continental League never launched. Shea then headed the movement for a new ballpark in New York City, and for his efforts the facility was named for him.

Shea Stadium was built, of course, to house the expansion New York Mets, who entered the National League in 1962. The Mets played in the Polo Grounds until Shea was ready in 1964, a full year behind schedule. In fact, the Mets held a going-away ceremony at the Polo Grounds at the end of the 1962 season in anticipation of moving into a new ballpark in 1963. But Shea Stadium wasn't completed in time, consigning the Mets to one final season at the venerable Polo Grounds. In retrospect, the timing was good as the team rode on the World's Fair momentum and drew 1.7 million fans that first year.

The most distinctive features of Shea Stadium are a right-center scoreboard that is still one of the largest in the majors and a Big Apple that rises from a black top hat when a Met hits a homer. Relatively few changes have been made to Shea Stadium over the years except for the addition of luxury boxes in 1985. Due to the circular design of the stadium, the arrangement does not allow for the luxury suite experience you expect to find in a modern stadium. In 2005, the Mets debuted four new full-color LED displays at Shea, including two new ribbon boards on the press level fascia and a color message center above the ticket windows between Gates D and E.

Interestingly enough, Shea Stadium is served by public transit but nearby LaGuardia Airport is not. This can be explained by the history of the area. Though Shea is surrounded by parking lots and auto-salvage businesses to the east, it was adjacent to the grand 1964 World's Fair when constructed, and the subway was one of the few ways to get out to the fair. You can still see remnants of the World Fair just south of Shea, including the landmark globe.

At one point architects drew up plans for a roof to cover Shea Stadium, but engineers determined the stadium's footings could not bear the added weight. Plans also were drawn up to increase the capacity of Shea to 90,000, mainly by filling in the opening in center field. They never proved economically viable.

Over the last decade the economics of major-league ballparks have shifted, with a goal to maximize profit margins from near-capacity crowds on a daily basis, not to fill mega-ballparks for special events. Shea Stadium's days are clearly numbered (the Mets have already announced plans for a new ballpark to be built next to the current Shea site). That day will likely mark the end of the cost-conscious, multipurpose "cookie-cutter" municipal facilities common in the 1960s and '70s.

The stadium has a remote and large picnic area in center field, catering to crowds of 100 to 1,400. On busy game days, this gate gets crowded and is slow-moving. Two newer picnic area features are the Dugout Shop souvenir stand and Long Ball Alley beverage service area located underneath the bleachers, with access to a ground-level view of the field. The design of the picnic area allows of multiple groups bookings for a given date. The area also includes two children's play areas, wheelchair-accessible game seating, and restrooms.

The stadium has expansive parking available on three sides, an attraction for tailgating before the game (technically, alcohol consumption in the parking lot is strictly prohibited by the team). Another nice feature is Mets Fan Fest—offered on weekends only—generating some excitement before games (see For the Kids below for a more-detailed description).

If you are sensing there isn't much of anything unique or impressive about Shea Stadium, you have the right idea about the place. On the other hand, there isn't much to complain about either—other than having too many seats with poor views. When it goes away, Shea Stadium will most likely be remembered as a symbol of the 1960s, not as a classic ballpark. To take a kinder view would be dishonest.

A leading Shea attraction is the popular Fan Fest beyond the right-field foul pole before weekend games—a lively scene viewed from the nearby subway station.

Ballpark Quirks

There are none in the conventional sense. The design of the stadium is so utterly free of quirks, one could make the case the strict symmetry is just one giant quirk.

Food and Drink

Food choices are fairly standard for the most part and you will pay New York prices, although at Shea concessions are typically about 25 cents lower than those at Yankee Stadium. You have your selection of dogs from Nathan's and Glatt ($4.50), as well as a foot long from Hebrew National ($5.75) or a corn dog ($3). For something slightly different, there are cheeseburgers ($5.75), chicken tenders with fries ($7), or Cascarino's Pizza ($5.25 to $5.75, depending on the topping selected). If you want authentic New York cuisine, try a tummy-filling Coney Island Gabilla's knish ($3.75).

Two ethnic stands are interesting and have some unusual offerings. For a Latino flare, get a Havana sandwich ($4.50) and wash it down with a Mexican Corona or pick one of our personal summertime favorites—Presidente cerveza from the Dominican Republic (either beer is $6.25). If you prefer sampling a local brew, Brooklyn Lager is a very good, full-bodied option; for something nonalcoholic and refreshing, the fresh lemonade ($4) from a stand down the third-base line features lemon, sugar, and a shot of soda. Mama's of Corona has Italian specialties including a delicious turkey or salami sandwich; the baskets include sides ($9.50). Mama's is also served in the Budwesier Backstop eatery located on the field level behind third base. The air-conditioned restaurant features Carvel ice cream, sushi, and beer. Featured prominently throughout the ballpark are Premio Italian sausages although you might want to think twice before asking for a small bag of chips ($2.50) to go with your order. If you need some caffeine, the generally underrated Dunkin Donuts coffee is sold at the ballpark.

A few additional food offerings are available at the Metropolitan Club level, including wraps, sushi rolls, and wine.

For the Kids
Perhaps the best aspect of Shea is the effort the Mets put into the Fan Fest area available for two-and-a-half hours prior to every Friday, Saturday, and Sunday home game. Although open to all, Fan Fest is primarily aimed at the youngster set with a big bouncy slide, electronic games, batting cages, and an obstacle course. Good staffing and security is assured in the tight, popular space. Fan Fest is located near the Subway station at Gate E, not far from the right-field foul pole.

Ballpark Tours
At this time, the Mets do not offer Shea Stadium tours to the public.

Handicapped Access
Limited seating for the disabled is located on the field level.

Local Baseball Attractions
Mets fans will want to drop by the Mets Hall of Fame exhibit on the Press Level in the Diamond Club lobby. It's not exactly a highlight for the team: Tommy Agee was the last inductee back in 2002 and there are only 21 inductees, including broadcasters Lindsey Nelson, Bob Murphy, and Ralph Kiner.

The New York Yankees play at Yankee Stadium in the Bronx. We cover the Yankees and Yankee Stadium in a separate chapter.

The business rivalry between the Mets and the Yankees is played out on a minor-league level with two short-season NY-Penn League teams playing within the five boroughs—the Brooklyn Cyclones and the Staten Island Yankees. Both teams play in ballparks worth visiting.

The Cyclones, a Mets farm team, play at KeySpan Park on Coney Island. The team name comes from the Coney Island Cyclone ride. Though Coney Island isn't the attraction it once was, Brooklynites and other New York City residents have taken to the Cyclones. The team is one of the top draws in the minor leagues, thanks to some cheap seats (the outfield bleachers are only $5) and the sense of baseball nostalgia in Brooklyn. The Cyclones and architect Jack L. Gordon were wise to avoid any visual reminders of Ebbets Field (the well-remembered former home of the Brooklyn Dodgers) and instead went with the amusement-park theme. If you go, spend some time in the area before hitting the ballpark. At the turn of the century, Coney Island was the region's summer playground, and though the most memorable rides are gone, you can still eat fried clams, salt-water taffy, and Nathan's hot dogs.

To get to KeySpan Park (1904 Surf Av.; *brooklyncyclones.com*): Take the D, F, or Q train to the last stop, Coney Island/Stillwell Avenue. At the corner of Stillwell and Surf Avenues (where Nathan's is located), turn right. Walk two blocks west along Surf Avenue to KeySpan Park. It's at the southern end of the boardwalk and is hard to miss.

Also at KeySpan Park is the Brooklyn Baseball Gallery, celebrating the history of Brooklyn baseball. The best-known team in Brooklyn baseball history (sorry, Cyclones) is the Brooklyn Dodgers, but the history of baseball in Brooklyn goes back to pre-Civil War days. Brooklynite Candy Cummings is credited with inventing the curveball, while Brooklyn newspaper reporter Henry Chadwick invented the box score and pushed a statistical approach to baseball.

The timeline features famous teams in Brooklyn baseball history, such as the Brooklyn Atlantics, Brooklyn Excelsiors, and the Brooklyn Bridegrooms. There is mention of Cummings and of Chadwick, but the emphasis is on Brooklyn Dodgers history and players like Jackie Robinson, Gil Hodges, Mickey Owen, and Roy Campanella.

The Staten Island Yankees play at Richmond County Bank Ballpark at St. George (75 Richmond Terrace, Staten Island; *siyankees.com*), a waterfront ballpark featuring views of lower Manhattan and the Statue of Liberty beyond the outfield walls. It's easy to get to the ballpark—just take the free Staten Island Ferry from the Battery Park terminal and walk to the ballpark from the Staten Island terminal. The ballpark is right on the waterfront, and the backdrop is stunning.

For more information on old New York City ballparks, check out the Yankee Stadium chapter for a look at former Brooklyn Dodgers ballparks and the San Francisco Giants chapter for a more extensive look at the Polo Grounds.

Getting There

Shea Stadium tends to be a favorite of suburban baseball fans for two very good reasons: it's easily accessible by car and there is a sea of parking surrounding the ballpark.

The ballpark is located between Grand Central Parkway and the Van Wyck Expressway. Both are major arteries; Grand Central Parkway goes into Manhattan (via the Triborough Bridge) from Queens. Whitestone Expressway, which runs north of the ballpark, is a major highway servicing Connecticut. From New

INSIDER'S TIP

Though a sellout crowd at Shea Stadium won't fill the many parking lots surrounding the ballpark, the combination of a Mets game and the U.S. Open, held next door at the USTA National Tennis Center and Arthur Ashe Stadium, will. If you're planning to attend a Mets game in August and drive to the ballpark, be sure to check whether U.S. Open matches are scheduled.

If you have any claustrophobic tendencies, the higher rows in Loge Reserved should be avoided at all costs.

Jersey, take the George Washington Bridge to the Deegan Expressway; from there go to the Triborough Bridge and onto the Grand Central Parkway to the ballpark. You don't need a lot of specialized instructions to find the ballpark via highway: it is easy to find.

By New York City standards, the parking is downright cheap: $12 for a car, $28 for campers and limos, and $32 for RVs.

INSIDER'S TIP

The #7 line has a reputation as a safe line, even later at night after Mets games and no matter what John Rocker says.

Of course, you can avoid the parking fee altogether and take the train to the ballpark. The #7 line goes to Queens and the ballpark. It starts at the Times Square station and goes through Grand Central Terminal before going into Queens. The Shea Stadium stop is the second-to-last on the line, and on a game day the vast majority of the folks riding that far are going to a Mets game. The station is located beyond the right-field fence.

The Long Island Railroad also serves Shea Stadium on game days via the Port Washington line.

Where to Stay

When you come to New York City, you really should treat yourself to all the city has to offer. That almost certainly means opting for a room in Manhattan rather than in Flushing near Shea Stadium and the airport. Sure, there are a slew of hotels near the ballpark because of LaGuardia, but you can't walk from any

INSIDER'S TIP
If you insist on staying near the ballpark, the Ramada Plaza LaGuardia Airport (37-10 114 St., Queens; *ramada.com*; $165-$200) is across the street from Shea Stadium. The Comfort Inn Flushing (133-43 37th Av., Flushing; *choicehotels.com*; $115-$150) is a short walk away.

of them to the ballpark and they are bland, corporate airport hotels. When we're talking about Flushing hotels, we're talking about modest establishments at best.

You will pay a little more to stay in a prime location, but the wide choices of hotels results in fair, competitive pricing. Go ahead and splurge: when you remember your New York City trip your primary memory won't be saving $40 a night by staying out by the airport instead of somewhere in Midtown. Besides, you're also close to the #7 subway line, which takes you right to Shea Stadium from Times Square and Grand Central Terminal via 42nd Street.

More often than not, you should be able to get a decent, no-frills room on the East Side of Midtown Manhattan for slightly under $200 a night, but you're not likely to find acceptable lodging in this prime location for much less. Overall, we were pleased with our accommodations at the Helmsley Middletowne Hotel (148 E. 48th St., *helmsleymiddletowne.com*, $160-$260) on a recent visit. The standard rooms with king-size beds are very spacious, the mid-block location is relatively quiet, and front-desk staffing is helpful although somewhat overworked. The hotel lacks a business center and wireless internet. The lobby is small, connecting to a quality Indian restaurant (see Diwan below in "While You're Here") that's open late. You can't beat this location for nearby food, sightseeing, entertainment, and culture. If you want to live big lounging in world-class hotel lobby, pick from any of three within a block and order a cocktail or two. They won't kick you out for visiting.

We've also stayed at the New York Helmsley (212 E. 42nd St.; *newyorkhelmsley.com*; $200-$300) and found it agreeable as well. It caters more to foreign tourists, but it's clean and the location is great.

Price would be the only reason not to stay at the legendary Waldorf=Astoria (301 Park Av.; *waldorfastoria.com*; $225-$600). It occupies an entire city block with over 1,000 rooms and a host of restaurants and bars. No two rooms are the same. Many are small (barely big enough for a bed and desk), but others are spacious and at times it seems like the luck of the draw as to where you end up. Over the years foreign dignitaries, kings and presidents have stay at the Waldorf, sometimes for long periods of time. You may actually be surprised when pricing a stay at the Waldorf: with so many rooms, there are times when prices are reasonable as management tries to fill the place. Generations have made the Waldorf=Astoria a highlight of their New York visit, and you could as well.

Even if you're not staying there, walk though the block-long lobby and linger awhile before stopping at the Bull and Bear for a cocktail. If you're from

Shea Stadium

An interesting view from Shea Stadium is along the right field side looking south where you can view the USTA National Tennis Center—home of the U.S. Open, and the Unisphere landmark from the 1964 World's Fair.

the provinces—as we are—you may not be aware of the importance of the lobby bar in New York City cultural life. At the turn of the century, hotels were the gathering places of New York City and virtually every important hotel featured a legendary bar of some sort. Take, for example, The St. Regis (2 E. 55th St.; *stregis.com*; $300-$500), another traditional New York City hotel, now part of the Starwood Hotels group. It's a Beaux Arts landmark dating back to 1904. Under most circumstances the room rates will be out of the range of most readers of this book. We mention it mostly as a place to stop by for what will surely be a memorable and expensive drink at the King Cole Room, home to the legendary Maxfield Parrish mural of Old King Cole. Similarly, most of you won't be springing for a room at the Carlyle (35 E. 76th St.; *thecarlyle.com*), but you could stop by Bemelmans Bar for a cocktail. The bar is named for Ludwig Bemelmans, who painted the mural in the bar and is best known for creating the Madeline series of children's books.

INSIDER'S TIP
The Empire Hotel Group (*newyorkhotel.com*) runs six hotels in the West Side and Times Square areas. The rooms they offer come at a variety of price points, ranging from $75 at the Americana Inn to the trendy $275 accommodations at the Lucerne Hotel. Of course, that $75 gets you a room barely bigger than a closet (literally, you'll have a bed and sink, with a shared bathroom down the hall), but the place is clean, quiet and safe. The other hotels in the chain have a reputation for cleanliness and safety as well.

The Hilton New York (1335 6th Av.; *hilton.com*; $250-$450) is a little more uptown (at 53rd) and gives good access to Central Park, the theater district and Midtown. It's predominantly a business, convention and event hotel, but most of the rooms have been remodeled in recent years and the lobby is a great place for a drink and people-watching.

The Dumont Hotel used to be one of those hidden New York City gems, featuring larger, slightly run-down rooms at an inexpensive rate. (You could also bet on running into a pro athlete, as Madison Square Garden books visiting NHL and NBA teams there.) It has been remodeled as the Affinia Dumont (150 E. 34th St.; *affinia.com*; $300-$500) and made trendy as a fitness-oriented hotel, with the rates going up accordingly. Luckily, the room rates didn't go up to the stratosphere and it's still a solid choice as a family hotel. You can find suites (with two double beds and a kitchenette) starting at $300 on most weekends, and it's in a quiet neighborhood.

That same area, especially along Lexington Avenue, features a number of old hotels geared for tourists and businesspeople alike, including the Radisson Lexington (511 Lexington Av.; *radisson.com*; $200-$300), Marriott New York Eastside (525 Lexington Av.; *marriott.com*; $200-$300), the spendy W New York (541 Lexington Av.; *whotels.com*; $300-$500), the inexpensive Doubletree Metropolitan (569 Lexington Av.; *hilton.com*; $200-$300), and more. These hotels tend to be pricy compared to their room sizes and amenities as you're paying for location, location, location.

Another good location—and one where the room rates tend to be a little cheaper—is the Times Square area, now cleaned up and catering to families. (You can catch a train going directly to Shea Stadium from the Times Square station.) Today's Times Square is all glitz and action, attracting tourists from around the world to walk around and gawk at one another, hoping to see a celebrity in the MTV studios. It's always noisy and bustling, with video displays and billboards brightly illuminating the night—bright lights, big city indeed. One good bet in this area is the fairly new Hilton Times Square (234 W. 42nd St.; *hilton.com*; $225-$400), close to the action of Times Square and Broadway theaters. Also worth checking out are the Westin New York at Times Square (270 W. 43rd St.; *westinnewyork.com*; $250-$450) and the all-suites Doubletree Times Square (1568 Broadway; *hilton.com*; $250-$450), which features a floor of kid-proofed suites complete with kitchenettes.

It's not easy to find hotel deals in New York City anymore, and we suspect the Internet is largely to blame. Once upon a time hotels like the Hotel Beacon on the Upper West Side were known mainly by locals and relied on lower prices to attract tourists. The rise of search engines and online travel services put hotels like the Beacon on an equal footing with the larger Midtown palaces. Today the Hotel Beacon is still a pleasant place to stay but not the insider's treat it once was—and certainly not the bargain.

Local Attractions
There is not much within walking distance of the ballpark. The remnants of the

1964 World's Fair, including the impressive Unisphere, are located south of the ballpark in Flushing Meadows-Corona Park. Originally a swampy area, the 1,200-acre parkland was drained in the 1930s so the site could host the 1939 World's Fair. Statues. Some commemorative markers are scattered through the grounds, but there aren't many remnants of the 1964 World's Fair, the Unisphere being the most prominent and famous. The New York Hall of Science (47-01 111th St., Queens; *nyhallsci.org*; 718/699-0005) is a hands-on science and technology center featuring more than 400 exhibits. The Queens Museum of Art (Flushing Meadows Corona Park, Queens; *queensmuseum.org*; 718/592-9700) was originally built for the 1939 World's Fair as the New York City Pavilion and served as a temporary home for the United Nations between 1946 and 1950. The art collection is modest; worth seeing is the Panorama of New York City, a diorama depicting every building, street, and park in the five boroughs, updated when needed. It was ordered by Robert Moses for the 1964 World's Fair. If you visit Flushing Meadows Corona Park, do it before the game—not after dark and certainly not after the park's closing time of 9 p.m.

INSIDER'S TIP

Downtown Flushing is close to the ballpark, but very few Mets fans make the short jaunt there across the Roosevelt Avenue Bridge or ride one more stop to the end of the #7 line. That's a shame: in a city filled with great ethnic restaurants, downtown Flushing stands out as a foodie's dream, with outstanding Chinese, Korean, and Malaysian diners within a short walk of the Main Street subway stop. It's the largest Chinatown in New York City and well worth a visit.

One sad fact: there's really no hangout in the general vicinity of Shea Stadium for Mets fans. Bobby V's sort of fit the bill when Bobby Valentine managed the Mets, but Valentine is long gone and Bobby V's is now a Italian restaurant called the Pine.

Team Ballpark History

The Mets have played at Shea Stadium since it opened in 1964. When the Mets entered the National League as an expansion team in 1962, the Amazins' played at the Polo Grounds. We discuss the Polo Grounds in our chapter on the San Francisco Giants and AT&T Park, and (to a lesser extent) in our chapter on the New York Yankees and Yankee Stadium: the New York Giants were closely identified with the Polo Grounds and the Yankees spent some important formative seasons there.

While You're There

There's just no way to see the best of New York City in a shorter trip, particularly if you're spending lots of time at the ballpark. And we won't presume to tell you the essentials of New York City. If you're spending any

Shea Stadium in a mid-1960s postcard, showing its original look.

amount of time there, we advise buying a guidebook. You'll look like a tourist as you wander around Times Square with your guidebook and map, but take heart in the fact you'll be surrounded by other tourists doing the same, and New York City residents are fairly friendly to tourists.

Having said that, there are some essential sites to see in the Big Apple, especially if you're staying in Midtown Manhattan or near Times Square.

The Empire State Building (350 5th Av.; *esbny.com*) has been an enduring symbol of New York since it opened in 1931, and the demise of the World Trade Towers on 9/11 made it once again the tallest building in New York City. A trip to the building's observation deck should be taken by everyone once, even through it can be a hassle (everyone is checked for security reasons and the lines can be long during popular tourism months) and expensive. The 86th Floor Observatory is surrounded by glass and wraps around the entire building; the view from 1,050 feet is stunning on a clear summer day. Kids of all ages will enjoy the high-speed elevator ride as well. While you're there, walk around the three-story lobby—it's like walking though an Art Deco museum.

INSIDER'S TIP
Buy tickets in advance on the *esbny.com* website to avoid the lines. You'll pay a small surcharge for the privilege, but if your time is limited in New York you can avoid a longer wait.

The observation deck is open 8:00 a.m. to midnight daily (except for holidays). Tickets are $14 for adults and youth (12-17), $13 for children (6-11) and $9 for seniors (62+).

Two museums are worth visiting, especially if you have children. The American Museum of Natural Museum (Central Park West; *amnh.org*) features one of the most impressive natural-history collections in the world. Kids will love the dinosaur exhibit—comprising the entire fourth floor of the museum—as well as the Hall of the Universe (featuring a 15-ton meteorite) and the Hall of Planet Earth. The Rose Center show in the Hayden Planetarium is a hot ticket; make arrangements in advance, otherwise you may be shut out if you try to buy a ticket the day of a show.

The Metropolitan Museum of Art (5th Av. at 82nd Street; *metmuseum.org*) is one of the great museums of the world, with a collection ranging from Egyptian antiquities to Old Master paintings to architectural gems designed by Frank Lloyd Wright. As you can tell from that short description, curators take a catholic view of art. You can spend one or two days there and not completely see the many offerings, so don't even try. Do a little research and hit the highlights. Kids will love seeing the complete Temple of Dendur, relocated from Egypt when a dam project was scheduled to flood its location. Architecture buffs will want to head to the Frank Lloyd Wright room lifted from a Minnesota lakeshore home before it was demolished. Wright was a diminutive fellow and everything he designed was at his scale. And art fans will want to head to the corner of the American Wing to view *Madame X* by John Singer Sargent, still capable of shocking more than 100 years after it was exhibited at the Paris Salon of 1884. The Met opens daily (except Mondays) at 9:30 a.m.

After visiting either museum, spend some time wandering through Central Park (*centralpark.org*). Contrary to appearances, most of the 843 acres of Central Park were not sculpted by nature, but rather laid out by Frederick Law Olmsted and Calvert Vaux after they won a public competition to design a park. Many think Central Park is one of the prime reasons New York City stays civilized: it adds much-needed green and park space to one of the most congested cities in the world. For the most part, Central Park is safe, particularly in the southern side. On a nice summer day, Central Park is bustling with walkers, tourists, runners, Frisbee players, dogs, and children. Worth a visit: Strawberry Field (on the west side of the park, at 72nd Street), the memorial to musician John Lennon, who was murdered across the street outside the Dakota apartments.

If you're staying in midtown, head to Rockefeller Center and visit the city within a city. Go there early: NBC's Today show broadcasts from the corner of Rockefeller Plaza and 49th Street weekdays at 7 a.m. (get there earlier to get a spot close to the action). Matt, Meredith, and Al don't always go outside, especially if the weather is bad, but you can bet they will be interacting with the crowd on a lovely summer morning.

Speaking of television, one of the hottest tickets in town isn't for Broadway but for CBS's David Letterman Show. If you plan ahead, you have a good chance of scoring tickets. You can request them up to four months in advance via the CBS Web site (*cbs.com/latenight/lateshow*; click on the Get Tickets link). If selected, a show staffer will call and perhaps ask you a trivia question about the show. Alternately, you can drop by the Ed Sullivan Theater (1697

Broadway) on weekday mornings and weekend days to request a ticket. If you really, really want a shot at a daily taping (the show tapes Monday through Thursday, with two tapings on Thursday), call 212/247-6497 at 11 a.m. and pray you can score a set of ducats.

A pleasant way to spend the better part of a day is a trip to the Statue of Liberty and Ellis Island (*statueoflibertyferry.com*). Millions of immigrants were welcomed to America by the Statue of Liberty, itself an immigrant, being a gift from the French people in 1886. Their destination was Ellis Island, the processing facility today restored as a museum honoring immigrants and the trials they endured to reach America. It's also a center for genealogy: you can search through government records to find when your ancestors arrived at Ellis Island and under what circumstances. Not everyone attempting to come to America made it in, and many were turned away by Ellis Island officials as well, lending a bittersweet tone to the museum. Ferries depart on the half hour from Castle Clinton in Battery Park. The wait to get on a ferry can easily take more than an hour starting from the time you get in line for tickets, even worse on weekends and holidays. However, you do get to occupy some of your time at historic Castle Clinton, originally built to protect New York City from the British. Admission for both attractions is free, but advance tickets cost $11.50 for adults and $4.50 for children (4-12). You can buy advance tickets from the Circle Line ferry website.

Earlier we mentioned Grand Central Terminal as a place to catch the subway to Shea Stadium; even if you do so, the grand structure is worth a gawk. The main concourse has been the crossroads of New York City since it opened, and a 1994 restoration cleaned the grime off the ceiling and windows, exposing a gorgeous (though inaccurate) constellation. Go ahead and stare at the ceiling; it's expected. If you're there at mealtime, head to the lower dining concourse to the Oyster Bar (*oysterbarny.com*), as the oysters are fresh, the selection of seafood is stunning, and the panroasts are as sinful as ever.

In fact, a big part of the attraction of Manhattan is the great variety of excellent dining available. Fulfilling the promise "you can find absolutely anything you want in New York City," we decided to seek out authentic southern barbecue near Times Square after the theater. In fact, that is easily accomplished by heading over to Virgil's Real Barbecue (152 W. 44th St.; *virgilsbbq.com*; 212/921-9494)—reservations suggested for this popular spot. Despite the quick turnover of tables, Virgil's fulfills the promise of real, slow-cooked BBQ and the place has a few dishes with unique flare. For instance, the Owensboro lamb melts in your mouth with a satisfying tangy kick, courtesy of the accompanying mustard BBQ sauce ($18.50 platter with two sides). You might think drinking margaritas in a southern BBQ place is a bad idea and you'd be right—they're super sweet and quite weak. Save your sweet tooth for dessert and pick from a very fine selection of authentic southern pies.

For a change of pace, try Indian fine dining at Diwan Restaurant (148 E. 48th St., 212/593-5425). As mentioned previously, this restaurant adjoins the Helmsley Middletowne Hotel, but that's the extent of the connection. Smartly appointed in ruby red and black, the restaurant specializes in tandoori, but it would be hard to go wrong with the curries and other menu selections. You'll also notice an attentive, friendly staff and an intelligently designed wine list featuring a good variety of price points. For lunch, an impressive, reasonably priced buffet is offered.

Remember one thing: New York City is full of great restaurants. Foodies will drool at the prospect of dining at Jean-Georges, Le Bernardin, or Babbo, but one of the true joys of New York City is stumbling across some small neighborhood joint and having a truly outstanding meal.

Shea Stadium   403

The Complete Guide to Big League Ballparks

Tampa Bay Devil Rays
Tropicana Field

Address: One Tropicana Drive, St. Petersburg, FL 33705.
Cost: $138 million; 1996-1998 renovation, $85 million.
Owner: City of St Petersburg.
Capacity: 45,000.
Dimensions: 315L, 370LC, 410LC, 404C, 404RC, 370RC, 322R.
Ticket Line: 888/326-7297.
Home Dugout Location: First-base side.
Playing Surface: AstroTurf (1998-1999), FieldTurf (2000-present).
Other Tenants: The NHL's Tampa Bay Lightning played there from 1993-1996, and the Arena Football League's Tampa Bay Storm from 1990-1997.
Previous Names: Florida Suncoast Dome (1990-1993), Thunderdome (1993-1996).
Nicknames: The Trop, The Juicer.
First Game: The Devil Rays began play on March 31, 1998 with an 11-6 loss to the Detroit Tigers before a crowd of 45,369. Wilson Alvarez gave up six runs in 2.1 innings and was tagged with the loss; Wade Boggs homered for the D-Rays in the sixth inning. The Devil Rays rebounded on April 1 for the first win in franchise history, 11-8.
Landmark Event: The New Kids on the Block drew the largest crowd in Tropicana Field history: 47,150 for an Aug. 11, 1990 concert. The Tampa Bay Lightning drew 28,183 for a 1996 playoff game. The 1994 NCAA Final Four basketball tournament drew crowds of 40,632 and 39,112.

Your Tropicana Field Seating Crib Sheet

The D-Rays employ a variable-pricing structure, the better to soak those Red Sox and Yankees fans who come out to the ballpark only when their favorite team is in town.

Best Sections to View a Game: The Kane's Club seats behind home plate are cushy, well-attended, and expensive—over $200 a pop. We like the young Devil Rays, but we don't like them well enough to lay down that kind of money to get close to the likes of Rocco Baldelli. Though attendance at Tropicana Field is better than it was a few years ago, it's still not to the point where you need to bypass a sold-out section. For the best balance between price and view, we recommend the Lower Reserve seats (between $22 and $35): they're close enough to the field to provide a great look at the D-Rays while not severely denting your checkbook.

Best Cheap Seats: The Beach is one of the best cheap-seat venues in the majors. It has its own entrance and its own festive party scheme. Prices are $11 or lower. It's basically an open area where you and your friends can go drink beer and watch the game.

Most Underrated Sections: The outfield bleachers may be a little overpriced—approaching $20 for popular games—but the views are pretty good. We deplore the high prices thrown onto previously affordable sections like the bleachers. The left-field bleachers seem to provide a better view of the action than do the right-field bleachers.

Seats to Avoid: Sitting too high in the grandstand puts the low-flung catwalks into play: they provide an unnecessary distraction. The corner seats at Tropicana Dome aren't angled very well toward the action.

Tropicana Field: Trying to Reverse History

There is no ballpark in baseball so vilified as Tropicana Field. Critics of domes seem to hate it even more than they hate Metrodome, saying it has all the life and soul of a Target store.

Yet both hated domes exist for a very good reason: weather. Some protection from the elements is needed in Minnesota in April and late September, and outdoor baseball in Florida during the hot summer months can be unbearable. When both facilities were designed, a dome was considered state-of-the-art.

Even though Tampa Bay is the youngest team in the American League, Tropicana Field is not a newer facility: it originally opened in 1990, less than a year after the unveiling of the first retractable-roof ballpark, SkyDome, in 1989. We take retractable roofs for granted, but back then they were still considered unproven technology, and St. Petersburg took the safe path in commissioning a fiberglass roof, especially when there was no guarantee of landing a major-league team. The roof was considered an engineering marvel of sorts, and today it's still one of the largest cable-supported domes in the world.

Tropicana Field—then called Florida Suncoast Dome—was built on spec as St. Petersburg city leaders pushed for its construction to land a major-league baseball team. It did work, but it took several years. The Chicago White Sox leveraged St. Petersburg to win public funding for U.S. Cellular Field, while an agreement to bring in the San Francisco Giants dissipated at the last second when local owners kept the team for the Bay. As a result, the first two major tenants of Tropicana Field were National Hockey League and Arena Football League teams.

Enter the expansion Devil Rays, whose short, brutish existence in the

Tropicana Field

American League has been marked by consistent losing records and a front office seemingly bent on alienating the few fans committed to the team. If there was a way for Vince Naimoli and crew to irritate the local baseball community, they managed to do so. Despite bringing in some talented people over the years—Lou Piniella on the field and Mike Veeck in the front office—the Devil Rays have never gained traction among Tampa-St. Pete residents. Fairly or unfairly, Tropicana Field was held as a symbol of the much-despised Naimoli regime.

You can imagine the joy when new ownership came into town after the 2005 season and announced sweeping changes as to how the team would be run and how fans would be treated. With new ownership comes a new commitment to the fan experience at Tropicana Field, as Stuart Sternberg and crew committed $10 million in facility upgrades for the 2006 season.

And, we will admit, the changes work. On a basic level, the new crew brought in a new mindset, with game-day employees trained in the fine art of customer service. You're bound to be greeted by several Devil Rays employees before you reach your seat.

Aesthetically, the team added a lot of nice little touches that add up to a more colorful experience. A large touch tank filled with cownose rays appeals to kids. The bathrooms were overhauled with new lighting and fixtures. Hundreds of flat-screen TVs in the Rotunda, concession areas, and the hallways keep you up-to-date when you leave your seat for a brew. Five palm trees were installed in the Rotunda, as well as a new floor mapping the Tropicana Field playing area. The whole place was power-washed. And the harsh cinder-block walls in the two main levels were replaced with stucco or drywall.

For hardcore baseball fans, the Ted Williams Museum and Hitters Hall of Fame has relocated from nearby Hernando, Fla., to Tropicana Field and combines some permanent exhibits featuring Teddy Ballgame with temporary installations. The museum opens two hours before game time and stays open through the end of the game. Though the museum was originally launched with Williams' participation as a way to honor great hitters, it's really more now about the accomplishments of Williams, which were many.

Although you may hate domes—and lord knows we do—you may not be as repulsed by Tropicana Field as you expect, but that will depend on how you view something like Center Field Street and the Grand Rotunda. The Grand Rotunda was designed as a homage to baseball history, incorporating the same dimensions (80 feet wide, five stories high) and based on the original blueprint for the legendary rotunda at Ebbets Field. Nice theory, but it doesn't work—it's impossible to conjure up the ghosts of Dem Bums in coastal Florida. Center Field Street is essentially a mall between the ballpark and the parking lots featuring services (banking, travel), outdoor activities, entertainment, and concessions. When a large crowd is on hand—say, when the Yankees are in town—the place can be festive. When a small crowd is on hand—say, when the Royals are in town on a Wednesday night—the place is boring.

Which is generally true of Tropicana Field as a whole. For baseball to

thrive in Tampa-St. Pete, some sort of retractable-roof ballpark with climate control (like Chase Field) is needed: 90-degree temperatures coupled with high humidity and a late-afternoon rainstorm led to the building of a dome in the first place, and those elements are still present as the Rays look to their future. In the meantime, Tropicana Field will do.

Ballpark Quirks

The entire ballpark is one big quirk. Take, for example, the roof. It sits slightly askew, an effect used by designers to better circulate cooled air throughout the ballpark. It also makes for a distinctive landmark.

Inside there are quirks galore. When there, look up at the catwalks, part of the support system for the fiberglass roof. It's not uncommon for a ball to end up clanging off a support or a light, leading to some of the most detailed ground rules in the majors. Basically, a ball hitting a catwalk or a light in foul territory will be judged first by where it hits (a ball hitting in foul territory is immediately a strike; play goes on for a ball that hits in fair territory) and then by where it lands. If it lands foul, it's a strike; if it lands fair, it's in play. If it stays on the catwalk it's a ground-rule double. However, a ball hitting either of the lower two catwalks, lights or suspended objects in fair territory is a home run.

The playing surface has a few quirks as well. The field combines artificial turf with all-dirt basepaths, the only ballpark in the majors to do so. (The Metrodome and Rogers Centre have dirt cutouts only around the bases.)

One final quirk: when the Devil Rays win, the dome is lit with orange light—an homage to the holder of the ballpark's naming rights.

Food and Drink

You won't need to fight the crowds to reach food and drink at Tropicana Field, as there are almost 300 points of sale in the ballpark.

Generally, the concession offerings are pretty decent, with local favorites on the menu. The new owners came in and slashed prices on most ballpark staples, such as hot dog and pop, and scrapped the hated policy preventing fans from bringing in their own water. A local outpost of the popular Columbia Restaurant chain offers Cuban fare. You can find local favorites like boiled peanuts in the Taste of Tampa Bay area in Center Field Street.

There are also four restaurants and bars within Tropicana Field. The Cuesta-Rey Cigar Bar is located in center field. Although the cigar craze has diminished nationally, the bar is a definite selling point for the D-Rays, especially in cigar-happy Tampa. This is most definitely not just a smoking lounge—in fact, pipes and cigarettes are expressly prohibited—but a clubby cigar lounge complete with leather seats and big-screen TVs for watching the game.

Those enjoying beer will probably enjoy the Budweiser Brew House, offering microbrewed specialties.

Also located in center field: the Batter's Eye Restaurant, behind (where else?) the center-field batter's eye. A special window tinting presents a black background to batters while allowing fans eating at the restaurant to view the game.

In left field you'll find the Beach at Tropicana Field, a place designed for those who prefer to casually hang around and watch a game: the area has its own concessions and an outdoor patio.

Finally, the Checkers Bullpen Café, located next to the Devil Rays' bullpen in right field, offers the fine cuisine you've come to expect from the Checkers Drive-In chain. It does seem a little odd to go indoors to eat food meant to be eaten outdoors in a car, but then again everything at Tropicana Field is a little odd.

Handicapped Access

There are 450 seats designated for disabled access.

For the Kids

The Devil Rays added a slew of attractions for children and families before the 2006 season. Older kinds will enjoy calling their own plays. Things like video pitching and batting cages may not be groundbreaking, but they had never been found before at Tropicana Field. And, for tired parents, there's a rest area filled with furniture and carpet for relaxation while the kids play.

Ballpark Tours

The Tampa Bay Devil Rays do not offer tours of Tropicana Field.

Getting There

Tropicana Field is right on I-275, the main freeway running through Tampa and St. Petersburg, so it's hard to miss. Exit 22 goes right to the Tropicana Field parking lots; just follow the signs.

Parking is not an issue for most Devil Rays games. There are over 7,000 parking spots in lots adjoining the ballpark and most of them are free of charge, though there is a $3 VIP lot reserved for season-ticket holders.

However, there's no mass transit servicing the ballpark. In general mass transit is lacking in the Tampa-St. Pete area, and this lack of an essential civic service extends to the ballpark. In past seasons the Looper Trolley ran to Tropicana Field when large crowds were expected (i.e., opening night and Yankee games).

Where to Stay

There are no hotels within walking distance of the ballpark; that is, within a mile or so. Given that the Devil Rays instituted free parking with the 2006 season, there's no reason to kill yourself to stay close to the ballpark when you can drive close to the door.

So feel free to stay anyplace in the greater Tampa-St. Pete area. Keep in mind the area is rapidly growing and the area freeway system hasn't kept up with demand. You don't want to stay on the outskirts of town unless you want to spend a lot of time on the road, and there are plenty of hotels within a relatively easy drive of the ballpark. We'd recommend you focus on three areas: downtown St. Pete, the airport area, and the Rocky Point Island area.

We're not going to list all the airport hotels for they are legion and corporate in their facelessness. Rocky Point Island has a little more character, as most of the hotels are on the waterfront and with restaurants nearby. Rocky Point Island is bisected by the Courtney Campbell Causeway, which connects Tampa and Clearwater, and is located on the north side of Tampa Bay. It's easy enough to get to the ballpark by driving through Clearwater or across the bay.

Hotels on Rocky Point Island include:

Hampton Inn, 3035 N. Rocky Point Dr., Tampa; *hamptoninn.com*.
Holiday Inn Express Rocky Point Island, 3025 N. Rocky Point Dr., Tampa; *holiday-inn.com*.
Days Inn Rocky Point, 7627 Courtney Campbell Causeway, Tampa; *daysinn.com*.
Radisson Bay Harbor, 7700 Courtney Campbell Causeway, Tampa; *radisson.com*.
Chase Suite Hotel, 3075 N. Rocky Point Dr., Tampa; *woodfinsuitehotels.com*.
Sailport Resort, 2506 N. Rocky Point Dr., Tampa; *sailport.com*.

Downtown St. Petersburg has improved immensely in recent years in terms of attractions and nightlife. There are not many hotels downtown, but three are worth noting if you're in search of an old-time Florida experience. The Pier

Hotel (253 2nd Av. N., St. Petersburg; *thepierhotel.com*; $150-$300) is one of those grand, historic Floridian hotels that are so rare these days. Originally built in the 1920s and then restored in 2000, the Pier Hotel is a throwback to the days when guests would spend weeks or months at a time at a hotel, vacationing at a much more leisurely pace. That pace is replicated at the Pier: the verandah is designed for lounging while nightly cocktails are served. Another 1920s gem undergoing a recent renovation is the Renaissance Vinoy Resort & Golf Club (501 5th Av. NE., St. Petersburg; *marriott.com*), named to the National Register of Historic Places because of its Mediterranean Revival architecture. It's also where visiting teams are housed. Holiday Inn Heritage (234 3rd Av. N., St. Petersburg; *holiday-inn.com*) isn't as nice as the Pier or the Vinoy, but it's still an old-style Florida hotel.

If you want a more corporate experience, check out the Hilton St. Petersburg (333 1st St. S., St. Petersburg; *hilton.com*; $100-$150) and the Hampton Inn and Suites (80 Beach Dr. NE., St. Petersburg; *hamptoninn.com*; $75-$125).

While You're There

There is not much surrounding the ballpark, though a trip to Ferg's Sports Bar and Grill—within walking distance of Tropicana Field—is an essential experience before a Rays game. Don't mess with the dining room: the real action is at the bar, where the hardcore Rays fans (and occasionally broadcasters and team officials) congregate. *Ferg's Sports Bar and Grill, 1320 Central Avenue, St. Pete; 727/822-4562.*

Otherwise, a visit to downtown St. Petersburg is recommended before or after the game. Start with a visit to The Pier, a five-story inverted pyramid jutting out a half-mile from the shoreline. Yes, it's touristy, but you're a tourist, so go ahead and enjoy the complex, complete with giant tubes bubbling with fish and creatures from the sea and a second-floor aquarium filled with native

The view from the Tiki Bar at Bright House Networks Field.

and tropical fish and sharks. Though there are a few shopping options—mostly Florida schlock—the reason to head to The Pier is for the food. You may experience crowds waiting to get into the local outpost of the century-old Columbia Restaurant (800 2nd Avenue NE.; *columbiarestaurant.com*; 727/822-8000), known for its seafood and Cuban delicacies. The fourth-floor location provides a great view of downtown Tampa across the bay.

BayWalk is an upscale shopping and dining area. Sports fans will enjoy Dan Marino's Fine Foods & Spirits, while the whole family will enjoy TooJay's Gourmet Deli.

The Pier is located at the end of Second Avenue N.E. on the downtown St. Petersburg waterfront; St. Petersburg; stpete-pier.com; 727/821-6443. BayWalk Center, 125 2nd Av. N., St. Petersburg; baywalkstpete.com; 727/895-9277.

Team Ballpark History
The Devil Rays have played at Tropicana Field for the team's entire history since joining the American League in 1998.

Local Baseball Attractions
An indoor game is not your only choice for baseball in Tampa. Three minor-league teams in the high Class A Florida State League play within a short drive of Tropicana Field.

Bright House Networks Field is best known as the spring home of the Philadelphia Phillies, but it's also the regular-season home of the Clearwater Threshers, the high Class A affiliate of the Phillies. Bright House Networks Field opened in March 2004 and it's a gem of a ballpark: the left-field Tiki Bar is a great place to down a tropical drink, the kids can stretch out on the outfield berm, and there's enough shade in the grandstand to keep you comfortable on a hot and muggy Florida night. It's easy enough to get to Bright House Networks Field from St. Pete and the Tropicana Field; Hwy. 19 runs north-south up to and through Clearwater. *Bright House Networks Field, 601 N. Old Coachman Rd., Clearwater; threshersbaseball.com.*

A little farther north is Knology Park, the spring home of the Toronto Blue Jays and the regular-season home of the Dunedin Blue Jays. It's not a classic ballpark and not exceptionally scenic, but the Blue Jays don't draw very well, so you'll not be fighting any crowds. We'd recommend dining in downtown Dunedin and then walking the Piniellas Trail to the ballpark. *Knology Park, 311 Douglas Av., Dunedin; dunedinbluejays.com.*

Head straight east from Clearwater on the Courtney Campbell Causeway, hang a left (north) on Dale Mabry, and you'll soon be at Legends Field, the spring home of the New York Yankees and the regular-season home of the Tampa Yankees. Legends Field feels like a big-league ballpark, which is a plus during spring training but a minus when you want to see prospects close-up. A Yankees fan will want to make the pilgrimage. The complex is also where many major-league Yankees rehab after an injury. *Legends Field, 1 Streinbrenner Dr., Tampa; legendsfieldtampa.com.*

Tampa has been a hotbed for spring training since the turn of the century. Twelve blocks from Tropicana Field is Al Lang Field, set in one of the most scenic ballpark locations in the country. (Technically, it's "Progress Energy Park, Home of Al Lang Field." It's a terrible name.) The Devil Rays play spring-training games there, but it sits unused the rest of the year. Too bad: with its waterfront location and scenic views, it would be the perfect place to take in a game. And with the Devil Rays slated to move spring-training operations in 2009, the future of the ballpark is in doubt.

It's worth a visit, however, for the history. Al Lang Field was the longtime spring home of the St. Louis Cardinals and the New York Mets, and that history is noted in a set of commemorative plaques surrounding the ballpark. Al Lang Field is the most historical ballpark in the Grapefruit League as the site has been used as a spring-training venue since 1916, when the Philadelphia Nationals first trained there from 1916-1921. Other teams calling Al Lang Field spring-training home include the Boston Braves (1922-1924), the New York Yankees (1925-1937), and the St. Louis Cardinals (1938-1997). The Al Lang moniker dates from the Cardinals years—1947, to be exact—and comes from the original Al Lang, St. Petersburg's local "father of baseball." When the Cardinals left, the Devil Rays became the first MLB team to train in its hometown since the 1919 St. Louis Cardinals and Philadelphia Athletics (save the wartime years of the 1940s, when spring training was interrupted). *Al Lang Field, 180 2nd Av. SE., St. Petersburg.*

Atlanta Braves
Turner Field

Address: 755 Hank Aaron Dr., Atlanta, GA 30315.
Cost: $235 million.
Architect: Atlanta Stadium Design Team.
Owner: City of Atlanta and Fulton County.
Capacity: 49,583.
Dimensions: 335L, 380LC, 401C, 390RC, 330R.
Ticket Line: 800/326-4000.
Home dugout location: First-base line.
Playing Surface: Prescription Athletic Turf, featuring a hybrid Bermuda grass.
Other Tenants: None.
Nickname: The Ted.
First Game: On April 4, 1997, the Atlanta Braves defeated the Chicago Cubs, 5-4. A sellout crowd of 45,044 was on hand to see reliever Brad Clontz pick up the win with 1.1 innings of scoreless work in relief of Braves starter Denny Neagle; Mark Wohlers picked up the save after Chipper Jones singled in Mike Mordecai with the game-winning run. Michael Tucker hit the first home run in Turner Field history in the third inning off Cubs starter Kevin Foster.
Landmark Event: Considering the Braves have made the postseason almost every year since Turner Field opened (the string was broken in 2006), it's fairly amazing only two World Series games have ever been played there, with the New York Yankees winning both in their 4-0 Series sweep of the Braves in the 1999 World Series.

Your Turner Field Seating Crib Sheet

The Braves use a variable-pricing scheme. We list the more expensive prices here; the actual price may be lower for a game not in heavy demand.

Best Sections to View a Game: In general, tickets to Atlanta Braves games aren't hard to acquire. We're of the opinion there are two things keeping attendance down at Turner Field: the lack of marketing to the local African-American community and the generic atmosphere at Turner Field. Either way, the lack of demand for tickets gives you plenty of opportunity to score the seats you want. If you're coming in for a single game, consider a splurge on the Lexus Level: prices, $35 and $29, are quite reasonable for an MLB club level. Plus, at the Lexus Level you'll have access to some air-conditioned comfort on a muggy night and a clear view of the center-field scoreboard.

Best Cheap Seats: Under the right circumstances, you can get into the ballpark for a buck as the Braves offer Skyline seats for $1 three hours before gametime. Those sections are in deep center and way down the left-field line. Go for the Skyline seats down the left-field line and then camp out at a Coca-Cola Sky Field table: the view is better. The only drawback: you won't have a good view of the mondo scoreboard.

Seats to Avoid: The $23 Field Pavilion seats are merely the outfield bleachers. Those seats provide a decent view of the action, but you won't have a good view of the scoreboard—and any seat over $20.

Most Underrated Sections: Upper Box seats are only $15. We want to hammer home this point: the center-field videoboard is impressive, and you should select seats that provide a clear view of it.

Turner Field: Good Design, Ordinary Presentation

We're not quite sure we'd write off Turner Field as just another retro ballpark, as some fans seem to have done. The Braves even advertise the ballpark as having "the nostalgia and atmosphere of old-time baseball," but that's not totally true: while there are some retro elements in the ballpark, from the seats Turner Field is pure business—a circus and plenty of sideshows surrounding an immaculately groomed playing field.

In fact, from the seats Turner really isn't retro at all. It's not an exceptionally intimate ballpark unless you're in the lower seating, and if anything the ballpark is on the modern side, with a high-tech scoreboard looming over the action and plenty of fireworks when a Braves player hits a homer.

Still, for many, retro represents pure nostalgia, and there's more than enough of it at Turner Field.

Turner Field began life as the main stadium for the 1996 Summer Olympics, constructed next to Atlanta-Fulton County Stadium. In that configuration, Olympic Stadium stretched out to accommodate a full track; the current grandstand was at one end of the oval, while the other end was torn down (you can see the pillars from the original stadium entrance at the Ralph David Abernathy side, with the rest of the old Olympic seating used as the Entry Plaza). After the Olympic games ended, it took eight months to retrofit the stadium to a baseball-only facility.

The designers did a pretty good job of hiding the ballpark's roots; you can sit almost anywhere in the stands and not be able to tell Turner Field began as an 85,000-seat track-and-field stadium. It could be argued these roots contributed to a certain blandness, however. Despite some brickwork, Turner

Dominating the view from the grandstand: the huge center-field scoreboard.

A bust of Henry Aaron, one of the several statues in the Entry Plaza.

Field isn't retro, but you can't really pin down any other distinctive style, either. It lacks any great places for fans to stand around and watch the game; the whole notion of exposed concourses and public spots is almost absent at Turner Field.

If you've not spent a lot of time going to baseball games in the South—and by that we mean basically anything south of the Mason-Dixon Line, excluding Florida—you need to know fans treat attending a game in those areas a little differently than the rest of the country. To wit: it's a great Southern tradition to stand around and chew the fat while keeping an eye on the game; a baseball game is really an excuse for community interaction. The best ballparks in the South contain plenty of places to mingle and visit.

If you look at the great retro parks—starting with Oriole Park at Camden Yards and going through Citizens Bank Park—you'll see they all have tons of places where fans can stand and watch the game. In Philadelphia, for example, most of the concourse ringing the field is wide-open; the opposite is true in Atlanta. When you walk away from your seat to grab a beer and a dog, you won't be able to see the game or just stand and stretch your legs.

Sadly, there's only one space at Turner Field that truly fills this need and, because of its location in the upper deck in left field, it won't be used by most Braves fans. Too bad, because it's a great space. The Coca-Cola Sky Field may be quite a distance from the action—435 feet from home plate and 80 feet above the field—but it's the perfect family space. There's a miniature diamond for the kids to run, and on a hot day the large row of misters will definitely be appreciated. Plus, the giant Coca-Cola bottles blast fireworks after a Braves home run; any kid who won't think it's cool to be close to an exploding Coke bottle isn't worth bringing to a ballgame. But we've never really seen a lot of folks gathered up there for the simple pleasure of talking during a game. Maybe the practice doesn't scale to the major-league level; maybe Atlanta is now a city with such a heavy influx of outsiders that many of the old Southern ways have been lost.

Indeed, we could have used a little more South—old or new—at Turner Field. We are fans of Atlanta and welcome every opportunity to spend time there. But you don't feel like you're in the South when you're at Turner Field. We don't expect the Dukes of Hazzard to come barreling through the infield or see the Confederate flag waving in center field, but the lack of any Southern food specialties at concession stands is troubling: your food choices are pretty much the same as in any big-league ballpark, sans anything local—no local microbrews, no local foods (save boiled peanuts), no local vendors, no soul food, no meat-and-three.

This gets us back to our central complaint about Turner Field: during the course of a game, you feel like you could be anywhere. The Braves complain about having a hard time attracting an African-American clientele—the racial balance in Atlanta is not reflected by the mostly white crowds at a Braves game—but in the end there's just nothing to attract them. Local is always good: a ballpark should be a place for a community to gather, but we see little of that at Braves games.

This is too bad, because overall Turner Field presents a decent, if not generic, game-day experience. Most fans will enter the ballpark via the Grand Entry Plaza, located in center field. As mentioned, it was part of the stadium's track-and-field configuration (the pillars close to the street show the original boundary of the Olympic stadium), but today it's a celebration of Atlanta and Southern baseball with statues of former Braves greats Henry Aaron and Phil Niekro and local legend Ty Cobb, originally installed at Atlanta-Fulton County Stadium. Also in the Plaza: a ceremonial magnolia tree and plaque honoring the minor-league Atlanta Crackers; and a statue of Phil Niekro, the winningest pitcher in Atlanta Braves history, but not franchise history—both Warren Spahn and the largely forgotten Kid Nichols won more games for the Braves.

The Grand Entry Plaza is designed to be a self-contained universe once the game starts, with a large-screen television showing game action. Also in the Entry Plaza: a Kids Zone featuring Cartoon Network characters (Tooner Alley), concession stands, pitching and batting cages (branded here as Scouts Alley), and a retail store. Tooner Alley is a rather shameless attempt to push the Cartoon Network brand with activities like Puffy Ami Tumi Karaoke and the Kids Next Door Treehouse.

Three levels comprise Turner Field. Most fans will stay in the main concourse as it does ring the ballpark. The Lexus Level is Turner Field's Club Level, containing 58 suites, club seating, and a private membership club, the 755 Club. The upper level is limited to the grandstand.

Even though there's an extra charge involved ($2 on a game day, $5 on non-game days), a visit to the Braves Museum and Hall of Fame is a must. As far as chronicling the history of the Braves franchise—which stretches back through Milwaukee and goes back to 1871 in Boston—the museum is superb. If you want to know what players were like at the turn of the century and how the Boston Braves played at South End Grounds, this museum is for you. You'll see reproduction uniforms of the various Braves teams (also known as the Red Stockings, Beaneaters, Doves, Rustlers, and Bees), as well as a reproduction of the contract Babe Ruth signed when he spent his last playing days in Boston.

There's a lot of emphasis on the Milwaukee Braves as well, the team where Hall-of-Famer Henry Aaron first came to prominence. Those Braves swaggered into Milwaukee's County Stadium and won the World Series in 1957 behind the pitching of Lew Burdette and the bat of Eddie Mathews. (It would be the last World Series won by the franchise until 1995.) Though the team started strong at the box office, attendance slipped dramatically (going from 2.2 million in 1957 to 555,584 in 1965) and the Braves left Milwaukee after only 13 seasons.

You could easily spend more than an hour walking through the exhibits (which include a dugout bench from Atlanta-Fulton County Stadium and a walk-through Pullman train car, to show how teams traveled before the advent of airplane trips) and the historical displays before the game. On a game day you'll need to enter the museum through a dedicated entrance in back of Section 134; on non-game days you can buy tickets at the main ticket office.

There is much to like at Turner Field. We just wish there was more Southern flavor to the ballpark.

Ballpark Quirks

There are none. This is a standard-issue corporate ballpark, with all the good and bad that entails.

Food and Drink

We've already complained about the concessions. Let's just say one more thing: the most unusual food item at Turner Field is bison. This is not because bison is especially popular in Atlanta, but because former owner Ted Turner is big into bison and runs a chain of restaurants featuring the lean meat. Can't get a meat-and-three at the ballpark, but you can get bison at the West Pavilion concession stands, along with notable food items from other ballparks.

The Chophouse, located in right-center field, serves barbecue and features a multilevel deck with plenty of seating.

In a nice touch, Pete Van Wieren or Skip Caray make a point of dropping by Skip & Pete's BBQ before the game to meet with fans.

For the Kids

There are plenty of distractions for kids uninterested in baseball. We've already mentioned the two most prominent option: Tooner Alley and Coca-Cola Sky Field.

Though we were a little cynical about the Tooner Alley branding earlier in this chapter, the fact is kids love Cartoon Network characters. In Tooner Alley (especially on a Sunday) you can find Cartoon Network characters like Scooby-

Doo and Johnny Bravo wandering around and interacting with the younger set. The activities are a welcome diversion and you're never too far away from a TV screen showing the game action.

The Coca-Sky Sky Field provides a diamond for kids to burn off energy, and the misters are welcome on a hot, muggy Atlanta day. Parents can watch the game from a picnic table while their kids build up a sweat running the bases and then cool down under the misters.

Ballpark Tours

Tours of Turner Field leave on the hour. During the season tours run between 9 a.m. and 3 p.m., Monday through Saturday, and 1 to 3 p.m. on Sundays, except when the Braves play an afternoon game. During the offseason tours run between 10 a.m. and 2 p.m., Mondays through Saturdays, with a holiday break at the end of the year.

The tour costs $10 for adults and $5 for children. They begin and end at the Braves Museum and Hall of Fame, with tickets available at the ticket office.

Local Baseball Attractions

Sadly, most fans won't be able to see the ballpark exhibits on the history of baseball in Atlanta, dating back to 1866: they're located on the Lexus (club) Level, restricted to anyone but those holding tickets to seats and suites on that level. There are also some tributes to former Braves greats in the Grand Entry Plaza, but there are only two tributes to Atlanta baseball history: a statue of local legend Ty Cobb, originally installed at Atlanta-Fulton County Stadium, and a ceremonial magnolia tree and plaque honoring the minor-league Atlanta

The Coca-Cola Sky Field at Turner Park features oversized seating, misters, exploding Coke bottles, and a generally good view of the action.

Crackers.

That's it.

Too bad, because there's a great baseball heritage in Georgia and the South. The Atlanta Crackers were just one of the great teams in Atlanta baseball history, playing at still-remembered Ponce de Leon Park. Baseball became popular in Atlanta right after the Civil War, with teams like the Gate City Nine and the Osceolas capturing wide followings. The Crackers, launched in 1901, were a cornerstone of the old Southern Association, and the Atlanta Black Crackers were a cornerstone of the Negro Leagues. Players like Luke Appling, Eddie Mathews, and Chuck Tanner spent time in a Crackers uniform, while Norman Lumpkin, and Sammy Haynes were famous Black Crackers. The Crackers left town after the 1965 season, forced out by the Braves; the Black Crackers folded before that.

Throughout the long history of both Crackers teams the home of Atlanta baseball was Ponce de Leon Park. The first Ponce de Leon Park opened in 1907 and could seat 9,000; it cost $60,000, a huge sum in those days. Alas, in 1923 the wooden structure fell prey to a foe more deadly than a wrecking ball—fire—but Crackers ownership rebuilt an even grander and expensive ($250,000) ballpark, which opened in 1924. Originally named Spiller Field, the ballpark seated over 14,000 and was expanded over time. It was best known for a mammoth magnolia tree in right-center field—462 feet away and in the field of play, which led to some special ground rules. Eddie Mathews and Babe Ruth were reportedly the only players to hit a ball into the tree.

Although the ballpark was torn down in 1965, the magnolia tree still stands

Turner Field

Ty Cobb and "Shoeless" Joe Jackson. The pair grew up in the same northern Georgia/southern South Carolina region. (Courtesy Library of Congress, LC-UCZ62-97880.)

at 650 Ponce de Leon Av. NE. It's now a century old, and there have been efforts to ensure the tree stays healthy. A plaque commemorating the tree's historical significance was dedicated in 2005.

Ty Cobb was known as the "Georgia Peach," though his demeanor and actions were anything but sweet and peachy. Teammates despised him, opponents hated him, and fans heckled him to their detriment, as he wasn't shy about heading into the stands to settle a score. Still, Cobb was revered as one of the greatest players of all time, as some savvy promotion from friend and legendary sportswriter Grantland Rice and some great hitting for the Detroit Tigers between 1905 and 1926 (he spent the last two years of his career with the Athletics) cemented his place in the Hall of Fame. The Ty Cobb Museum, located in his hometown of Royston, is housed in a hospital he launched with a gift of $100,000 in 1950. Today that hospital has grown into the Ty Cobb Healthcare System; the museum in the hospital's Joe A. Adams Professional Building contains exhibits on his life and a theater showing filmed highlights. Royston is located northeast of Atlanta; take I-85 to the Royston exit. *Ty Cobb Museum, 461 Cook St. Royston, GA; 706/245-1825; tycobbmuseum.org. Adults, $5; seniors, $4; children 4 and older, $3.*

As long as you're headed out of Atlanta on I-85, take some time to drive further north into South Carolina and take in a game at West End Field, home of the Sally League's Greenville Drive. West End Field is one of the most notable ballparks in the minor leagues: it's stunning in how it reflects Greenville past and present, celebrating the city's rich baseball history while serving as a solid building block as Greenville plans for the future.

There's a rich baseball tradition in Greenville: "Shoeless" Joe Jackson grew up there and played for one of the city's many textile mill teams before turning pro. While there's been minor-league baseball in Greenville for decades, those mill teams were just as important—or maybe more important—to the average Greenville citizen, and the many photos of local mill teams pay homage to that tradition.

Most of the mills are gone and, as they've left town, Greenville has been forced to remake itself. Some Southern textile towns merely withered away or went the tourist route; Greenville city leaders decided to attract the businesses of tomorrow (banks, high tech) and provide an elevated quality of life.

And much of that centers on Main Street, where office buildings, trendy restaurants, shops, art galleries, and parks coexist. Main Street extends from downtown south past the Reedy River to the West End, where it is now anchored by West End Field.

It is one of the most intimate ballparks you'll find at this level of baseball: all 5,700 seats are between the foul poles, as lot constraints in the form of office buildings and condos beyond left field and a railroad track beyond right field left no room for seating past the outfield fences. No grandstand seat is more than 13 rows away from the field. In an homage to the Drive's parent team, the dimensions of the outfield fences match those in Fenway Park; there's even a Pesky Pole down the right-field line and a miniature (30-foot-high) version of the Green Monster, complete with a manual scoreboard. For those who like color, there's also a 15x20 video screen in right field.

And West End Field is very much a Southern ballpark. One of the great pleasures of baseball in the South is the role of the ballpark as a community gathering space—the ultimate third place—and chewing the fat at a ballgame is a time-honored tradition. There's an extra-wide concourse in the back of the grandstand, allowing for plenty of fans to stand around while others head to the concessions. A large plaza down the left-field line provides more space for standing around, as does a picnic area down the right-field line. *West End Field, 945 S. Main St., Greenville; greenvilledrive.com; 864/240-4500. West End Field is located on the city block bordered by Main Street, Field Street and Markley Street. Main Street runs directly through downtown Greenville; West End is actually at the southern end of Main Street.*

Getting There

It's hard to miss Turner Field as it sits right next to I-75/85, about a mile south of downtown Atlanta.

Getting there is another matter. For some reason, exceptional freeway access to the ballpark has never been constructed, at least from the north. If you're coming from the north on I-75/85, there are two exits serving the ballpark. From exit #248A (marked as the Martin Luther King Dr./State Capitol/Turner Field exit), turn right onto Martin Luther King Drive and then left onto Pryor Street, noting the State Capitol on your left. Stay on Pryor until you hit Fulton Street; turn right onto Capitol Avenue/Hank Aaron Drive. This is a scenic, albeit slow-moving route; there are signs to point the way. You can also take exit #246 and make a left on Fulton Street. Stay on it until hanging a right on Capitol Avenue/Hank Aaron Drive. If you follow the signs you'll be okay.

From the south on I-75/85, take exit #246 and make a right on Fulton Street. Stay on it until hanging a right on Capitol Avenue/Hank Aaron Drive. Again, follow the signs.

Those of us who remember Atlanta-Fulton County Stadium have fond memories of the sea of parking surrounding the old stadium, but much of that parking has been lost to development. Today there are only 1,200 or so parking spaces surrounding Turner Field available to the general public. The two closest lots to the Grand Entry Plaza are reserved for season-ticket owners and Lexus owners. That's right: if you drive a Lexus to the game you can park it at the Lexus Lot east of the Grand Entry Plaza. It's a primo spot, but it's not free: $12. Otherwise, most lot parking north of the ballpark goes for $12, with far-off Silver lots going for $8.

A more logical approach is to take the MARTA Braves Express bus to the game. The bus runs every 15 minutes from the Underground Atlanta/World of Coca-Cola Plaza beginning 90 minutes before each game. The last bus back from Turner Field leaves one hour after the game. Up through the seventh inning the bus goes back to the Underground/World of Coca-Cola Plaza; after that it returns to the Forsyth Street entrance to the Five Points Rail Station. (The point: the shuttle route encourages you to spend some time hanging out at Underground Atlanta before going to the game. We concur with this strategy and will discuss both attractions elsewhere in this chapter.) The cost is $2.75 (kids 6 and younger ride for free) and tickets are available at the sales booth at Underground Atlanta. For more information, check out *itsmarta.com/getthere/braves.htm*.

If you plan on flying in: Turner Field is eight miles from Hartford-Jackson Atlanta International Airport. It's now the world's largest and busiest passenger airport. There's good and bad in this: it's good because competition usually yields some low-priced fares on almost any carrier; it's bad because it can take quite a while to make it from your gate to baggage claim and then to a rental car. Give yourself plenty of time to make your way through the airport maze.

Where to Stay

There are two hotels on the south side of Turner Field: Country Inn and Suites (759 Pollard Blvd.; *countryinns.com*; $100-$160) and Comfort Inn at Turner Field (795 Pollard Blvd.; *choicehotels.com*; $80-$170). Given the lack of amenities in the general ballpark area (restaurants, other attractions), be prepared to spend a lot of time at the ballpark if you stay there. Both hotels are nice enough and geared for families wanting to immerse themselves in the Braves experience.

There are also a host of hotels in downtown Atlanta. Don't be fooled by what seems to be a short distance between downtown and the ballpark: Turner Field is not a downtown venue, and most hotels are on the other side of downtown from the ballpark. Because Atlanta is a major convention city—even in the summer—you'd be best off arranging your hotel room well in advance, both for the cheaper rates and the better choice. There's the usual list of suspects among downtown convention-oriented hotels: the Ritz-Carlton Atlanta (181 Peachtree St. NE.; *ritzcarlton.com*; $350-$700), Hilton (255 Courtland St.; *hilton.com*; $175-$250), Marriott Marquis (265 Peachtree Center Av.;

marriott.com; $125-$250), Hyatt Regency Atlanta (265 Peachtree St. NE.; *hyatt.com*; $195-$265), and the Westin Peachtree Plaza (210 Peachtree St. NE.; *westin.com*; $200-$400). There's a fairly high level of entertainment at most of these establishments: kids will enjoy Trader Vic's at the Hilton, while the revolving bar on the 73rd floor of the Westin provides a great view of the region. A good buy among downtown hotels is the Residence Inn Atlanta-Downtown (134 Peachtree St. NW.; *marriott.com*; $85-$240): while the building is older by Atlanta standards, the rooms are large and more like apartments than hotel suites.

Still, don't feel compelled to stay downtown: while there are some downtown attractions we'll recommend in the next section, they don't require you stay there, and the ballpark's location pretty much dictates spending time in a car anyway. The Buckhead area of Atlanta features upscale dining, shopping, and hotels in a wide range of prices, including the J.W. Marriott Hotel Lenox (3300 Lenox Rd. NE.; *marriott.com*; $170-$325), the Homewood Suites (3566 Piedmont Rd.; *homewood-suites.com*; $129-$225), Crowne Plaza Buckhead (3777 Peachtree Rd. NE.; *crowneplaza.com*; $100-$350), W Atlanta (111 Perimeter Center W.; *starwood.com*; $200-$350), and Marriott Residence Inn Buckhead (2960 Piedmont Rd. NE.; *marriott.com*; $120-$200).

Turner Field is only eight miles away from Hartford-Jackson International Airport. There is the usual cluster of airport hotels nearby.

While You're There

We admit it openly: we love Atlanta. Yes, the air is more than a little sticky in the summer, but an early- or late-season trip to Atlanta to catch some Braves games at Turner Field is one of the best baseball vacations out there.

While a lot of downtown Atlanta isn't much to write home about, there are two attractions the whole family will love: Underground Atlanta and the World of Coca-Cola. (In fact, we'd recommend spending the day at these two attractions and then heading to the Braves game via shuttle bus in the evening.)

Atlanta was literally born next to Underground Atlanta, as the location was the terminus for the Western & Atlantic Railroad, serving central Georgia with service to Chattanooga. Businesses soon popped up around the terminus to serve the farmers bringing product to market, and a community—which went by the names Terminus, Thrasherville, Marthasville, and, ultimately, Atlanta—grew rapidly, becoming a vital crossroads of the South. By the advent of the Civil War, Atlanta had grown to 10,000 residents and was an important player in the regional economy.

So important that when the Civil War ended and Gen. William T. Sherman made his famous march through the South, Atlanta was directly in his crosshairs. The railroad terminal on the site of Underground Atlanta was destroyed along with most of Atlanta.

Sherman failed to defeat the spirit of the city, and soon afterward Atlantans began the long process of rebuilding, centering their efforts around the railroad terminus. A new railroad depot—Union Station, still standing—was built, as were the city streets in the area. By 1887, Atlanta had 22,000 residents, and the business district was thriving.

Growth continued, and in the 1920s city streets were raised to accommodate car traffic above the train tracks. While not the intended effect, the move to raise the streets preserved the original storefronts from the turn of the century under city streets. During the boom era of the late 1960s—the same boom era that attracted Braves ownership—city fathers opened up those closed-up properties in the first iteration of Underground Atlanta, but it failed. Thirty years later Underground Atlanta reopened as a retail/shopping/entertainment complex.

You can get a healthy dose of Atlanta history at Underground Atlanta: interspersed with stores and restaurants are displays showing life in the antebellum South and how Atlanta looked and worked at the turn of the century. Guided tours of Underground Atlanta are offered on Fridays, Saturdays, and Sundays, but you can download information from the *underground-atlanta.com* Web site and tour on your own.

The shopping is a mix of chain stores and local establishments, while a mix of fast-food vendors and sit-down restaurants should fit most visitors' needs. *Underground Atlanta, 50 Upper Alabama St., Atlanta; underground-atlanta.com; 404/523-2311.*

It's appropriate that the World of Coca-Cola is next to Underground Atlanta, for Coca-Cola was invented in downtown Atlanta and has always been a key part of Atlanta's economic growth. It's just sugared water, but the interesting thing about Coca-Cola is how the firm pushed the envelope when it came to advertising and marketing. Plus, a visit to Club Coca-Cola, where various Coke products from around the world can be sampled, is fascinating. (Be warned, a new World of Coca-Cola is scheduled to open in Spring 2007, so check out the Website or call for information.) *World of Coca-Cola, 55 Martin Luther King Jr. Dr., Atlanta; woccatlanta.com; 404/676-5151. Adults, $9; seniors (60 & above), $8; children ages 4-11, $5.*

Team Ballpark History

The wandering Braves have quite the ballpark history.

The Braves began life in 1871 and mainly played until 1914 in three ballparks under the South End Grounds name, occupying the same location near the current Ruggles T Station at Columbus and Walpole and the former site of Huntington Avenue Grounds, a previous home of the Boston Red Sox. Why did both Boston baseball teams once play so close to one another? Proximity to mass transit—in this case, the New York, New Haven and Hartford Railroad line—was a huge consideration in ballpark locations before the advent of the automotive age.

The first South End Grounds wasn't distinguished, but the rapid growth in popularity of baseball and large crowds wanting to see the likes of King Kelly led Braves owner James Gaffney to build one of the most distinctive ballparks in baseball history. The second South End Grounds was the first double-decked ballpark in Boston history and featured spires at both ends easily visible from a distance. The fanciful design featured intricate brick work and unique finishing touches, and the second-level pavilion was the first Club Level in baseball, offering fans a place to spread out and watch the game in a more relaxed fashion. The ballpark also featured what some argue was the first electric scoreboard: wires were placed underneath the playing field to lights mounted on the outfield wall to indicate the status of the game. Braves ownership put up screens down the first-base line to keep freeloaders from watching games for free from the rooftops of adjacent houses.

Baseball was king in Boston in the South End Grounds era: the Braves (or Red Stockings, Doves, Rustlers, Beaneaters, or Bees, depending on the year) won 13 pennants while playing there, and a World Series. Box-office attractions like King Kelly, John Clarkson, and Kid Nichols provided a steady stream of working-class patrons to the ballpark.

That second South End Grounds burned down in the Great Roxbury Fire in 1894, replaced by a plain, single-deck fire-resistant structure because Braves ownership underinsured the grand structure. Despite the less-than-grand surroundings, the Braves continued to draw at South End Grounds, and by 1914 it was apparent the team would need a new, grander structure to keep up with the Red Sox and their spanking-new Fenway Park. (In fact, South End Grounds closed on Aug. 11, 1915, and over the next year the Braves played home games at Fenway Park.) Braves ownership knew they could draw huge crowds—in

After it opened, Braves Field was the temple of baseball in Boston, outshining Fenway Park for many years.

fact, they rented Fenway Park for the 1914 World Series to accommodate crowds larger than South End Grounds could handle—and they set out to build a facility that would out-do Fenway.

And, in many ways, they did. Braves Field opened on August 18, 1915, and was instantly hailed as a monumental accomplishment. Holding 43,500, Braves Field was larger than Fenway—the largest in the United States, as a matter of fact. (It would hold that distinction until the opening of Yankee Stadium.) The covered grandstand served as a blueprint for a generation of ballparks. Like many ballparks of the era, it featured a vast outfield with the center field fence 550 feet out: Ty Cobb hated the place and said no one would ever hit a home run there, but he was wrong. Walton Cruise hit the first home to right field some seven years later, and Frank "Pancho" Snyder homered to left field in 1925. (Remember, this was at a time when "bounce homers"—that is, balls bouncing over the fence—counted as home runs and not ground-rule doubles. There were three bounce homers hit at Braves Field in 1921.) By 1928 it was clear fans wanted to see home runs, and so Braves ownership relented and moved the fences in while adding bleachers.

While the Braves could count on a certain number of rabid fans to fill up the "Jury Box" bleachers (so named because fans held court on the proceedings of the game), over time the Braves' appeal dwindled. Part of that was because it wasn't a great place to watch a game: smoke and grime from a nearby railroad switching yard spilled into the ballpark and cool winds off the Charles River kept balls inside the fences. By the time Ted Williams came along, it was clear the Red Sox ruled Boston.

Though, ironically, the Red Sox used Braves Field often. In 1929 Boston city officials finally allowed Sunday baseball, but because Fenway Park was located close to a church, the team still couldn't break the Sabbath. So the Red Sox played Sunday games at Braves Field between 1929 and 1932. The Red Sox also moved 1915 and 1916 World Series games to Braves Field to accommodate larger crowds.

TRIVIA
Felipe Alou was the first Atlanta Brave to bat at Atlanta Stadium, and his son Moises Alou was the last to bat in the regular season when playing for the Montreal Expos.

Parts of Braves Field still stand. Boston University's Nickerson Field (once the home of BU football) is on the ballpark site, and the Gaffney Street entrance to the field and the ticket booth date from Braves Field. Nickerson Field served as the first home of the AFL's Boston Patriots and the home of the ill-fated Boston Breakers of the United States Football League. A marker outside Nickerson Field commemorates the Braves Field era. (Nickerson Field is on Harry Agganis Way at Commonwealth Avenue on the Boston University campus.)

In 1953 it was clear Major League Baseball would move westward, and Braves owner Lou Perini beat Bill Veeck to Milwaukee, moving the team to County Stadium. We discuss County Stadium in our look at Miller Park, home of the Milwaukee Brewers.

The Braves had a relatively short run in Milwaukee: 1953-1965. The team was a smash in the early years, drawing 1,826,397 in 1953 and setting a National League record, and later drawing 2.2 million in a single year. Milwaukee had wanted baseball bad enough to use county money to build a ballpark—County Stadium was the first publicly funded major-league ballpark, though certainly not the last—and its citizens were eager to support the team. Though you could argue a better ownership group might have saved baseball in Brewtown, the allure of Atlanta and its increasing pool of corporate support and affluent citizens was too much to ignore.

When the Braves moved to Atlanta in 1966, the team's first home was Atlanta Stadium, renamed Atlanta-Fulton County Stadium in 1975. It was an $18-million circular cookie-cutter ballpark built to attract major-league sports (it worked; the NFL's Atlanta Falcons soon took up residence as well), and because of the relatively high altitude of Atlanta the ballpark was soon tagged with a nickname of the "Launching Pad." It was located directly north of the current Turner Field site. Besides being the home of the Braves it was also the home of the NFL's Atlanta Braves and the baseball venue for the 1996 Summer Olympics.

The Braves initially played the American Indian angle heavily. Big Victor was a popular feature when the team moved to town: the totem-pole figure had eyes that rolled when the Braves hit a homer. He lasted a season until mechanical problems forced his retirement, and he was replaced by Chief Noc-A-Homa and his wigwam.

The Braves retired Atlanta-Fulton County Stadium on a sad note: the final match there was Game 5 of the 1996 World Series, won by the New York Yankees 1-0. Though the ballpark is gone, it is memorialized in the Turner Park parking lot: a blue fence marks the outfield fence, brickwork in the asphalt shows the infield and bases, and a marker pinpoints where Hank Aaron's record-breaking 715th home run landed.

Chicago White Sox
U.S. Cellular Field

Address: 333 W. 35th St., Chicago IL 60616.
Cost: $137 million; $80 million in renovations.
Architect: Original design, HOK Sport; 2004-2005 renovations, HKS.
Owner: Illinois Sports Facilities Authority.
Capacity: 40,615.
Dimensions: 330L, 377LC, 400C, 372RC, 335R.
Ticket Line: 866/769-4263.
Home Dugout Location: Third-base side.
Playing Surface: Bluegrass with eight different blends of grass. The infield dirt was transported from the original Comiskey Park.
Other Tenants: None.
Previous Names: Comiskey Park (1991-2003).
Nicknames: The Cell.
First Game: On April 18, 1991, the White Sox inaugurated what was then called the new Comiskey Park in a most inauspicious fashion, dropping a 16-0 decision to the Detroit Tigers. Frank Tanana threw the complete-game shutout, with Rob Deer homering twice and Cecil Fielder and Tony Phillips each hitting one as well. Both Deer and Fielder drove in four runs on the day.
Landmark Event: The Chicago White Sox won the 2005 World Series in a rather methodical fashion, sweeping the Houston Astros four games to

none. The White Sox won both games played at US Cellular Field: 5-3 in the opener and 7-6 in Game Two. On the way to the Series the White Sox swept the Red Sox 3-0 in the first round of the playoffs, with the first two games played at the Cell. The following round saw the ChiSox defeat the Angels four games to one, with the only loss coming in the series opener at U.S. Cellular Field. Overall the White Sox went 5-1 at home during the playoffs. The White Sox made the American League Championship Series in 1993 and the American League Divisional playoffs in 2000. It was the first World Series win for the White Sox since 1917. The Cell has also hosted concerts by the Rolling Stones and Bruce Springsteen.

Your U.S. Cellular Field Crib Sheet

Best Sections to View a Game: Unless you have some connections, you won't see the game from the best seats in the park: the ChiSox sold out all season tickets for the 2006 season and are likely to sell them out for 2007.

Best Cheap Seats: The Center Field Bleachers are only $16 ($7 for children). Like the Left Field Bleachers, you have good accessibility to the center-field concessions on both the field and promenade levels. One caveat: after drunken fans rushed the field and attacked a Kansas City Royals coach, the White Sox instituted some strict rules about where fans can move during a game. Fans who buy the cheap seats aren't allowed in the rest of the ballpark, so forget about moving down to the good seats near the end of the game.

Most Underrated Sections: The bleachers are great. We highly recommend them.

Seats to Avoid: The Arcade seats in right field aren't as good as you'd think: you're right in front of the standing-room-only (SRO) area, and you'll have plenty of folks standing right beside you, no matter how many security guards are out there. Those seats work better in theory than in reality. Speaking of the SRO tickets: the rowdies tend to gather out there and we've come upon more than one incident involving an intoxicated fan and security guards. So unless you really, really want to be at a sold-out game or are part of a large crowd, we do not recommend them.

U.S. Cellular Field: The Second Time's the Charm

Commonly referred to as Chicago's "other" baseball team, the American League White Sox reside at 35th Street and Shields and play at U.S. Cellular Field. While the Cell does not have nearly the romantic history of its rival in Wrigleyville or the original Comiskey Park, it's a vastly underrated ballpark. And with the White Sox winning the 2005 World Series, locals are shedding that "other" label and embracing their Pale Hose.

When the day finally came for the ChiSox to build a new ballpark in the late 1980s, those in charge were dealt the impossible task of bringing those memories from the old park across the street to a modernized setting.

You may not have wanted to see Comiskey Park go, but there's no doubt the franchise received a boost with a move to the Cell. The White Sox drew 2.34 million fans in 2005, the fourth best in ballpark history; the three best years attendance-wise came in 1991-1993, the first three years the ballpark was open. The 1994 strike took the wind out the South Side's sails, and it's only now that the ChiSox are drawing the fans back.

In some ways the construction of the new Comiskey Park was an amazing thing: it was the first new sports facility build in Chicago proper since Chicago Stadium opened in 1929. (Think about it. The NHL's Chicago Blackhawks, the NBA's Chicago Bulls, the Cubs, and the White Sox, all spent over 60 seasons playing in the same facilities. Never let it be said the good citizens of the Windy City spent too much on sports facilities between 1929 and 1991.) Still, the timing was bad. Many believe the new Comiskey came a year too soon and when Oriole Park at Camden Yards ushered in a new era of retro ballparks in 1992, the Sox' facility quickly became an outdated structure. Some say a lack of entertainment in the surrounding neighborhood and the ballpark's steep

U.S. Cellular Field

upper deck also dampen attendance.

In 2001, the White Sox began renovating Comiskey Park in hopes of turning the stadium's image around. The Sox again spent money in 2002 to improve the park.

On January 31, 2003, the White Sox announced a naming-rights deal with U.S. Cellular for $68 million to be spread over 20 years. To validate the deal with fans of the sacred Comiskey Park moniker, the franchise vowed to only use that money to remodel the ballpark. They began using it immediately, spending $20 million that offseason to install a new videoboard and ribbon boards on the upper-deck façade, while constructing a Fan Deck in centerfield. A later series of renovations removed the last eight rows of the upper deck, enclosed both the club level and the upper concourse, and expanded and relocated the FUNdamentals skills area. The overhauls continue: in 2006 all the blue seating was replaced with green seats, the same as in the original Comiskey.

The capacity of U.S. Cellular Field decreased as the White Sox made changes. When it opened, U.S. Cellular Field held 44,321. That was increased to 47,522 in 2001, 47,098 in 2002-2003, and 40,615 from 2004 on.

Over the past five seasons, the bland and boring Comiskey Park has been transformed into the architecturally attractive U.S. Cellular Field, and that's just the outside. Inside the park the Sox have added plenty of fan amenities and given the South Side a facility with its own personality.

The exploding scoreboard, reminiscent of the exploding scoreboard first installed by legendary owner Bill Veeck in the original Comiskey Park, is

obviously the Cell's trademark feature and that hasn't changed. The Sox toyed
with idea of moving it to left or right field at one time but thankfully they
haven't. Its prominence in centerfield is the best part of the stadium, not to
mention you have a good view of it from anywhere in the park. Veeck loved to
tinker with his ballparks and some of the other innovations he installed in the
original Comiskey Park—like the right-field Rain Room—can be found at U.S.
Cellular Field.

   The Fan Deck is a great touch. Imagine a great big patio with all kinds of
seating that sits high above the centerfield seating area. The view is great and
fairly unique in baseball and the setting is perfect if you feel stuffy in your
middle-of-the-aisle seats. At the bottom of the deck is a concession stand, so
you aren't too far from refreshing yourself with snacks or drinks.

   Unfortunately, any seat at the Cell is pretty expensive. If you want to sit
anywhere in the lower bowl it's going to cost you at least $24 and up to $33,
depending on whom the team's playing and the day of the week. And that will
only get you into the outfield bleachers. If you want your own seat in the lower
bowl, that will cost you $26 on the low end. The cheapest seat in the ballpark is
$14, with a not-so-great view from the top of the upper deck.

   The other big catch with buying upper-deck seats is you are doomed to
spend the rest of your evening at that altitude as you are not allowed to set foot
on the lower concourse. This means an upper-deck seat does not grant you
access to the centerfield fan deck, the Hall of Fame shop, the Rain Room, or the
plethora of great concession stands on the lower concourse. However, you do
still get to enjoy the immensely popular FUNdamentals section.

If you happen to have the cash to get yourself a seat in the lower deck, not only are you granted access to nearly all of the Cell's fan amenities, you get a great view no matter where you sit. The sight lines are fantastic and you're right on top of the field. The lower-deck concourses are wide and loaded with a wide variety of concession stands. Even on a packed night you don't have to wait long to get what you want. Another plus is being able to see the action on the field from anywhere on the concourse.

The Cell's facelift has pushed it into the upper half of ballparks in terms of respectability. If they want to push their attendance figures in that direction, they should consider making a game at U.S. Cellular Field a bit more affordable.

Ballpark Quirks

Nothing that wasn't designed to be there, but we don't say this in any pejorative way. Though the new Comiskey Park might have been a generic ballpark when it opened, the White Sox have done a lot to add some personality to U.S. Cellular Field. It works, but there's still a whiff of the corporate at the ballpark.

One interesting quirk really has nothing to do with the game of baseball. The White Sox offer a Pet Check where they'll kennel your animals for a $3 fee. Only service animals are allowed in the ballpark. Reservations are requested; call 312/674-1000, ext. 5503 for information.

Food and Drink

The Cell offers a wide range of ballpark food, from your traditional hot dogs (as well as kosher dogs), burgers and popcorn to Chicago-style pizza, beef sandwiches, funnel cakes, meatball sandwiches, and sausage. The concession stands are named after former Sox greats, including Luis Aparicio, Tony LaRussa, and the 1983 Winning Ugly White Sox. There is plenty of variety at the park, including desserts and coffee for those day-after-night games.

A tip for all you vegetarians: head to the Fan Deck in center field to find some of the best veggie hot dogs and gardenburgers in the majors. The best thing about the food is it's extremely affordable by ballpark standards. Two people can eat pretty liberally for less than $20—and that's saying something.

Handicapped Access

There are just over 400 wheelchair-accessible seats at the Cell. Parking for vehicles displaying a valid handicapped placard or license plate is located in Lot D; enter it through the 37th Street entrance to the parking lots.

Ballpark Tours

Tours of U.S. Cellular Field are limited to groups of 10 or more; no individual tours are offered. These group tours are presented on Tuesdays and Fridays at 10:30 a.m., with a 1:30 p.m. also offered on non-game days. Reservations are required; call 312/674-1000 for more information.

For the Kids

The FUNdamentals station in left field is a dream come true for any kid. The area is free of charge and offers plenty of baseball activities and instruction for kids including a speed pitch, baserunning station, a youth-sized diamond for instruction and batting and pitching cages.

The souvenir shop/museum located behind home plate on the lower concourse is a nice touch. They have gear from every era of White Sox baseball including those hideous early 90s curly-c hats, collared jerseys from the late 70s, and the immensely popular 80s "SOX" shirts.

The Rain Room, another Bill Veeck invention that made the move across the street from the old Comiskey Park, is on the outfield concourse. Great on hot days, it's the place to rejuvenate tired toddlers and irritable adults.

The Sox offer two stands with kid-oriented concessions; the Rookie's Club stands can be found near sections 100 and 538.

Parents should consider taking their children to any Guest Relations Booth, where kids will receive a free ID bracelet personalized with their seat location. While there aren't many cases of lost kids at the ballpark, the wristband can help you avoid the situation completely.

Where to Stay

You won't be staying near the ballpark. Since that's a given, you should book your lodging to fit within any other plans you make. In theory, you could fly into O'Hare Airport, stay at an airport hotel, and drive to the game, but that makes for many miles in the car. You could fly into Midway Airport, but you won't be staying out there either.

Most of Chicago's great attractions are located downtown, about four miles from the ballpark. There are three major parts to downtown: the Grant Park area, the Loop, and the Magnificent Mile. If you envision downtown Chicago running north to south, the Magnificent Mile is at the north end, the Loop is in the middle, and the Grant Park area is to the south. All three have their attractions and advantages.

The northern downtown area features the city's most luxurious hotels, but there are also more casual establishments for families on a budget. The selection ranges from affordable joints like the Hampton Inn (33 W. Illinois; *hilton.com*; $150-$350) and the Holiday Inn-Chicago City Centre (300 E. Ohio St.; *chicc.com*; $100-$270) to larger establishments like the Sofitel Chicago Water Tower (20 E. Chestnut St.; *sofitel.com*; $150-$300), the legendary Drake (140 E. Walton Place; *thedrakehotel.com*; $255-$600), Crowne Plaza Chicago Metro (733 W. Madison; *ichotelsgroup.com*; $200-$600), the Four Seasons (120 E. Delaware Place; *fourseasons.com*; $400-$3,500), the spendy but oh-so-chic Peninsula Chicago (108 E. Superior St.; *peninsula.com*; $450-$5,000), and the Ritz-Carlton (160 E. Pearson St.; *fourseasons.com*; $400-$4,000). When looking for a hotel in the Magnificent Mile area, your most important consideration should be location: generally speaking, if you're spending a few days in Chicago and plan to hit the sights of downtown, you'll want to stay as close as possible to Michigan Avenue.

The Loop is the old core of downtown and the business center of the city. (The elevated train tracks form a loop and anything within those boundaries or nearby is considered to be in the Loop.) It features many of the attractions that made Chicago famous. Alas, the Berghoff Restaurant is no more (though the bar is still open), but Macy's—the grand doyenne of department stores that began life as Marshall Field's—still stands. Marshall Field's was one of the first temples of shopping, a huge department store featuring Corinthian columns and a Tiffany skylight. It's not the same since Federated Department Stores committed the ultimate sin of buying Field's and renaming every store in the chain, but still worth a visit.

There is one grand old hotel still standing inside the Loop. The Palmer House Hilton (17 E. Monroe St.; hilton.com; $130-$300) is billed as the longest continuously operating hotel in North America and served as the blueprint of the hotel as a city within the city, featuring multiple restaurants, shops, and ballrooms. Though many of the 1,700-plus rooms are in need of updating, the public spaces—particularly the lobby's grand ceiling, which contains 21 large murals and paintings—are spectacular. It's spendy, but there are plenty of amenities for the family (pool, casual dining).

Not to say there aren't other great hotels in the Loop—specifically, on the northern edge of the river. Two bonuses to staying in the Loop: hotel prices tend to be a little lower than on the Magnificent Mile or the Gold Coast, and because many of these hotels cater to conventioneers, you can find cheap weekend rates and packages. Of late the Loop has become a location for boutique lodging like the Hotel Burnham (1 W. Washington St.; *hotelburnham.com*; $150-$350) and the Hotel Monaco (225 N. Wabash Av.; *monaco-chicago.com*; $150-$400), but the real emphasis is on luxury joints: the Fairmont Hotel (200 N. Columbus Dr.; *fairmont.com*; $130-$500), the Renaissance Chicago (1 W. Wacker Dr.;

INSIDER'S TIP
Alas, you won't be able to avoid some pretty high parking charges no matter where you stay in Chicago. Be prepared to pay upwards of $35 per night for parking in major hotels, less in more casual establishments. Don't dream of street parking along a major thoroughfare.

marriott.com; $160-$500), the Crowne Plaza Silversmith (10 S. Wabash St.; *crownplaza.com*; $150-$300), and the Swissotel Chicago (323 E. Wacker Dr.; *swissotel.com*; $160-$2,500). Though it's a little off the Loop, families will want to check out the funky House of Blues Hotel (333. N. Dearborn Av.; *loewshotel.com*; $140-$1,200) and its legendary Sunday brunch.

Michigan Avenue (next to Grant Park) used to be home to many of the great hotels of Chicago, but most have been torn down or, as in the case of the late, lamented Blackstone, converted to condos. The Chicago Hilton (720 S. Michigan Av.; *hilton.com*; $175-$290) still stands and, while it's primarily a convention hotel, you can find some good weekend specials. Like the Palmer House, the Chicago Hilton is a grand old "city within a city" hotel, billed as the largest in the world when it opened.

The Chicago Hilton has one advantage: it's within a short walk of the Art Institute of Chicago and long walks from the Field Museum and the John G. Shedd Aquarium. The three are among the best institutions in the world and anyone visiting Chicago needs to see at least one of these great attractions. We discuss them further in the Wrigley Field chapter.

Local Attractions

Cubs fans have Wrigleyville. Sox fans have tailgating. Unfortunately, there is no sprawl of bars and restaurants near U.S. Cellular Field like there is near Wrigley Field. There are some establishments near the ballpark geared toward White Sox fans; if it's true you shouldn't wear Sox colors at Addison and Clark, it's equally true you shouldn't wear the blue and red of the north siders at these fine establishments.

Across the street from the northern parking lot of U.S. Cellular Field is Jimbo's Lounge (3258 S. Princeton; 312/326-3253; *jimboslounge.com*) where Jimbo and Joey hold court before and after Sox games. It's a working-class establishment; there's no martini list or beer on tap (really, Pabst Blue Ribbon *should* be drunk out of a can), and the menu is dominated by processed meats. We love it, but admit we were a little disappointed to see Jimbo went high-tech with a Web site. When this book went to press Jimbo and crew were fighting an eviction notice, so don't be surprised if the Lounge been replaced by some gentrified bistro.

Schaller's Pump (3714 S. Halsted St.; 773/376-6332) is a family-run bar and restaurant where many Sox fans gather before and after the game. Steak, barbecue, and pork chops are the specialties of the house. If you're lucky there will be an accordion player in the house. Shinnik's (3758 S. Union; 773/523-

8591) is known as a hangout for cops and firefighters; many Sox fans make it a regular stop before and after the game. A great beer selection can be found at Puffers (3356 S. Halsted St.; 773/927-6073); the back deck is a fine place to savor a Sox win or lament a South Side loss.

Take a trip north on the CTA Red Line and you'll be in downtown Chicago in no time. A little further north on the Red Line to Addison and one could be so inclined to head to Wrigleyville, although expect to hear comments if you come wearing White Sox gear.

Getting There

Rush hour in Chicago can be an ordeal, so driving is not the recommended way to get to U.S. Cellular Field. The CTA Red Line stops near the ballpark at 35th Street, leaving you with a short walk to the gates. Though the south side of Chicago doesn't have the best of reputations, you won't be hassled taking the train to the game. In 2008, the local Metra train line will institute local service to U.S. Cellular Field as well.

If you drive, be prepared to fight the traffic. No matter where you're coming from, you'll want to make your way to the Dan Ryan Expressway (I-94). From the north, northwest, or O'Hare Airport, you can take I-94 all the way in; from the south, take Highways 55 or 57 to the Ryan Expressway; from the west, take Highway 290 east to the southbound Ryan Expressway. Once on the Dan Ryan Expressway watch for the 35th Street exit and follow the signs to the ballpark. Parking is $18.

Team Ballpark History

The Chicago White Sox were an original franchise in the American League in 1901. Back then professional baseball didn't bother too much with the niceties of trademark, and White Sox owner Charles Comiskey cleverly appropriated the name of a formerly popular National League team, A.G. Spalding's Chicago White Stockings, for his pirate crew.

The relocated St. Paul Saints played at the third iteration of South Side Park (39th and Princeton), a 7,500-seat ballpark that perhaps ended up being better known as the home of Negro League baseball in Chicago for decades. It began life as a cricket field built for the Chicago Wanderers to take advantage of the huge crowds descending on Chicago for the 1893 Chicago World's Fair. Comiskey added a grandstand but kept control of the facility, leasing it to John Schorling, owner of a Negro Leagues team. That ballpark was town down in the late 1940s; public housing sits on the site.

Comiskey was one of the great promoters in baseball, taking the minor Western League and turning it into the major American League, helped by great players like Shoeless Joe Jackson and Ty Cobb and operators like Clark Griffith and Frank Navin. He built White Sox Park (as it was known in 1910-1912 and again in 1962-1975) as a shrine to baseball, and when it opened for the 1910 season it was hailed as the greatest ballpark on the face of the earth. It could have been greater: Comiskey rejected the plans of architect Zachary Taylor Davis for a column-free grandstand and a Neoclassic exterior. The end result— a symmetrical grandstand, extensive brickwork and forward-looking Prairie

Over the years Comiskey Park hosted events other than baseball, including the sport of auto polo, where a duo would drive in a customized auto and attempt to score goals using a basketball.

School detailing—served as a model for ballparks across the nation. Comiskey knew the power of the grand gesture: when Comiskey Park opened the capacity was 28,800 (the largest ballpark in baseball) and cost $750,000, and by 1927 he was adding 27,000 more seats and enclosing the entire ballpark. It could have been a groundbreaker in another way: in 1910 it hosted a night game played under experimental lights, drawing 20,000 fans to an amateur game.

A former city dump (a game was once delayed after Luke Appling tripped on a copper kettle that worked its way through the fill), Comiskey Park was one

Bill Veeck and Hank Greenberg, the former Tiger great who ended up owning part of the White Sox.

of the most colorful venues in baseball. The foul lines weren't painted on with chalk, but rather hoses painted white and dug into the turf. In 1969, artificial turf—Sox sod—was installed only in the infield with grass left in the outfield. With generous foul areas and distant fences, it was a definite pitchers' ballpark. Comiskey Park was the toast of the town when it opened, and the White Sox regularly outdrew the Cubs in those early years.

It was also a ballpark where the White Sox played every trick to gain a home-field advantage, led by the legendary Bossard family of groundskeepers: Emil, Gene, and Roger. The infield was dramatically watered down when White Sox sinkerballers were on the mound; when an opposing ground-ball pitcher was in town, the infield was packed with clay and gasoline—burned before the game to ensure a hard surface. To compensate for a poor-fielding shortstop or outfielder, the grass would be left long; similarly, the grass would be cut short when a great defensive outfielder or second baseman played for the Sox. Home plate was moved 14 feet closer to the fences when Al Simmons played for the Sox, then moved back when the experiment didn't work.

In baseball history, it would take a great personality to upstage the Comiskey family, but a later owner of the White Sox did just that. When Bill Veeck bought the White Sox in 1959, he embarked on a series of ballpark renovations designed to please the entire family. He was a tinkerer by inclination and a baseball promoter by trade, and he combined both passions in some very colorful ways at Comiskey Park. He added fireworks, sound effects, and aerial bombs to the huge center-field scoreboard in 1960. Being at the ballpark on a hot day could be unpleasant, so Veeck installed a Rain Room to cool off patrons. He ordered then Sox broadcaster Harry Caray to lead the crowd in "Take Me Out to the Ballgame" years before Caray made it a tradition at Wrigley Field. Realizing not every fan wanted to spend all nine innings in the same seat, he installed a picnic area in left field.

Veeck was also a legendary promoter. Perhaps the most legendary promoter in baseball, he loved the grand gesture to stir up attention in the newspapers—and if they brought out a few fans to the ballpark, that was okay, too. Some of the promotions seem tame today—like giving away stockings in an attempt to bring more women to the ballpark when he owned the Cleveland Indians—but others ended poorly. The most notorious promotion in Major League Baseball was a Bill Veeck stunt gone awry. On July 12, 1979, the Disco Demolition Night promotion led to a fan riot when drunken rowdies stormed the field and interrupted the destruction of disco records. Police never really restored order to the ballpark and the White Sox forfeited the nightcap to the Detroit Tigers.

Comiskey Park was also the home of the NFL's Chicago Cardinals from 1922 to 1958, the site of the first All-Star Game in 1933, and the 50th anniversary All-Star Game in 1983. When Forbes Field was abandoned by the Pittsburgh Pirates in mid-1970, Comiskey Park became the oldest ballpark in the majors.

Today we expect our ballparks to have picnic areas, promotions, and special effects, but before Bill Veeck those things simply didn't exist. He was a visionary who greatly impacted the way we experience a baseball game. There's not much mention of him at U.S. Cellular Field, and when he left baseball he was hated by several of his former team owners—and you can still find animosity toward the Veeck name in baseball today.

However, the White Sox have done a pretty good job of honoring Comiskey Park at U.S. Cellular Field. Many of the most noteworthy features of the old ballpark—the exploding scoreboard, the Rain Room, the outfield picnic area—are part of today's facility in a direct homage. The White Sox Hall of Fame (closed for remodeling during the 2006 season) is located in the ballpark's gift shop. The site of the original Comiskey Park is now a parking lot next to the new ballpark, with home plate marked by a bronze plaque in the sidewalk.

Local Baseball Attractions

Wrigley Field is, of course, the most popular baseball attraction in the city and state. (Sorry: no getting around it, Sox fans.) We cover it in its own chapter.

Milwaukee is less than two hours from Chicago and many Cubs and White Sox fans head to Miller Park when their team faces the Brewers. We cover Miller Park in its own chapter.

We're not sure if it's a White Sox hangout any longer, but Miller's Pub (134 S. Wabash Av.; 312/645-5377) in the Loop is an essential stop for White Sox fans, thanks to the extensive photo collection and obvious devotion to preserving the memory of Bill Veeck and former White Sox and Cubs players. Veeck was a regular at Miller's well after selling the White Sox. The food isn't great, but it's served late—and finding late-night food service in the Loop can be tricky.

Chicago is a great area for minor-league baseball as well, though you'll need to venture outside the city limits to see it. The Kane County Cougars of the Class A Midwest League play at Philip B. Elfstrom Stadium in Geneva. It is a prototypical Midwest League ballpark. Built before advanced ballpark design reached the minor leagues, Elfstrom Stadium is a pedestrian ballpark with some nice touches. While we're not sure it's worth a lot of effort to attend a Cougars game, it's worth a visit should your travel take you in that direction. (34W002 Cherry Lane, Geneva; *kccougars.com*; 630/232-8811.)

A ballpark definitely worth the drive: Silver Cross Field, home of the Northern League's Joliet JackHammers. Opening in 2002, Silver Cross Field is one of the nicer ballparks in the Northern League and in Illinois. Fitting nicely into its surroundings—which includes a historic train station and a fortress-like high school—Silver Cross Field is a great place to watch a baseball game.

Built in a slightly retro style (though not enough so that it's a distraction), the brick-and-steel façade of Silver Cross Field fits nicely within downtown Joliet. Most patrons will reach the ballpark from lots to the west, which means they pass underneath a railroad overpass to reach the park. This setting somewhat lessens the impact of the park's multi-story entrance (which is shown in the photo at the top of this page; the steel-beam facade was designed to be reminiscent of the many bridges crossing the nearby Des Plaines River), which is a shame. The ballpark's architects could have done a better job in creating a more dramatic entrance to the ballpark, instead of one mostly obscured by railroad tracks.

Once inside the ballpark there's a lot to catch the eye. The design is fairly conventional. The playing surface sits at ground level, while a second-floor open concourse contains concessions. A third level contains 14 suites and press facilities. There are grassy berms located down each line, while an outdoor concession building features rooftop seating and a covered picnic area designed for larger groups. A children's play area is located down the third-base line and a covered picnic area is located down the first-base line. All in all, it's a great place to watch a ballgame. (One Mayor Art Schultz Drive, Joliet; *jackhammersbaseball.com*; 815/726-2255.)

Two other independent baseball teams play in the Chicago area. The Northern League's Schaumburg Flyers play at Alexian Field (1999 S. Springinsguth Rd., Schaumburg; 847/891-2255; *flyersbaseball.com*) in the western suburb of Schaumburg, while the Frontier League's Windy City ThunderBolts play at Hawkinson Ford Field (14011 S. Kenton Av., Crestwood; 708/489-BALL; *wcthunderbolts.com*) in the southern suburb of Crestwood.

The Complete Guide to Big League Ballparks

Chicago Cubs
Wrigley Field

Address: 1060 W. Addison, Chicago, IL 60613.
Cost: $250,000.
Architect: Zachary Taylor Davis.
Owner: Chicago Cubs.
Capacity: 41,118.
Dimensions: 355L, 368LC, 400C, 368RC, 353R.
Ticket Line: 773/404-CUBS.
Home Dugout Location: Third-base side.
Playing Surface: Grass.
Other Tenants: The NFL's Chicago Staleys (better known by the name they adopted in 1922: the Chicago Bears) played at Wrigley Field from 1921 to 1970.
Previous Names: Weeghman Park (1914-1919), Cubs Park (1920-1925), Wrigley Field (1926-present).
First Game: On April 23, 1914, the Chicago Whales defeated the Kansas City Packers, 9-1 behind the pitching of Claude Hendrix and two home runs off the bat of Art Wilson. Hendrix, who had a long career in the majors, was the best pitcher that season in the Federal League, compiling a 29-11 record with a 1.69 ERA. A crowd of 21,000 was on hand. The first National League game at Weeghman Park came on April 20, 1916, with the Cubs defeating the Cincinnati Reds 7-6 in 11 innings.
Landmark Events: The lovable Cubs have long been synonymous with futility,

so there have not been many postseason games played at Wrigley Field, especially after 1938. (In fact, the Cubs have never won a World Series while playing at Wrigley Field; their last world championship came in 1908.) The 1932 World Series was notable for the actions of Babe Ruth in the third game of the series. According to some eyewitnesses Ruth appeared to point to center field right before hitting a home run to that area; whether or not he actually did is still a matter of vigorous debate. Of course, a history of Wrigley Field wouldn't be complete without a mention of poor Steve Bartman, who in the sixth game of the 2003 playoffs reached over the railing for a foul ball off the bat of the Marlins' Luis Castillo that could have been caught by Cubs outfielder Moises Alou. Castillo ended up walking and the Marlins erased a 3-0 Cubs lead by scoring eight in the eighth, forcing a Game 7. The Fish won that game and ended up winning the World Series. Cubs are fans still upset about Bartman's botched attempt, but then again it wasn't Bartman who folded after the play—Cubs pitcher Mark Prior withered away—and Bartman certainly didn't cause the Cubs to lose Game 7.

Your Wrigley Field Seating Crib Sheet

The Cubs use a complicated variable ticket pricing scheme, with value games, regular games, and prime dates priced differently. There is quite a difference between value and prime dates, with most prime-date seats priced more than double the value games. Here we use the pricing for the prime dates; be warned the pricing for the game you plan on attending may be dramatically less.

Best Sections to View a Game: Just being in the ballpark will be rewarding. Here's one of the dirty secrets about Wrigley Field: it is actually a fairly uncomfortable place to watch a ballgame. The aisles are narrow, the rows are crammed together, and the seats are tight, designed for the smaller posteriors of 1914 baseball fans, not the more rotund—or robust, depending on your viewpoint—fans of today. Given the number of games the Cubs sell out, any day you can get into the ballpark is a good day. A bleacher seat, of course, is pure nirvana.

Best Cheap Seats: The cheapest seats at Wrigley Field are $17, and those are the Upper Deck Reserved Outfield seats located in the back rows of the grandstand. Given the intimate nature of Wrigley Field, these seats are still more than acceptable, although you'll be a distance away from decent concessions—be prepared to walk. Pay the extra buck and go for Upper Deck Reserved Infield if you have the option.

Most Underrated Sections: We're not huge fans of the Terrace Reserved Outfield seats ($28) down each line; you'll need to crane your neck to see the action for most of the game. Move to the upper deck as close to home plate as you can get for a better seat.

Wrigley Field: The Friendly Confines

Like so many other Cubs fans, we can vividly remember our first visit to the Friendly Confines of Wrigley Field. After a slight rain delay, the sun broke through the clouds and an Andy Frain usher led us to our seats, despite there being only about a hundred fans in the ballpark. With great pomp he cleaned the excess water off the old-fashioned seats with a chamois cloth, leaving us alone in a section behind home plate. We were in heaven.

The only thing better would have been if the usher had been wearing a traditional blue-and-gold Andy Frain uniform instead of a bland windbreaker. At times it seems the ushers' uniforms are about the only thing that has changed at Wrigley Field over the years; that sense of tradition is one of the many great things about attending a game at Wrigley Field.

Ironically, Wrigley Field has indeed changed much over the years and continues to do so today. Despite the changes, fans continue to flock to Wrigley Field for all the right reasons: watching a Cubs game there is a timeless experience, uniting the fans of today with those of yesteryear. There's no reason to manufacture nostalgia here—like it's awkwardly manufactured in new ballparks—as Wrigley Field literally drips with the stuff.

Each major league has an historic landmark ballpark. In the case of the American League it's Fenway Park; in the National League it's Wrigley Field. Though the ballpark has evolved into a National League institution, it began life as a haven for outlaws. Charles Weeghman commissioned Zachary Taylor Davis—who had earlier designed Comiskey Park—to design a 16,000-seat ballpark at the corner of Clark and Addison for the Chicago Whales of the outlaw Federal League, a rival to the American and National Leagues. (Team names being a more fluid thing in those days, the team was also known as the Chicago Federals and the Chifeds.)

Davis designed a single-level steel-and-concrete grandstand, meeting Chicago's stringent fire codes (Mrs. O'Leary's cow and all that), adding wooden bleachers in the outfield. It took only two months to build the structure and it would have taken less time had a two-day strike not interrupted construction. He called it Weeghman Park, but it was also referred to as Federal League Park in postcards and newspaper articles of the era.

Though Weeghman was suffering under some severe disadvantages—at the time Clark and Addison was far off the beaten path, and Charlie Comiskey's White Sox drew 644,501 fans in 1913, leading the American League in attendance. The decision to sink a quarter-million dollars into Weeghman Park was sound financially, and by the end of the season the Whales were outdrawing the Pale Hose, with the Cubs trailing both. (It also helped that Weeghman was tied into the Chicago underworld to some degree, connected to gambler Arnold Rothstein, who famously fixed the 1919 World Series. Weeghman Park quickly became known as the place for those in the know to gather.)

Weeghman was a restaurateur, not a baseball insider, so he took a different approach to a ballgame. Instead of relying solely upon roaming vendors to sell

food and beer, he installed concession stands within the Weeghman Park concourse. And he did something that shook baseball owners: he allowed fans to keep baseballs hit into the stands. (Giddy with this freedom, over time the legendary Bleacher Bums developed the habit of throwing home runs hit by opponents back onto the field.)

Alas, after building eight new ballparks in three years, the rest of the Federal League wasn't as financially secure as Weeghman, and by the end of the 1915 season it folded. Weeghman was invited to take over the ailing Chicago Cubs from Charles Taft, and he did so along with eight other investors, including chewing-gum magnate William Wrigley, Jr. The Cubs moved from West End Grounds to Weeghman Park for the 1916 season.

In 1920 the Wrigley family purchased the Cubs from Weeghman and renamed the ballpark Cubs Park. William Wrigley, Jr. renamed the park Wrigley Field in 1926, despite some opposition from baseball officials; at the time it was against baseball rules to name a ballpark after a corporation, but Wrigley argued he was naming the ballpark after himself and not the Wrigley chewing-gum empire.

Earlier we said Wrigley Field has always been a work in progress. Weeghman himself continually tinkered with the ballpark, adding 2,000 seats after taking over the Cubs; later a second deck was added to the structure. Major changes took place in 1937 when the outfield bleachers were expanded and a massive center-field scoreboard, still in use, was erected. Plus, a young Bill Veeck—whose father ran the Cubs for Bill Wrigley—planted bittersweet and ivy on the outfield wall in a first rough attempt to pad the brick fence. Although he never owned the Cubs, Veeck is still an important figure in

TRIVIA
Wrigley Field was named for William Wrigley, Jr., the team's owner. His was a prototypical Horatio Alger story: in 1891 he moved to Chicago from Philadelphia and began selling soap and baking powder before hitting on gum as a well-selling item. He devoted himself to manufacturing gum, coming up with the Juicy Fruit line.

More importantly, Wrigley was a devotee of the power of advertising, and by 1920 his company was selling 20 million pieces of gum a year behind brands like Doublemint, Wrigley's Spearmint, and Juicy Fruit.

franchise history: besides making those changes to the ballpark, he became a fixture in the outfield bleachers after selling the Chicago White Sox, quaffing brews with fellow Bleacher Bums and using his artificial leg as an ashtray.

Before the 2006 season, the famed Wrigley Field bleachers were expanded and a restaurant was added underneath the center-field scoreboard.

The hand-operated scoreboard is still a trademark of Wrigley Field, with the innings and pitchers' numbers manually changed. Because of the scoreboard's location in deep center field, no ball has ever hit it, though Bill Nicholson (who reached Sheffield Avenue to the right of the scoreboard in 1948) and Roberto Clemente (who reached Waveland Avenue to the left of the scoreboard in 1959) have come closest. One trademark of the scoreboard: the many flags flying above. The flags show the National League divisional standings. After a Cubs game the scoreboard indicates whether the home team

Wrigley Field

won or lost by which flag is flying: a white flag with a blue "W" celebrates a victory, while a blue flag with a white "L" mourns a loss.

For many years Wrigley Field was the only ballpark in the majors without lights, forcing the team to play afternoon home games until 1988. (The Cubs are still limited to a set number of night games to minimize the impact on local residents.) Residents of the surrounding neighborhood liked it that way—fans departed the area before residents returned from work—and a clubby, informal atmosphere evolved, forever immortalized in the classic "Bleacher Bums" from Chicago's Organic Theater Company.

Alas, those special moments can't last forever, and when the Tribune Company bought the Cubs in 1981 things changed, with the dreaded "corporate synergy" seeping through the famous outfield vines. The Cubs and Tribune Company had a preexisting relationship—with WGN Radio serving at the team's home since going on the air in 1924 and WGN-TV broadcasting Cubs games since going on the air in 1948—and the $20.5 million purchase made sense as the Tribune Company sought to expand Superstation WGN nationwide. Cubs games became a cornerstone of WGN's national schedule and, with the ever-entertaining Harry Caray behind the mike, Cubs broadcasts became must-see events for hardcore and casual sports fans. With Caray extolling the virtues of suds in the bleachers, celebrities with Chicago ties singing "Take Me Out to the Ballgame" during the seventh-inning stretch, and director Arnie Harris cutting to bikini-topped cuties in the stands wherever possible, there's no way a Cubs broadcast could be ignored.

Which, in a true show of synergy, made Wrigley Field a destination for hardcore and casual sports fans. Some say it ruined Cubs baseball, making Wrigley Field a haven for partiers who didn't really care what happened on the field. There's a measure of truth there: go to a Cubs game today and it really does seems like the game result doesn't matter so long as the Bud is flowing and the sun is out. But we're tired of baseball purists who throw a hissy fit when the masses show interest in a ballpark, and the great thing about Wrigley Field these days is there's always a buzz on game day, no matter how the Cubbies are doing.

Ballpark Quirks

The outfield ivy is unique both in the majors and minors. It is responsible for the most unusual—and therefore quirkiest—ground rule in the majors: play is stopped when a ball is "lost" in the ivy, with the batter awarded a ground-rule double. We say "lost" because smart outfielders know enough to throw their arms up and claim the ball can't be found when the ball makes it into the ivy.

There's also one other quirky ground rule: the dugout steps are off-limits to players chasing down a foul pop-up.

MLB is pretty strict about foul poles being pristine, but the Cubs spiced them up by adding Jack Brickhouse's trademark "Hey Hey" saying to both. Harry Caray may have the greater national name recognition from his days in

Wrigley Field 457

Some of the famed rooftop bleachers outside of Wrigley Field proper. They were formerly a point of contention between the Cubs and owners, but an agreement gives them official sanction and city supervision—and the Cubs a cut of the revene.

the Wrigley Field broadcasting booth, but for generations of Cubs fans in Chicago Brickhouse was truly the voice of the Cubs, working games between 1948 and 1981. He began his Chicago broadcasting career in 1940 and was also a radio personality at WGN Radio, interviewing the likes of Ronald Reagan and Pope Paul VI, and serving as the voice of the Chicago Bears from 1953 through 1976. After Brickhouse retired he was replaced by Caray.

Also honored on the foul poles: flags representing retired numbers of Cubs greats. On the left-field pole: #14 (honoring Ernie Banks) and #10 (honoring Ron Santo). On the right-field pole, #26 (honoring Billy Williams) and #23 (honoring Ryne Sandberg).

The Cubs also hang a number of flags on the upper-deck roof to commemorate players and events in Wrigley Field history. The left-field flags mark the post-season appearances by the Cubs, including the 1908 World Series win, the most recent World Series appearance in 1945, and the last postseason appearance in 2003. The right-field flags honor Jackie Robinson (every MLB team has retired Robinson's #42), Andre Dawson's #8, former owner Philip K. Wrigley (PKW), Hack Wilson's 190-RBI season in 1930 (HACK-190), Ferguson Jenkins' #31, Sammy Sosa's 66-homer season in 1998, Kerry Woods' 20-strikeout game in 1998, and Greg Maddux's 300 career wins (MADDUX 300).

Food and Drink
The food offerings at Wrigley Field have been overhauled in recent years, with Levy Restaurants coming in and making some huge changes in the 23 concession stands. Previously, every concession stand sold pretty much the same thing, but now stands are themed.

Having said that, there are really only two food items worth seeking out at Wrigley Field: Old Style beer and a Chicago red hot. We know Budweiser spends a lot of money marketing to Cubs fans, and lord knows we sat through enough instances of Harry Caray shamelessly shilling Bud during Cubs broadcasts, but we're old enough to remember when Bud wasn't the most popular beer in Chicago—when you found most neighborhood taverns sporting Old Style or Augsburger signs. Today, Augsburger is virtually impossible to find in Chicago, while Old Style is an endangered species. Hell, it's not even made in La Crosse, Wisconsin any longer, but you can still find it at Wrigley Field. We suspect Harry would approve.

Chicagoans know how to prepare and eat their hot dogs. A Chicago-style hot dog has been "dragged through the garden"—a Vienna Beef frank topped with mustard, relish, chopped onion, chopped tomato, a kosher dill-pickle spear, sport peppers, and celery salt, all tucked into an oversized poppy-seed bun. Ketchup? Only the ignorant put ketchup on their hot dog in Chicago.

And that is all the people need to know.

For the Kids
There is little at Wrigley Field for kids. You will find a lot of kids in the stands at Wrigley Field, but they're being brought up the right way: to appreciate the game of baseball and Wrigley Field as the perfect place to watch that game.

Handicapped Access
There are 249 wheelchair-accessible seats at Wrigley Field. That's less than almost any new park, but it's a lot more than you'd expect for a ballpark that opened in 1914.

Ballpark Tours
A tour of Wrigley Field costs a whopping $20. Supply once again meets demand: tours are given only on Fridays and Saturdays.

Local Baseball Attractions
The Chicago White Sox play on the south side of Chicago at U.S. Cellular Field. We cover this ballpark in a separate chapter.

Milwaukee is less than two hours from Chicago, and many Cubs and White Sox fans head to Miller Park when their teams face the Brewers. We cover Miller Park in its own chapter.

Wrigleyville is an attraction in its own right. The area surrounding Wrigley Field swells with crowds on game days; even Cubs fans who don't have tickets to a game head to a local watering hole to watch on the big screen.

Interestingly, we find the patrons in these local watering holes to be a little more passionate about how the Cubs do than the fans in the ballpark: Wrigley Field may be a great open-air bar, but the folks in the local taverns are true, hardcore Cubs fans.

Murphy's Bleachers (3655 N. Sheffield Av.; *murphysbleachers.com*; 773/281-5356), located past right-center field, has an impressive lineage. Bill Veeck used to hang out there before and after Cubs games, and more than a few Cubs, past and present, were known to knock down a few after afternoon games. The sports bar features a rooftop reserved for groups.

The Cubby Bear (1059 W. Addison St.; *cubbybear.com*; 773/327-1662) may not be as charming as in the past—today it's a loud sports bar with over 100 blaring TV sets—but for many Cubs fans it's a mandatory stop before and after the game. We're not overly impressed with the Cubby Bear these days, but others are.

Across the street from the Cubby Bear is Bar Louie Wrigley (3545 N. Clark St.; *barlouieamerica.com/wrigley.html*; 773/296-2500), best described as an upscale sports bar. It features the usual trappings of a sports bar—lots of beers on tap and a menu featuring bar staples like burgers and chili dogs—with an upscale twist or three.

If beer and great food is what you want, your best destination is Goose Island Wrigleyville (3535 N. Clark St.; *gooseisland.com*; 773/832-9040). Folks in the Upper Midwest know about the quality Goose Island microbrews, and this expansive Wrigleyville outpost features them all on tap plus many dishes incorporating beer. The Waveland Melt is tremendous, the beer-batter-coated cod and calamari are heavenly, and the family will enjoy a fondue made with Blonde Ale. Sit outside if you can.

If you didn't have enough Old Style at the ballpark, head to Sluggers (3450 N. Clark St.; *sluggersbar.com*; 773/248-0055) and knock down a few more while listening to the dueling pianos or playing skee-ball upstairs.

The best Chicago hot dog we've ever experienced was at Clark St. Dog (3040 N. Clark St.; 773/281-6690), less than a mile south of Wrigley Field. Of course, it came after a few Old Styles at the ballpark.

One thing about Chicago: it's a city of neighborhood bars and hard to go wrong at any of them, even if you're not a regular. Take, for instance, Sterch's (2238 N. Lincoln Av.), located a few miles south of the ballpark. From the outside, Sterch's looks like a dive bar geared toward locals, but go there and you'll be treated like a regular; yes, the tap-beer selection is limited (but who cares when Guinness is one of them?) and the mixed drinks veer toward the roadhouse variety.

Many out-of-town Cubs fans make the pilgrimage to Harry Caray's Restaurant in Chicago's River North neighborhood (33 W. Kinzie St.; *harrycarays.com*; 773/HOLY-COW). Harry may be gone, but his trademark glasses are still with us, along with a lot of other Cubs memorabilia: a ball used during Kerry Woods' 20-strikeout game, four seats from Comiskey Park, photos from the George Brace collection, and more. The four-story building has a

colorful background, opening in 1895 as the home of a varnish distributor and
later serving as the home of Frank Nitti, the enforcer of the Al Capone gang.
(Nitti's apartment is still intact on the fourth floor.) Unlike most celebrity
restaurants, the food at Caray's is pretty decent: steaks, chops, and Italian
specialties dominate the menu.

Chicago is a good area for minor-league baseball as well, though you'll
need to venture outside the city limits to see it. We discuss the minor-league
offerings of the area in our chapter on U.S. Cellular Field.

Downtown Attractions

Downtown Chicago is one of the great architectural treasures of the world.
Only New York City takes its architecture so seriously; the great surroundings
makes it a treat to tour on foot.

Michigan Avenue—known on the north side as the Magnificent Mile—runs
north-south through downtown Chicago. You can center a walk on Michigan
Avenue and see some of Chicago's great attractions. We'll begin at the north
and work our way south.

The **Old Chicago Water Tower** at Michigan and Chicago may not be flashy,
but it occupies a unique position in Chicago history: it was one of the few
surviving buildings from the Great Chicago Fire of 1871, constructed in
1869 from Joliet limestone. The fire was one of the most destructive urban
disasters, causing $200 million in damage and leading the city of Chicago
to enact stringent building codes. (For the record: the fire did start in Mrs.

O'Leary's barn on DeKoven Street.) The Water Tower is dwarfed by surrounding skyscrapers and now serves as the Chicago Convention and Tourism Bureau Visitor's Welcome Center.

One of those skyscrapers dwarfing the Water Tower is the **John Hancock Center** (875 N. Michigan Av.; *hancock-observatory.com*). Though not as tall and famous as the Sears Tower, the Hancock Center has a great location and a screened observation area that allows you to feel why Chicago is known as the Windy City. (Indeed, one of the biggest challenges that faced designers of both the Hancock Center and the Sears Tower was allowing enough "give" so both would bend in the powerful breezes.) You can see three states from the observation deck on the 94th floor. *The Hancock Observatory is open daily from 9:00 a.m. to 11:00 p.m.; the price is $9.95 for adults, $6 for children, and $7.50 for seniors (plus sales tax).*

Michigan Avenue between Water Tower Place (located next to the Old Chicago Water Tower, natch) and the Chicago River is one of the world's great shopping areas. Brothers can wait impatiently while their sisters swoon over the offerings at **American Girl Place** (111 E. Chicago Av.; *americangirlplace.com*) and have the favor returned when they pig out at **Ghirardelli Chocolate Shop & Soda Fountain** (830 N. Michigan Av.; *ghirardelli.com*). All the leading department stores have outposts on the **Magnificent Mile**: **Macy's**, **Bloomingdale's**, **Lord & Taylor**, and **Neiman Marcus**.

As you approach the Chicago River from the north, you'll reach two notable office buildings on the Chicago River marking the southernmost point of the Magnificent Mile. **The Wrigley Building** (400 N. Michigan Av.) has been the home of the Wm. Wrigley Jr. Company since 1920, including the entire period when the firm owned the Chicago Cubs. (Yes, chewing gum is that profitable.) It is especially striking at night when illuminated by the floodlights across the street.

In the middle of your jaunt, be sure to stop at the **Billy Goat Tavern** (430 N. Michigan Av., lower level; *billygoattavern.com*; 312/222-1525), for it occupies a huge place in Cubbies lore. William "Billy Goat" Sianis opened his original Billy Goat Tavern across the street from Chicago Stadium in 1934. In a city of big shoulders and larger-than-life characters, Sianis needed some sort of gimmick to stand out and, when a goat ostensibly walked into his tavern, he adopted it, grew a goatee, and dubbed himself Billy Goat. When, in a shameless act of self-promotion, he unsuccessfully attempted to bring a billy goat into Game 6 of the 1945 World Series, he vowed his revenge upon the Cubs, saying the team would never win another Series until a billy goat was allowed into Wrigley Field. Unfortunately, a 1984 attempt to lift the curse didn't work—nephew Sam Sianis brought a billy goat into Wrigley Field to great ceremony—and the Cubs still have not won a World Series since 1908. Legendary Tribune columnist Mike Royko adopted the Billy Goat Tavern as his own haunt when it moved to its present Michigan Avenue location in 1964, and it's still regarded as a media hangout. In a weird pop-culture confluence, the Billy Goat Tavern may be better known through a Saturday Night Live skit where the likes of John Belushi, Dan Aykroyd, and Bill Murray served up cheeseburgers, Pepsi, and chips—no fries, no Coke—in a series of skits.

Getting There

It's easy to remember: Clark and Addison.

Clark and Addison are two major streets in Chicago; West Addison Street running east-west and North Clark Street running northwest from downtown. You can catch Addison at the Kennedy Expressway or Lake Shore Drive and make your way to the ballpark, which is about four miles from the north end of downtown.

We don't recommend you drive unless you're coming in from out of town and don't mind paying for parking. There is truly a limited amount of parking near Wrigley Field; restrictions on street parking in Wrigleyville mean you need to pay close attention to the signs, and you will be ticketed and towed if in violation of said restrictions. (Basically, forget about parking on Wrigleyville streets during night games unless you have a resident permit sticker.) Many businesses in Wrigleyville will do you the favor of providing a parking spot, usually costing $10 or more. The farther away from Wrigley Field the less restrictive the street parking, so your choice is hoofing it from many blocks away or ponying up for lot parking. For an afternoon game, a pregame lunch at the likes of the Cubby Bear is in order, so arrive early and park a distance from the ballpark.

The Cubs offer lot parking at DeVry University at Addison and Western—about six blocks west of Wrigley Field—during weekend and evening games. The $6 cost covers parking and shuttle service to the ballpark.

If you're staying in downtown Chicago—a practice we recommend, as you'll find later in this chapter—you can take the CTA Red Line or the Cubs bus to the ballpark. The Red Line runs from the South Side through the Loop and up to Skokie, but you won't need to go that far: the Addison stop next to Wrigley Field will do just fine.

For weekend and night games, the Cubs run double-decker buses between select downtown stops and Wrigley Field. The downtown buses start at the Chicago Hilton and Towers, stops at the Tribune Towers and the Old Chicago Water Tower, and then run to Wrigley Field. The cost: $5 roundtrip.

Many fans in the area ride bikes to games; the Cubs make it easy to do by offering a secured bike-check service near Gate K on Waveland Avenue.

Where to Stay

A few hotels are near the ballpark, but choose wisely: the hotels closest, like the Sheffield Hotel or the Chateau Hotel, are not the nicest places to stay.

Billed as the hotel closest to Wrigley Field, the Best Western Hawthorne Terrace (3434 N. Broadway Av.; *bestwestern.com*; $150-$250) is an older property nestled in the Lakeview neighborhood of Chicago. It's not flashy but it's clean, and the location can't be beat.

The Majestic Hotel (528 W. Brompton Place; *cityinns.com*; $100-$300) is a hidden gem for those attending Cubs games: a boutique hotel about 10 minutes away from the ballpark. The Majestic is not fancy, but it's clean and definitely unique. It's not necessarily someplace to take the kids—there's no pool, though you can tire kids out at the waterfront park two blocks away—but for someone just taking in a weekend of Cubs games it's perfect.

The owners of the Majestic also own and run City Suites Hotel (933 W. Belmont, *cityinns.com*; $100-$300), slightly further away from Wrigley Field but still within a walkable distance. Like the Majestic, City Suites is a boutique hotel, but where the Majestic has a English manor feel, City Suites has an Art Deco theme. We're not talking about anything fancy here: it's clean and convenient to train and bus lines. (It's also located just off Clark, so you can walk through the heart of Wrigleyville on your way in.)

Most of Chicago's great attractions are located downtown, about four miles from the ballpark. Staying there makes a lot of sense if you're attending a Cubbies game: you can easily take a train or shuttle from downtown to Wrigley Field. We won't cover all the downtown hotels here—we provide an overview of the major hotels in our chapter on U.S. Cellular Field—but we will note one hotel that makes a lot of sense for Cubs fans: the Chicago Hilton (720 S.

Michigan Av.; *hilton.com*; $175-$290). It's on the south end of Michigan Avenue and a good distance from the downtown attractions. However, the Chicago Hilton and Towers has two advantages: you can catch a bus from there to Wrigley Field for weekend and night games, and it's within a short walk of the Art Institute of Chicago and long walks from the Field Museum and the John G. Shedd Aquarium. The three are among the best museums in the world, and any one visiting Chicago needs to visit at least one of these great attractions.

The Art Institute of Chicago (111 S. Michigan Av.; *artic.edu*; 312/443-3600) is one of the world's outstanding museums, a place where you could spend all day and still not see everything noteworthy on display. The best items, though, are regional in nature. Some of the world's great architects, such as Daniel Burnham, Bruce Goff, Louis Sullivan, Ludwig Mies van der Rohe, and Frank Lloyd Wright were based in Chicago at important points in their careers, and examples of their works are highlighted in the collections. The paintings collection is strong in most historic periods, though realism is a particular strength; this is the place to see *American Gothic* from Iowa's Grant Wood and Edward Hopper's *Nighthawks*.

The Field Museum (1400 S. Lake Shore Dr.; *fieldmuseum.org*; 312/922-9410) combines a high level of scholarship with lots of cool attractions, such as dinosaurs (including Sue, the best-preserved T Rex on display anywhere) and mummies, for the kids. You could easily spend the day at the Field and never bore anyone in your party.

Though located on the shores of Lake Michigan, the John G. Shedd Aquarium (1200 S. Lake Shore Dr.; *sheddaquarium.com*; 312/939-2438) presents exhibits on finny critters from around the world, including sharks and marine mammals.

Team Ballpark History

Though it seems like the Cubs have been at Wrigley Field forever, the Friendly Confines is actually the team's seventh or eighth home, depending on who you ask.

The Cubs trace their history back to 1876 when they were originally known as the Chicago White Stockings and a charter member of the National League. Some baseball historians put the team's roots farther back to 1871 when the original Chicago White Stockings competed in the National Association against the likes of the Boston Red Stockings (who later became the Boston Braves), the Troy Haymakers, and the Fort Wayne Kekiongas. We're not going to settle that issue here (some MLB teams recognize the National Association; others, like the Cubs, don't), but we will point out the original Chicago White Stockings played 16 home games at the first iteration of Lake Front Park (or Lakefront Park) in 1871. That 7,000-seat ballpark, also known as Union Base-Ball Grounds, burned down in the Great Chicago Fire after that season, and the White Stockings disappeared until the 1874 season. The team resurfaced at the 23rd Street Grounds at 23rd and State streets, about two miles north of the

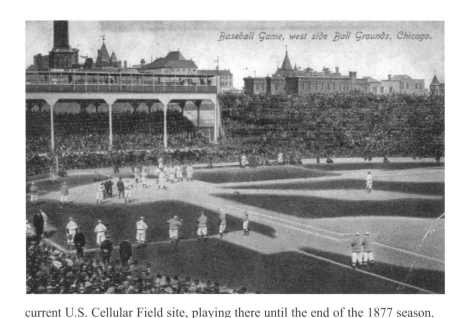
Baseball Game, west side Ball Grounds, Chicago.

current U.S. Cellular Field site, playing there until the end of the 1877 season.
The White Stockings moved to the second version of Lakefront Park in 1878, playing there through 1884. That ballpark, located south of Randolph Street between Michigan Avenue and the Illinois Central Railroad tracks, was known for its cozy dimensions. The 5,000-seat ballpark sported the smallest field ever used for major-league baseball, with the left-field foul pole only 186 feet from home plate (later moved in to 180 feet) and the right-field pole just 196 feet from home plate. Because of this, a ball hit over the fence was only a double, at least in 1883; in 1884 it was a home run. (That change made a huge difference in how many runs the White Stockings scored: the team hit 13 homers in 1883 and 142 in 1884.)

Moving to West Side Park at Congress and Throop streets in 1885 gave the White Stockings a slightly larger ballpark, both in terms of capacity and field size. West Side Park was also used as a bicycle track, so the design was oval-shaped a la the Polo Grounds. In 1891 the Colts (after undergoing a name change prior to the 1890 season) played Monday, Wednesday, and Friday games at West Side Park, while playing Tuesday, Thursday, and Saturday games at South Side Park, located at 35th and Wentworth. If that's a familiar address, it's because South Side Park was located next to the original Comiskey Park, with some of the playing fields of both facilities overlapping. For the 1892 season, the Colts played all their home games at South Side Park, but in 1893 they once again hung their hats at two different ballparks, playing Sunday games at West Side Grounds and the rest at South Side Park.

West Side Grounds was a larger ballpark at Polk and Wolcott (then Lincoln) streets, seating 16,000. (The location is now part of the University of Illinois at Chicago campus just west of downtown Chicago.) Whereas only a decade earlier the White Stockings were playing in the coziest ballpark in major-league history, the Colts were playing in one of the most spacious, with the center-field fence a whopping 560 feet from home plate. (The large expanse in center field gave fans a place to stand and watch the game in the field of play.) The Cubs played at West Side Grounds until they moved to Weeghman Park in 1915.

New York Yankees
Yankee Stadium

Address: E. 161st St. and River Av., Bronx, NY 10451.
Cost: $2.5 million in 1923 original; at least $48 million in 1976 reconstruction.
Architect: Osborn Engineering in 1923; Praeger-Kavanaugh-Waterbury in 1976.
Owner: City of New York.
Capacity: 56,546.
Dimensions: 318L, 399LC, 408C, 385RC, 314R.
Ticket Line: 718/293-6000.
Home Dugout Location: First-base side.
Playing Surface: Grass.
Other Tenants: One other professional baseball team has called Yankee
Stadium home. The National Negro League's New York Black Yankees,
owned by entertainer Bill "Bojangles" Robinson and underworld figure
"Soldier Boy" Semler, played from 1936 up to 1948 when the league
disbanded. Despite drawing well over the years, the Black Yankees finished
last in the league more often than not. Several other Negro Leagues games
were played in Yankee Stadium with the first coming on July 5, 1930; a
doubleheader split between the Baltimore Black Sox and Lincoln Giants
drew 18,000 paid to benefit the Brotherhood of Sleeping Car Porters. Two
professional football teams called Yankee Stadium home: the All-American
Football Conference's New York Yankees played there in 1946-1949 (both
Yankees teams were owned by Dan Topping; hence the connection), and
the NFL's New York Giants called Yankee Stadium home from 1956 to
1973. The North American Soccer League's New York Cosmos played at
Yankee Stadium in 1971 and 1976. Also, the stadium was used for many
high-profile boxing matches over the years, including Joe Louis's victory
over Max Schmeling in 1938 and Louis's victory over Max Baer in 1935.

Boxing matches were common enough that a brick vault was constructed under second base to house the various electrical and telephone equipment needed for such events.

Other Names: Nothing official; unofficially, "The House That Ruth Built."

First Game: On April 23, 1923, as though scripted for a Broadway stage, the Yankees defeated the Boston Red Sox 4-1 on the strength of a third-inning Babe Ruth three-run home run, and the "House that Ruth Built" moniker was forever firmly established. Before the game, John Phillip Sousa and the Seventh Regiment Band brought musical fanfare to the flag-raising ceremony in deep center field, while Gov. Al Smith was on hand to throw out the first pitch. An estimated crowd of 100,000 came to the stadium grounds that day, but "only" a capacity crowd of 74,200 was allowed through the gates.

Landmark Event: Where exactly would you like to start? The first Yankee World Championship came in Yankee Stadium's first year of existence, four games to two, over intercity rival Giants, who had defeated the Yanks in the two previous World Series. Since then the Pinstripers have collected another 25 World Series titles. Two of the most notable World Series were lost by the Yankees in seventh games on the road. In 1960, the Yankees came into the October Classic as the heavy favorite against the Pittsburgh Pirates, but a thrilling see-saw game ended with Bill Mazeroski's walk-off homer in the bottom of the ninth in Game 7. If ever the Yanks were America's sentimental favorite, it was in 2001 when the Bronx Bombers claimed the Eastern Division title by 13.5 games barely a month after Sept. 11 brought down the World Trade Center, rattling New York City and the entire nation. Although the Yankees historical biography describes the 2001 team as "very much a team in transition," it looked like they would claim another World Championship until the Arizona Diamondbacks staged a come-from-behind ninth-inning rally to win Game 7 for Randy Johnson, pitching in relief. Finally, on July 4, 1939, Lou Gehrig proclaimed himself the luckiest man on the face of the earth, a month after his consecutive-game streak ended and he was diagnosed with amyotrophic lateral sclerosis, now known as Lou Gehrig's disease. Not every landmark event has to do with baseball. Notre Dame football coach Knute Rockne made his famous "win one for the Gipper" speech at the halftime of an Irish-Army game in 1928, eight years after George Gipper passed away. The speech worked; the Irish rallied for a win. Joe Louis defeated Max Schmeling in what is considered one of the best heavyweight fights of all time. Pope Paul VI celebrated Mass there on Oct. 4, 1965 (the first papal Mass in America), and evangelist Billy Graham attracted more than 100,000 (with 20,000 more turned away) to a 1957 crusade.

Your Yankee Stadium Seating Crib Sheet

Best Sections to View a Game: The best Yankee tickets are difficult to score—at least through conventional channels. Season tickets at the seven highest levels, from Field Championship to Main Reserved MVP, are all sold out in advance. However, for a price you should be able to locate some quality ticket offers by contacting a broker. For most games, the best selection of tickets available will be at the spacious Tier level (third deck). All Tier Box MVP tickets ($45 in advance) give you a good view of the action.

Best Cheap Seats: Since the 1976 reconstruction, every seat is nicely angled toward the infield action so you have a good view from all locations. The stadium is essentially divided into two areas—the main stadium horseshoe and the bleacher area. Although the right-field bleachers are relatively good seats for $12, you have no access to the main stadium area and you'll go without beer. The Yankee bleacher bums made those cheap seats infamous over the years, but the no-alcohol policy has pretty well cleaned up the situation. In the main stadium, Tier Reserved sections 13-14 are also non-alcohol—and value-priced at $19. Rows A-E are especially desirable—fewer seats to the row and closest to the action. Oddly enough, fans find the Tier Reserved seats at the far ends of the horseshoe in the left- and right-field corners (sections 31-36) are pretty good vantage points. The far right-field seats are nearly as close to first base as Tier Reserved behind home plate due to the overall configuration of the field and grandstand. You might want to avoid Tier level seating, especially if you have any fear of heights. The steep angle is conducive to viewing the game, but prompts some fans to complain of vertigo. Your best value in the lower levels are Main Reserved ($40), especially sections 19-22 near first and third bases, and sections 33-36 at either end of the horseshoe inside the foul lines. All Main Reserved seats offer you shade and weather protection from the overhang. The Yankees provide many good seating opportunities for fans in wheelchairs and their companions at a significant discount. Without commenting on the owner himself, this is one of several classy touches provided by the Yankees management.

Seats to Avoid: The Left Field Bleachers are truly seats of last resort, not a good value at $12. If you sit in the low rows you are stuck looking through Monument Park and the bullpens. In the higher rows, you are far away—very far away—from the action, and you can't drown your sorrows because these are non-alcohol sections. And you don't have access to the main ballpark seating. The best you can say is you're in Yankee Stadium and it was not expensive. The worst seats in the main ballpark are $19 Tier Reserved sections 26-28 in left and corresponding sections 25-27 in right; they are the most remote and not as well angled as the other areas. A significant number of rows, sections, and boxes have been identified by the Yankees as obstructed due to pedestrian walkways and the impact of the flagpole. These tickets are offered for sale at the Yankee advance ticket sale window.

Yankee Stadium: Thanks for the Memories

As we all know, baseball is about far more than the game you are attending at the moment or the tangible comforts of the place. If you seek the ultimate sense of baseball history and enjoy being with passionate and remarkably knowledgeable fans, it's no surprise Yankee Stadium can be your ultimate baseball experience. No one comes here with misplaced expectations of finding the most-modern conveniences and a pampered existence.

Yankee Stadium and the cast of characters that come with it will provide you with a unique New York experience. Obviously, the die-hard baseball fan will drink in every facet of the visit (possibly literally), but the experience will be equally entertaining for the novice and casual observer, as well. Keep in mind, things will change as of 2009 when the Yankees are expected to begin play in a new, much-cozier 50,800-capacity ballpark located across the street to the north in Macombs Dam Park and part of John Mullaly Park. And no matter how faithfully some of the traditions are restored, it will be a different place in a new space. Let's just hope Bob Sheppard, the P.A. announcer at Yankee Stadium since 1951 (Joe DiMaggio's last season and Mickey Mantle's first), will be around to open the new ballpark.

The most storied ballpark in major-league baseball, Yankee Stadium has served as home to the legendary New York Yankees teams of the 20th century as well as most of the brightest stars in baseball, including Babe Ruth, Lou Gehrig, Joe DiMaggio, Mickey Mantle, Roger Maris, Ron Guidry, Derek Jeter, and Reggie Jackson. It was at Yankee Stadium where Gehrig began his streak of 2,130 straight games played in 1925, a record unchallenged until the days of Cal Ripken more than a half-century later. Still standing, of course, is the longest-standing major-league hitting record—DiMaggio's 56-game hitting streak in 1941.

Yankee Stadium was conceived out of dire necessity in 1921 after the team was booted from its shared home at the Polo Grounds by the New York Giants. With the Yankees and Ruth outdrawing their counterparts, Giants management informed the Yankees the team must leave the Polo Grounds as soon as possible. Yankees ownership went out and bought 10 acres formerly housing a lumberyard in the Bronx from the estate of William Astor. Flush with box-office revenues thanks to Ruth, Yankees management originally planned a massive stadium seating over 100,000. The first plans for Yankee Stadium were on the imposing side: a triple-decked, roofed stadium. This design was scaled back to the current layout: three decks in the horseshoe, with bleachers and scoreboards in the outfield. The price was a then-astronomical $2.5 million. At one point Yankee Stadium could house 80,000, but eventually that number decreased to 70,000; the 1976 remodel included replacement of tight 18-inch seats with spacious new 22-inch chairs, bringing capacity down to the current 57,546.

Some definite quirks existed in the original Yankee Stadium. For instance, in 1932 the Yankees placed a monument to manager Miller Huggins in the spacious center field that originally measured 490 feet and was nicknamed

"Death Valley," the place where fly balls went to die. As the years went by and more Yankees notables passed away, the team constructed additional shrines in Monument Park. Balls hit here were in play, and more than once a center fielder was frustrated as a deep shot bounced around among the monuments. On the flip side, the original Yankee Stadium was constructed for a lefty slugger like Babe Ruth: the official distance of the right-field foul pole was 280 feet with a four-foot-high fence, but some argue the real distance was closer to 260 feet the first season Yankee Stadium was open. (Interestingly, Ruth hit less than half his career homers at his two main home ballparks: Yankee Stadium and the Polo Grounds. Perhaps he focused more on the road.)

Over the years the Yankees tinkered with the ballpark (adding permanent bleachers and extending the grandstand before the 1937 season), but Yankee Stadium remained relatively unchanged until 1973 when the Yankees vacated their aging home field for two years (playing at Shea Stadium) while the ballpark was redone from top to bottom. Very little of the old stadium remained: the actual playing surface was lowered; steel supports were removed and the upper decks were cantilevered for a better view of the field; wider seats were installed, leading to far less of them; the original roof was removed; a replica facade was placed on the upper deck; three escalator towers were added; and a "telescreen" was added for instant replays.

Monument Park was preserved to the greatest extent possible with the monuments kept in place behind the center-field wall. You will want to get to the ballpark early in order to see the display. With any ticket other than the Bleachers, you can visit Monument Park as soon as the gates open (two hours prior to game time) and up to 45 minutes before the first pitch. Access is via the staircase at the end of the aisles between the Field and Main level seats at Section 36. In total, the Yankees have retired the numbers of 16 players, not too

surprising when you consider their better than two dozen World Championships.

The essence of Monument Park will be kept in its entirety at the new ballpark location. Heavens, you shouldn't disturb the spirits of Maris, Mantle, Gehrig, and Ruth—even if the Curse of the Bambino was vanquished in 2004.

The best thing about the Yankee Stadium rebuilding in 1976 was improved seating. Unlike the original design, not a single seat is poorly situated or obstructed. At the same time, you get a pretty good sense of the original stadium by simply walking the extremely narrow concourses. You might want to get to your seat early because the tight quarters make it difficult to navigate quickly as game time approaches. Yankee fans have many endearing attributes—and getting to the game early is one of them. Consequently, the squeeze presented by narrow concourses is considerably alleviated.

You can't help but admire typical Yankee fans. They are students of the game and they certainly don't lose interest if the Yanks fall behind. The fans know their team and they deeply respect the legacy, though they're not above a little fun; the grounds crew dances to "YMCA" while grooming the infield and gets a chuckle from the crowd. On our most recent visit, an older fan brought his young granddaughter. He got riled for good reason watching some sloppy play resulting in a first-inning deficit to Baltimore. "Are you angry?" the youngster asked Grandpa. In a sweet and soothing voice he responded, "Not at you, baby." Just as calmly, the Yankees came back to defeat the fast-fading Orioles, 3-2.

The roaming vendors are another highlight. They know what's going on and many of them enjoy entertaining. Some make tosses several rows up (not the beer vendors, mind you). One fellow announces batters—for home and away players—and provides insightful commentary worthy of a radio color analyst. At Yankee Stadium, you are more likely to stay in your seat than hunt for concessions along the narrow corridors.

The original Yankee Stadium was a nightmare if you needed to use the bathroom—there weren't nearly enough of them. The 1976 renovation somewhat improved the situation, but you still have a tight squeeze here compared to other modern venues. An interesting touch is finding the women's restrooms in baby pink wall tiles and flooring. The reaction from my companion was, "very 1950s." Frankly, the place is not clean inside or out. You will likely smell the garbage, but the smell of smoke is highly unlikely. Smoking is prohibited, and the Yankees aren't subtle about it with signs stating, "Smokers will be ejected."

Still, we're talking Yankee Stadium here. While we're sure the new ballpark will have all the necessary amenities, luxury boxes, and revenue-enhancing features found in a modern ballpark, we hope a little of the trademark New York City street grime is included—otherwise, it just wouldn't be Yankee Stadium.

Ballpark Quirks

This is Yankee Stadium, so the standard definition of quirk in this context is instantly incongruous. In fact, most history buffs would argue removal of many distinctive aspects from the original configuration has made the current stadium seem quirky. Perhaps the most visible reminder of that is the signature Yankee frieze (the famous Roman-style lattice hanging from the roof rimming the main stadium grandstand). The reproduction frieze in the current version of the stadium seems entirely forced and out-of-place in its isolated outfield location. The original frieze was copper but had been painted white in the 1960s—and that's how most fans still remember it. In the new stadium, the original frieze (put into storage before the 1970s renovation) will appear in original copper and in its proper location.

This isn't necessarily a quirk, but it is a signature installation: the giant 120-foot-high replica of Babe Ruth's bat outside Gate 4. If you're meeting friends at the game, this is a popular gathering spot.

Food and Drink

Food choices are fairly standard, for the most part, and you will pay New York prices (typically 25 cents higher than the prices at Shea). The selection of hot dogs and sausages is especially broad with quality Hebrew National kosher wieners a featured item ($4.75). Frankly, the other wiener selections are less popular and a quality notch below. Hamburgers and cheeseburgers ($6.50) are more reasonably priced, as are the large, filling Gabilla's knishes ($3.75) found at Glatt's hot dog stands.

With some effort, you can find some more exotic fare, including Wok & Roll Chinese (near Section 6 on Main Level) and sushi. A small stand features "Imported Beers of the World" (as well as premium domestic brands); the offerings include standards like Corona, Heineken, and Amstel Light, as well as a few slightly unusual ones—Sapporo, Pilsner Urquell, and Yuengling. (If you look around you can find local favorites like Brooklyn Lager as well.) At $7.50 for a 12-ounce bottle, this is not the best deal around. In fact, the Yankees tend to give you price breaks for buying grande. For instance, you can get a 24-ounce Foster's tap for $9.50—a good deal, relatively speaking; a domestic 24-ouncer is $1 cheaper; the same amount of water goes for $4.50. You can get a literally huge deal on a 44-ounce soda ($6). Near the Tier Level beer stands only, you'll also find a very popular fresh-squeezed lemonade stand ($4.75). You'll find few takers for the Arbor Mist wines offered ($7.50); this is Yankee Stadium, after all.

Tier Level concessions are on par or better than the Main and Field level; Loge Level offerings are limited (with most food service provided within the restricted club and loge seating areas).

For the Kids

Other than playing catch in the park near the ballpark, you won't find much to keep the kids entertained at this venue. The highlight might be food—pick from a variety of hot dogs, lots of ice-cream offerings such as Dippin' Dots ($4.50, $5.50 in a helmet) and the tasty, fresh-squeezed lemonade.

Ballpark Tours

As you might suspect, the tour put on by the Yankees is not standard issue. In fact, this is not one-size-fits-all—you choose from one of three levels of offerings. No matter which level you choose, it will be heavy on the history of Yankee legends. The Classic Tour ($14 adults, $7 children/seniors) lasts an hour and delivers on all the highlights, including Monument Park, the field, dugout and typically the clubhouse; the Champions Tour ($20 adults, $14 children/seniors) extends to 80 minutes and adds an historical short film; the Champions Plus Tour ($25/$17) includes a Club Level tour and a souvenir. During the off-season, the tours are set for noon every day (except major holidays). Due to the popularity of the tours, it is advisable to obtain tickets in advance. A variety of options are available by checking *yankees.com*.

Local Baseball Attractions

The New York Mets play at Shea Stadium, located in Flushing near LaGuardia Airport. We cover the Mets and Shea Stadium in a separate chapter.

The business rivalry between the Mets and the Yankees is played out on a minor-league level with two short-season NY-Penn League teams playing within the five boroughs: the Brooklyn Cyclones and the Staten Island Yankees. Both teams play in ballparks worth visiting; we cover both in our earlier chapter

Yankee Stadium

covering Shea Stadium.

There are remnants of many old ballparks in the greater New York City area. Later in this chapter we'll discuss the marker commemorating the location of home plate at the Yankees' original home, Hilltop Park, but with five major-league teams calling New York home over the years, there are an abundance of sites to visit.

The second Washington Park was built by team owner Charlie Ebbets to be the home of the Brooklyn Superbas (who later became the Brooklyn Trolley Dodgers and then the Brooklyn Dodgers) between 1898 and 1912. The Dodgers moved to Ebbets Field, but Washington Park lived on for a few years as the home of the Federal League's Brooklyn Tip Tops (named for Tip-Top Bread) before being most of the park was demolished in 1926.

If you're in the vicinity of Third Avenue at First Street in Brooklyn, take a look at the 20-foot-high wall on Third Avenue. It once served as the left-field wall for Washington Park and is now owned by the Con Edison power company. Though Washington Park was rebuilt after the Dodgers moved to Ebbets Field, some baseball historians now think the walls date back to the original Washington Park, dating from the 1899-1908 period—before the construction of Fenway Park, Tiger Stadium, or Wrigley Field. We're not talking anything special here, as there's no marker and nothing about the wall that particularly screams baseball.

After the New York Mets moved from the Polo Grounds to Shea Stadium, the Polo Grounds ballpark was torn down in April 1964, utilizing the same wrecking ball (painted to look like a baseball) used to tear down Ebbets Field. The Polo Grounds Towers now stands on the site, and all that's left is a small

Macombs Dam Park, adjacent to Yankee Stadium, will be part of the redevelopment surrounding the new ballpark when it opens in the 2009 season.

marker in front of Tower D showing where home plate once stood and a staircase that once transported fans down from Edgecombe Avenue to the Polo Grounds. (If you poke around you can see a marker commemorating the John T. Brush stairway, presented by the New York Giants. The Polo Grounds was originally called Brush Stadium after team owner John T. Brush.)

Similarly under-commemorated is the location of Ebbets Field, now home to the Ebbets Field Apartments. If you want to head to Brooklyn and see the site, prepare to be underwhelmed: the only marker is at the corner of Bedford and Sullivan where a cornerstone is set into the way, with a baseball and the words "THIS IS THE FORMER SITE OF EBBETS FIELD" engraved.

Even though Mickey Mantle grew up in Oklahoma, he came to personify the Yankees for a generation of fans and became an essential part of the Big Apple fabric. Later in life he was surrounded by much sadness, as he fought alcohol and health problems and the pressure of being Mickey Mantle, taking refuge in his restaurant, Mickey Mantle's (42 Central Park South). Mickey has passed on but the restaurant remains. It's filled with Yankee and Mantle memorabilia, but the food isn't very good; Mickey's favorite was chicken-fried steak, which is probably the menu highlight.

Getting There
If you are coming from Manhattan, the subway will be your quickest and least expensive option, although you will likely stand most of the way due to the convergence of rush hour with weekday night games. The 4, B (weekdays only), and D lines bring you to the 161st St. station right at Yankee Stadium (look for the orange and green stripes on the NYC Subway Map). These are much busier subway lines than the ones taking you to Shea Stadium, but the ride to Yankee Stadium from Manhattan typically is less than a half hour. Fares are $2 each way; buy a MetroCard if you plan on taking multiple trips.

The #4 line runs from Brooklyn to Wall Street and then north along Lexington Avenue to the ballpark and points north. (You can catch the #4 at Grand Central Terminal, which we'll discuss later in this chapter.) The B and D lines run on the western side of Central Park and 6th Avenue from Brooklyn to the Bronx.

The Yankees website lists the best routes to get to the game if you're driving. An abundance of parking lots are available next to the ballpark, some offering valet parking.

Where to Stay
When you come to New York City, you really should treat yourself to all the city has to offer. That almost certainly means you should opt for a room in Manhattan rather than the Bronx. Of course you will pay a little more for staying in a prime location, but the wide choices of hotels here results in fair, competitive pricing. Go ahead and splurge: when you remember your New York City trip your primary memory won't be saving $40 a night by staying in the Bronx instead of somewhere in midtown. You're also close to the Lexington

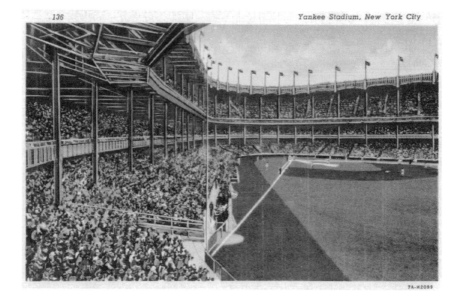

Yankee Stadium, New York City

7A-H2099

subway line, which takes you right to Yankee Stadium.

We discuss New York City hotels in our chapter on Shea Stadium. The advice in that chapter also holds true here: staying close to a subway line in Midtown Manhattan or the Times Square area means you're never too far away from an easy trip to the ballpark.

Local Attractions

You can take your pick of bars, restaurants, and souvenir stands catering to Yankee fans along River Avenue directly across from the stadium. Two of the more popular watering holes are Stan's Sports Bar and Restaurant (836 River Av.) and the Yankee Tavern (72 161st St.). The Yankee Tavern dates back to 1928 and the Babe was known to down a beer or two there. Your best bet for a truly New York deli sandwich experience (but not open after a night game) is the Court Deli—located two short blocks east of the stadium at 161st St. and Walton Avenue. The Bronx courthouse is located across the street. Quite a wide variety of restaurants are available in this area, but none nearly as popular as the Court Deli.

Also popular with Yankee fans and some players: Frankie and Johnnie's Pine Restaurant (1913 Bronxdale Av., between Matthews and Muliner avenues; 718/792-5956). To be honest, it's not in the best of neighborhoods. Bring your cash; no credit cards accepted.

As for other areas around the stadium, you won't find much interesting to do and some parts of the neighborhood are not very safe. This will probably change once the area around the ballpark is gentrified and a new Yankee Stadium comes online.

Team Ballpark History

New York entered the upstart American League in 1903 when Bill Devery and Frank Ferrell bought the Baltimore Orioles franchise and moved the team to Manhattan, but they did so without one crucial component: they lacked a ballpark. They hastily constructed an all-wood ballpark at Broadway and 168th Street, opening play there on April 30. The ballpark was named Hilltop Park, and the team was known as the Highlanders.

Hilltop Park might have had a great location—it was so named because it was one of the highest points in the area—but it wasn't much of a ballpark, holding just 16,000 in a single-deck grandstand. (Then again, it was built in just six weeks.) Hilltop Park was torn down soon after the Highlanders moved; Columbia-Presbyterian Medical Center was built on the site and a marker commemorates the location of home plate in a courtyard on the grounds.

So much of the tradition surrounding the Yankees dates back to those years. In 1912 the team began wearing pinstriped uniforms, but the biggest changes took place in 1913 when the team adopted the Yankees moniker after moving to the Polo Grounds. Both moves proved to be successful.

There actually were four versions of the Polo Grounds, with the Yankees playing in the final version. Polo was indeed played at the original Polo Grounds, located north of Central Park between 110th and 112 streets and 5th and 6th avenues, but by the early 1880s baseball was the prime use of the area. Both the original New York Giants of the National League and the New York Metropolitans of the American Association played there. After the Giants were evicted from the first Polo Grounds, the team moved to land further uptown (at

Yankee Stadium on Opening Day: April 19, 1923. (Courtesy Library of Congress, LC-B2- 5973-10[P&P].)

Assorted dignitaries were on hand for the opening of Yankee Stadium on April 19, 1923, including Yankees co-owner Col. Jacob Ruppert, Commissioner Kenesaw Mountain Landis, Yankees co-owner Tillinghast Huston, and Red Sox owner Harry Frazee. (Courtesy of the Library of Congress, LC-B2-2286-13[P&P].)

155th) and built the new Polo Grounds at the southern end of Coogan's Hollow.

It was such a good site the Giants were soon followed by the Players League, whose New York Giants (yes, both teams used the New York Giants nickname) built Brotherhood Park on the northern side of Coogan's Hollow. After the Players League collapsed, the Giants moved into Brotherhood Park and renamed it the Polo Grounds. That ballpark burned down (with the Giants finishing the season in Hilltop Park), but it was replaced by a concrete structure for the 1912 season; that ballpark became the Polo Grounds everyone associates with professional baseball.

The Yankees were a smash at the Polo Grounds, outdrawing the National League rival and earning the wrath of Giants management, who finally kicked the team out. Flush with success and a solid box-office draw in Babe Ruth, team owner Col. Jacob Ruppert began construction on a new ballpark.

The new facility served the Yankees well until the 1970s when the team and the city embarked on a reconstruction. In 1974 and 1975 the Yankees played at Shea Stadium; you can read all about Shea in its own chapter.

While You're There

There's just no way to see the best of New York City in a shorter trip, particularly if you're spending lots of time at the ballpark. And we won't presume to telling you the essentials of New York City. We discuss essential New York City experiences in our chapter covering Shea Stadium.

Index

Beckett, Josh 148
Beckett, Sam 213
Belanger, Mark 227
Bell, David 85
Bell, James "Cool Papa" 68
Beloit Snappers 264
Bench, Johnny 185, 192
Benes, Andy 69
Bennett, Charlie 114
Bennett, James Gordon 44
Bennett Park (Detroit) 114
Benny, Jack 24
Bertman's Stadium Mustard 199
Bernie Brewer 263
Bierbauer, Louis 329
Big Victor 433
Biggio, Craig 1
Billy Goat Tavern 464-465
Blair, Jack 36-37
Blair County Ballpark (Altoona, Penn.) 324
Blair Field (Long Beach State) 24
Blass, Steve 331
Blue Ash Sports Center 192
Blues Stadium (Kansas City) *see Municipal Stadium (Kansas City)*
Bluege, Ossie 356
Bobby Maduro Stadium *see Miami Stadium*
Boggs, Wade 405
Bonds, Barry 29, 32, 35, 36
Boog's BBQ 288-289
Boone, Aaron 315
Borchert Field 263-264
Bossard family 447
Boston Braves 66, 160, 163-164, 175, 176, 416, 423, 431-433 *see also Atlanta Braves*
Boston Braves (NFL) 160
Boston Breakers 433
Boston Patriots 176, 433
Boston Pilgrims 175 *see also Boston Red Sox*
Boston Red Sox 159-177, 431-433
Boston Red Stockings 467
Boston Redskins 160
Boston Yanks 160
Boucher, Joseph A. 164
Boudreau, Lou 199
Boundary Field (Washington, D.C.) 359
Bouton, Jim 268
Bowa, Larry 103
Bowie Baysox 297
Bragan, Bobby 7
Braves Field (Boston) 176, 223, 238, 432-433
Braves Museum and Hall of Fame 422-423
Breadon, Sam 65
Briggs Stadium *see Tiger Stadium*
Bright House Networks Field (Clearwater, Fl.) 414, 415
Brett, George 211, 221
Brickhouse, Jack 459-460
Brito, Mike 135
Brock, Lou 45, 66
Brockton Rox 176
Brodie, John 49
Brooklyn Atlantics 392
Brooklyn Bridegrooms 392
Brooklyn Dodgers 133, 141-145, 157, 281, 357, 478 *see also Los Angeles Dodgers*
Brooklyn Excelsiors 392
Brooklyn Robins 141, 208

Deer, Rob 245, 435
Delahanty, Ed 102
Delmarva Shorebirds 297
Denver Broncos 128
Denver Zephyrs 128
Derringer, Paul 189
Detroit Tigers 105-116, 426
Detroit Wolverines 115-116
Devery, Bill 481
Diamond, The (Lake Elsinore, Cal.) 24
Dierker, Larry 277
DiMaggio, Joe 33, 49, 473
"Dirty Water" 165
Disney, Walt 23
District of Columbia Stadium *see RFK Stadium*
Doby, Larry 199, 225
Dodger Stadium 17, 23, 129-146, 213, 350
Dolphin Stadium 147-157
Dolphins Stadium *see Dolphin Stadium*
Duffy's Cliff 163
Dugdale Park (Seattle) 380
Duluth Huskies 256
Dunedin Blue Jays 415
Dunn, Jack 286
Dunn IV, Jack 288
Dunn Field 206 *see also League Park (Cleveland)*
Dunn Tire Park (Buffalo, N.Y.) 285

Earnshaw, George 235
Easter, Luke 45
Eastern Shore Baseball Hall of Fame 297
Eau Claire Express 254
Ebbets, Charlie 143, 144, 478
Ebbets Field *x*, 48, 141-145, 237, 289, 391, 409, 478, 479
Eckersley, Dennis 130
Edison Field 15
Elfstrom Stadium (Geneva, Ill.) 448
Ellerbe Becket 69
Elster, Kevin 29
Enron Field 271 *see also Minute Maid Park*
Epicenter (Rancho Cucamonga, Cal.) 24
Erskine, Carl 7
Everett AquaSox 384
Everett Memorial Stadium 384
EwingCole architects 85
Ewing Field (San Francisco) 49
Exhibition Stadium (Toronto) 338, 340, 345-346
Exposition Park (Pittsburgh) 330, 331

Faan, Paul I. 49
Falconi Field (Washington, Penn.) 324
Farrell, Frank 481
Farrell, Wes 208
Federal League Park 455 *see also Wrigley Field*
Feller, Bob 199
Fenway Park 119, 159-177, 229, 237, 289, 431-433, 455
Fielder, Cecil 435
Fifth Third Field (Dayton) 193
Fingers, Rollie 261, 305
Finley, Charlie O. 223-224, 230, 238-239
Fisk, Carlton 162, 165
Florence Freedom 192-193
Florida Marlins 147-157
Forbes Field (Pittsburgh) 237, 289, 316, 319, 323, *329*, 330-331

Roseboro, John 129
Rothstein, Arnold 455
Royals Hall of Fame 224
Royals Stadium *see Kauffman Stadium*
Ruppert, Jacob *482*
Ruppert Stadium (Kansas City) *see Municipal Stadium (Kansas City)*
Ruth, Babe 286, 287, 288, 290-291, 319, 346, 423, 425, 454, 470, 473, 474, 475, 476, 482
Ryan, Nolan 276, 277

Saarinen, Eero 63
Sacramento River Cats 50, 233
Safeco Field 367-384
San Diego Chargers 313
San Diego Hall of Champions 308
San Diego Jack Murphy Stadium 313
San Diego Padres 299-314
San Diego Padres (PCL) 305, 313
San Diego Stadium 313
San Diego Surf Dawgs 310
San Francisco Giants 29-51, 383
San Francisco Seals 33, 48, 49, 50, 383
San Jose Giants 50-51
Sandberg, Ryne 460
Sanders, Reggie 179
Santana, Johan 244
Santo, Ron 460
St. George Grounds (Staten Island) 44
St. Joseph Blacksnakes 225
St. Louis Brown Stockings *see St. Louis Browns*
St. Louis Browns 24, 62, 64-66, 146, 295-296
St. Louis Cardinals 53-68, 157, 246, 295, 416
St. Louis Cardinals Hall of Fame and Museum 56, 62
St. Louis Perfectos *see St. Louis Browns*
St. Paul Saints (current) 254, 255
St. Paul Saints (former) 256, 445
Schaumburg Flyers 449
Schmeling, Max 469
Schmidt, Mike 87, 103
Schorling, John 445
Scioscia, Mike 20
Seals Stadium (San Francisco) 33, 48, 49, 50, *51,* 383
Seattle Indians 380-381
Seattle Mariners 367-384
Seattle Pilots 268, 379-381, 382
Seattle Rainiers 379-381, 382, 383
Segui, Cory 382
Segui, Diego 382
Selig, Allan "Bud" 257, 261, 268, 379
Shannon, Mike 62-63, 66
Shea, William 388
Shea Stadium 45, 49, 385-403, 474, 482
Sheppard, Bob 473
Shibe, Ben 230, 235, 236, 237
Shibe Park (Philadelphia) *88*, 93, 100, *102*, 235-238, 239, 289
Sick, Emil *379*, 380-381
Sick's Seattle Stadium 268, 379-381, 382
Silver Cross Field (Joliet, Ill.) 448
Simmons, Al 235, 447
Simmons, Ted 66
Simon, Randall 260
Sisler, George 66
Skidmore, Owings & Merrill 227, 241
Sky Sox Stadium (Colorado Springs, Col.) 128
SkyDome *see Rogers Centre*

Toronto Blue Jays 333-346
Toronto Maple Leafs (IL) 346
Toronto Maple Leafs (NHL) 345
Torre, Joe 66
T.R. Hughes Ballpark (O'Fallon, Mo.) 68
Traynor, Pie 318
Tropicana Field 338, 405-416
Troy Haymakers 467
Truman, Harry S. 222-223
Truman Sports Complex (Kansas City) 211, 213
Tucker, Michael 417
Tucson Electric Park 83
Tucson Sidewinders 83
Turner Field 417-434
Turner, Ted 423
Turnpike Stadium (Arlington, Texas) 13
Ty Cobb Museum 426

Uecker, Bob 261, 263
Union Baseball Grounds (Chicago) 467-468
Union Park (Pittsburgh) 330
U.S. Cellular Field 336, 435-449, 468

Valentine, Bobby 398
Vancouver Canadians 384
Vancouver Capilanos 384
Vander Meer, Johnny 189
Vander Wal, John 315
Vaughn, Joe "Arky" 318
Veeck, Bill 66, 156, 197, 208-209, 254, 295, 433, 438, 439, 446, 447, 456-457
Veeck, Mike 409
Vernon, Mickey 347
Veterans Stadium (Philadelphia) 49, 87, 89, 100, 102-103, 238
Von der Ahe, Chris 64-65

Wade Stadium (Duluth, Minn.) 256
Wagner, Honus 318, 319, 330
Walberg, Rube 235
Walters, Bucky 189
Wambsganss, Bill 208
Waner, Lloyd 318
Waner, Paul 318
Warner Park (Madison, Wis.) 264
Washington Park (Brooklyn), 141, 478
Washington Nationals 90, 235, 347-365
Washington Redskins 347, 348, 350, 352
Washington Senators 13, 225, 253, 347, 350, 351, 355-357
Washington Wild Things 324
Western Metal Supply Co. 303, 305, 306
Western Pennsylvania Sports Museum 324
Weaver, Earl 288
Weeghman, Charles 455-457
Weeghman Park see Wrigley Field
Weil, Sid 191
West, Sam 356
West End Field (Greenville, S.C.) 426-427
West Side Grounds (Chicago) 468-469
West Side Park (Chicago) 468
WGN 458-460
White Sox Park 445 see also Comiskey Park
Williams, Billy 460
Williams, Ted 160, 162, 164-165, 207, 256, 305, 351, 409, 432
Williamsburg 165
Wills, Maury 7